second edition

# CourseTutor
# CoreMicroeconomics

Executive Editor: Charles Linsmeier
Development Editor: Bruce Kaplan
Media and Supplements Editor: Tom Acox
Executive Marketing Manager: Scott Guile
Associate Managing Editor: Tracey Kuehn
Project Editors: Vivien Weiss and TSI Graphics
Art Director: Babs Reingold
Senior Designer: Kevin Kall
Interior Designer: Lissi Sigillo
Photo Editor: Christine Buese
Photo Researcher: Deborah Anderson
Production Manager: Barbara Anne Seixas
Composition and Illustrations: TSI Graphics
Printing and Binding: RR Donnelley

ISBN-13: 978-1-4292-6286-6
ISBN-10: 1-4292-6286-9

First printing 2011

Worth Publishers
41 Madison Avenue
New York, NY 10010
www.worthpublishers.com
www.wortheconomics.com

*t*he study of microeconomics is no easy task. You have to work carefully to follow the arguments presented in the text. Next, work through the tutorials and the questions and problems in this *CourseTutor,* checking your progress as you go along.

At the end of this course, if you do this work diligently, you will be able to analyze with more sophistication your everyday life. This will result in better decisions in areas ranging from career choice to studying, and from consumer purchases to marriage. You will be in a better position to analyze public policy issues such as taxation, education, antitrust, government spending, and foreign trade.

A good knowledge of microeconomics means few public policymakers will be able to con you with talk of a free government lunch. You will always be on the lookout for unintended consequences of any public policy change. You will look at the incentives inherent in any transaction and from that review you will be able to generate expectations about the future.

Microeconomics is an exciting subject to study. Less than 20 percent of Americans have ever taken a course in economics, so you will be in an elite crowd. Most of us know a lot about how the political system works and why we need to vote every couple of years. But not enough of us understand how our economy works.

Many people work and live in an economic environment 24/7, but often have little idea of how it works. Our ideas of how the economy sets prices and produces products vary from conspiracy theories involving multinational corporations to beliefs that government provides or regulates everything.

Because many of us end up working for corporations, we must be part of the conspiracy. But most of us wouldn't consider doing the things that corporations and businesses are often accused of doing. There is an inherent contradiction in what we see continually in the media. Furthermore, without corporations, much of what we enjoy today simply would not exist.

You will not find any conspiracy theories in this book. My goal is to give you the tools you need to do your own analysis of any economic situation.

Economists, like everyone else, are spread all across the political spectrum. The vast majority of economic analysis is agreed upon by the profession. But we all have different value systems, so it is not surprising that economists differ on which policy to use to solve a specific situation. Different policies have different side effects and it is often the nature of the side effects that lead economists to advocate different policy approaches to the same problem.

I hope you find microeconomics as exciting and as interesting as I did when I was a college sophomore. Microconomics pervades our lives and a good understanding of economic principles is essential. Enjoy the book and the course.

One more thing. This *CourseTutor* has been set up as your guide throughout the term. Each chapter of *CourseTutor* starts with a brief description of the chapter's contents, a list of key objectives, and a review of key terms. After studying these, move on to the tutorials. Start with the Frequently Asked Questions (FAQs). You will find that there is a FAQs section for each section of the chapter. Following each FAQs, there is a Quick Check of usually ten questions, designed to test your knowledge of the key concepts in each section. If you get all of these questions correct, go on to the next section. If you miss a few questions in a section, *CourseTutor* will give you further study suggestions, and often you will be given additional problems to work and solved problems to analyze. In this way, the tutorials are a buffet: Use what you need to obtain concept mastery, but move on to the next section if you know the material.

After you finish the tutorial portion of *CourseTutor,* you will find further hints and reminders to help you with chapter material, and Core Graphs and Core Equations will be presented for your review. Each chapter usually contains 20 homework questions and problems. If your instructor requests, you can work these Homework Questions in the book and hand in individual answer sheets, or work the questions online. Then, examine the ExamPrep sheet for each chapter, which gives you a framework for thinking about the chapter. Fill out the ExamPrep sheet to help you study for exams.

After this material, every chapter contains the standard study guide material for your review, should you need additional help. There are matching questions, fill-in questions, true-false questions, multiple choice questions and problems, and essay questions. Answers to these questions and problems are provided to help you assess your progress through the text.

I personally cannot be with you every step of this journey. This *CourseTutor* is my attempt to be your guide.

Gerald W. Stone

# CONTENTS

# Exploring Economics

Jack Hollingsworth/Getty Images

## Economics Is a Rich Discipline of Wide Scope

In this first chapter, you are given a general introduction to economics. You will see the scope of economics as a way of thinking about the world, then you will look at how economists go about doing economics. Next, you will be presented with the key ideas in economics; you will meet these ideas throughout the course.

This is an introductory chapter. You are not expected to memorize all the ideas and issues covered in this first chapter. Rather, use this chapter as a way of familiarizing yourself with the general outline and process of economics.

| This Is What You Need to Know | STEP 1 |
| --- | --- |

**After studying this chapter you should be able to**

- Explain the scope of economics and economic analysis.
- Differentiate between microeconomics and macroeconomics.
- Describe how economists use models.
- Describe the *ceteris paribus* assumption.
- Discuss the difference between efficiency and equity.
- Describe the key ideas in economics.

## STEP 2                     Review the Key Terms

**Microeconomics:** The decision making by individuals, businesses, industries, and governments.

**Macroeconomics:** The broader issues in the economy such as inflation, unemployment, and national output of goods and services.

*Ceteris paribus:* Assumption used in economics (and other disciplines as well), where other relevant factors or variables are held constant.

**Efficiency:** How well resources are used and allocated. Do people get the goods and services they want at the lowest possible resource cost? This is the chief focus of efficiency.

**Equity:** The fairness of various issues and policies.

**Scarcity:** Our unlimited wants clash with limited resources, leading to scarcity. Everyone faces scarcity (rich and poor) because, at a minimum, our time is limited on earth. Economics focuses on the allocation of scarce resources to satisfy unlimited wants.

**Opportunity costs:** The next best alternative; what you give up to do something or purchase something.

## STEP 3                     Work Through the Chapter Tutorials

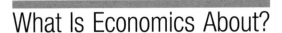

# What Is Economics About?

### Frequently Asked Questions

Q:  **What topics encompass economics?**
A:  Economics is about almost everything. Economic analysis can be usefully applied to topics as diverse as how businesses make decisions to how college students allocate their time between studying and relaxing, from how individuals determine whether to "invest in themselves" by taking additional courses while on the job to how government deals with recessions and inflation.

Q:  **How is economics divided as a subject?**
A:  Economics is separated into two broad categories: microeconomics and macroeconomics.

Q:  **What is the subject matter of microeconomics?**
A:  Microeconomics deals with individual, firm, industry, and public decision making. For example, microeconomics deals with issues such as whether you should attend a concert or study, and if you study, how you allocate your study time among all your courses. Business firms consider issues such as how much output to produce and how many people to hire to produce the output. Policymakers might use microeconomics to determine the appropriate caps on $CO_2$ discharges to mitigate climate change.

Q:  **What is the subject matter of macroeconomics?**
A:  Macroeconomics focuses on the broader economic issues confronting the nation such as inflation (a general increase in prices economy-wide), employment and

unemployment, economic growth, and policies to pull the economy out of a recession.

**Q:** How does model building characterize economics?

**A:** Economics uses a stylized approach to a number of issues. Stylized models boil issues and facts down to their basic relevant elements. Then, using assumptions, stylized (simple) models are developed. Not all situations are covered by the models because economists seek to generalize about economic behavior and reach generally applicable results.

**Q:** What is the *ceteris paribus* assumption, and when is it used?

**A:** Models often make use of holding some important variables constant (the *ceteris paribus* assumption). For example, to determine how much gasoline people will buy at different prices, we hold their income constant.

**Q:** How are efficiency and equity related?

**A:** Economists and policymakers often confront the tradeoff between efficiency and equity. Efficiency reflects how well resources are used and allocated; economic analysis often focuses on ensuring that efficient outcomes result from public policy. Sometimes the equity or fairness of the outcome is questioned. Because equity and fairness are subjective matters, there are differences of opinion about fairness, except at the extremes where people generally agree. For public policy issues, economics illuminates the tradeoffs between equity and efficiency. Economists have a lot to say about efficiency, but they tend to avoid the subjective issue of equity.

## What Is Economics About? Quick Check

### Circle the Correct Answer

1. (T/F) Microeconomics concentrates on such aggregates as economic growth and inflation.
2. (T/F) *Ceteris paribus* means that economists do economics by creating models.
3. Macroeconomics covers all *except* which one of the following?
   a. the inflation rate
   b. the unemployment rate
   c. productivity rates
   d. sales of Nike athletic shoes compared to Reeboks
4. Models are
   a. useless because they are too simple.
   b. stylized, simple representations of reality that can lead to important insights.
   c. exact, careful representations of reality.
   d. quite limited in their usefulness.
5. Concerning the efficiency versus equity tradeoff
   a. economists have much to say about both efficiency and equity.
   b. economists have much more to say about equity than efficiency.
   c. economists have much to say about efficiency but little to say about equity.
   d. economists have much to say about equity but nothing to say about efficiency.

Score: ____

Answers: 1. F; 2. F; 3. d; 4. b; 5. c

### If You Got All 5 Correct

You have a good sense of what economics is about. Go on to Key Ideas of Economics in the next section.

### If You Didn't Get All of Them Correct

Spend a little time reviewing this material. It is not hard, but it provides a foundation for the remainder of this chapter. If you do not get this material straight, you might get lost later. Make a quick trip through the first section of the chapter again, looking at each heading and making sure you know what is covered under each topic. When you have a better sense of what economics is and how economists do what they do, go on to Key Ideas of Economics. ■

# Key Ideas of Economics

## Frequently Asked Questions

**Q: How is economics often defined?**

A: Our economy has limited resources. Our wants are limitless. This means that we face scarcity and must make tradeoffs in everything we do. Economics is often defined as the study of the allocation of scarce resources to competing wants.

**Q: What are opportunity costs?**

A: Everything we do involves opportunity costs. All activities require that we spend resources (e.g., time and money) that could be used in another activity. This other activity represents the opportunity cost of the current activity chosen. Opportunity costs apply to us as individuals and to societies as a whole.

**Q: What is thinking at the margin?**

A: Rational thinking requires that you think and make decisions at the margin. For example, making decisions at the margin for most businesses means deciding on the next employee to hire or the next advertising campaign, and for consumers it means deciding on the next product to purchase. Businesses use marginal analysis to determine how much output to produce and how many employees to hire. People use marginal analysis to determine which products to buy. Governments use marginal analysis to determine levels of regulation.

**Q: How do incentives affect people?**

A: People follow incentives. If society wants to discourage some behavior, society can tax it, punish it, or do a host of other things that increases its costs. Conversely, society can provide things such as tax benefits for behaviors it wishes to encourage.

**Q: What do markets do?**

A: Markets bring buyers and sellers together. Competition for the consumer's dollar forces firms to provide products at the lowest possible price, or some other firm will undercut their price. New products are introduced to the market and old products disappear. This dynamism is what makes markets efficient.

**Q: What is market failure, and how is it treated?**

A: Though markets are usually efficient, there are recognized times when they are not. Pollution is an example of this. Government action is often needed to provide a solution to problems of market failure.

**Q: What happens when people have information superiorities?**

A: Information is important. Superior information gives economic actors a decided advantage. Sometimes this is simply a facet of life. At other times, information advantages can result in dysfunctional markets. Sellers of used cars know more about the condition of their car than buyers. This is why buyers often take a used car to a mechanic for testing before the purchase is finalized.

**Q: What benefits do specialization and trade bring?**

A: Trading with other countries leads to better products for consumers at lower prices. Economies grow by producing those products where they have an advantage over other countries. This is why much of what we buy today comes from other countries. Specialization leads to tangible benefits.

**Q:** **Why is productivity important?**

**A:** Countries with the highest average per capita income are also the most productive. Their labor forces are highly skilled and firms employ huge amounts of capital with these workforces. This results in immense productivity and correspondingly high wages for the workers. High productivity growth results in high economic growth, which leads to high wages and high incomes, which stimulate large investments in education and research. All of this activity leads to higher standards of living.

**Q:** **What can be done to deal with fluctuations in the overall economy?**

**A:** The overall economy moves from growth spurts to recessions, then back to growth spurts. Economists have provided analyses that have helped governments smooth fluctuations in the overall economy.

## Key Ideas of Economics Quick Check

### Circle the Correct Answer

1. (T/F) Opportunity costs arise only when money is exchanged.
2. (T/F) Government can do things to make overall economic fluctuations less severe.
3. Which one of the following statements is *not* an underlying idea of economics?
   a. Markets are efficient.
   b. When markets fail, government can provide a solution.
   c. Individuals are always rational and always follow their incentives.
   d. Scarcity is the economic problem.
4. Which one of the following does *not* improve our standard of living?
   a. trade
   b. specialization
   c. productivity
   d. market failure
5. When we have two soft drinks on a hot day and turn down the offer of a free third soft drink because we feel this might be too much and leave us waterlogged, we are
   a. thinking irrationally because it is free.
   b. helping alleviate scarcity by leaving something for someone else.
   c. thinking on the margin.
   d. using information to gain an advantage in the market.

Score: _____

Answers: 1. F; 2. T; 3. c; 4. d; 5. c

### If You Got All 5 Correct

You have a good sense of the bedrock ideas in economics. Spend a few moments with Hints, Tips, and Reminders.

### If You Didn't Get All of Them Correct

Review the material. Then go to the text and read through each heading in this section. Be sure you understand what concept is being discussed. If you are unclear about any of the ideas, reread the relevant passage in the text, then continue. ∎

## STEP 4      Consider These Hints, Tips, and Reminders

1. This chapter represents your *introduction* to the study of economics; treat it that way. No need to try and memorize all of the terms and topics—you will see them several times again throughout the course. Just read this chapter to get a sense of the breadth of economics.

2. Reading and using graphs are a different story. The Appendix to the chapter introduces you to the graphical methods you will encounter as you learn economics. Pick up any periodical such as the *New York Times, Wall Street Journal, Financial Times, Newsweek, Business Week,* and so on, and you will find them filled with graphs and figures that are part of the articles. Focus more of your study time on the Appendix and learn to interpret and read graphs—it will save you a lot of grief.

Do the Homework for Chapter 1
Exploring Economics

**STEP 5**

Instructor _____ Time _____ Student _____

**Use the answer key below to record your answers to these homework questions.**

1. _____   6. _____   11. _____   16. _____
2. _____   7. _____   12. _____   17. _____
3. _____   8. _____   13. _____   18. _____
4. _____   9. _____   14. _____   19. _____
5. _____   10. _____   15. _____   20. _____

1. Microeconomics focuses on
   a. what causes unemployment.
   b. what causes inflation around the world.
   c. decisions by firms.
   d. government deficits.

2. Macroeconomics is *not* generally concerned with
   a. what causes unemployment.
   b. what causes inflation around the world.
   c. pricing decisions by corporations.
   d. government deficits.

3. *Ceteris paribus* is
   a. an assumption used by economists to complicate models.
   b. the assumption that business maximizes profits.
   c. the assumption used by economists that all labor is equally productive.
   d. an assumption used by economists that holds all else constant.

4. Efficiency
   a. reflects how often economists make assumptions about important variables.
   b. reflects how well resources are allocated.
   c. reflects the fact that all labor is equally productive.
   d. is an assumption used by economists that holds important variables constant.

5. Equity refers to
   a. an assumption used by economists to complicate models.

   b. an individual's subjective judgment about fairness of policies.
   c. an assumption used by economists that all labor is equally productive.
   d. an assumption used by economists that holds important variables constant.

6. When you cannot go to a movie and play tennis at the same time, you are facing
   a. the fact that you cannot talk and chew gum at the same time.
   b. equity tradeoffs.
   c. an efficiency versus equity tradeoff.
   d. opportunity costs.

7. Over a long period of time, our standard of living is determined by
   a. government regulation.
   b. productivity.
   c. opportunity costs.
   d. minimum wage laws.

8. We trade with other countries because
   a. the law requires us to.
   b. we can exploit developing nations, reducing their incomes.
   c. we are unable to produce most products ourselves.
   d. consumers get better products at lower prices.

Note to Student: There are 8 questions in this homework assignment.

## Use the ExamPrep to Get Ready for Exams STEP 6

This sheet (front and back) is designed to help you prepare for your exams. The chapter has been boiled down to its key concepts. You are asked to answer questions, define terms, draw graphs, and, if you wish, add summaries of class notes.

### What Is Economics About?

Describe the following:

Microeconomics:

Macroeconomics:

Describe what *ceteris paribus* is and how it is used in economics:

Describe the tradeoff between efficiency and equity:

### Key Ideas of Economics

List the 10 key ideas in economics and give an example of each:

| Key Idea | Example |
| --- | --- |
| | |
| | |
| | |
| | |
| | |
| | |
| | |
| | |
| | |
| | |

## Additional Study Help Chapterwide Practice Questions

### Matching

Match the description with the corresponding term.

___ 1. Microeconomics
___ 2. Macroeconomics
___ 3. Models
___ 4. *Ceteris paribus*
___ 5. Efficiency
___ 6. Equity
___ 7. Scarcity
___ 8. Opportunity costs
___ 9. Thinking at the margin
___ 10. Productivity
___ 11. Market failure
___ 12. Business cycles
___ 13. Specialization
___ 14. Trade

a. Occurs when markets do not do what they are supposed to do.
b. Fairness.
c. When someone considers whether to eat an additional ice cream cone. Summed up in the phrase "the straw that broke the camel's back."
d. Simple, stylized descriptions of issues.
e. Considered the economic problem, resulting from our wants being greater than available resources.
f. Markets that provide the best quality products for the lowest possible cost.
g. How much output we produce over a specific period; the greater the amount, the higher our standard of living will be.
h. Fluctuations in the overall economy, such as recessions.
i. The exchange of goods and services between countries or individuals.
j. When each of us concentrates on doing fewer things well rather than many things not as well.
k. All other relevant factors held constant.
l. The cost of what you have to give up.
m. A part of economics that looks at the decisions of individual consumers and businesses.
n. A part of economics that looks at the decisions of all consumers and all businesses.

### Fill-In

Circle the word(s) in parentheses that complete the sentence.

1. (Macroeconomics, Microeconomics) _____ focuses on decision making by individuals, compa-nies, and governments while (macroeconomics, microeconomics) _____ addresses problems such as unemployment and inflation.

2. In creating models to determine how efficient and equitable policies are, economists use the concept of (efficiency, equity, *ceteris paribus*) _____ to focus attention on the important variables. How well resources are used and allocated are issues of (efficiency, equity, *ceteris paribus*) _____, while (efficiency, equity, *ceteris paribus*) _____ deals with the fairness of policies.

### True-False

Circle the correct answer.

T / F 1. Analyzing whether you will buy more Vera Bradley handbags if the price drops would be considered part of microeconomics.

T / F 2. Analyzing whether everyone will buy more Vera Bradley handbags if the price drops would be considered part of macroeconomics.

T / F 3. *Ceteris paribus* means that models should be as simple as possible, but no simpler.

T / F 4. Because models are stylized versions of issues, they rarely have anything useful to say.

T / F 5. Economists generally have more to say about equity than efficiency.

T / F 6. Only people who are not rich are forced to make tradeoffs.

T / F 7. The opportunity cost of going to a concert is the price of the concert ticket.

T / F 8. Thinking "I am full, I cannot eat another mouthful" is an example of thinking at the margin.

T / F 9. Government policymakers find little use for economics when determining how to bring about desired changes.

T / F 10. Government is helpless in the face of recessions.

T / F   11. Markets are inefficient because someone is always better informed than someone else.

T / F   12. Trade is a one-way street: Rich nations benefit at the expense of poor nations.

T / F   13. Our standard of living is linked to productivity growth.

T / F   14. The opportunity cost of parking at school includes the amount of time I have to search for a parking space.

T / F   15. If I study for chemistry rather than history, I incur no opportunity cost because no monetary transaction takes place.

## Multiple Choice

Circle the correct answer.

1. Which of the following is *not* a concern of micro-economics?
   a. The German firm BMW builds a new auto plant in North Carolina.
   b. You buy a music CD.
   c. Unemployment falls in the United States.
   d. Your sister finds a job after college.

2. Which of the following is *not* a concern of macro-economics?
   a. Inflation climbs to 5% per year.
   b. Unemployment rates tumble.
   c. Coca-Cola expands overseas.
   d. Productivity rises in most businesses.

3. What does *ceteris paribus* mean?
   a. All people are considered equal.
   b. All relevant factors are held constant.
   c. Only important things are considered.
   d. The number of variables has to be kept under control.

4. What special insights can economics tell us about equity?
   a. Many things, because economics is a powerful way of looking at the world.
   b. Some things, because economics considers people to be rational.
   c. Not much, because each of us has to determine what is fair; economics has no special competence here.
   d. Only limited insights, in the special case when markets are completely competitive.

5. Which of the following is *not* an opportunity cost you incur if you see a Yankees baseball game?
   a. the parking fee, if you drive to the park
   b. the time spent in the after-game traffic jam
   c. the exorbitant price paid for hot dogs
   d. the $50 tickets that were given to you by a friend who could not go to the game

6. All *except* which one of the following is an example of thinking at the margin at an all-you-can-eat buffet?
   a. I am almost full, so I will have one dessert.
   b. If I eat five more egg rolls, I will be so full that I cannot eat a dessert.
   c. I have eaten seven egg rolls already.
   d. To eat another egg roll, I have to loosen my belt.

7. Pollution is an example of
   a. an inequitable outcome of markets.
   b. market failure.
   c. the problems that can arise with specialization.
   d. not thinking on the margin.

8. A company believing that offering airline frequent flyer miles with their product will lead to increased sales is following which key economic idea?
   a. People think at the margin.
   b. Information is important.
   c. People follow incentives.
   d. Government can deal with market failure.

9. A person who believes that you should hire an automotive expert to help you negotiate with a car dealer about the purchase of a used car is following which key economic idea?
   a. Markets are efficient.
   b. Government can deal with market failure.
   c. People follow incentives.
   d. Information is important.

## Essay-Problem

Answer in the space provided.

The questions below extend the material covered in this chapter. The answers you give may not correspond completely with ours; don't worry as long as they are fairly close.

1. Do you have a driver's license? If so, you probably had to wait for various lengths of time to take your initial driving test or get your license renewed. There are people who will wait in line for you if you pay them a fee. Why would you pay other people to do something that does not cost you in the first place?

2. Why should we *not* expect tax law to be as economically efficient in outcome as possible?

3. Is *ceteris paribus* unique to economics?

## What's Next

You now have an introduction to economics. You have a sense of what economics is concerned with and how economists actually do economics. You also have been given an introduction to key ideas in economics. You are now ready to put this knowledge to work.

In the next chapter, we bring in several of the concepts from this chapter in looking at the crucial importance of economic growth. We present a simple stylized model of an economy and look at the major things that generate economic growth and higher living standards.

## Answers to Chapterwide Practice Questions

### Matching

| | | | |
|---|---|---|---|
| 1. m | 5. f | 9. c | 13. j |
| 2. n | 6. b | 10. g | 14. i |
| 3. d | 7. e | 11. a | |
| 4. k | 8. l | 12. h | |

### Fill-In

1. Microeconomics, macroeconomics
2. *ceteris paribus*, efficiency, equity

### True-False

| | | | |
|---|---|---|---|
| 1. T | 5. F | 9. F | 13. T |
| 2. F | 6. F | 10. F | 14. T |
| 3. F | 7. F | 11. F | 15. F |
| 4. F | 8. T | 12. F | |

### Multiple Choice

| | | |
|---|---|---|
| 1. c | 4. c | 7. b |
| 2. c | 5. d | 8. c |
| 3. b | 6. c | 9. d |

## Essay-Problem

1. Time is an opportunity cost. You could be doing other things with your time. For especially lengthy waits incurred by busy business people, it is often worth it for them to pay someone to wait in line. Highly paid individuals often have personal assistants to run their lives.

2. There is an efficiency versus equity tradeoff. Economists can propose the most economically efficient tax laws, but these have to go through a political process to become law. The political process ensures that equity considerations come into play. In other words, economists can propose various tax laws, but as soon as someone says that the proposed law is unfair to some person or some group, politicians will take notice and factor this in to the degree they think warranted.

3. No. It is common to the sciences. For example, physicists hold everything constant, then change one variable when they run various experiments. This is the logic behind taking one particle and seeing what happens under normal speeds, then taking the same particle and accelerating it to speeds near the speed of light.

# Appendix:
# Working with Graphs
# and Formulas

## Graphs, Charts, Tables, and Equations Are the Language of Economics

Your study of economics will use a lot of graphs, some charts and tables, and a few simple equations. Knowing how to read, interpret, and use these methods of representing ideas and data will make your study of economics easier and make reading ordinary publications more enjoyable.

| This Is What You Need to Know | STEP 1 |
| --- | --- |

**After studying this appendix you should be able to**

- Describe the four simple forms of data graphs.

- Make use of a straightforward approach to reading graphs.

- Read linear and nonlinear graphs and know how to compute their slopes.

- Use simple linear equations to describe a line and a shift in the line.

- Explain why correlation is not the same as causation.

| Work Through the Appendix Tutorial | STEP 2 |
| --- | --- |

## Frequently Asked Questions

Q: What are the main types of graphs used to display economic data, and how do they differ?

A: There are four main types of graphs used to display and analyze economic data: time series, scatter plots, pie charts, and bar charts. Time series graphs plot data measures over time, whereas scatter plots plot two series (neither axis measures time) against each other. Pie charts split data into percentage parts of the whole and display them like pie slices. Bar charts present discrete data values as bars, which can be shown either vertically or horizontally.

**Q:  Are there any rules for reading graphs?**

**A:**  There are no formal rules, but a few simple suggestions might help. First, check the title to see what is being presented, then look to see what is measured on each axis, and look at the graph to see if it makes logical sense. Now look carefully at the graph to see if any interesting relationships shine through. Finally, read the caption associated with the graph to ensure you have not missed anything important.

**Q:  What is a linear relationship, and how is its slope computed?**

**A:**  A linear relationship is represented by a straight line. To compute the slope of a straight line, pick two points on the line and compute the ratio of the change in the variable on the vertical axis to the change in the variable on the horizontal axis (rise over run). In Figure APX-1, the slope of the line is computed by selecting two points such as $a$ and $b$, then computing the ratio of changes in each variable:

$$(20 - 15) / (40 - 20) = 5 / 20 = 0.25$$

In this simple graph, when the number of cars on the road rises by 20, the commute time grows by 5 minutes, or 15 seconds for each additional car.

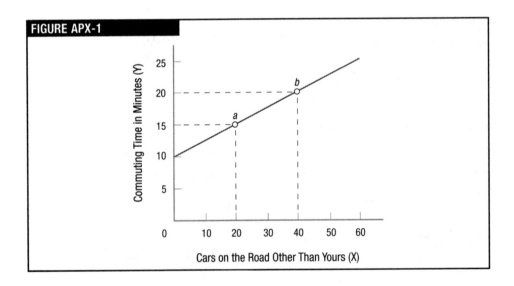

**FIGURE APX-1**

**Q:  How is slope computed when the relationship is nonlinear?**

**A:**  To find the slope of a nonlinear curve, pick a point and find the slope of a line tangent to that point. In Figure APX-2, the slope at point $a$ is equal to

$$(16 - 13) / (30 - 20) = 3 / 10 = 0.3$$

Notice that in this case the rate of congestion gets worse as each additional car enters the road (the slope gets steeper as more cars travel the road). This is a crucial difference from the linear curve where the slope was constant.

FIGURE APX-2

**Q: What simple equation represents a linear relationship?**

A: Straight lines can be represented by a simple equation of the form: $Y = a + bX$. In Figure APX-3 (Figure APX-1 reproduced), $Y$ equals commuting time, $a$ equals the vertical intercept of 10 minutes (the commute time when you are the only car on the road), $b$ is equal to the slope of .025, and $X$ is equal to the number of other cars on the road. Thus, the full equation is

$$Y = 10 + 0.25X$$

FIGURE APX-3

$Y = 10 + 0.25X$

**Q: How can *ceteris paribus* be represented in both graphs and equations?**

A: The term *ceteris paribus* means to hold some additional important variables constant. So, for instance, in the commuting time model above, we might be assuming that the number of lanes available for travel is held constant. Assume that adding another lane reduces commuting time by 5 minutes, and removing a lane increases commute time by 5 minutes. We can add a variable $L$ to our equation, representing lane additions or decreases, so that our new equation becomes

$$Y = 10 + 0.25X + L$$

where $L$ is equal to $-5$ when a lane is added and $+5$ when a lane is reduced due to road work. Figure APX-4 on the next page shows the impact of this new variable on the commute time. Adding a new lane reduces commute time for all levels of traffic, while eliminating a lane increases commute time in all traffic conditions.

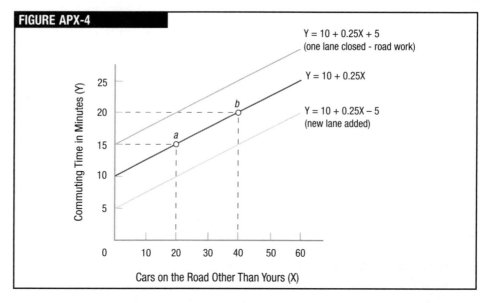

**FIGURE APX-4**

$Y = 10 + 0.25X + 5$
(one lane closed - road work)

$Y = 10 + 0.25X$

$Y = 10 + 0.25X - 5$
(new lane added)

Commuting Time in Minutes (Y)

Cars on the Road Other Than Yours (X)

Q:   **Why does correlation not imply causality?**

A:   Just because two variables are related to each other does not mean one variable causes the other to change.

## Key Point to Remember

Graphs, tables, charts, and equations are just other ways to view data and relationships between variables.

# Working with Graphs and Formulas Quick Check

1. Figure APX-5 shows 2006 GDP per capita for selected countries, and the country's corresponding years of life expectancy at birth for both men and women. Russia's per capita GDP is roughly what percent of America's?

   a. 100%
   b. 1%
   c. 15%
   d. 50%

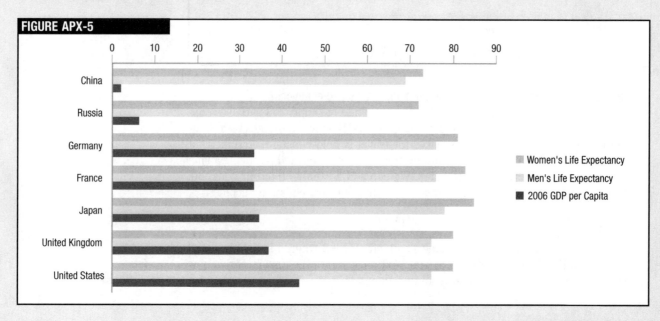

**FIGURE APX-5**

China
Russia
Germany
France
Japan
United Kingdom
United States

Women's Life Expectancy
Men's Life Expectancy
2006 GDP per Capita

2. Using the same Figure APX-5, which country has the highest life expectancy for males/females?
   a. France/Germany
   b. United Kingdom/United States
   c. Japan/United Kingdom
   d. Japan/Japan
3. Figure APX-6 shows the median (middle person) duration of unemployment in weeks for each month for 2002–2004. Notice that there is a spike in how long people have been unemployed each June. Which of the following is probably the best explanation for these spikes in how long people have been unemployed?

   a. Employers do not like to hire people in June because they don't want to have to let new people go on vacation.
   b. The unemployed see the arrival of summer as a chance to surf and do not bother to look for a job.
   c. May and June represent graduation in both high school and college, so the job market becomes crowded and many unemployed individuals can't find work.
   d. Federal law restricts the number of people who can interview for federal jobs in the summer because of budget limitations.

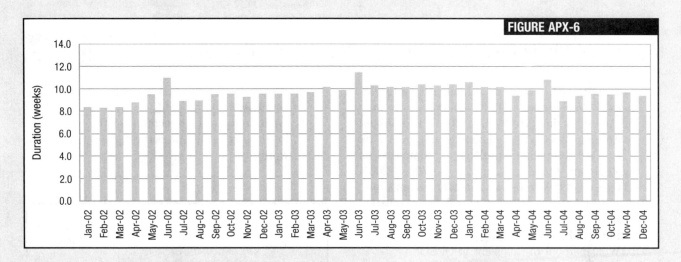

**FIGURE APX-6**

4. Figure APX-7 shows the relationship between the size of a video file in megabytes and the download time in minutes. What is the slope of the line?
   a. 0.4
   b. 0.3
   c. 0.2
   d. 0.1

5. Assume the line (relationship) in Figure APX-7 is for your medium-speed DSL line. Now assume you get a high-speed broadband network connection. How does that affect the line in Figure APX-7?
   a. No impact.
   b. The line will rotate downward with a smaller slope.
   c. The line will rotate upward with a larger slope.
   d. Broadband is so fast that the line will equal the horizontal axis.

Score: ____

**FIGURE APX-7**

### If You Got All 5 Correct

You have a good working knowledge of how to read graphs, how to describe linear relationships, and how to calculate the slope of a line. Enjoy the rest of the course.

### If You Didn't Get All of Them Correct

You should review this material again. You are going to see graphs throughout this course. Over the course of the semester you will be computing percentages, interpreting simple graphs, and on a rare occasion looking at simple equations such as those described in this section. Don't worry about it at this point. You will get a lot of practice as the semester unfolds, and soon you won't give it a second thought. Good luck in the course. ■

# Additional Study Help Working with Graphs and Formulas

1. Figure SH APX-1, from data in an article in *Business Week*, February 24, 2003, shows the source of America's imported oil in 2001. The United States consumed a total of 25 million barrels of oil a day or 9.125 billion barrels a year. Imported oil as a percent of total consumption was 70% in 2001. The pie chart below shows where that oil came from.
   a. With oil prices at $30 a barrel, approximately how much did the United States pay in 2001 for imported oil? _____
   b. What percent of this went to OPEC?

   _____

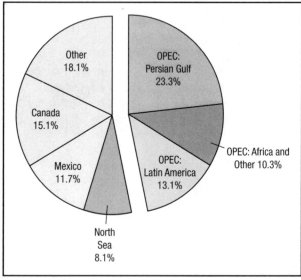

**SH APX-1**

2. Figure SH APX-2 is based on data in *The Wall Street Journal*, January 24, 2003. It shows the average number of children born to women during the early 1980s and the early 2000s in selected countries.

   a. How is the United States unique among these countries? _____
   b. What factors might account for the wide-ranging drop in fertility rates throughout most of the world?

   _____

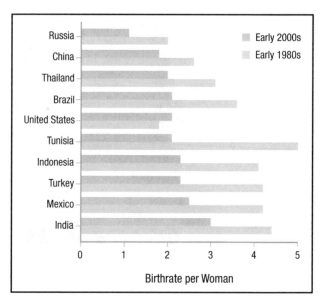

**SH APX-2**

3. Figure SH APX-3 shows educational attainment of Latinos in Los Angeles, California, in 2001. These data were included in a special survey in the *Economist*, November 2, 2002.
   a. What percent of foreign born have no college at all? _____
   b. By the third generation, what percent have not been to college? _____
   c. Between the second and third generations, what is the major change?

   _____

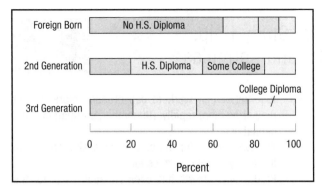

**SH APX-3**

4. Figure SH APX-4 graphs productivity change (output per hour worked) to changes in aggregate output (GDP) for the last several decades.
   a. Draw a smooth curve (or line) on the graph that shows the normal relationship between these two variables.
   b. Is this a positive or negative relationship that you graphed? _____
   c. State the relationship in words. Does it seem to make sense?

   _____

   d. Notice the two open circles. They represent years 2000 and 2001. Are these points above or below the line you drew on the graph?

   _____

   e. Could this help explain why job growth was slow in the years following the last two recessions? How?

   _____

   _____

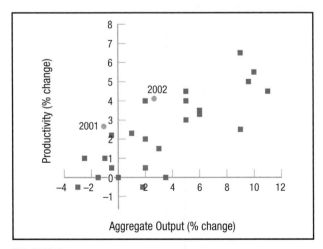

**SH APX-4**

5. Figure SH APX-5, using World Bank data, shows the population in the world living on under $1 a day.
   a. As a percent of the world's population, has poverty (as defined by living on $1 a day) declined? _____
   b. Where is poverty growing the fastest?

   _____

   c. Where has poverty declined the fastest?

   _____

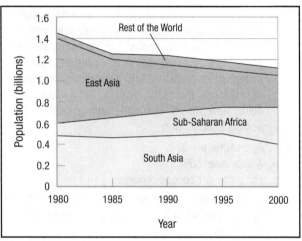

**SH APX-5**

6. Use the grid to answer the following questions.
   a. Plot the following equation: $Y = 2 + 0.5X$
   b. Plot the following equation: $Y = 10 - 1.5X$
   c. At what value of $X$ is the value of $Y$ equal for both equations? _____
   d. If $X = 2$, what would be the difference between the values for $Y$ in equations a and b?

   _____

# Answers to Additional Study Help: Working with Graphs and Formulas

1. a. (9.125 billion $\times$ 0.70) $\times$ \$30 = 6.3875 $\times$ \$30 = \$191.625 billion.
   b. The percent of imports from OPEC equals 23.3 + 10.3 + 13.1 = 46.7%.

2. a. Fertility rates have actually risen for the United States, unlike the remainder of the countries, where it has dropped.
   b. Fertility rates may be declining in developing nations for many reasons, including increases in income, better access to birth control (better communications such as telephones, satellite television, etc., have increased awareness about birth control in developing nations), increased urbanization (urban households have fewer children), and possibly greater access to education.

3. a. Approximately 82%
   b. A little over 50%
   c. Far more get college diplomas

4. a. A smooth line would be positively sloped and go roughly through the origin and up toward point $Y = 5; X = 10$.
   b. Positive relationship
   c. This positive relationship suggests that when aggregate output is changing very rapidly, productivity is changing rapidly as well. Alternatively, rapidly growing aggregate output is associated with rapidly growing productivity. Yes, it makes sense that productivity change and aggregate output change would go together. When workers can produce more, output may grow more rapidly. Remember, correlation is not causation.
   d. The two circles for the current recession are above the line you drew in question a.
   e. Productivity growth has been unusually high for the given change in output. This could be due to the possibility that the rapid technological buildup (computers, telecommunications, etc.) during the late 1990s is taking a while to be integrated into the economy. This could partly explain the rapid growth the economy experienced in 2004 and 2005. Productivity growth could hold back job growth in the sense that businesses can meet growing needs with their current number of workers—there is no need to hire more workers.

5. a. Yes. World population has grown in the last two decades, but world poverty has declined. One snag in these data is that they are not adjusted for inflation. One dollar in 1980 probably translates into two dollars today.
   b. Sub-Saharan Africa
   c. East Asia

6. a and b: See Figure SHA APX-1.
   c. $X = 4$
   d. The difference is 4, as shown in Figure SHA APX-1 (vertical arrow).

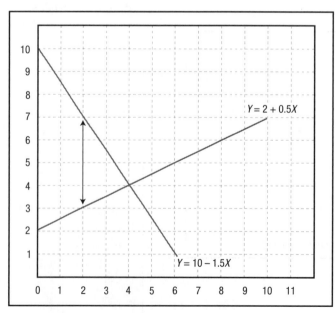

**SHA APX-1**

# Production, Economic Growth, and Trade

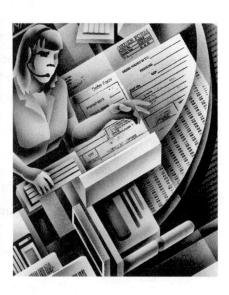

Boris Lyubner/Getty Images

## Economic Growth and Trade Improve Our Standard of Living

Economic growth is crucial. It brings poor countries out of poverty and helps people in all countries better their conditions. We will return to the concept of growth again and again in this course. To understand how growth comes about, you need to understand the determinants of growth. Also, you need to know the benefits of trade.

| | |
|---|---|
| This Is What You Need to Know | STEP 1 |

**After studying this chapter you should be able to**

■ Describe the three basic questions that must be answered for any economy.

■ Describe production and the factors that go into producing various goods and services.

■ Describe the opportunity cost an economy incurs to increase the production of one product.

■ Use a production possibilities frontier (PPF) or curve to analyze the limits of production.

■ Describe economic growth and the impacts of expanding resources through increasing human resources, capital accumulation, and technological improvements.

■ Describe the concepts of absolute and comparative advantage and explain what they tell us about the gains from trade when countries specialize in certain products.

■ Describe the practical constraints on free trade and how some industries might be affected.

## STEP 2 — Review the Key Terms

**Production:** The process of converting resources (factors of production)—land, labor, capital, and entrepreneurial ability—into goods and services.

**Resources:** Productive resources include land (land and natural resources), labor (mental and physical talents of people), capital (manufactured products used to produce other products), and entrepreneurial ability (the combining of the other factors to produce products and assume the risk of the business).

**Land:** Includes natural resources such as mineral deposits, oil, natural gas, water, and land in the usual sense of the word. The payment to land as a resource is called rent.

**Labor:** Includes the mental and physical talents of individuals who produce goods and services. The payment to labor is called wages.

**Capital:** Includes manufactured products such as welding machines, computers, and cellular phones that are used to produce other goods and services. The payment to capital is referred to as interest.

**Entrepreneurs:** Entrepreneurs combine land, labor, and capital to produce goods and services. Entrepreneurs absorb the risk of being in business, and they receive profits in return.

**Production efficiency:** Goods and services are produced at their lowest resource (opportunity) cost.

**Allocative efficiency:** The mix of goods and services produced is just what the society desires.

**Production possibilities frontier (PPF):** Shows the combinations of two goods that are possible for a society to produce at full employment. Points on or inside the PPF are feasible, and those outside of the frontier are unattainable.

**Opportunity cost:** The cost paid for one product in terms of the output (or consumption) of another product that must be forgone.

**Absolute advantage:** One country can produce more of a good than another country.

**Comparative advantage:** One country has a lower opportunity cost of producing a good than another country.

## STEP 3 — Work Through the Chapter Tutorials

# Basic Economic Questions and Production

### Frequently Asked Questions

Q: **What questions must every economy answer?**

A: *Every* economy must decide *what* to produce, *how* to produce it, and *who* will get the goods and services produced. The answers to these questions depend on how an economy is organized, whether capitalist, socialist, or communist.

Q:  What is the process by which goods and services are produced?

A:  Goods and services are produced by combining resources—the factors of production (land, labor, capital, and entrepreneurship)—into products. Land includes all natural resources, labor includes the physical and mental talents of humans, capital represents all manufactured products used to produce other products, and the entrepreneur assumes the risk of production and combines the other three factors of production to produce goods and services.

## Basic Economic Questions and Production Quick Check

### Circle the Correct Answer

1. (T/F) In a capitalist economy, the distribution of most goods is determined by private markets.
2. (T/F) Land as a resource would include timber in a national forest, shale oil deposits in Colorado, and farm land in Iowa.
3. Which of the following is *not* a payment for a factor of production?
   a. interest
   b. wages
   c. rents
   d. capital gains on stock
4. Which of the following is *not* a form of capital as a factor of production?
   a. office computer
   b. stock certificates
   c. company car
   d. screwdriver for fastening parts on an assembly line
5. Producing the right mix of products for society is known as what?
   a. production efficiency
   b. factors of production
   c. basic economic questions
   d. allocative efficiency

Score: ____

Answers: 1. T; 2. T; 3. d; 4. b; 5. d

### If You Got All 5 Correct

You have a good grasp of the concepts of production, the three basic economic questions, and efficiency. Go on to Production Possibilities and Economic Growth in the next section.

### If You Didn't Get All of Them Correct

Take a moment and review the first part of the chapter in the book. This material is very simple, so when you have completed this review, go on to Production Possibilities and Economic Growth in the next section. But keep in mind that each new section builds on the previous ones. ∎

# Production Possibilities and Economic Growth

## Frequently Asked Questions

Q:  What does a production possibilities frontier (PPF) show?

A:  The production possibilities frontier (PPF) or curve shows the different combinations of goods and services that a fully employed economy can produce, given available resources and current technology, with both factors assumed to be fixed in the short run. Production mixes inside and on the frontier are possible, but combinations that lie outside the curve are unattainable. In Figure 1, points *a*, *b*, and *d* are attainable, but point *c* is not.

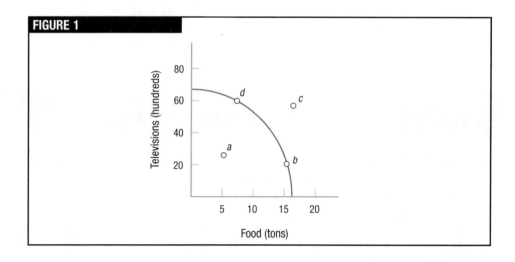

**FIGURE 1**

*Televisions (hundreds)* — *Food (tons)*

**Q:  What do points along the PPF represent?**

**A:**  Production on the frontier represents the maximum output attainable by the economy when all resources are fully employed.

**Q:  How is the concept of opportunity cost portrayed by the PPF?**

**A:**  Reallocating production from one product to another involves *opportunity costs*: The output of one product must be reduced to get the added output of the other. Producing more and more of one product eventually raises the opportunity costs for this product because of the unsuitability of some resources.

**Q:  What does the PPF model tell us about economic growth?**

**A:**  The production possibilities model suggests that economic growth comes from an expansion in resources or from improvements in technology. Expansions in resources expand the production possibilities frontier for all commodities. Technological advances in one industry directly expand production only in that industry, but nonetheless allow more of all types of goods to be produced. The new technology allows previous output to be produced using fewer resources, thus leaving some resources available for use in other industries.

**Q:  Can economic growth result from population growth?**

**A:**  Economic growth can be enhanced by increasing the quantity or quality of labor available for production. Population growth, caused by higher birthrates or immigration, increases the quantity of labor available. Investments in human capital such as education improves labor's quality.

**Q:  Does the type of products produced and consumed affect economic growth?**

**A:**  Greater capital accumulation further improves labor's productivity and thus increases growth rates. This is shown in Figure 2 as a movement from point *a* outward, in contrast to a movement from point *b* outward—note how much greater is the growth when a society invests more in capital goods rather than consumes more.

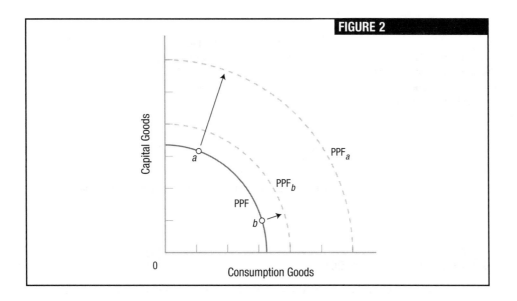

**FIGURE 2**

# Production Possibilities and Economic Growth Quick Check

## Circle the Correct Answer

1. (T/F) A PPF curve identifies the best mix of products for a given society to produce.
2. (T/F) Production choices on, or to the left of, the PPF curve are attainable by the economy in question.
3. (T/F) If an economy can produce 10 more computerized drill presses only by producing 500 fewer jelly rolls, the opportunity cost of a drill press is 50 jelly rolls.
4. Opportunity cost is a measure of
   a. what it costs a firm to break into a new market.
   b. the increase in output that comes from adding inputs to the production process.
   c. the inputs a firm must purchase to be able to produce some good.
   d. the goods an individual or economy must forego to produce or consume more of some other good.
5. If an economy permits more immigration and invests in its school system, we would expect its PPF curve ($PPF_0$) in Figure 3 to
   a. shift in toward the origin to $PPF_1$.
   b. shift out away from the origin to $PPF_2$.
   c. remain in about the same place.
   d. react in any of the above ways—we cannot predict which.
6. Which economic policy is most likely to promote strong economic growth in the long run?
   a. more consumption goods and fewer capital goods
   b. producing more computerized drill presses and fewer jelly rolls
   c. high tax rates on capital investment by business
   d. more government retirement programs that encourage early retirement to make way for younger workers

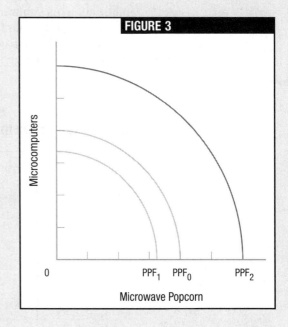

**FIGURE 3**

7. If an economy is producing a mix of goods that lies directly on its production possibilities frontier, this indicates which of the following?
   a. Consumers are happy.
   b. The economy is operating at full employment.
   c. The economy is leaving some resources unused.
   d. The economy is growing.
8. The primary factors underlying economic growth are
   a. falling consumer demand but improving technology.
   b. expanding resources and rising interest rates.

c. rising exports and imports.

d. expanding resources and improving technology.

9. If an economy produces computers and pizzas, and a technological innovation makes the production of computers cheaper, we would expect the economy's production of pizzas to

a. decrease.

b. not change.

c. increase.

d. decrease by an amount equal to the increase in computers.

10. Which production factors are easiest to influence through government policies?

a. land

b. entrepreneurial talent

c. capital and labor

d. none can be influenced

Score: ____

**Answers: 1. F; 2. T; 3. T; 4. d; 5. b; 6. b; 7. b; 8. d; 9. c; 10. c**

## If You Got 9 or 10 Correct

You get the idea about the concepts of production possibilities frontiers and the determinants of economic growth. Go on to Specialization, Comparative Advantage, and Trade in the next section.

## If You Didn't Get at Least 9 Correct

The next section on comparative advantage and trade builds on the concepts in this section. As you work through it, some of the concepts from these first two sections will begin to take hold. Take a moment to go back and review this section in the book. When you have completed this review, and before you move on, take a moment and work through the following solved problem.

## Solved Problem: Production Possibilities

a. Using the grid, plot a typical PPF for apples and office furniture, putting office furniture on the horizontal axis.

b. Draw a new PPF that reflects the economy a year after apple blight has killed nearly half of all apple trees.

c. Using the original PPF curve from part a, draw the new curve resulting from a technological breakthrough in apple production that greatly improves yields.

d. Explain why economies that produce more capital goods and fewer consumer goods have higher growth rates in the future.

## Solution-Discussion: See Figure 4.

**FIGURE 4**

a. Your curve should be concave (bowed-out) from the origin with apples on the vertical axis and office furniture on the horizontal axis.

b. The new curve should be under the curve in part a but with the same end point on office furniture. The impact is on apple production only. Office furniture is unaffected.

c. The new curve should be outside the curve in part a but with the same end point on office furniture. The impact is on apple production only. Office furniture is unaffected.

d. Producing more capital goods represents investment in future production that expands the PPF in the future because capital makes labor more productive.

## Keep in Mind

This simple production possibilities model is based on the following simple assumptions:

■ Resources are fixed and limited.
■ Technology is given.
■ Production is efficient.
■ Two goods are assumed for simplicity.

From this simple set of assumptions, we get several important conclusions:

■ The economy faces a PPF curve and a tradeoff in the production of both goods.
■ Producing more of one good results in rising opportunity costs for that good.
■ Along the PPF, resources in the economy are fully employed.
■ Points inside the PPF represent unemployment.
■ Points outside the PPF are unattainable.

But most important, this simple, stylized model provides a guide to the kinds of policies that enhance economic growth:

■ Any policy that expands the quantity or improves the quality of resources will improve economic growth.
■ Any policy that improves technical progress will enhance growth.

Public policy can be viewed and analyzed through the lens of this simple PPF model. ■

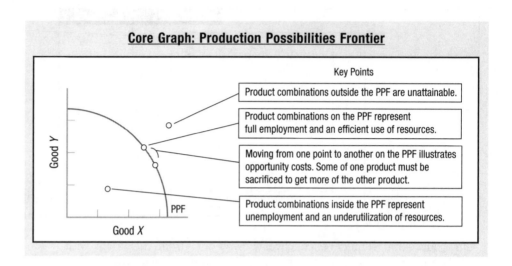

### Core Graph: Production Possibilities Frontier

Key Points

Product combinations outside the PPF are unattainable.

Product combinations on the PPF represent full employment and an efficient use of resources.

Moving from one point to another on the PPF illustrates opportunity costs. Some of one product must be sacrificed to get more of the other product.

Product combinations inside the PPF represent unemployment and an underutilization of resources.

Good Y

Good X

PPF

# Specialization, Comparative Advantage, and Trade

## Frequently Asked Questions

Q: **What is absolute advantage?**
A: An absolute advantage exists when one country can produce more of some good than another country.

Q: **What is comparative advantage?**
A: A country has a comparative advantage if its opportunity costs to produce a good are lower than another country's.

Q: **What is the importance of comparative advantage for trade?**
A: Countries gain from voluntary trade if each specializes in producing those goods at which it enjoys a comparative advantage. Voluntary trade is thus a positive-sum game: Both countries stand to benefit from it.

# Specialization, Comparative Advantage, and Trade Quick Check

## Circle the Correct Answer

1. (T/F) If two countries engage in voluntary trade, both can hope to gain from this trade, even though one country may have a much larger and more technologically advanced economy than the other.
2. (T/F) Countries that have an absolute advantage over other countries would not benefit from trade with them.
3. If one country has a comparative advantage over another, this means
   a. it can produce more of all products than the other country.
   b. it can produce one product at a lower opportunity cost than can the other country.
   c. its products are the best in the world.
   d. it has a bigger market share than the other country.
4. Two countries will benefit from trading with one another if
   a. each country concentrates on producing those goods at which it has an absolute advantage.
   b. the country with the greatest productive capacity does all of the production.
   c. each country concentrates on producing those goods at which it has the lowest opportunity cost.
   d. each country produces only goods that the other cannot.
5. In the table below, what is the opportunity cost for Japan of producing cameras rather than commercial airplanes?
   a. 27,500
   b. 5/6
   c. 50,000 to 1
   d. 1 to 500,000

|               | Aircraft | Cameras |
|---------------|----------|---------|
| United States | 300      | 600,000 |
| Japan         | 10       | 500,000 |

6. Which of the following does *not* typically limit international trade?
   a. transportation costs
   b. the risks of a falling standard of living as a result of trade
   c. the risks associated with overspecialization
   d. the prospect of short-term job losses in some sectors

7. In a zero-sum game involving two parties
   a. neither party can hope to make any gains.
   b. both parties can be expected to make positive gains.
   c. one party can gain only if the other party also gains.
   d. one party can gain only if the other party loses.

Use the table below to answer Questions 8, 9, and 10.

|               | Athletic Shoes (pairs) | Music CDs |
|---------------|------------------------|-----------|
| United States | 10,000                 | 20,000    |
| Great Britain | 5,000                  | 15,000    |

8. What is the opportunity cost for Britain producing athletic shoes compared to music CDs?
   a. 2/3
   b. 3
   c. 2
   d. 1/2
9. If Britain produced music CDs only, then traded with the United States, which would occur?
   a. It would not benefit because the United States would still have an absolute advantage in producing athletic shoes.
   b. It would not benefit because its opportunity cost for producing music CDs is higher than that of the United States.
   c. It would not benefit because it does not have a comparative advantage.
   d. Both countries would benefit.
10. If Britain produced athletic shoes only, then traded with the United States, which would occur?
    a. It would not benefit because the United States would still have an absolute advantage in producing music CDs.
    b. It would not benefit because its opportunity cost for producing athletic shoes is higher than that of the United States.
    c. It would benefit because it has a comparative advantage.
    d. Neither country would benefit.

Score: ____

### If You Got 9 or 10 Correct

You understand the concepts of specialization, comparative advantage, and voluntary trade. This chapter introduced the concepts of scarcity, production, tradeoffs, opportunity cost, and the benefits of specialization and voluntary trade. Most of this material is fairly straightforward, and you have probably mastered it. Just to be on the safe side, take a few moments and review the section on Hints, Tips, and Reminders.

### If You Didn't Get at Least 9 Correct

You should have scored 8 or better in this exercise even though questions 8–10 are difficult.

- Don't panic. Comparative advantage and voluntary trade are some of the more difficult concepts in the chapter and the book. It often takes students several attempts at this material to really master it.
- Take a moment and review this section in the book.
- Remember that people and nations voluntarily trade because each expects to benefit. Not many people would voluntarily trade (goods, hours worked, babysitting, or anything else) with someone else if they did not expect to benefit.
- Also, keep in mind that within countries there are winners and losers from trade. Typically, consumers (a large group) benefit from trade and specific industries, and occupations (a smaller group) may lose. But overall, there are net gains from trade.

When you have completed this review, continue on, but you will probably want to review this chapter again. Maybe going through the Hints, Tips, and Reminders section that follows will help. ■

---

## STEP 4    Consider These Hints, Tips, and Reminders

1. Opportunity cost is an important concept that will resurface throughout the remainder of the course. Keep in mind that it is the value of your next-best alternative. The costs of going to a movie are your next-best alternative—what you could have done with your money and time. The PPF makes this tradeoff clear—moving from one point to another involves opportunity costs.

2. The PPF is a really simple model of national economies but illustrates several important concepts:
   - **Scarcity**: Output possibilities beyond the boundary are impossible.
   - **Increasing opportunity cost**: As more of one good is produced, the opportunity cost of producing it rises because resources are not equally suitable for producing two different goods.
   - **Choice**: Societies must choose levels of output.
   - **Tradeoffs**: To pick one point on the PPF is to give up a different level of production.
   - **Opportunity cost**: Choices involve tradeoffs that involve opportunity costs—what society must give up to have more of another commodity or service.
   - **Full employment versus unemployment**: Along the PPF, resources are fully employed, while inside the PPF there is unemployment of resources.

■ **Economic growth**: Expanding the curve outward represents economic growth. Growth comes from improved technology and increases in resources

Keep in mind that this is a very simple model, but it provides insights into a lot of important issues.

3. The issues of specialization and trade are difficult to see at first, but keep in mind the following:
   ■ The basis for trade is comparative advantage and specialization. Whoever has the lowest opportunity costs to produce a given product or service has a comparative advantage.
   ■ This was Ricardo's main insight, so keep the principle of comparative advantage in mind as you work through problems.
   ■ Trade is controversial because there are winners and losers from trade. The winners are usually a large number of consumers, who each gain a little. The losers are typically a specific industry and its workers, who each lose a lot. There lies the controversy—many of us gain at the expense of a few.
   ■ Remember that comparative advantage applies to both people and resources. James Patterson and Stephen King have a comparative advantage over almost everyone when it comes to writing novels. Some land, for example, can produce crops more cheaply (in terms of resource cost) than other acreage.
   ■ It is important to remember that absolute advantage is irrelevant for trade. Comparative advantages confer the benefits of trade between parties.
   ■ Comparative advantage and trade allow individuals and nations to consume levels of goods and services beyond their PPF. This is why people voluntarily trade! This principle holds true for individuals, communities, and nations. To make the point, look at an absurd set of examples: How would your life change if
     1. you could only buy American-made goods?
     2. you could only buy goods made in your state?
     3. you could only buy goods made in the city where you live?
     4. you could only buy goods made by those living on your block?
     5. you couldn't buy goods from anyone, but you had to produce everything you consume yourself?

As you move down this list, most of us would agree that the quality of life as we know it today would decline.

| Do the Homework for Chapter 2 Production, Economic Growth, and Trade | **STEP 5** |

Instructor _____ Time _____ Student _____

**Use the answer key below to record your answers to these homework questions.**

1. _____    6. _____    11. _____    16. _____
2. _____    7. _____    12. _____    17. _____
3. _____    8. _____    13. _____    18. _____
4. _____    9. _____    14. _____    19. _____
5. _____    10. _____   15. _____    20. _____

Use these paragraphs and Figure HW-1 to answer questions 1–8.

On January 25, 2009, *The New York Times* reported that Taiwanese computer manufacturers that had heretofore designed and produced high-end laptop computers for Apple, Dell, and others had decided to launch their own brands of netbooks. Netbooks are stripped-down smaller versions of laptops using the free Linux operating system. They have slower processors, limited memory, and small hard drives with wireless internet capability designed for "cloud" computing, which means users work with online programs such as the word processing and spreadsheet software provided by Google and others.

Assume that if Taiwan directed all its resources to producing netbooks, 30 million could be made. Also, let's assume it has a robust (no pun intended) coffee industry and if all its resources went to coffee, 20 million bags could be produced. To keep this problem simple, assume that resources can be seamlessly switched from one industry to the next without loss of productivity (the PPF is a straight line).

1. In Figure HW-1, which curve represents the PPF for these two goods in Taiwan?

2. What is the opportunity cost for Taiwan to produce one added netbook?

3. Now assume that Taiwanese coffee farmers import a new hybrid coffee tree that doubles production.
   a. In Figure HW-1, which curve represents the new PPF for Taiwan?
   b. What is the new opportunity cost to produce an added netbook?

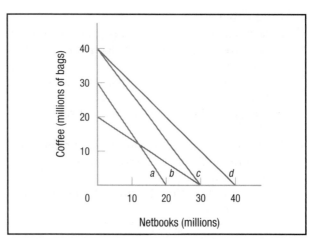

**HW-1**

|   | (in millions) | |
|---|---|---|
|   | **Netbooks** | **Coffee** |
| a | 20 | 30 |
| b | 30 | 20 |
| c | 30 | 40 |
| d | 40 | 40 |

Now, as you knew we would, let's introduce a trading partner. Brazil is world-renowned for its coffee, but it also has a small computer-manufacturing capability. If Brazil employed all of its resources to coffee production it could grow 50 million bags, but applying all resources to computer production would only result in 10 million netbooks. Again for simplicity, assume that resources can be seamlessly moved between industries.

4. Does Brazil have a higher or lower opportunity cost of coffee than Taiwan?
   a. higher
   b. lower

5. Assume that Taiwan is operating on its original PPF of 20 million bags of coffee and 30 million netbooks. Further assume that both countries are splitting their resources equally between coffee and netbooks.
   a. How many netbooks total (both countries combined) would be produced?
   b. How many bags of coffee total (both countries combined) would be produced?

6. Now assume that Brazil devotes all of its resources to coffee and Taiwan uses all of its resources to build netbooks. They agree to trade half of what they produce to each other.
   a. How many *additional* netbooks does Brazil end up with?
   b. How many *additional* bags of coffee does Taiwan get to consume?

7. Who are the winners in this trade scenario?
   a. Brazil's computer makers
   b. Taiwan's coffee growers
   c. Consumers in both countries
   d. Only Brazilian coffee growers

8. Who are the losers if these countries trade? (Write down the letters of all that apply.)
   a. Brazilian coffee growers
   b. Taiwanese coffee growers
   c. Brazilian computers makers
   d. Taiwanese computer makers
   e. Taiwanese consumers
   f. Nobody loses

Use Figure HW-2 to answer questions 9–11.

9. In the PPF curve shown in Figure HW-2, which points are attainable?
   a. *a* and *b*
   b. *b* and *c*
   c. *c*
   d. *b* only

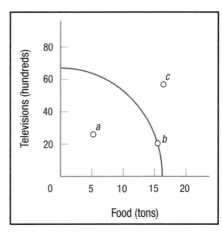

**HW-2**

10. Point *c* represents
    a. how much more it costs to produce more food.
    b. negative returns to the production possibilities frontier.
    c. an impossible level of output for this economy to attain.
    d. unemployed or underutilization of resources.

11. Moving from point *a* to point *b* would represent
    a. a more inefficient use of resources.
    b. diminishing returns.
    c. a losing situation because fewer TVs are produced.
    d. a reduction in unemployment as the economy moves to full employment.

Use the table on the right to answer questions 12–13.

12. What is the opportunity cost of producing 800 tons of soybeans instead of 600 tons?
    a. There is no opportunity cost; this country can easily produce more tons of soybeans.
    b. 100 PDAs
    c. four PDAs for every ton of soybeans produced
    d. 50 PDAs

13. What is the opportunity cost of producing 175 PDAs instead of 150?
    a. eight tons of soybeans for every additional PDA produced
    b. 200 tons of soybeans
    c. the amount of soybeans that must be given up for the additional PDAs
    d. all of the above

**Production Possibilities**

| Combination | Soybeans (tons) | Handheld PDAs |
|---|---|---|
| A | 1,000 | 0 |
| B | 800 | 100 |
| C | 600 | 150 |
| D | 400 | 175 |
| E | 200 | 190 |
| F | 0 | 200 |

14. In a country with low standards of living and low levels of human capital, we would expect this country to focus on which of the following products?
    a. computers
    b. cellular phones
    c. clothing
    d. HDTV sets

15. If country A has an absolute advantage over country B in the production of a particular good, this means that
    a. country A has a technological advantage over country B.
    b. country A can produce more of a product than can country B.
    c. country A can produce a product at a lower opportunity cost than country B.
    d. country A is the market leader in producing the product.

Note to Student: There are 15 questions in this homework assignment.

| | Use the ExamPrep to Get Ready for Exams | **STEP 6** |
|---|---|---|

This sheet (front and back) is designed to help you prepare for your exams. The chapter has been boiled down to its key concepts. You are asked to answer questions, define terms, draw graphs, and, if you wish, add summaries of class notes.

## Basic Economic Questions and Production

Describe the following.

A production function:

Increasing returns:

Diminishing returns:

Negative returns:

Constant returns:

## Production Possibilities and Economic Growth

Use the grid below to diagram a typical production possibilities curve with increasing opportunity costs.

Add three points to the figure: full employment, underutilization of resources, and production that is not possible under the given constraints.

Describe how opportunity costs are shown on this diagram.

Describe the way economic growth can happen in the economy and show economic growth in the grid on the previous page.

## Specialization, Comparative Advantage, and Trade

Define the following.

Absolute advantage:

Comparative advantage:

Describe the gains from trade associated with comparative advantage.

Describe some of the limits to trade and specialization.

## Additional Study Help Chapterwide Practice Questions

### Matching

Match the description with the corresponding term.

___ 1. Production
___ 2. Inputs
___ 3. Land
___ 4. Entrepreneurship
___ 5. Production possibilities frontier (PPF)
___ 6. Opportunity costs
___ 7. Economic growth
___ 8. Absolute advantage
___ 9. Comparative advantage

a. The price an economy or an individual must pay, measured in units of one product, to increase its production (or consumption) of another product.

b. That which goes into the production process to create finished products: land, labor, capital, and entrepreneurial ability.

c. Delineates the different possible mixes of goods an economy can produce when it is fully employing its resources.

d. When one country can produce a particular good at a lower opportunity cost than can the other county, trade will be beneficial.

e. A vacant, unimproved parking lot in the middle of Omaha, Nebraska.

f. The process of transforming inputs into outputs, or of turning factors of production—land, labor, capital, and entrepreneurial ability—into products and services.

g. When people and firms are continually increasing their production and consumption. Two primary explanations for this are expanding resources and improving technologies.

h. When one country can produce more of a particular good than another country.

i. Earns profits for its part in the production process.

### Fill-In

Circle the word(s) in parentheses that complete the sentence.

1. No matter how the economy is structured, every economy must answer three basic questions—what goods and services to produce, who will get these goods and services, and (who will be in charge of the economy, how will the goods and services be produced, how will income will be distributed) _____.

2. Production involves turning (technology, resources) _____ into goods and services. Resources consist of land, entrepreneurship, labor, and (energy, capital, profits) _____. Entrepreneurial ability is paid (profit, interest, rents) _____ for its efforts in assuming risk and combining the other factors of production to produce products and services for the market.

3. When the correct mix of goods and services are produced, the economy is said to be (capitalistic, allocatively efficient, productively efficient) _____. When goods and services are produced at their lowest opportunity cost, (allocative efficiency, productive efficiency) _____ prevails.

4. All points on the PPF represent output combinations that are (attainable, unattainable) _____; while points outside of the PPF are said to be (attainable, unattainable) _____. Points inside the PPF represent (unemployment, full employment) _____; while points on the PPF represent (unemployment, full employment) _____.

5. Moving from one point to another on the PPF results in (gains, opportunity costs) _____ as one product is traded for another. When the PPF is bowed out from the origin, opportunity costs are (increasing, decreasing, constant) _____.

6. When the PPF expands outward, the economy has experienced (full employment, economic growth) _____, and this occurs because (government, costs, resources) _____ has/have expanded. Another source of economic growth according to the PPF model is (income redistribution, technology) _____.

7. An/A (absolute, comparative) _____ advantage occurs when one individual or nation can produce more of a good or service than another. An/A (absolute, comparative) _____ advantage occurs when one individual or nation can produce a good or service at a lower opportunity cost than another. An/A (absolute, comparative) _____ advantage is the reason why so many nations are trading with other nations.

## True-False

Circle the correct answer.

T / F     1. Only socialist economies have to consider how goods and services will be produced.

T / F     2. Production involves turning land, labor, capital, and entrepreneurship into goods and services.

T / F     3. If an economy can produce 10,000 more gallons of peanut butter only by producing 5000 gallons less of jelly, the opportunity cost of 1 gallon of peanut butter is 2 gallons of jelly.

T / F     4. A PPF curve will identify the best mix of products for a given society to produce.

T / F     5. If an economy is operating at full employment, it can increase its production of one good only by decreasing its production of another.

T / F     6. If an economy initially produces a balanced mix of agricultural and manufactured goods, it could probably double its production of agricultural goods by devoting all of its productive resources to agriculture.

T / F     7. The two primary determinants of economic growth are expanding resources and improving technology.

T / F     8. In an economy that produces automobiles and video games, a technological advance in automobile manufacturing will likely have no effect on video game production levels.

T / F     9. The labor factor can be increased either by expanding the workforce or by making investments in human capital, such as offering on-the-job training.

T / F     10. The more an economy favors the production of consumption goods over capital goods, the stronger its economic growth is likely to be over time.

## Multiple Choice

Circle the correct answer.

1. Which of the following is *not* one of the three basic questions any economy must answer?
   a. How are goods and services to be produced?
   b. Who will receive these goods and services?
   c. How is the political leadership to be determined?
   d. What goods and services are to be produced?

2. What are the primary factors of production for any industry?
   a. political power, public relations, and advertising
   b. land, labor, capital, and entrepreneurship
   c. oil, coal, gas, and steel
   d. business owners, workers, consumers, and government regulators

3. Production is about the relationship between
   a. inputs and outputs.
   b. workers and management.
   c. firms and consumers.
   d. the decisions of individual producers and the growth of the economy as a whole.

4. In production possibility frontier analysis, which mixes of goods are considered to be attainable by an economy?
   a. only those mixes falling on the PPF curve
   b. those mixes on, or to the left of, the PPF curve
   c. those mixes on, or to the right of, the PPF curve
   d. only those mixes falling to the left of the PPF curve

5. What does the PPF curve show?
   a. the various levels of output producers are willing to supply at different price levels
   b. the quantity of output an economy will produce at varying levels of labor or some other input
   c. the best mix of goods for an economy to produce
   d. the various mixes of goods an economy can produce at full employment of its resources

6. If an economy is producing a mix of goods that falls directly on its production possibilities frontier, this indicates that
   a. consumers must be happy with the mix of goods produced.
   b. the economy is operating at full employment.
   c. the economy is leaving some resources unused.
   d. the economy is growing.

7. Opportunity cost is a measure of
   a. what it costs a firm to break into a new market.
   b. the increase in output that comes from adding inputs to the production process.
   c. the inputs a firm must purchase to be able to produce some good.
   d. the goods an individual or economy must forgo to produce or consume more of some other good.

8. If an economy must forgo building 700 new homes to produce 3500 new automobiles, what is the opportunity cost of one automobile?
   a. 0.2 home
   b. 1 home
   c. 5 homes
   d. 700 homes

9. An economy that devotes half of its resources to producing guns and half to producing butter turns out 1000 guns and 1000 pounds of butter every year. If this economy were to begin devoting all of its resources to producing guns, how many guns would we expect it to produce annually?
   a. something less than 2000 guns
   b. right around 2000 guns
   c. something more than 2000 guns
   d. We have no grounds for making any predictions.

10. The primary factors underlying economic growth are
    a. decreasing consumer demand and improving technology.
    b. expanding resources and rising interest rates.
    c. rising exports and declining imports.
    d. expanding resources and improving technology.

11. Which of the following would *not* be an investment in human capital?
    a. researching automated production techniques
    b. putting more money into the education system
    c. beginning a job-training program
    d. launching an employee physical fitness campaign

12. Which of the following would *not* be an expected outcome of investing in human capital?
    a. higher wages
    b. increased worker productivity
    c. an expanded PPF
    d. higher rates of workplace injuries

13. Which economic policy is most likely to promote strong economic growth in the long run? (Ignore the possibilities of international trade.)
    a. more consumption goods and fewer capital goods
    b. more capital goods and fewer consumption goods
    c. exclusively consumption goods
    d. more TIVO recorders

14. If an economy produces guns and butter, and a technological innovation makes the production of guns cheaper, we would expect the economy's production of butter to
    a. decrease.

b. remain about the same.
c. increase.
d. be unpredictable.

15. Additional capital means
    a. that each unit of labor become less efficient.
    b. higher possible production throughout the economy.
    c. high production, but only in a few parts of the economy.
    d. little difference in production or efficiency.

16. Which change would *not* be a way of stimulating economic growth?
    a. using more resources
    b. raising educational levels
    c. improving incentives for private firms to increase production
    d. restricting trade to protect the automobile industry

17. Which answer would *not* be an outcome of the ripple effect of technological change?
    a. new products
    b. improved goods and services
    c. increased efficiency
    d. improving efficiency in one industry, but not others

18. In Figure MC-1, assume that an economy starts with a PPF curve at $PPF_0$. Economic growth occurs when the economy
    a. moves on the $PPF_0$ curve from consumer goods to capital goods (point $b$ to point $a$).
    b. moves from $PPF_0$ to $PPF_1$.
    c. moves from $PPF_0$ to $PPF_2$.
    d. moves on the $PPF_0$ curve from capital goods to consumer goods (point $a$ to point $b$).

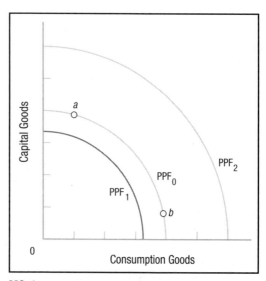

**MC-1**

19. In a positive-sum game involving two parties, which of the following is true?t
    a. Both parties can and generally do make positive gains.
    b. For one party to gain, the other party must lose.
    c. Neither party can hope to make any gains.
    d. Both parties will invariably make equal gains.

20. If one country has a comparative advantage over another, which of the following can happen?
    a. It can produce more of some product than the other country.
    b. It can produce some product at a lower opportunity cost than can the other country.
    c. It produces higher-quality products than the other country.
    d. It markets its products more quickly than the other country.

21. If one country has an absolute advantage over another, which of the following can happen?
    a. It can produce more of some product than the other country.
    b. It can produce some product at a lower opportunity cost than can the other country.
    c. It produces higher-quality products than the other country.
    d. It markets its products more quickly than the other country.

22. Two countries will benefit from trading with one another if
    a. each country concentrates on producing those goods at which it has an absolute advantage.
    b. the country with the greatest productive capacity does all of the production.
    c. each country concentrates on producing those goods at which it has a comparative advantage.
    d. each country produces only goods that the other cannot.

23. An economy with a highly educated workforce and large supply of capital, but relatively little land, would probably fare best in the global market by focusing on the production of which of these?
    a. wheat
    b. coal
    c. microcomputers
    d. timber

24. American standards of living have increased over the second half of the last century because of
    a. control of immigration.
    b. restrictions on trade.
    c. expansion of resources and technological progress.
    d. reductions in our trade deficit.

25. A likely outcome of signing the North American Free Trade Agreement (NAFTA) would be
    a. lower growth in the United States.
    b. job losses in some industries but increased potential for overall growth.
    c. job losses throughout the U.S. economy.
    d. no job losses in any part of the economy.

## Essay-Problem

Answer in the space provided.

Some of the questions below are challenging. Don't get discouraged if your answers are not always the same as those we suggest. Use these as another way to assess your progress, but more important, to discover and learn some of the subtleties surrounding production, economic growth, and trade.

1. What is the essence of the three basic economic questions?

2. Describe the specific resources (factors of production) that a typical Apple computer store might use. Be specific in your description—do not just suggest "land, labor, capital, and entrepreneurial talent."

3. Is it likely that any country produces on its PPF?

4. If an economy that initially produces a balanced mix of corn and computers begins shifting more and more of its resources into the production of computers, why does the opportunity cost of computers eventually begin rising?

5. Has the Internet generated economic growth?

6. If expanding resources help an economy to grow, name some ways to expand resources.

7. How have computers spurred economic growth?

8. Name some of the short-term costs and long-term benefits of expanding international trade.

9. If international trade benefits both trading partners, why would countries erect trade barriers?

10. Explain how cell phones have helped countries around the world achieve quicker economic growth.

11. Using the information from the table below, draw a PPF curve for an economy that produces cars and boats. (Put cars on the horizontal axis.)

**Possible Combinations**

| Cars | Boats |
| --- | --- |
| 0 | 125 |
| 60 | 120 |
| 120 | 105 |
| 170 | 80 |
| 200 | 60 |
| 225 | 30 |
| 250 | 0 |

Which of the following mixes are attainable by the economy, and which are unattainable?
    a. 100 cars; 100 boats
    b. 200 cars; 75 boats
    c. 50 cars; 125 boats

## What's Next

This chapter provided an introduction to how economic growth arises and how comparative advantage and international trade spur economic growth. We took individual and societal preferences for granted. In the next chapter, we look at demand and supply, the bedrock concept in economics. We will explore how individuals signal their demands for goods and services, and how firms respond to these signals.

## Answers to Chapterwide Practice Questions

### Matching

| | | | |
|---|---|---|---|
| 1. f | 4. i | 6. a | 8. h |
| 2. b | 5. c | 7. g | 9. d |
| 3. e | | | |

### Fill-In

1. how will the goods and services be produced
2. resources, capital, profit
3. allocatively efficient, productive efficiency
4. attainable, unattainable, unemployment, full employment
5. opportunity costs, increasing
6. economic growth, resources, technology
7. absolute, comparative, comparative

### True-False

| | | | |
|---|---|---|---|
| 1. F | 4. F | 7. T | 9. T |
| 2. T | 5. T | 8. F | 10. F |
| 3. F | 6. F | | |

### Multiple Choice

| | | | |
|---|---|---|---|
| 1. c | 8. a | 14. c | 20. b |
| 2. b | 9. a | 15. b | 21. a |
| 3. a | 10. d | 16. d | 22. c |
| 4. b | 11. a | 17. d | 23. c |
| 5. d | 12. d | 18. c | 24. c |
| 6. b | 13. b | 19. a | 25. b |
| 7. d | | | |

### Essay-Problem

1. All economic systems have to answer the questions of what to produce, how to produce it, and who gets goods and services, but the answers can differ.
2. The typical Apple computer store hires labor (sales staff who are very familiar with Apple products and computer technicians). Typically, they rent space in retail centers, the land component. Inside the stores are considerable fixtures, working products, inventory, and

other capital-including lights, registers, and phones. Some individual manages each store, and to this extent that person represents the entrepreneur.

3. Production possibilities analysis is very stylized and assumes that all inputs are used efficiently, a highly unlikely situation. Nevertheless, PPF analysis is still useful for thinking about production and growth.

4. In the initial situation, the economy likely uses those resources most suitable to corn production for producing corn, and those resources more suitable to computer production for producing computers. Most of the economy's low-skilled labor, for instance, will probably be working in the cornfields, whereas its high-skilled workers will be laboring efficiently in the computer industry. As ever more computers get produced, however, resources must be drawn from the corn industry, many of them suited more to corn production than to computer production. Low-skilled field hands, for instance, may suddenly find themselves in microchip factories, where they may be ill-suited to working efficiently. Such resource shifts significantly reduce the quantity of corn the economy can produce, while only marginally improving its output of computers. Thus, the more computers produced, the higher their opportunity cost will be, measured in terms of corn.

5. Among many specific answers, here is one. The Internet has enabled shoppers to compare prices of goods quickly. This has facilitated consumption, especially in less developed areas of the world. Increasing consumption has often been a motor to growth. The Internet has also significantly reduced transactions costs for many products. Auction firms like eBay have opened up huge markets for goods that were heretofore extremely difficult to obtain. Finding old books and obscure items previously involved incredible search costs.

6. One general way an economy can expand its labor factor is by increasing the number of people in the workforce. It might do this by increasing immigration, raising the national birthrate, or encouraging more potential workers to enter the workforce. By reducing discrimination in labor markets, the government was able to expand the labor force as more women and minorities entered. The second general way an economy can expand the labor factor is by raising the skill level of workers already employed, thereby increasing their productivity. This is known as investing in human capital. Some examples of investments in human capital are improving the educational system, providing on-the-job training, and improving employee health care.

7. Computers have spurred economic growth in many ways. Robotics, highly dependent on computers, have made production of products such as automobiles and snow blowers much more efficient and improved product quality. Computers have made planning much easier because making changes to numbers is not the cumbersome task it was before computerized spreadsheets. Computers have also become major communication devices, especially around the globe.

8. When a country expands its trade, it generally increases its production of those goods at which it has a comparative advantage, shipping many of them abroad, while increasing its import of those goods at which it is at a comparative disadvantage. Domestic producers of the latter goods will see their profits fall when cheaper imports begin flooding the market; they may have to close down or lay off workers. The short-term pain for these firms and individuals is real. Nevertheless, if both entrepreneurs and workers begin moving into production sectors that are enjoying strong foreign sales, they stand to see their profits and wages rise in the long run. With global production and consumption rising as countries everywhere produce more of those goods at which they have comparative advantages, all of those who participate in expanded international trade should experience positive gains in the long run.

9. Trade, while beneficial to a country overall, may hurt specific industries that are now at a comparative disadvantage. These specific industries may seek political recourse. The political bark of a harmed industry often is much louder than the satisfaction of individuals benefiting from trade because the benefit may be small to each person, though great when summed together. Industries harmed by trade have an easier time focusing resources and lobbying efforts than can consumers.

10. Twenty years ago, telephone communication required huge expenditures in infrastructure: Telephone cable had to be laid or strung up on telephone poles. Today, cell-phone towers are much, much cheaper to produce. Cell phones have spurred communication without massive expenditures in infrastructure.

11.

(a) attainable
(b) unattainable
(c) unattainable

# Supply and Demand

Illustration Works/Alamy

## Most Economic Issues Involve Supply and Demand in Some Way

Supply and demand form the foundation of economics. You will use these concepts throughout the remainder of the semester. To understand how market economies operate, you will need to have a firm grasp of supply and demand analysis. Nearly every economic problem you confront will be clarified in some way by this analysis.

| This Is What You Need to Know | STEP 1 |
|---|---|

**After studying this chapter you should be able to**

- Describe the nature and purposes of markets.

- Describe the nature of demand, demand curves, and the law of demand.

- Describe the determinants of demand and be able to forecast how a change in one or more of these determinants will change demand.

- Describe the difference between a change in demand and a change in quantity demanded.

- Describe the nature of supply, supply curves, and the law of supply.

- Describe the determinants of supply and be able to forecast how a change in one or more of these determinants will change supply.

- Describe the difference between a change in supply and a change in quantity supplied.

- Determine market equilibrium price and output.

■ Determine and predict how price and output will change given changes to supply and demand in the market.

■ Understand the impacts of government intervention in markets.

## STEP 2          Review the Key Terms

**Markets:** Institutions that bring buyers and sellers together so they can interact and transact with each other.

**Price system:** A name given to the market economy because prices provide considerable information to both buyers and sellers.

**Demand:** The maximum amount of a product that buyers are willing and able to purchase over some time period at various prices, holding all other relevant factors constant (the *ceteris paribus* condition).

**Law of demand:** Holding all other relevant factors constant, as price increases, quantity demanded falls, and as price decreases, quantity demanded rises.

**Demand curve:** Demand schedule information translated to a graph.

**Horizontal summation:** Market demand and supply curves are found by adding together how many units of the product will be purchased or supplied at each price.

**Determinants of demand:** Nonprice factors that affect demand, including tastes and preferences, income, prices of related goods, number of buyers, and expectations.

**Normal good:** A good for which an increase in income results in rising demand.

**Inferior good:** A good for which an increase in income results in declining demand.

**Substitute goods:** Goods consumers will substitute for one another depending on their relative prices.

**Complementary goods:** Goods that are typically consumed together.

**Change in demand:** Occurs when one or more of the determinants of demand changes, shown as a shift in the entire demand curve.

**Change in quantity demanded:** Occurs when the price of the product changes, shown as a movement along an existing demand curve.

**Supply:** The maximum amount of a product that sellers are willing and able to provide for sale over some time period at various prices, holding all other relevant factors constant (the *ceteris paribus* condition).

**Law of supply:** Holding all other relevant factors constant, as price increases, quantity supplied will rise, and as price declines, quantity supplied will fall.

**Supply curve:** Supply schedule information translated to a graph.

**Determinants of supply:** Nonprice factors that affect supply, including production technology, costs of resources, prices of other commodities, expectations, number of sellers, and taxes and subsidies.

**Change in supply:** Occurs when one or more of the determinants of supply change, shown as a shift in the entire supply curve.

**Change in quantity supplied:** Occurs when the price of the product changes, shown as a movement along an existing supply curve.

**Equilibrium:** Market forces are in balance when the quantities demanded by consumers just equal the quantities supplied by producers.

**Equilibrium price:** Market equilibrium price is the price that results when quantity demanded is just equal to quantity supplied.

**Equilibrium quantity:** Market equilibrium quantity is the output that results when quantity demanded is just equal to quantity supplied.

**Surplus:** Occurs when the price is above market equilibrium, and quantity supplied exceeds quantity demanded.

**Shortage:** Occurs when the price is below market equilibrium, and quantity demanded exceeds quantity supplied.

**Price ceiling:** A government-set maximum price that can be charged for a product or service. When the price ceiling is set below equilibrium, it leads to shortages.

**Price floor:** A government-set minimum price that can be charged for a product or service. When the price floor is set above equilibrium, it leads to surpluses.

## Work Through the Chapter Tutorials            STEP 3

# Demand

## Frequently Asked Questions

**Q: What are markets, and why are they important?**

A: Markets are institutions that enable buyers and sellers to interact and transact business with one another. Through their purchases, consumers signal their willingness to buy particular products at particular prices. These signals help businesses to decide what and how much to produce.

**Q: What is demand, and how are price and quantity demanded related?**

A: *Demand* refers to the quantity of products people are willing and able to purchase at various prices during some specific time period, all other relevant factors held constant. The *demand curve* shown in Figure 1 depicts the relationship between price and quantity demanded. Price and quantity demanded are negatively (inversely) related: As prices rise, consumers buy less, and vice versa. This inverse relation is known as the *law of demand.*

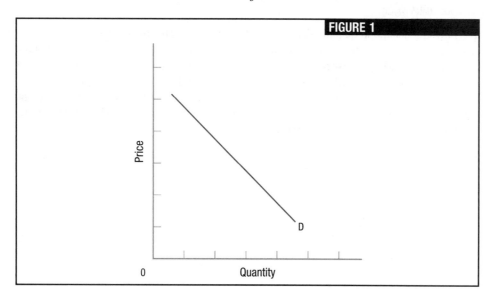

FIGURE 1

Q:  **What are the determinants of demand?**

A:  The *determinants of demand* include the following:
-  Consumer tastes and preferences
-  Income
-  Prices of substitutes and complements
-  The number of buyers in the market
-  Expectations regarding future prices, incomes, and product availability

Q:  **What causes the demand curve to shift?**

A:  *Demand changes (shifts)* when one or more of these determinants change. In Figure 2 a new popular ad campaign for Nalgene bottles would shift demand from $D_0$ to $D_1$. Alternatively, the ease of making digital copies could reduce the demand for music CDs, as shown by the demand curve declining from $D_0$ to $D_2$.

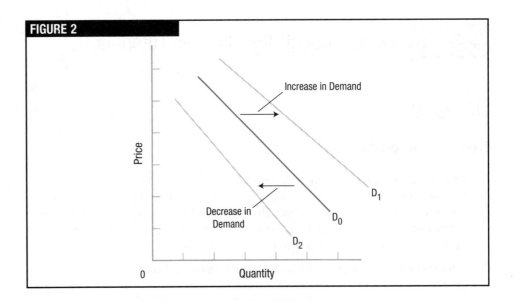

**FIGURE 2**

Q:  **How are market demand curves determined?**

A:  *Market demand curves* are found by horizontally summing individual demand curves. We simply add the total quantities demanded by all consumers for each possible price.

Q:  **How is a change in quantity demanded different from a change in demand?**

A:  A *change in quantity demanded* occurs only when the *price* of a product changes, leading consumers to adjust their purchases along an existing demand curve. This is shown in Figure 3 as a movement from point *a* to point *b*. Note in this case that a reduced price of $P_2$ was required to increase sales. Contrast this with the movement from point *a* to point *c* (an increase in demand), where much more is sold at the same price, $P_0$.

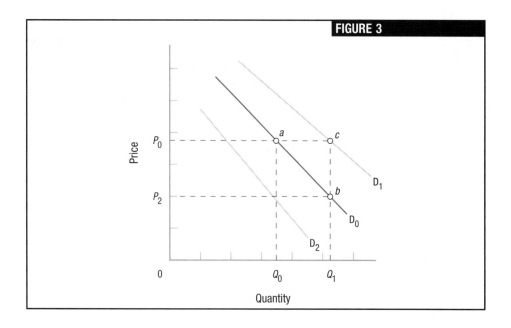

**FIGURE 3**

## Demand Quick Check

### Circle the Correct Answer

1. (T/F) The major benefit of markets is that they bring sellers and buyers together to transact business.
2. (T/F) The law of demand states that demand increases (demand curves shift to the right) when income increases.
3. (T/F) All markets have roughly the same number of buyers and sellers.
4. (T/F) Demand curves always have positive slopes reflecting the law of demand.
5. Which of the following is *not* a determinant of demand for orange juice?
   a. consumer after-tax income
   b. price of tomato juice
   c. medical research on the benefits of orange juice
   d. agricultural subsides (government payments) to farmers to grow more oranges
6. Which of the following will cause an increase in the demand for steel?
   a. Price of automobile tires increases because of a shortage of rubber from Malaysia.
   b. Concrete steel reinforcing rods are replaced by aluminum to reduce rust along the Atlantic seaboard.
   c. Gasoline prices are reduced by 50% because OPEC countries (the Middle East oil cartel) break into a quarrel and all countries expand production.
   d. McDonald's increases its production of hamburgers and fries to meet demand when a medical study concludes that fries are healthy alternatives to vegetables.
7. Which of the following is *not* a determinant of demand for MP3 players?
   a. the price of television sets
   b. consumer income
   c. the quality of music available in MP3 format
   d. the quantity of music available in MP3 format
8. An increase in demand means that
   a. the demand curve shifts upward and to the left.
   b. the demand curve shifts downward and to the right.
   c. more goods are purchased at the same price.
   d. fewer sellers are willing to sell the good.

9. The essence of a sale is (see Figure 4)
   a. reducing price to increase the quantity demanded.
   b. an attempt by sellers to increase consumer satisfaction.
   c. a movement from point *a* to point *c* in the figure.
   d. a shift in the demand curve from $D_0$ to $D_1$ in the figure.

10. A decrease in quantity demanded in Figure 4 can be characterized by
    a. a shift in the demand curve from $D_0$ to $D_1$.
    b. a movement from point *a* to point *c*.
    c. a shift in the demand curve from $D_0$ to $D_2$.
    d. a movement from point *b* to point *a*.

Score: ____

**FIGURE 4**

## If You Got 9 or 10 Correct

You have the concepts of demand, changes in demand, and changes in quantity demanded under control. Keep in mind that a change in one or more of the determinants of demand *shifts* the demand curve and is a *change in demand*, while a *change in quantity demanded* is caused by a change in the price of the product and is a movement *along* an existing demand curve. Go on to the next section, Supply.

## If You Didn't Get at Least 9 Correct

Keep in mind that it may take more than a cursory reading of the text to capture these concepts. To be able to use the analysis presented, it may take some time and effort. But given the importance of demand and supply analysis to the study of economics, give it a little more time than usual. Take a moment and go back and review the section on demand.

## Keep in Mind

■ Demand refers to
  □ the amount of a product . . .
  □ that people are willing and able to buy . . .
  □ at various prices . . .
  □ over some time period . . .
  □ holding all other relevant factors constant.
■ The other relevant factors are the determinants of demand:
  □ tastes and preferences
  □ income

□ prices of substitutes and complements
□ number of buyers in the market
□ expectations of future prices, income, and product availability
■ When a determinant changes, the demand curve shifts.
■ A change in one or more of the determinants *shifts* the demand curve and is a *change in demand*, while a *change in quantity demanded* is caused by a change in the product's *price* and is a movement *along* an existing demand curve.

Now that you have reread the section, take a crack at the problem below. Once you have answered the questions yourself, follow along as the solution to the problem takes you through getting from individual demands to a market demand curve. ■

## Solved Problem: Market Demands from Individual Demands

Use the table below, assuming the market consists only of the three people given. First, fill in the table by determining the market demand curve. Next, use the grid to construct the individual demand curves. Finally,

| | Quantity Demanded | | | | | |
|---|---|---|---|---|---|---|
| Price | Lisa | Mildred | Nan | Market | 50% | 200% |
| $100 | 0 | 1 | 1 | _____ | _____ | _____ |
| 80 | 1 | 2 | 3 | _____ | _____ | _____ |
| 60 | 2 | 3 | 5 | _____ | _____ | _____ |
| 40 | 3 | 4 | 7 | _____ | _____ | _____ |
| 20 | 4 | 5 | 9 | _____ | _____ | _____ |

construct the market demand curve. Now assume some event reduces the market demand by one-half (50%). Complete the table and show the new demand curve on the graph. Next, assume that just the opposite occurs and the market doubles (200%). Again, complete the table and show the new market demand on the graph.

## Solution-Discussion

The market demand curve is the horizontal summation of individual demands. When the price is $100, adding up the quantities demanded by each of the three individuals gives 2 (Mildred and Nan each are willing and able to buy one apiece, and Lisa wants none). When the price is $60, Lisa buys 2 (point $a$); Mildred, 3 (point $b$); and Nan, 5 (point $c$). Adding all three quantities demanded equals 10 (point $d$) on the market demand curve. Doing the same for all five prices yields the market demand as shown. All four curves are plotted in Figure 5. Next, when demand drops by 50%, it equals half of the total of the original market demand, which in this instance is just equal to Nan's demand. When demand doubles (200%), all values double; demand shifts outward by twice the original demand curve and is shown as $D_{200\%}$.

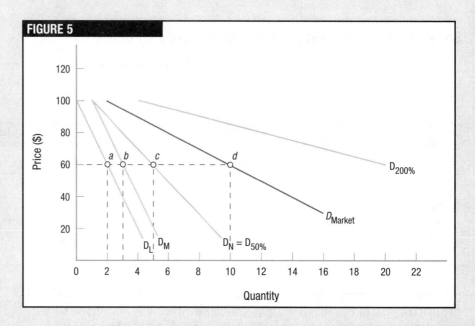

**FIGURE 5**

| Quantity Demanded | | | | | |
|---|---|---|---|---|---|
| Price | Lisa | Mildred | Nan | Market | 50% | 200% |
| $100 | 0 | 1 | 1 | 2 | 1 | 4 |
| 80 | 1 | 2 | 3 | 6 | 3 | 12 |
| 60 | 2 | 3 | 5 | 10 | 5 | 20 |
| 40 | 3 | 4 | 7 | 14 | 7 | 28 |
| 20 | 4 | 5 | 9 | 18 | 9 | 36 |

Ideally, you now see the logic behind demand. If you are not comfortable with this section on demand, reread the Frequently Asked Questions, then retake the quick quiz above. Because the supply section is quite similar in structure to demand, you will in all likelihood begin to see the pattern. Good luck with supply.

# Supply

## Frequently Asked Questions

Q: **What is supply, and how are price and quantity supplied related?**

A: *Supply* represents the quantity of a product producers are willing and able to put on the market at various prices, when all other relevant factors are held constant. The *law of supply* reflects the positive relationship between price and quantity supplied: As the supply curve in Figure 6 shows, the higher the market price, the more goods supplied, and vice versa. *Market supply*, as with market demand, is arrived at by horizontally summing the individual supplies of all firms.

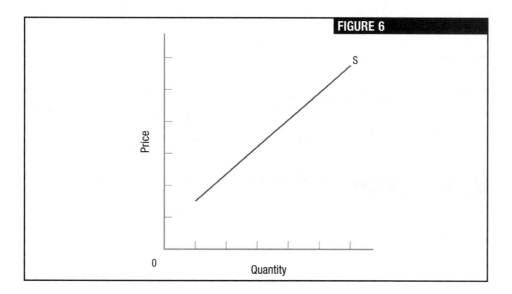

**FIGURE 6**

Q: **What are the determinants of supply?**

A: The *determinants of supply* are the following:
- production technology
- the cost of resource inputs
- prices of other commodities
- expectations
- number of sellers or producers in the market
- taxes and subsidies

Q: **How is a change in supply defined?**

A: A *change in supply* results when one or more of the determinants of supply change. A shift to the right, as shown in Figure 7 on the next page, reflects an increase in supply (from $S_0$ to $S_1$), whereas a shift to the left (from $S_0$ to $S_2$) represents a decrease in supply.

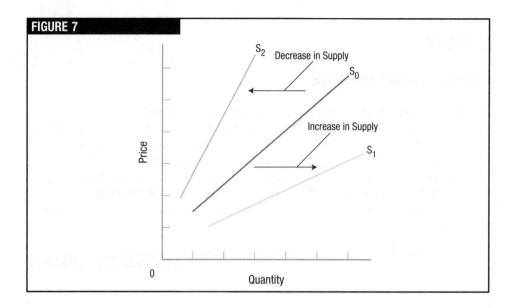

**FIGURE 7**

**Q:** **How does a change in quantity supplied differ from a change in supply?**

**A:** A *change in quantity supplied* is only caused by a change in the *price* of the product; it is a movement along an existing supply curve. A reduction in price results in a reduction of quantity supplied. This is shown in Figure 8 as a

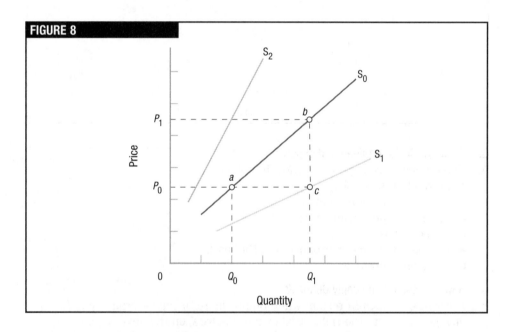

**FIGURE 8**

movement from point $b$ to point $a$, on supply curve $S_0$. A price increase leads to an increase in quantity supplied. This is shown as the reverse movement from point $a$ to point $b$.

Contrast this with the movement from point $a$ to point $c$ (an increase in supply) where much more is sold, even though the price is held to $P_0$.

## Supply Quick Check

### Circle the Correct Answer

1. (T/F) The law of supply states that higher prices will lead producers to offer less of their product for sale during a given period.
2. (T/F) A supply curve always slopes up and to the right to show that quantity supplied increases with price.
3. (T/F) If producers expect higher prices, that usually leads to an increase in supply.
4. Which of the following is *not* a determinant of supply?
   a. costs of resources
   b. consumer tastes and preferences
   c. production technology
   d. the number of sellers (producers) in the market
5. A decrease in supply will cause the supply curve to shift
   a. up and to the left.
   b. up and to the right.
   c. down and to the left.
   d. down and to the right.
6. When the price of a product increases from $P_0$ to $P_1$ in Figure 9,
   a. quantity supplied decreases from $S_0$ to $S_2$.
   b. quantity supplied increases from $Q_0$ to $Q_1$.
   c. supply decreases to $S_2$.
   d. supply increases to $S_1$.

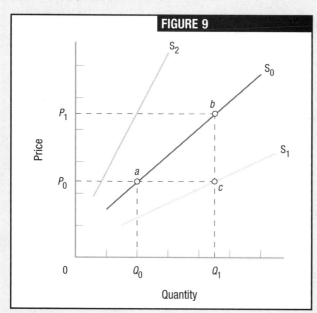

**FIGURE 9**

7. The prices of other commodities affect supply because
   a. producers will switch to produce a more profitable commodity.
   b. consumers will buy more of a cheaper commodity.
   c. consumers will switch to complementary goods.

d. producers will increase their price to keep pace with other commodities.

8. A change in supply of HDTV sets
   a. results from a change in consumer tastes and preferences.
   b. results from a price change.
   c. results in a change in the amount of HDTVs offered at every price.
   d. leads to a corresponding change in demand for HDTV sets.
   e. results from an improved picture aspect ratio.
9. Determinants of supply affect
   a. the entire supply curve.
   b. the quantity supplied only.
   c. the number of consumers who want the product.
   d. the quantity demanded.
10. Which of the following is correct concerning the market for baseball gloves shown in Figure 10?
    a. If glove manufacturers raise the price of their gloves from $P_0$ to $P_1$, quantity supplied decreases from $S_0$ to $S_2$.
    b. Excess livestock production leads to falling leather prices, so quantity supplied increases from $Q_0$ to $Q_1$.
    c. Excess livestock production leads to falling leather prices, resulting in supply decreasing to $S_2$.
    d. Excess livestock production leads to falling leather prices, so supply increases to $S_1$.

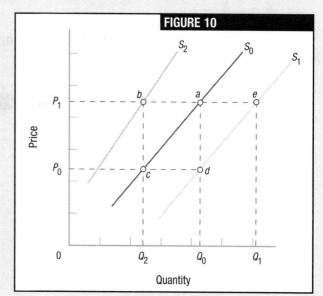

**FIGURE 10**

Score: ____

## If You Got 9 or 10 Correct

You have mastered the concepts of supply, changes in supply, and changes in quantity supplied. You obviously noticed how closely the concepts of supply and demand structurally parallel each other. Keep in mind that a change in one or more of the determinants of supply *shifts* the supply curve and is a *change in supply*, while a *change in quantity supplied* is caused by a change in the product's price and is a movement *along* an existing supply curve. Go on to the next section, Market Equilibrium.

## If You Didn't Get at Least 9 Correct

You probably didn't do well on the previous section either. Both demand and supply follow the same general principles for different sides of the market. Demand focuses on consumers' decisions and what they wish and are able and willing to purchase, while supply looks at business decisions to supply goods, but in a quite similar way.

### Keep in Mind

Changes in demand and changes in supply are defined in a similar fashion: They are caused by a change in one (or more) of the determinants. Similarly, a change in quantity demanded or a change in quantity supplied are both caused by just a change in the price of that product. A change in quantity demanded or supplied means a movement from one point on the curve to another. In contrast, a change in demand or supply means that the market now faces an entirely new demand or supply curve.

Before you move on, work through the solved problem below. ∎

---

## Solved Problem: Supply

Use Figure 11 to answer the questions that follow.

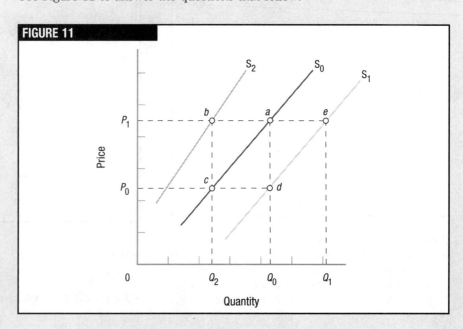

FIGURE 11

a. Assume the market is initially at point $a$ on $S_0$. A decline in quantity supplied would be represented by what point? _____

b. If the market was initially at point $a$ and production technology underwent substantial improvement, which curve would represent the resulting increase in supply? _____

c. Assume the market is initially at point $d$. An increase in quantity supplied would be represented by which point? _____

d. If supply is initially $S_0$, which curve represents a decline in supply?

_____

e. A move from point $a$ to point $c$ represents a _____.

f. A movement from point $c$ to point $b$ represents a _____.

## Solution-Discussion

a. A decline in quantity supplied is a movement along an existing supply curve, so quantity supplied declines from point $a$ to point $c$, and this is caused by a reduction in price from $P_1$ to $P_0$.

b. Supply curve $S_1$ would represent an improvement in technology increasing supplies to the market.

c. An increase in quantity supplied is caused by a change in price from point $d$ to point $e$.

d. Supply curve $S_2$ represents a decrease in supply. Increases in input costs, for example, will shift the supply curve to the left.

e. A decrease in quantity supplied, because it is a movement along an existing supply curve.

f. A decrease in supply, since the curve has shifted to the left. Note that on supply curve $S_2$, less is provided to the market at each price.

Now that you have worked through this solved problem, see if you can complete the following exercise before you go on to the next section on market equilibrium. This short exercise asks you to create both demand and supply curves and explain some of their features.

## Exercise for You to Complete

1. Using the blank grid on the next page, draw the axis lines and label the vertical axis "price" and the horizontal axis "quantity."

2. Draw a demand curve on this graph and label it $D_0$. Pick any point on the demand curve and label it point $a$. Pick another point on the demand curve with a lower price and label it point $b$.

3. Explain how points $a$ and $b$ illustrate the law of demand. _____

_____

_____

4. When price rises from point $b$ to point $a$ and quantity demanded drops, economists refer to this as a(n) _____.

5. Recessions tend to put a damper on demand. Draw a new demand curve that represents a decrease in demand and label it $D_1$. How is this different from what you described in question 4?

_____

_____

6. Again, using the blank grid below, draw the axis lines and label the vertical axis "price" and the horizontal axis "quantity."

7. Draw a supply curve on this graph and label it $S_0$. Pick any point on the supply curve and label it point $c$. Pick another point on the supply curve with a higher price and label it point $d$.

8. Explain how points $c$ and $d$ illustrate the law of supply.

_____

_____

9. When price rises from point $c$ to point $d$ and quantity supplied grows, economists refer to this as a(n) _____.

10. When the cost of microcomputer chips falls, it increases supply. Draw a new supply curve in the graph reflecting this increase. How is this different from what you described in question 9?

_____

_____

## Answers

(3) When the price of a product is reduced from point $a$ to point $b$, quantity demanded increases. This is the law of demand. (4) Decrease in quantity demanded. (5) Shifting to a new curve is a decrease in demand: At all prices, consumers want to buy less of the product. (8) When the price of a product is increased from point $c$ to point $d$, quantity supplied increases. This is the law of supply. (9) Increase in quantity supplied. (10) Shifting to a new curve (the supply curve shifts rightward) is an increase in supply: At all prices, firms are willing to provide more of the product to the market.

Keep in mind that supply and demand form the foundation of most of what you will study this semester. At this point, you may want to reread both of these sections in the text, then rework the previous two sections again. The next section on equilibrium brings the concepts of supply and demand together, and the level of complexity grows. Spend a little extra time here; it will pay dividends throughout the remainder of the course.

# Market Equilibrium

## Frequently Asked Questions

Q:  **What is market equilibrium?**
A:  Supply and demand together determine *market equilibrium*. Equilibrium occurs when quantity demanded and quantity supplied are equal. Equilibrium is shown in Figure 12 on the next page as point $e$. This means that producers offer for sale precisely the quantity that consumers are willing to purchase at that price. Equilibrium price, $P_0$, is that price where the market clears the equilibrium quantity of $Q_0$. If price temporarily gets above market equilibrium, inventories accumulate as consumers buy less than suppliers want to provide, so the market price drops to equilibrium. If price is temporarily below equilibrium, buyers want more than sellers are willing to sell, so prices begin rising toward equilibrium at point $e$.

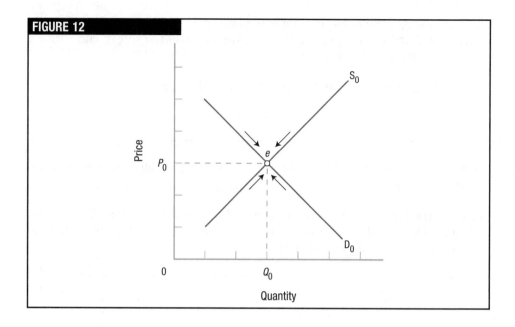

**FIGURE 12**

Q: **When supply or demand change, what can be predicted?**

A: When supply and demand change (a shift in the curves), equilibrium price and output change. When only *one* curve shifts, both resulting changes in equilibrium price and quantity can be predicted. For example, in Figure 13, if demand increases from $D_0$ to $D_1$, both equilibrium output and price will rise as equilibrium moves from point $e$ to point $c$.

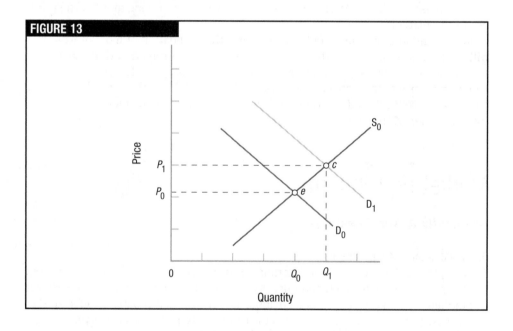

**FIGURE 13**

Q: **When supply and demand both change, what can be predicted?**

A: When *both* curves shift, the change in equilibrium price can be forecast in some instances, and the change in equilibrium output in others, but in no case can both be forecast without more information. For example, when demand rises and supply falls, the equilibrium price will rise to $P_2$ (point $b$ in Figure 14), but the change in equilibrium output is uncertain. Whether output will rise or fall depends on the relative size of the shifts between demand and supply.

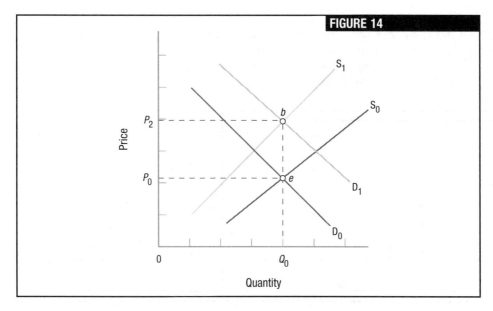

**FIGURE 14**

Alternatively, when demand rises and supply rises (people want more and more is available), equilibrium output will rise, but the change in equilibrium price is indeterminate without knowing about the relative size of the shifts between demand and supply.

## Solved Problem: When Both Supply and Demand Curves Shift

1. Consider a scenario in which consumer demand for influenza vaccine increases because of a more severe than normal winter flu epidemic, while drug manufacturers are using new DNA techniques that permit them to produce vaccines more quickly and cheaply.

   Graph the three possible price and output scenarios for the flu vaccine market in the grids below.

   a.   What will happen to the price of vaccines? (rise, fall, uncertain)

   _____

   b.   What will happen to the output of vaccines? (rise, fall, uncertain)

   _____

2. Now consider what happens in the cellular phone market if cell phone use is shown to have serious detrimental health effects if used more than 10 minutes a day. At the same time, microchip production confronts the

end of Moore's Law (the speed of microchips doubles every 18 months at lower costs) and costs rise substantially.

Graph the three possible price and output scenarios for the cell phone market in the grids below.

  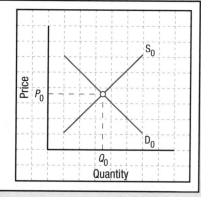

a.  What will happen to the price of cell phones? (rise, fall, uncertain)

_____

b.  What will happen to the output of cell phones? (rise, fall, uncertain) _____

3. Now consider the market for Toyota's vehicles if China offers high prices for steel and absorbs most of the world's output for its own development efforts, increasing the price of steel. Toyota, however, develops a plug-in hybrid that averages over 100 miles per gallon, goes 100 miles on a charge, and sells for under $20,000.

Graph the three possible price and output scenarios for Toyota cars in the grids below.

  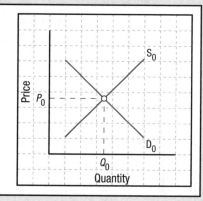

a.  What will happen to the price of Toyota cars? (rise, fall, uncertain)

_____

b.  What will happen to the output of Toyota cars? (rise, fall, uncertain) _____

4. Finally, let's look at the market for tape recorders and their decline in the digital age. However, costs to manufacture these devices have also fallen given changing production technology.

Graph the three possible price and output scenarios for the tape recorder market in the grids below.

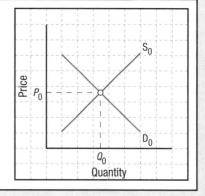

a. What will happen to the price of tape recorders? (rise, fall, uncertain) _____

b. What will happen to the output of tape recorders? (rise, fall, uncertain) _____

## Solution-Discussion

1. See Figure 15 below. In this situation both demand and supply increase and output will rise. What will happen to equilibrium price is uncertain. If demand and supply increase at the same rate, the price will remain the same (panel B). If the change in demand is larger than the change in supply, the price will rise (panel A), and the price will drop when supply increases more than demand (panel C).

**FIGURE 15**

2. See Figure 16 on the next page. In this situation both demand and supply for cell phones decline and output will fall. Again, what will happen to equilibrium price is uncertain. If demand and supply decline at the same rate, the price will remain the same (panel B). If the drop in demand is larger than the drop in supply, the price will fall (panel A), but if supply drops more than demand, price will rise (panel C).

**FIGURE 16**

Panel A
Change in Demand > Change in Supply

Panel B
Change in Demand = Change in Supply

Panel C
Change in Demand < Change in Supply

3. See Figure 17 below. In this situation the supply of Toyotas declines because a input into production costs more, but the development of the plug-in hybrid results in an increase in demand. In this case, price will clearly rise, but what happens to equilibrium output is uncertain. If demand and supply change at the same rate, output will remain the same (panel B). If the increase in demand is larger than the drop in supply, output will rise (panel A), and if supply drops more than the increase in demand, output will fall (panel C).

**FIGURE 17**

Panel A
Change in Demand > Change in Supply

Panel B
Change in Demand = Change in Supply

Panel C
Change in Demand < Change in Supply

4. See Figure 18. In this situation the supply of tape recorders increases due to technology, but the demand declines given the digital alternatives. In this case, price will fall, but again, what happens to equilibrium output is uncertain. If demand and supply change at the same rate, output will remain the same (panel B). If the drop in demand is larger than the increase in supply, output will fall (panel A), and if supply increases more than the decrease in demand, output will rise (panel C).

**FIGURE 18**

Panel A
**Change in Demand > Change in Supply**

Panel B
**Change in Demand = Change in Supply**

Panel C
**Change in Demand < Change in Supply**

# Market Equilibrium Quick Check

## Circle the Correct Answer

1. (T/F) Markets clear at the equilibrium price.
2. (T/F) A product's equilibrium price found where the demand curve intersects the supply curve.
3. At equilibrium
   a. producers store surpluses for times of shortage.
   b. producers offer the exact amount of a product consumers want.
   c. producers switch to substitution products.
   d. consumers switch to complementary products.

Use Figure 19 to answer questions 4, 5, and 6. For questions 4 and 5, begin each question with market supply and demand equal to $S_0$ and $D_0$, respectively, with the market in equilibrium at point $e$. If demand or supply changes, assume it shifts to either $D_1$ or $S_1$.

4. If supply decreases and demand increases, what is the new equilibrium output?
5. The economic boom of the late 1990s caused incomes to rise dramatically in California. Assume the figure represents the housing market in San Jose, California. What is the new equilibrium price for housing?
6. (T/F) The movement from point $a$ to point $c$ in the figure is caused by an increase in both demand and supply.
7. Which of the following is *not* how markets adjust to shocks and disturbances?
   a. almost instantaneously
   b. after a period of adjustment
   c. only with government intervention
   d. differently

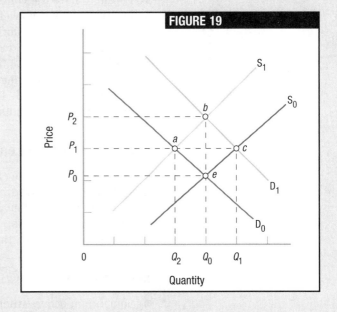

**FIGURE 19**

Use Figure 20 on the next page to answer questions 8, 9, and 10. For questions 8 and 9, begin each question with market supply and demand equal to $S_0$ and $D_0$, respectively, with the market in equilibrium at point $e$.

8. If supply increases and demand decreases, what is the new equilibrium price? _____
9. Nextel walkie-talkies are shown to increase worker productivity in auto glass delivery. This reduces costs to auto glass repair shops. Assume the figure represents the auto glass repair business. What is the impact on

**FIGURE 20**

equilibrium price for auto glass repairs? _____
_____

10. Describe what causes this market in the figure to move
from point *a* to point *c*. _____
_____

Score: ____

## If You Got 9 or 10 Correct

You seem to have the concepts of demand, supply, changes in supply and demand, and market equilibrium well in hand. Keep in mind that supply and demand together determine market equilibrium. If supply *or* demand change, you can predict the change in *both* price and quantity sold. If both of the supply *and* demand curves shift, *either* price or quantity sold can be predicted, but not both; one will be indeterminate without information on the relative size of the shifts between demand and supply. This is a little tricky, but you seem to have mastered it. Take a moment to review the section Hints, Tips, and Reminders.

## If You Didn't Get at Least 9 Correct

Don't panic. This is some of the most difficult material in the chapter and the book. It often takes students several attempts at this material to really master it. But keep in mind that it is probably the most important material in the book. Five years from now when you are moving up in your career, this is one of the three to four things you will remember from this course.

## Keep in Mind

- Equilibrium occurs where quantity supplied equals quantity demanded.
- When supply or demand (one or the other curve) shifts, you can determine the change in *both* price and quantity sold. The table below summarizes the predicted changes from an initial equilibrium when either the supply or demand curve shifts.

| Change in Demand or Supply | Change in Price | Change in Quantity Sold |
| --- | --- | --- |
| Demand increases | Increase | Increase |
| Demand decreases | Decrease | Decrease |
| Supply increases | Decrease | Increase |
| Supply decreases | Increase | Decrease |

■ When both curves shift, you can only predict the change in either price or quantity sold, but not both. The table below summarizes which variable (price or quantity sold) is predictable given that both curves have shifted.

| Change in Demand | Change in Supply | Change in Price | Change in Quantity Sold |
|---|---|---|---|
| Increase | Increase | Indeterminate | Increase |
| Decrease | Decrease | Indeterminate | Decrease |
| Increase | Decrease | Increase | Indeterminate |
| Decrease | Increase | Decrease | Indeterminate |

Before you move on, take some time to work through the solved problem below. Also, when you read the daily newspaper or the *Wall Street Journal*, look for articles where you can apply the concepts of supply and demand. You will find that there are several each week. This solved problem takes you through all that you have studied in this chapter. Pay particular attention to the description of the solution. ■

## Solved Problem

The monthly supply and demand data for MP3 players is outlined in the table below.

| Price | Quantity Demanded | Quantity Supplied | New Supply |
|---|---|---|---|
| $130 | 600 | 1,200 | _____ |
| 120 | 700 | 1,100 | _____ |
| 110 | 800 | 1,000 | _____ |
| 100 | 900 | 900 | _____ |
| 90 | 1,000 | 800 | _____ |
| 80 | 1,100 | 700 | _____ |
| 70 | 1,200 | 600 | _____ |

Use the grid and data in the table to answer the following questions.

a. Graph the curves in the grid above. Label the curves $S_0$ and $D_0$.

b. Equilibrium price is equal to _____.

c. Equilibrium output is equal to _____.

d. Assume initially that the price of MP3 players was set at $120. Would there be a shortage or surplus in this market? _____ How large would the shortage or surplus be? _____

Describe the kind of pressures that would exist in this market to move the price toward equilibrium. _____ _____

e. Now, assume, as is so often the case in these types of markets, that technological improvements in electronics manufacturing mean that supply increases by 25%. List the new supply values for each price in the last column of the table. Plot the new supply curve and label it S₁.

f. What is the new equilibrium price? _____

g. What is the new equilibrium output? _____

## Solution-Discussion

a.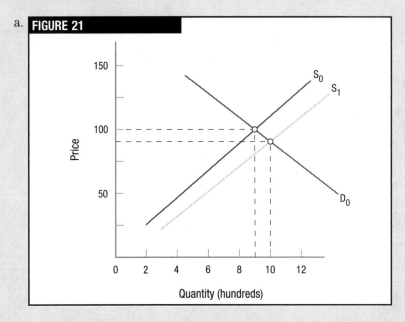

**FIGURE 21**

b. $100. At $100, quantity supplied (900) is equal to quantity demanded (900).

c. 900

d. Surplus, 400. Excess inventories lead to sales and other actions that would reduce prices.

e. See Figure 21. At every price, quantity supplied has increased by 25% (see table below).

| Price | Quantity Demanded | Quantity Supplied | New Supply |
|-------|-------------------|-------------------|------------|
| $130  | 600               | 1,200             | 1,500      |
| 120   | 700               | 1,100             | 1,375      |
| 110   | 800               | 1,000             | 1,250      |
| 100   | 900               | 900               | 1,125      |
| 90    | 1,000             | 800               | 1,000      |
| 80    | 1,100             | 700               | 875        |
| 70    | 1,200             | 600               | 750        |

f. $90

g. 1,000

As a final exercise, check to see what the new equilibrium price and output would be if demand now increased by 40%. This answer is that price rises to nearly $110, and output grows to around 1,200. Simple numerical problems like this provide the kind of insight you need when the questions get complicated. Always draw the original supply and demand curves and then work out the shifts (always the hard part), and the answers will be clear.

# Price Ceilings and Price Floors

## Frequently Asked Questions

Q: **When does government use price ceilings and price floors?**

A: When competitive markets are left to determine equilibrium price and output, they clear; that is, businesses provide consumers with the quantity of goods they want to purchase at the established prices. Nevertheless, the equilibrium price may not be what many people consider fair. The government may then use price ceilings or price floors to keep prices below or above the market equilibrium.

Q: **What are price ceilings, and what can happen with them?**

A: A price ceiling is the *maximum* legal price that can be charged for a product. Price ceilings set below market equilibrium result in shortages. In Figure 22, a price ceiling set at $P_1$ when the equilibrium price is $P_e$ will result in shortage $Q_2 - Q_1$.

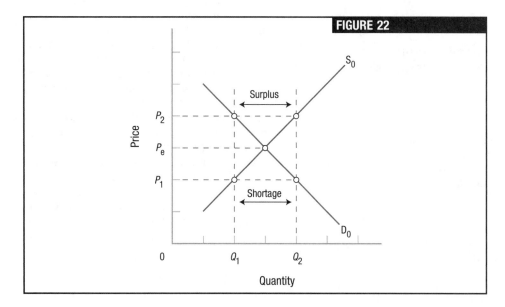

**FIGURE 22**

Q:   **What are price floors, and what can happen with them?**

A:   A price floor is the *minimum* legal price that can be charged for a product. Price floors set above market equilibrium result in surpluses. In Figure 22, a price floor set at $P_2$ when the equilibrium price is $P_e$ will result in surplus $Q_2 - Q_1$.

Q:   **Why do taxes cause a deadweight loss?**

A:   Taxes drive a wedge between what consumers pay for a product and what business receives. They raise the price of products and reduce the quantity sold. The result is that some transactions that would have occurred in the absence of taxation do not, and this means that some consumer and producer surplus are lost to society.

## Price Ceilings and Price Floors Quick Check

### Circle the Correct Answer

1. (T/F) Governments use price ceilings or price floors when markets do not clear.
2. (T/F) When price ceilings are set above the equilibrium price, shortages occur.
3. (T/F) Governments will use price ceilings when markets do not work.
4. If the government sets a price floor above an equilibrium price, this means
   a. shortages will occur.
   b. surpluses will occur.
   c. nothing will happen.
   d. the market will quickly return to equilibrium.
5. If the government sets a price ceiling below an equilibrium price, this means
   a. shortages will occur.
   b. surpluses will occur.
   c. nothing will happen.
   d. the market will quickly return to equilibrium.
6. If the government sets a price floor below an equilibrium price, this means
   a. shortages will occur.
   b. surpluses will occur.
   c. nothing will happen.
   d. the market will quickly return to equilibrium.
7. New York City politicians believe that private parking rates in Manhattan are too high, so they institute price ceilings below the current price. What happens to private parking spaces?
   a. Shortages occur.
   b. Surpluses occur.
   c. Nothing.
   d. The market adjusts quickly back to equilibrium.
8. Hospital orderlies convince the local government that they are being paid poorly for the work they do. The government decides to set a minimum wage that all hospitals must pay. After much discussion, the minimum wage is set $2.00 below the current wage. What happens to the number of hospital orderlies?
   a. There are fewer orderlies than wanted by hospitals.
   b. There are more orderlies than wanted by hospitals.
   c. Nothing.
   d. Dislocation happens at first, and then the market returns to equilibrium.
9. Now consider that the government sets the minimum wage at $2.00 above the current wage. What happens?
   a. There are fewer orderlies than wanted by hospitals.
   b. There are more orderlies than wanted by hospitals.
   c. Nothing.
   d. Dislocation happens at first, and then the market returns to equilibrium.
10. Some consumers convince state politicians that electricity is priced too high. They claim that families are being hurt by greedy utilities. The politicians then set a price ceiling at the current equilibrium price. Suddenly, the weather turns brutally hot in June, and people run their air conditioners much more. What happens?
    a. There is a surplus of electricity because the greedy utilities provide more in the hopes of making money from the situation.
    b. There is a shortage of electricity because utilities cannot meet the increased demand because of the price ceiling. There may be brownouts.
    c. Equilibrium is maintained because increased demand is a signal for utilities to increase supply.
    d. There are shortages at first because the utilities face an information problem of figuring out what demand is going to be, but this is solved quickly.

Score: ____

**Answers: 1. F; 2. F; 3. F; 4. b; 5. a; 6. c; 7. a; 8. c; 9. b; 10. b**

## If You Got 9 or 10 Correct

You picked up the concepts of price ceilings, price floors, and the impact of taxes on consumer and producer surplus and the resulting deadweight loss. Even so, you might find it useful to take a quick look at the section titled Hints, Tips, and Reminders.

## If You Didn't Get at Least 9 Correct

You need to review this material slowly because the principles are straightforward:

- Start by looking again at Figure 22. Put your pencil above and then below the equilibrium price, and ask yourself what happens when the government institutes a price ceiling or a price floor. Remember that price ceilings are the highest price a firm can charge, and price floors are the lowest price a firm can charge or pay.
- Go back to the text and review the two Figures 13 and 14; they separate price ceilings from price floors. This may help you see why shortages and surpluses can result.

## Key Point to Remember

Effective price ceilings and floors have an impact on markets. An effective price ceiling is the maximum price that can be charged, but if it is set below the equilibrium price, it will cause shortages. An effective price floor is the minimum price that can be charged or paid, but if it is set above equilibrium, it will cause surpluses.

Some of the questions in this section were a little difficult. Go back and reason out why you missed a question. Then take some time to work through the Hints, Tips, and Reminders section below. You will find some suggestions that will make studying this chapter easier. ■

## Consider These Hints, Tips, and Reminders                    STEP 4

1. **Reminder:** A change in one or more of the determinants of demand shifts the demand curve and is a change in demand, while a change in quantity demanded is caused by a change in the product's price and is a movement along an existing demand curve.

2. **Reminder:** A change in one or more of the determinants of supply shifts the supply curve and is a change in supply, while a change in quantity supplied is caused by a change in the product's price and is a movement along an existing supply curve.

3. **Reminder:** Supply and demand together determine market equilibrium. If supply or demand (one curve) changes (shifts), you can predict the change in both price and quantity sold. If both curves change (shift), either price or quantity sold can be predicted, not both; one variable will be indeterminate without more information on the relative size of the shifts between demand and supply.

4. The core graph on the next page shows market equilibrium along with a surplus and shortage. Shortages (surpluses) result when the price is temporarily below (above) equilibrium price.

5. One of the areas where students tend to falter is drawing graphs and working through changes in supply and demand in markets. One good approach to this issue is to always draw a graph when you are confronted with a question or

## Core Graph: Market Equilibrium

**Key Points**

When price is temporarily *above* equilibrium, there is a surplus since quantity supplied exceeds quantity demanded.

When supply and demand intersect and quantity demanded equals quantity supplied, the market is in equilibrium.

When price is temporarily *below* equilibrium, there is a shortage since quantity demanded exceeds quantity supplied.

problem involving supply and demand. To begin your analysis, start with a graph like that for the video cell phone market shown here.

Use the subscript 0 for the original position. Begin with equilibrium labeled "e"; then ask "Is only price changing?" If so, you know that you are moving along an original supply or demand curve. If the answer is no, then ask "Do the facts of the question mean that a determinant is changing?" Note that the question could be such that nothing relevant is changing (this can be tricky). So, if a determinant is changing, is the impact on supply or demand? Figure out which, then shift the curve in the graph. Draw in the dot for the new equilibrium point, and make your conclusions. It may seem a little complex at first, but once you do it a few times, it will become commonplace.

**6.** To help you see the correct direction for shifts in supply and demand caused by changing determinants, exaggerate the change! For example, if you are looking at the demand for high-mileage hybrid cars, and gasoline prices rise, assume that gas prices jump by $5.00 a gallon. In this way it becomes obvious that demand for hybrid cars increases. By exaggerating the degree of change, the shift in the curve jumps out at you.

**7.** Here is another trap to avoid. When the price of a good rises (or falls), students (and commentators) often are heard to say that demand has fallen (risen) when they should be saying that quantity demanded has fallen (risen). The terminology is precise for a reason. Moving along an existing curve and selling more when price falls (a sale is in progress) is much different from selling more at the previous price because demand has risen (the entire demand curve shifts to the right). This also applies to supplies.

**8.** Here is one final trap to avoid. Supply and demand both increase when the curves shift to the right and decline when they shift to the left. Don't be tempted to think that an upward shift in the supply curve is an increase (as it is for demand) and that a shift downward in the supply curve is a decline (again this is true for demand). Thinking this way will lead to errors when you are faced with changes in the supply curve. Note that an upward shift in supply is a decrease in supply, and vice versa! Think of an increase as a shift to the right and a decrease as a shift to the left.

| | Do the Homework for Chapter 3 | **STEP 5** |
|---|---|---|
| | Supply and Demand | |

Instructor _____ Time _____ Student _____

---

**Use the answer key below to record your answers to these homework questions.**

1. _____   6. _____   11. _____   16. _____
2. _____   7. _____   12. _____   17. _____
3. _____   8. _____   13. _____   18. _____
4. _____   9. _____   14. _____   19. _____
5. _____   10. _____   15. _____   20. _____

---

Use these paragraphs and Figure HW-1 to answer question 1.

On December 8, 2007, *The Economist* reported that, adjusted for inflation, food prices had risen by 75% between 2005 and 2007. Without stopping, the prices of food and other commodities (oil, aluminum, steel, etc.) continued rising at a quicker pace for most of 2008. Much of these higher prices have been driven by growth and development of the emerging markets of India and China. Higher incomes result in changing diets and a higher demand for manufactured goods. Questions 1–6 explore many of the specific changes that took place in particular markets in the first half of 2008 and then the changes that the recession of 2008–2009 imposed on these same markets.

For example, worldwide, roughly 90% of rice grown is consumed in the home country. One exception is Australia, which exports most of the rice it grows. But the *New York Times,* April 17, 2008, reported that Australia has faced a serious drought since 2000.

Rice is a very water-intensive crop and the extended drought resulted in a reduction of rice exports from 1.7 million metric tons in 2000 to less than 100,000 metric tons in 2008. Most of Australia's rice lands have now been converted to wine grapes, requiring far less water.

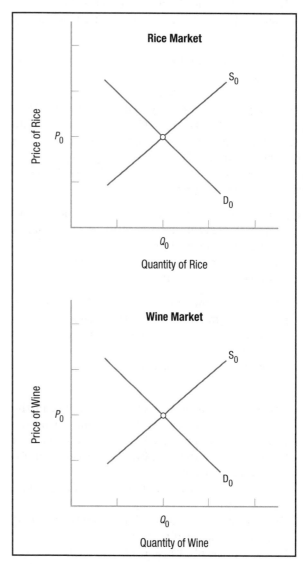

1. Use Figure HW-1 to visualize the impact of these developments in Australia on both the rice and wine markets.

   What would you expect happened to
   I. the price of rice? ((a) rise, (b) fall, (c) no change)
   II. the price of wine? ((a) rise, (b) fall, (c) no change)
   III. the quantity of rice produced? ((a) rise, (b) fall, (c) no change)
   IV. the quantity of wine produced? ((a) rise, (b) fall, (c) no change)

**HW-1**

2. Researchers are looking to genetically modify rice seeds so they bloom earlier in the day (to counter the effects of global warming) and do not need as much water. Assume these new varieties of rice are capable of producing current yields in adverse conditions. What will be the impact on

    I. the price of rice? ((a) rise, (b) fall, (c) no change)

    II. the price of wine grapes? ((a) rise, (b) fall, (c) no change)

    III. the quantity of rice produced? ((a) rise, (b) fall, (c) no change)

    IV. the quantity of wine grapes produced ((a) rise, (b) fall, (c) no change)

3. The drought in Australia is being felt across Europe. Europe has been "confronted by plummeting prices due to overproduction and competition from well-marketed and moderately priced New World wines," and prices have fallen by a quarter (*New York Times*, August 4, 2007).

Europe subsidizes wine production and this has contributed to the glut of grapes. Which of the following policy changes could help European wineries by reducing the amount of grapes and wine in the marketplace resulting in higher average prices for European wine? (Write down the letters of all that apply.)

a. Increase subsidies to wineries

b. Lower tariffs on imported wine

c. Increase excise taxes on European wine

d. Exempt European wines for VAT taxes (VAT taxes act like sales taxes)

e. Raise tariffs on Australian and American wines

f. Institute an advertising program that encourages Europeans to drink more domestically produced wine

g. Pay wineries to destroy grape vines

h. Institute an advertising campaign in the United States encouraging Americans to drink more French wine

i. Begin a grape ethanol program in Europe

---

Use this paragraph and Figure HW-2 to answer questions 4 and 5.

Congress passed an energy bill in 2005 and then updated it in 2007. The net effect was to heavily subsidize the building and expansion of corn-based ethanol plants and to mandate a rising percent of gasoline be composed of ethanol. Use Figure HW-2 to answer the following questions.

4. Assume these congressional changes result in a doubling of demand for corn in 2010. Assume initially that supply remains the same. What will be the new equilibrium price and output in the market?

    I. Price          II. Output

5. Given this new demand, farmers convert to genetically modified seed that triples output. What will be the new equilibrium price and output in this market?

    I. Price          II. Output

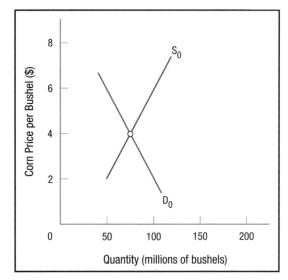

**HW-2**

---

6. The price of gasoline rose to $4 a gallon in the summer of 2008. What will be the impact on the following markets if the financial crisis of 2008–2009 and the worldwide recession lasts for two to three years?

    I. The price of gasoline ((a) rise, (b) fall, (c) no change)

    II. The number of new ethanol plants built ((a) rise, (b) fall, (c) no change)

    III. The price of farmland ((a) rise, (b) fall, (c) no change)

    IV. The number of BMWs sold ((a) rise, (b) fall, (c) no change)

7. Market demand curves are

a. the average demand faced by business.

b. the horizontal sum of individual demand curves.

c. not a very useful concept; individual demands are most important.

d. easily estimated for nearly all products and services.

Use Figure HW-3 to answer questions 8 and 9.

8. Assume the market is initially at point $c$ with $Q_1$ sold at a price of $P_0$. An increase in quantity demanded would be represented by which of the following?
   a. a movement to point $a$
   b. a shift in the demand curve to $D_1$
   c. a movement to point $b$
   d. a shift in the demand curve to $D_2$

9. Assume the market is initially at point $c$ with $Q_1$ sold at a price of $P_0$. An increase in demand would be represented by which of the following?
   a. a movement from point $a$ to point $c$
   b. a shift in the demand curve to $D_1$
   c. a movement to point $b$
   d. a shift in the demand curve to $D_2$

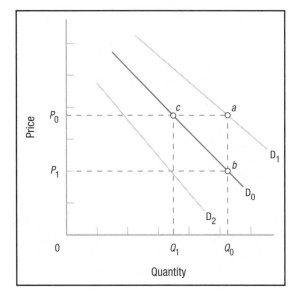

**HW-3**

10. The law of supply suggests that
    a. more will be demanded as the price falls.
    b. higher prices lead to greater quantity supplied.
    c. more advertising leads to consumers buying more.
    d. as prices rise, consumers find other (cheaper) products to buy.

Use Figure HW-4 to answer questions 11 and 12.

11. Assume the market is initially at point $a$. An increase in quantity supplied would be represented by a
    a. movement to point $d$.
    b. movement to point $c$.
    c. movement to point $b$.
    d. shift in the supply curve to $S_2$.

12. Assume the market is initially at point $a$. An increase in supply would be represented by a
    a. movement to point $d$.
    b. movement to point $c$.
    c. movement to point $b$.
    d. shift in the supply curve to $S_2$.

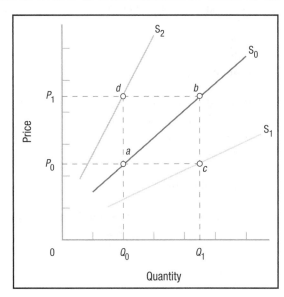

**HW-4**

13. Determinants of supply affect
    a. the quantity supplied.
    b. how much consumers demand.
    c. the entire supply curve.
    d. the quantity demanded.

14. A change in supply results from
    a. a change in one of the determinants of demand.
    b. a change in the price of the product.
    c. a shift in the demand curve.
    d. a change in one of the determinants of supply.

Use Figure HW-5 to answer questions 15 and 16.

15. Assume the market for cell phones is initially in equilibrium at point $b$ with $Q_0$ units sold at a price of $P_2$. Now assume that the Surgeon General releases a report that says that extensive use of cellular phones has a negative impact on hearing. The new equilibrium
   a. will be at point $e$.
   b. will be at point $c$.
   c. will be at point $a$.
   d. will not change.

16. Assume the market for cell phones is initially in equilibrium at point $c$ with $Q_2$ units sold at a price of $P_1$. Now assume that the industry develops a new method of producing phones that halves the cost. The new equilibrium
   a. will be at point $e$.
   b. will be at point $b$.
   c. will be at point $a$.
   d. will not change.

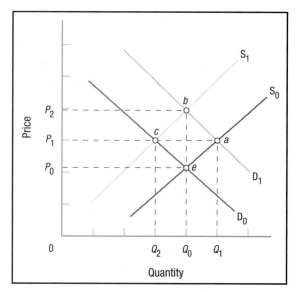

**HW-5**

Use Figure HW-6 to answer questions 17–20. In each case assume that the market begins in equilibrium at point $e$.

17. How much will consumers purchase if the government placed a price floor of $8 on this market?
   a. 300
   b. 200
   c. 400
   d. none

18. What will be the impact if the government places a price floor of $4 on this market?
   a. a shortage equal to 200
   b. no impact at all
   c. equilibrium price would fall to $4
   d. a surplus equal to 200

19. How much will consumers purchase if the government places a price ceiling of $6 on this market?
   a. 300
   b. 400
   c. 200
   d. none

20. What would be the impact if the government placed a price ceiling of $4 on this market?
   a. a shortage equal to 200
   b. no impact at all
   c. a shortage equal to 300
   d. a surplus equal to 200

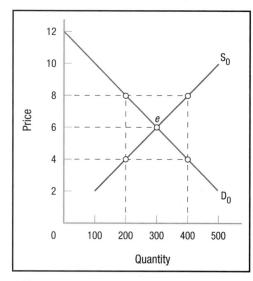

**HW-6**

| | |
|---|---|
| ## Use the ExamPrep to Get Ready for Exams | ## STEP 6 |

This sheet (front and back) is designed to help you prepare for your exams. The chapter has been boiled down to its key concepts. You are asked to answer questions, define terms, draw graphs, and, if you wish, add summaries of class notes.

## Markets

Describe markets and their role:

## Demand

Describe a demand curve:

Describe the law of demand:

Describe how we calculate market demand:

List the determinants of demand:

1. _____   2. _____
3. _____   4. _____

Define a change in quantity demanded:

Define a change in demand:

Now in Figure EP-1, draw a demand curve, show a change in quantity demanded, and show a change in demand.

**EP-1**

## Supply

Describe a supply curve:

Describe the law of supply:

Describe how we calculate market supply:

List the determinants of supply:

1. _____   2. _____
3. _____   4. _____

Define a change in quantity supplied:

Define a change in supply:

Now in Figure EP-2, draw a supply curve, show a change in quantity supplied, and show a change in supply.

**EP-2**

## Market Equilibrium

Define market equilibrium:

Show market equilibrium in Figure EP-3.

Now draw a shortage in the figure. What causes a shortage?

Now draw a surplus in the figure. What causes a surplus?

**EP-3**

## Predicting a New Market Equilibrium

### When Only One Curve Shifts

Complete Figures EP-4 and EP-5
and the tables below (indicate
whether equilibrium price and
output increase or decrease).
Start with an initial equilibrium
where $D_0$ and $S_0$ cross at point $e$.
In Figure EP-4 only shift demand,
and in Figure EP-5 only shift supply.

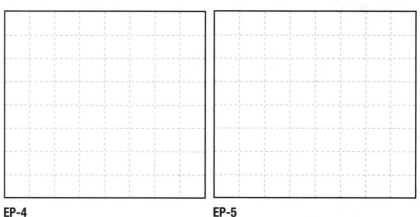

EP-4                                    EP-5

| Only Demand Changes | Price | Quantity |
| --- | --- | --- |
| Demand increases to $D_1$ | | |
| Demand decreases to $D_2$ | | |

| Only Supply Changes | Price | Quantity |
| --- | --- | --- |
| Supply increases to $S_1$ | | |
| Supply decreases to $S_2$ | | |

### When Both Curves Shift

Complete Figures EP-6 and EP-7
and the tables below (indicate
whether equilibrium price and
output increase or decrease). Start
with an initial equilibrium where
$D_0$ and $S_0$ cross at point $e$. In
Figure EP-6, show supply increasing,
and have demand first increase and
then decrease. In Figure EP-7,
show supply decreasing, and have
demand first increase and then
decrease.

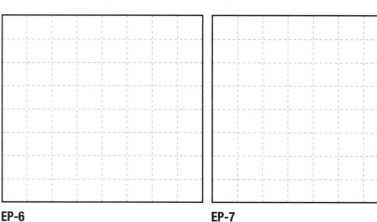

EP-6                                    EP-7

| Supply Increases | Price | Quantity |
| --- | --- | --- |
| Demand decreases to $D_1$ | | |
| Demand decreases to $D_2$ | | |

| Supply Decreases | Price | Quantity |
| --- | --- | --- |
| Demand increases to $D_1$ | | |
| Demand decreases to $D_2$ | | |

## Price Ceilings and Price Floors

Use Figure EP-8 to describe price ceilings and floors. Begin with
initial supply and demand curves labeled $S_0$ and $D_0$.

### Price Ceilings

Draw a price ceiling below equilibrium price. What are the implications
for the market?
List some examples of price ceilings:

### Price Floors

Draw a price floor above the initial equilibrium price. What are the
implications for the market?
List some examples of price floors:

EP-8

## Additional Study Help Chapterwide Practice Questions

### Matching

Match the description with the corresponding term.

___    1. Markets
___    2. Demand
___    3. Supply
___    4. Substitutes
___    5. Complements
___    6. Equilibrium
___    7. Shortage
___    8. Surplus

a. The amount of output that businesses are willing to produce and offer at various prices.

b. A balance between supply and demand where producers make exactly the amount of product that consumers want to buy.

c. An excess of a product caused by supply exceeding demand.

d. Institutions that bring buyers and sellers together to make transactions.

e. The amounts of a good or service that consumers are willing and able to buy at various prices.

f. Products that are used together.

g. Too little of a product is available in the market at current prices.

h. A competing product that consumers will switch to if the price of the original product rises.

### Fill-In

Circle the word(s) in parentheses that complete the sentence.

1. Markets are institutions that permit (buyers and sellers, government and consumers) _____ to transact with each other, and the market is often referred to as (capitalism, socialism, the price system) _____.

2. Demand refers to the goods and services that people (want, are willing and able) _____ to buy during some period of time. A negative relationship exists between price and (demand, quantity demanded) _____. This is known as the law of demand, which states that as price increases, (demand, quantity demanded) _____ falls, and vice versa.

3. Market demand curves are the (horizontal, vertical) _____ summation of individual demand curves. Market demands will change if one or more of the determinants change. These include tastes and preferences, income, (costs of resources, prices of related goods) _____, and expectations regarding future prices, income, the number of buyers and product availability.

4. When income rises and demand for a given product rises, that product is a(n) (normal, inferior) _____ good. But if demand declines when income grows, the product is a(n) (normal, inferior) _____ good.

5. Movies and sporting events are (substitute, complementary) _____ goods, while coffee and cinnamon rolls are (substitute, complementary) _____ goods.

6. A change in price will result in a change in (demand, quantity demanded) _____, while a change in income will cause a change in (demand, quantity demanded) _____. When Taco Bell drops the price of its burritos to 50 cents, the demand for McDonald's hamburgers will (rise, fall) _____ because these two products are generally considered (substitutes, complements) _____. But when McDonald's raises the price of its hamburgers by 50 cents, its sales will fall because demand (falls, rises, remains constant) _____.

7. The law of supply states that there is a (direct, inverse) _____ relationship between price and quantity supplied. A change in price will result in a change in (supply, quantity supplied) _____, while a change in resource costs will cause a change in (supply, quantity supplied) _____. When General Motors finds that the price of steel has risen by 10%, its supply curve for Chevy Trucks will (shift to the right, shift to the left, not change) _____.

8. Market equilibrium results when quantity supplied equals quantity demanded. If price is set temporarily above equilibrium, a (surplus, shortage) _____ results, but if the price is set below equilibrium, a (surplus, shortage) _____ results.

9. When either the supply or demand curve shifts (one curve only), you are able to predict the new (price, quantity sold, both price and quantity sold) _____. If demand increases, equilibrium price will (rise, fall) _____, and equilibrium output will (rise, fall) _____. If supply increases, equilibrium price will (rise, fall)

_____, and equilibrium output will (rise, fall) _____.

10. When both the supply and demand curves shift, you are able to predict the new (price, quantity sold, either price or quantity sold but not both) _____. If demand increases and supply falls, equilibrium price will (rise, fall, be indeterminate) _____, and equilibrium output will (rise, fall, be indeterminate) _____. If both supply and demand increase, equilibrium price will (rise, fall, be indeterminate) _____, and equilibrium output will (rise, fall, be indeterminate) _____.

## True-False

Circle the correct answer.

T / F  1. All markets offer a wide variety of products for sale.

T / F  2. You can only buy products in markets. Services are traded through a different mechanism.

T / F  3. The most basic component of markets is transactions.

T / F  4. According to the law of demand, quantity demanded is inversely related to price changes.

T / F  5. A demand curve always slopes up and to the right to show that quantity demanded increases with price.

T / F  6. When prices rise, demand decreases.

T / F  7. Demand refers to the goods and services people are willing and able to buy during a certain period of time.

T / F  8. According to the law of demand, all other factors held constant, as price increases, quantity demanded falls.

T / F  9. A supply curve shows the maximum amount of a good or service that businesses will offer at various prices.

T / F  10. If producers expect higher prices, that _usually_ leads to an increase in supply.

T / F  11. A change in product price leads to a change in supply.

T / F  12. Signing a new union contract with substantial increases in wages and benefits typically will result in an increase in supply.

T / F  13. An improvement in technology only results in an increase in quantity supplied.

T / F  14. A product's equilibrium price is fully determined by the demand for that product.

T / F  15. A cleared market is a market in equilibrium.

T / F  16. The equilibrium price is also called the market clearing price.

T / F  17. All other relevant factors held constant, an increase in supply will lead to an increase in output and a decrease in price.

T / F  18. All other relevant factors held constant, if supply and demand both rise, price will necessarily rise.

T / F  19. If both the supply curve and the demand curve for a product change, you can't calculate either the new price or the new quantity produced.

T / F  20. When supply and demand move in opposite directions, it is easy to predict a change in output.

T / F  21. To be effective, a price floor must be set below the equilibrium price.

T / F  22. Price ceilings typically give rise to product shortages.

T / F  23. Price ceilings and floors are meant to achieve socially beneficial results, but they often have unintended detrimental consequences.

T / F  24. A raise in the minimum wage typically reduces unemployment among lower-skilled workers.

## Multiple Choice

Circle the correct answer.

1. All markets
   a. offer the same basics products.
   b. bring buyers and sellers together to transact business.
   c. are the same size.
   d. offer either products or services, but not both.

2. How do markets best help buyers and sellers to communicate?
   a. by providing a place for buyers and sellers to interact online
   b. by providing information about the quality and quantity of government goods and services
   c. through price
   d. by providing technology for communication

3. Quantity demanded changes as a result of a change in
   a. demand.
   b. supply.
   c. product quality.
   d. product price.

4. The law of demand states that
   a. quantity demanded rises as price falls.
   b. quantity demanded rises as price rises.
   c. demand rises as price rises.
   d. demand falls as price falls.

5. A demand curve always slopes
   a. up and to the right.
   b. down and to the right.
   c. consistent with the corresponding supply curve.
   d. parallel to the corresponding supply curve.

6. Which of the following is a determinant of demand?
   a. production technology
   b. resource input cost
   c. income
   d. number of sellers

7. Substitute goods are
   a. goods that are consumed together.
   b. goods whose quantity demanded does not fluctuate with price changes.
   c. related goods that consumers will turn to when prices rise.
   d. related goods that consumers will turn to when prices fall.

8. An increase in the number of buyers
   a. decreases demand.
   b. increases demand.
   c. decreases quantity demanded.
   d. increases quantity demanded.

9. Market demand curves are
   a. the horizontal sum of individual demand curves.
   b. the vertical sum of individual demand curves.
   c. the statistical average of individual demand curves.
   d. a graph of business demand for resources and employees.

10. An increase in demand means
    a. consumers will pay the same price for more output.
    b. consumers will buy more output at every price.
    c. consumers will only buy more output at the current price.
    d. consumers will only pay more for the current output.

11. Change in quantity demanded is caused by
    a. a change in consumer tastes.
    b. an increase in buyers.
    c. a change in income levels.
    d. a change in price.

12. Which statement best describes the law of demand?
    a. The higher the price of the product, the more of the product is likely to be produced.
    b. The lower a product's price, the more of that product consumers will purchase during a given time period.
    c. The greater the need, the greater the demand.
    d. Demand is related to many different factors.

13. Use Figure MC-1 to answer the questions that follow.

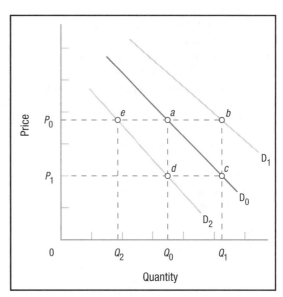

**MC-1**

a. Assume the market is initially at point $a$ on $D_0$. An increase in quantity demanded would be represented by what point? _____
b. If the market was initially at point $a$ and consumer income increased, an increase in demand would be represented by _____.
c. Assume the market is initially at point $d$. A decrease in quantity demanded would be represented by which point? _____
d. If demand is initially $D_0$, which curve represents a decline in demand? _____
e. A movement from point $a$ to point $d$ represents a(n) _____.

f. A movement from point *c* to point *b* represents a(n) _____.

14. Supply is
    a. dependent on consumer demand.
    b. the minimum amount of output producers will offer at a given price.
    c. the maximum amount of output producers will offer at various prices.
    d. an unimportant aspect of markets.

15. When the price of a product increases,
    a. quantity supplied decreases.
    b. quantity supplied increases.
    c. supply decreases.
    d. supply increases.

16. The idea that higher prices will lead to higher quantity supplied is part of
    a. the law of quantity supplied.
    b. the law of quantity demanded.
    c. the law of demand.
    d. the law of supply.

17. A supply curve shows
    a. the minimum amount of output businesses will make at various prices.
    b. the maximum amount of output businesses will offer for sale at various prices.
    c. the value consumers place on a good or service.
    d. the cost of the inputs required to sell a good or service.

18. Determinants of supply affect
    a. the entire supply curve.
    b. the quantity supplied.
    c. the number of consumers.
    d. the quantity demanded.

19. Improvements in production technology
    a. generally increase production cost.
    b. often allow for the creation of new products.
    c. have no effect on supply.
    d. generally decrease demand.

20. The prices of other commodities affect supply because
    a. when possible, producers will switch to produce a more profitable commodity.
    b. consumers will buy more of a cheaper commodity.
    c. consumers will switch to complementary goods.
    d. producers will increase their price to keep pace with other commodities.

21. An increase in the number of sellers of a product
    a. increases product price.
    b. has no long-term effect on supply.
    c. increases supply.
    d. decreases supply.

22. A change in supply
    a. results from a change of one of the determinants of demand.
    b. results in a price change.
    c. results in a change in the amount of product offered at every price level.
    d. leads to a corresponding change in demand.

23. A change in the price of a product causes a change in
    a. quantity supplied.
    b. supply.
    c. input cost.
    d. expectations.

24. When a market clears,
    a. producers bring more of a product to market than consumers are willing to purchase at the market price.
    b. producers bring less of a product to market than consumers would be willing to purchase at the market price.
    c. producers bring precisely the amount of a product to market that consumers wish to purchase at the market price.
    d. the price of a particular good is higher than the market will bear.

25. If there is a *surplus* of sports cars on the market, which of the following statements will *not* be true?
    a. Producer inventories of sports cars are rising.
    b. The market price of sports cars lies below their equilibrium price.
    c. Producers are bringing more sports cars to market than consumers are willing to purchase at the market price.
    d. The market price of sport cars exceeds their equilibrium price.

26. When the real estate market is in a "seller's market," which of the following can occur?
    a. Homebuyers can expect to find a wide selection of relatively inexpensive homes.
    b. There is a surplus of homes on the market.
    c. All real estate transactions take place in realtors' offices.
    d. There is a shortage of homes on the market.

27. All other relevant factors held constant, if there is a decrease in demand,
    a. price and output will drop.
    b. price will drop, but output will rise.
    c. price and output will rise.
    d. price will rise, but output will drop.

28. All other relevant factors held constant, if supply and demand both decrease,
    a. output will rise, but price will fall.
    b. output will fall, with the effect on price being indeterminate.

c. output will rise, with the effect on price being indeterminate.

d. price will rise, with the effect on output being indeterminate.

29. At equilibrium,
   a. producers store surpluses for times of shortage.
   b. producers offer the exact amount of a product consumers want.
   c. producers switch to substitution products.
   d. consumers switch to complementary products.

30. All markets respond to disturbances in equilibrium
   a. instantly.
   b. after a long period of adjustment.
   c. only when government intervenes.
   d. differently.

31. A cleared market is one that
   a. has a surplus.
   b. has a shortage.
   c. has an artificial price limit.
   d. is in equilibrium.

32. The market response to a surplus is
   a. increased demand.
   b. decreased demand.
   c. increased prices.
   d. decreased prices.

33. Equilibrium prices are
   a. *not* determined by the forces of supply and demand.
   b. easily determined by businesses.
   c. set by the government.
   d. the natural outcome of market forces.

34. If demand increases,
   a. equilibrium price and output increase.
   b. equilibrium price and output decrease.
   c. equilibrium price increases, and output decreases.
   d. equilibrium price decreases, and output increases.

35. Which of the following is an example of a price ceiling?
   a. the minimum wage
   b. agricultural price supports
   c. rent controls
   d. unemployment insurance

36. Which of the following is an example of a price floor?
   a. rent controls
   b. caps on the Medicare payments made to doctors and hospitals
   c. a private company running a sale on its products
   d. agricultural price supports

37. A price ceiling set above a product's equilibrium price will generally result in
   a. a product shortage.
   b. a product surplus.

c. the product being sold at its equilibrium price and clearing the market.

d. none of the above.

38. A price floor set above a product's equilibrium price will generally result in
   a. a product shortage.
   b. a product surplus.
   c. the product being sold at its equilibrium price and clearing the market.
   d. none of the above.

39. A price ceiling set below a product's equilibrium price will generally result in
   a. a product shortage.
   b. a product surplus.
   c. the product being sold at its equilibrium price and clearing the market.
   d. none of the above.

Use Figure MC-2 to answer Questions 40–43. Equilibrium occurs at price $P_e$.

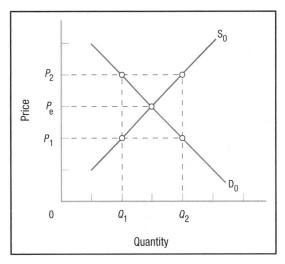

**MC-2**

40. What happens if the government sets a price ceiling at price $P_2$?
   a. Nothing.
   b. There will be a surplus of $Q_2 - Q_1$.
   c. There will be a shortage of $Q_2 - Q_1$.
   d. The market will settle back to equilibrium in a short period of time.

41. What happens if the government sets a price ceiling at price $P_1$?
   a. Nothing.
   b. There will be a surplus of $Q_2 - Q_1$.
   c. There will be a shortage of $Q_2 - Q_1$.
   d. The market will settle back to equilibrium in a short period of time.

42. What happens if the government sets a price floor at price $P_2$?
    a. Nothing.
    b. There will be a surplus of $Q_2 - Q_1$.
    c. There will be a shortage of $Q_2 - Q_1$.
    d. The market will settle back to equilibrium in a short period of time.

43. What happens if the government sets a price floor at price $P_1$?
    a. Nothing.
    b. There will be a surplus of $Q_2 - Q_1$.
    c. There will be a shortage of $Q_2 - Q_1$.
    d. The market will settle back to equilibrium in a short period of time.

## Essay-Problem

Answer in the space provided.

Some of the questions below can be challenging. Don't get discouraged if your answers are not always the same as those we suggest. Use these sample answers as another way to assess your progress but, more important, to discover and learn some of the subtleties surrounding markets and supply and demand.

1. What is the essence of markets?

2. Explain how the laws of demand and supply differ.

3. Prices of related goods or other commodities are determinants for both demand and supply. How do they differ?

In the table below, use the spaces provided to answer whether, in the market specified, demand, supply, equilibrium quantity, and equilibrium price increases ($\uparrow$), decreases ($\downarrow$), remains the same (NC), or is indeterminate (?). In the Comment-Discussion column briefly state the reasons for your answer.

| Market Changes | Demand | Supply | Equilibrium Quantity | Equilibrium Price | Comment-Discussion |
|---|---|---|---|---|---|
| 4. Assume there is a freeze in Florida that ruins its orange crop this year. What happens in the market for tomato juice? | | | | | |
| 5. gain, assume there is a freeze in Florida that ruins its orange crop this year. Now what happens in the market for orange juice? | | | | | |
| 6. Again, assume there is a freeze in Florida that ruins its orange crop this year. In addition, an extended drought in California significantly reduces the tomato crop. Now what happens in the market for tomato juice? | | | | | |
| 7. Hard bargaining by southern California grocery unions results in higher wages and expanded health benefits for all workers in all stores. What will be the impact on the grocery market? | | | | | |
| 8. Growth hormones are scientifically shown to increase vigor and quality of life without significant side effects. Advances in chip design make manufacturing these hormones nearly costless. What happens in the market for mountain bikes? | | | | | |

| Market Changes | Demand | Supply | Equilibrium Quantity | Equilibrium Price | Comment-Discussion |
|---|---|---|---|---|---|
| 9. Growth hormones are scientifically shown to increase vigor and quality of life without significant side effects. Advances in chip design make manufacturing these hormones nearly costless. What happens in the market for televisions? | | | | | |
| 10. The Federal Reserve, becoming concerned with inflation, raises interest rates too high, accidentally driving the economy into a deep recession. At the same time, improved technology drives the costs of memory chips lower and lower. What happens in the MP3 player market? | | | | | |

## What's Next

You now have a good understanding of how markets work using supply and demand analysis. We have assumed throughout this chapter that markets have large numbers of buyers and sellers and are highly competitive. In addition, we assumed that both buyers and sellers had good information about prices and the products themselves.

In the next chapter, we look at some of the imperfections in markets and how our competitive market supply and demand analysis must be adjusted to account for these problems. For example, sometimes sellers have better information than buyers (used cars), and they use this knowledge to gain an edge on buyers. These issues do not, however, negate the usefulness of the analysis. Just be aware that the conclusions may have to be modified.

## Answers to Chapterwide Practice Questions

### Matching

| | | | |
|---|---|---|---|
| 1. d | 3. a | 5. f | 7. g |
| 2. e | 4. h | 6. b | 8. c |

### Fill-In

1. buyers and sellers, the price system
2. are willing and able, quantity demanded, quantity demanded
3. horizontal, prices of related goods
4. normal, inferior
5. substitute, complementary
6. quantity demanded, demand, fall, substitutes, remains constant
7. direct, quantity supplied, supply, shift to the left
8. surplus, shortage
9. both price and quantity sold, rise, rise, fall, rise
10. either price or quantity sold but not both, rise, be indeterminate, be indeterminate, rise

## True-False

| | | | |
|---|---|---|---|
| 1. F | 7. T | 13. F | 19. F |
| 2. F | 8. T | 14. F | 20. F |
| 3. T | 9. T | 15. T | 21. F |
| 4. T | 10. T | 16. T | 22. T |
| 5. F | 11. F | 17. T | 23. T |
| 6. F | 12. F | 18. F | 24. F |

## Multiple Choice

| | | | |
|---|---|---|---|
| 1. b | 13. b. $D_1$ | 20. a | 33. d |
| 2. c | 13. c. e | 21. c | 34. a |
| 3. d | 13. d. $D_2$ | 22. c | 35. c |
| 4. a | 13. e. decrease in | 23. a | 36. d |
| 5. b |       demand | 24. c | 37. c |
| 6. c | 13. f. increase in | 25. b | 38. b |
| 7. c |       demand | 26. d | 39. a |
| 8. b | 14. c | 27. a | 40. a |
| 9. a | 15. b | 28. b | 41. c |
| 10. b | 16. d | 29. b | 42. b |
| 11. d | 17. b | 30. d | 43. a |
| 12. b | 18. a | 31. d | |
| 13. a. c | 19. b | 32. d | |

## Essay-Problem

1. They bring buyers and sellers together.
2. Demand curves are negatively sloped while supply curves are positively sloped, and the two laws reflect these differences.
3. Price of related goods for demand refers to prices of substitutes or complements in consumption. The price of hamburger affects the demand for chicken. On the supply side, the prices of related commodities refer to substitutes in production. If firms can produce either of two commodities, and the market price of one rises, firms will produce more of that product and its supply will rise. This is an important distinction that you should analyze carefully when looking at changes to demand and supply caused by changes in determinants.

| Market Changes | Demand | Supply | Equilibrium Quantity | Equilibrium Price | Comment-Discussion |
|---|---|---|---|---|---|
| 4. Assume there is a freeze in Florida that ruins its orange crop this year. What happens in the market for tomato juice? | ↑ | NC | ↑ | ↑ | Demand for a substitute rises. |
| 5. Again, assume there is a freeze in Florida that ruins its orange crop this year. Now what happens in the market for orange juice? | NC | ↓ | ↓ | ↑ | Supply of orange juice declines due to freeze. |

| Market Changes | Demand | Supply | Equilibrium Quantity | Equilibrium Price | Comment-Discussion |
|---|---|---|---|---|---|
| 6. Again, assume there is a freeze in Florida that ruins its orange crop this year. In addition, an extended drought in California significantly reduces the tomato crop. Now what happens in the market for tomato juice? | ↑ | ↓ | ? | ↑ | Demand for substitute rises (tomato juice), drought reduces the supply of tomato juice. Price rises, but impact on output sold is indeterminate. |
| 7. Hard bargaining by southern California grocery unions results in higher wages and expanded health benefits for all workers in all stores. What will be the impact on the grocery market? | NC | ↓ | ↓ | ↑ | Input costs (labor) rise, so supply declines. |
| 8. Growth hormones are scientifically shown to increase vigor and quality of life without significant side effects. Advances in chip design make manufacturing these hormones nearly costless. What happens in the market for mountain bikes? | ↑ | NC | ↑ | ↑ | More healthy people will engage in mountain biking. |
| 9. Growth hormones are scientifically shown to increase vigor and quality of life without significant side effects. Advances in chip design make manufacturing these hormones nearly costless. What happens in the market for televisions? | NC | NC | NC | NC | No impact. Television demand is unaffected by health issues. |
| 10. The Federal Reserve, becoming concerned with inflation, raises interest rates too high, accidentally driving the economy into a deep recession. At the same time, improved technology drives the costs of memory chips lower and lower. What happens in the MP3 player market? | ↓ | ↑ | ? | ↓ | The recession lowers income and demand, while technology reduces cost, increasing supply. |

# Market Efficiency, Market Failure, and Government 4

Panoramic Images/Getty Images

## Buyers and Sellers Come Together in Markets

In the previous chapter, you learned the important tool of supply and demand analysis. In describing the workings of supply and demand, we used a stylized view of competitive markets, where buyers and sellers easily come together. Reality is not so clear cut. In this chapter, we explore the complexities inherent to most markets. This does not mean you have to toss out what you have just learned about supply and demand. Rather, market complexities will force you to adjust your supply and demand analysis: You still use it; you just have to adjust it.

| This Is What You Need to Know | STEP 1 |
|---|---|

**After studying this chapter you should be able to**

- Understand how markets allocate resources.

- Define the conditions needed for markets to be efficient.

- Understand how markets impose discipline on producers and consumers.

- Understand and be able to use the concepts of consumer and producer surplus.

- Understand what market failure is, and when it occurs.

- Describe the different types of market failure.

- Develop a basic understanding of U.S. economic history.

93

STEP 2      Review the Key Terms

**Property rights:** The clear delineation of ownership of property backed by government enforcement.

**Consumer surplus:** The difference between market price and what consumers (as individuals or the market) are willing to pay. It is equal to the area above market price and below the demand curve.

**Producer surplus:** The difference between market price and the price at which firms are willing to supply the product. It is equal to the area below market price and above the supply curve.

**Asymmetric information:** Occurs when one party to a transaction has significantly better information than another party.

**Adverse selection:** Occurs when products of different qualities are sold at the same price because of asymmetric information.

**Moral hazard:** Asymmetric information problem that occurs when an insurance policy or some other arrangement changes the economic incentives and leads to a change in behavior.

**Public goods:** Goods that, once provided, no one person can be excluded from consuming (nonexclusion), and one person's consumption does not diminish the benefit to others from consuming the good (nonrivalry).

**Free rider:** When a public good is provided, consumers cannot be excluded from enjoying the product, so some consume the product without paying.

**Common property resources:** Resources that are owned by the community at large (parks, ocean fish, and the atmosphere) and therefore tend to be over-exploited because individuals have little incentive to use them in a sustainable fashion.

**External cost (or negative externality):** Occurs when a transaction between two parties has an impact on a third party not involved with the transaction. External costs are negative, such as pollution or congestion. The market provides too much of a product with negative externalities at too low a cost.

**External benefits:** Positive externalities, such as education and vaccinations. Private markets provide too little at too high a price of goods with external benefits.

STEP 3      Work Through the Chapter Tutorials

# Markets and Efficiency

### Frequently Asked Questions

Q:   What causes markets to be efficient?

A:   Markets are efficient mechanisms for allocating resources. The prices and profits characteristic of market systems provide incentives and signals that are nonexistent or seriously flawed in other systems of resource allocation.

Q: **What conditions must be met for markets to be efficient?**

A: For markets to be efficient, they must have well-structured institutions. These include the requirements that (1) information is widely available; (2) property rights are protected; (3) private contracts are enforced; (4) spillovers are minimal; and (5) competition prevails.

Q: **How do markets impose discipline on producers and consumers?**

A: Producers would like to charge higher prices and earn greater profits. But their economic survival depends on turning out quality goods at reasonable prices. As consumers, we would all like to engage in frequent extravagant purchases. But given our limited resources, each of us must decide which products are most important to us. As a result, markets are also rationing devices.

Q: **What are consumer and producer surplus?**

A: Because many consumers are willing to pay more than equilibrium prices for goods, they receive a consumer surplus equal to what they would have been willing to pay and what the market sets as a price. In a similar way, producers receive a producer surplus. The difference between market price and what a firm would have been willing to provide products for (the area under market price but above the supply curve) is producer surplus.

## Key Point to Remember

Competitive markets impose efficiency on both consumers and producers. Firms must produce what consumers want at reasonable prices in order to survive, or some other firm will, and consumers have limited resources, so they must allocate their income efficiently between competing products.

## Markets and Efficiency Quick Check

### Circle the Correct Answer

1. (T/F) Markets are only as efficient as the central government rules setting them up.

2. (T/F) Prices and profits are market signals to entrepreneurs in market systems.

3. (T/F) Efficient markets are markets where information is readily available to both buyers and sellers.

4. (T/F) Consumer surplus is the difference between what you would have been willing to pay to obtain a product and market price.

5. Which of the following describes producer surplus?
   a. The difference between what people are willing to pay and what firms are willing to supply the product for.
   b. The excess that producers earn from providing the product above market prices.
   c. The excess inventory that firms keep on hand to adjust to changing consumer tastes.
   d. The difference in price between what producers are willing to supply the product for and market price.

6. Which of the following is *not* a condition for markets to act efficiently?
   a. Contracts are enforced.
   b. Competitive markets prevail.

c. Property rights are protected.
   d. Economic agents provide positive external benefits.

7. Which of the following describes the discipline imposed by markets?
   a. Producers would prefer to provide shoddy goods, but they are prevented by law from doing so.
   b. Consumers would prefer to purchase extravagant items, but the market system makes them too poor to spend profligately.
   c. If producers provide low-quality goods at high prices, they will go out of business.
   d. If consumers want something, they can buy it.

8. For markets to act efficiently, accurate information must be widely available because
   a. it is only fair.
   b. it reduces transactions costs.
   c. it is better to be open than secretive.
   d. all products have high informational requirements.

9. Which of the following is *not* correct?
   a. Property rights provide incentives for the optimal use of resources.
   b. Pollution is a negative externality and causes markets to work inefficiently.

c. If a legal system is running well, informal rules are not needed to keep markets efficient.

d. For markets to be efficient, they must be open to the entry of new participants and the exit of current participants.

10. The market is a rationing device for consumers because

a. it forces each of us to decide which products are most important because our resources are limited.

b. producers often provide shoddy goods.

c. the rich take the good products, leaving us with a limited number of things from which to choose.

d. producers are in business to make profits.

Score: ____

Answers: 1. F; 2. T; 3. T; 4. T; 5. d; 6. d; 7. c; 8. b; 9. c; 10. a

## If You Got 9 or 10 Correct

You have a good handle on the way markets provide efficiency, and of the conditions needed for markets to work efficiently. Go on to Market Failures in the next section.

## If You Didn't Get at Least 9 Correct

A simple review should be all that you need. And as you do so, jot down the conditions needed for markets to work efficiently. Take a moment and review why consumer and producer surplus exist and how they are measured.

## Keep in Mind

The most difficult material in this section deals with consumer and producer surplus. Remember that consumer surplus is equal to the difference between what consumers would be willing to pay for the product (found on the demand curve) and what they actually have to pay (market price). Producer surplus in a similar fashion is the difference between market price and what producers would have been willing to provide the product for (found on the supply curve). Work through the problem that follows to make sure that you have these concepts down pat. ∎

## Solved Problem: Producer and Consumer Surplus

The table below contains supply and demand data.

| Price | Quantity Demanded | Quantity Supplied |
|-------|-------------------|-------------------|
| 20 | 0 | 36 |
| 18 | 2 | 32 |
| 16 | 4 | 28 |
| 14 | 6 | 24 |
| 12 | 8 | 20 |
| 10 | 10 | 16 |
| 8 | 12 | 12 |
| 6 | 14 | 8 |
| 4 | 16 | 4 |
| 2 | 18 | 0 |

In the grid above, graph both supply and demand.

a. What do equilibrium price and output equal?

b. How large are consumer and producer surplus?

Now, assume that resource cost (labor and raw materials) used to produce this good increased rapidly, adding $3 per unit to the cost of production.

c. Plot the new supply curve and label it $S_1$.

d. What is the new equilibrium price and output?

e. How much has consumer surplus and producer surplus declined?

## Solution-Discussion

The original supply and demand curves are plotted in Figure 1 (labeled $S_0$ and $D_0$, respectively).

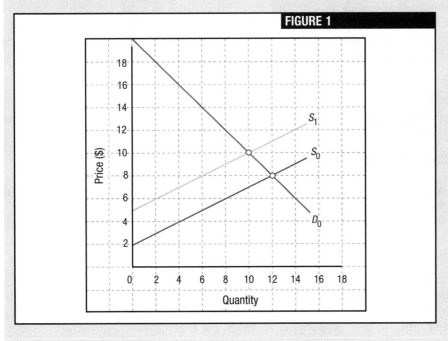

FIGURE 1

a. Original equilibrium price is $8, and equilibrium output is 12.

b. Computing consumer surplus involves computing the area below the demand curve and above equilibrium price, and producer surplus is the area above the supply curve and below equilibrium price. We do this by computing consumer surplus or producer surplus for each unit sold (price off the demand curve minus equilibrium price or price off the supply curve for producer surplus), or we can compute it by computing the area of the triangles. Remember that the area of a triangle is found by computing one-half base times its height. It is this latter process we will use here:

Consumer surplus: [($20 − $8) × 12] ÷ 2 = ($12 × 12) ÷ 2 = $144 ÷ 2 = $72

Producer surplus: [($8 − $2) × 12] ÷ 2 = ($6 × 12) ÷ 2 = $72 ÷ 2 = $36

c. See the figure on the previous page.

d. Equilibrium price is $10, and equilibrium output is 10.

e. The new consumer and producer surplus values are:

Consumer surplus: [($20 − $10) × 10] ÷ 2 = ($10 × 10) ÷ 2 = $100 ÷ 2 = $50

Producer surplus: [($10 − $5) × 10] ÷ 2 = ($5 × 10) ÷ 2 = $50 ÷ 2 = $25

Thus, consumer surplus has fallen by $22, and producer surplus has fallen by $11.

---

Ideally, the solved problem has cemented in your mind how consumer and producer surplus are computed. If this is not the case, continue on, but be prepared to review this section again. Most of these are not difficult concepts (only consumer and producer surplus are a little difficult). The next section on market failures builds on this section and deals with the same issues. As you work through it, you will begin to see the pattern of what it takes to have an efficient market and how the absence of each of these elements leads to market failure. Keep this simple framework in mind as you read the next section.

# Market Failures

## Frequently Asked Questions

Q: What happens if markets do not meet one or more of the five requirements discussed in the previous section?

A: For markets to be efficient, they must meet the five institutional requirements identified above. When one or more of these conditions is not met, the market is said to fail.

Q: Is market failure catastrophic?

A: Market failure generally does not mean that a market totally collapses or fails to exist, but that it fails to provide the socially optimal goods and services. The exception to this are pure public goods, because the market may totally fail to provide the goods.

Q: **What is asymmetric information?**

A: In some markets, one party to a transaction may have better information than the other. In this case, the market is said to fail because of asymmetric information. Asymmetric information can result in the inability of sellers to find buyers for the products, but it usually just involves adjustments in contracting methods.

Q: **What is adverse selection, and when does it occur?**

A: Adverse selection occurs when products of different qualities are sold at one price and involve asymmetric information. Individuals, for instance, know far more about their own health than do insurance companies. And because high-risk individuals are those who are most likely to purchase insurance, adverse selection skews the insurance pool, giving it a risk level higher than average.

Q: **What is moral hazard, and when does it occur?**

A: Moral hazard occurs when an insurance policy or some other arrangement changes the economic incentives people face, leading people to change their behavior, usually in a way detrimental to the market. The presence of lifeguards on the beach may cause people to take greater risks in the waves, and nets permit trapeze artists to perform more risky stunts.

Q: **What are private and public goods?**

A: Private goods are those goods that can be consumed only by the individuals who purchase them. Private goods are rival and exclusive. Public goods, in contrast, are nonrival and nonexclusive, meaning my consumption does not diminish your consumption and that once such a good has been provided for one person, others cannot be excluded from enjoying it.

Q: **What problem is caused by public goods, and how can it be overcome?**

A: Public goods give rise to the free rider problem. Once a public good has been provided, other consumers cannot be excluded from it, so many people will choose to enjoy the benefit without paying for it: They will free ride. And because of the possibility of free riding, the danger is that no one will pay for the public good, so it will no longer be provided by private markets, even though it is publicly desired. Pure public goods usually require public provision.

Q: **What happens to contracts when the legal system is inefficient?**

A: When an efficient legal system for the enforcement of contracts is lacking, contracts will be small because large contracts with complex financial provisions are difficult to enforce informally.

Q: **What happens to markets when external costs or benefits are present?**

A: Markets rarely produce the socially optimal output when external costs or benefits are present. The market overproduces goods with external costs, selling them at too low a price. Conversely, markets tend to provide too little of products that have external benefits.

Q: **How do monopolies make markets inefficient, and what can be done to overcome this problem?**

A: Some markets tend toward monopoly, and when a monopoly does control the market, prices go up. In the late nineteenth century, the monopolistic practices of the "robber barons" spurred passage of a series of antitrust laws that are still used today to promote competitive markets.

## Core Graph: Externalities

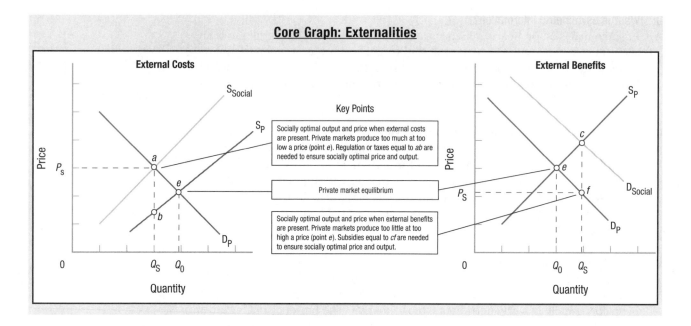

## Key Point to Remember

Market failure occurs when information for buyers and sellers is not widely available, the market involves public goods, contracts are not enforced, externalities are present, or markets are not competitive. Market failure means that private markets will fail to provide the socially optimal output and price, so government intervention (typically rules or regulations) may be necessary. In the case of pure public goods, government often must provide them.

# Market Failures Quick Check

## Circle the Correct Answer

1. (T/F) When market failures occur, markets totally collapse and need government help.
2. (T/F) Asymmetric information causes markets to fail because sellers always have more information about products than buyers.
3. (T/F) Adverse selection occurs when insurance encourages high-risk individuals to obtain insurance but drives out low-risk individuals.
4. Which one of the following is an example of moral hazard?
   a. People prone to injuries obtain medical insurance, and the insurance company has no way of knowing about this tendency.
   b. People become less cautious about securing their property, saying, "Don't worry about it. It's insured."
   c. People think that all used cars are lemons.
   d. People prone to illness take out high-deductible health insurance policies.
5. Which one of the following is *not* an example of a public good?
   a. national defense

   b. local radio music broadcasts
   c. weather forecasts
   d. cell phone towers
6. Markets rarely produce the socially optimal output when negative externalities are present because
   a. externalities are nonrival and nonexclusive.
   b. producers and consumers do not pay all costs.
   c. consumers would balk at paying more.
   d. people cannot recognize a negative externality.
7. Public goods give rise to the free rider problem because
   a. not enough people pledge to give to public television.
   b. of the lemons problem.
   c. once a public good has been provided, other consumers cannot be excluded from it.
   d. when we consume them, we prevent other people from consuming them.
8. To overcome a problem of negative externalities, governments can use all except which one of the following?
   a. regulation
   b. taxation

c. markets

d. strict enforcement of contracts

9. Monopolies can hamper market efficiency because

a. prices go up when monopolies control markets.

b. the government is hampered by law from dealing with monopolies.

c. antitrust polices have been ineffective against monopolies.

d. of adverse selection and moral hazard.

10. Market failures are caused by all *except* which one of the following?

a. Information is widely available, but not everyone makes use of it.

b. There are long delays in the legal system to enforce contracts.

c. Externalities are present.

d. Extensive monopoly power is present.

Score: ____

## If You Got 9 or 10 Correct

Your understanding of why markets are efficient, why they sometimes fail, and how market failure might be remedied, is solid. Move on to the next section, Market Failure, Government Intervention, and U.S. Economic History.

## If You Didn't Get at Least 9 Correct

You should carefully review the material, keeping distinct the different types of market failure.

■ Take a moment and jot down the different types of market failure.

■ Contrast these with those conditions needed for markets to be efficient from the first section.

■ Then, go back and check the text, making sure your jotting did not leave out any type of market failure.

■ Describe a remedy for each type of market failure.

Now might be a good time to spend some time reviewing the first two sections again. The heart of our economy is markets and their efficient operation. A lot of government programs stem from the types of institutional failures discussed in this section.

The next section, on government intervention, shows what can happen when government steps in to regulate markets. In these instances, market failure may not be the reason for the intervention. Some people view market outcomes as unfair to many and encourage government to correct for this unfairness. The next section builds on concepts in the first two sections. If you have missed some of the concepts in the first two parts of this chapter, you will have to review them again. But first, work through the next section and see if it doesn't help you see some of what you missed in the earlier sections. ■

# Market Failure, Government Intervention, and U.S. Economic History

Our economic history has been characterized by periods of remarkable growth in productivity and output from thriving private markets, followed by various kinds of market failures. These spectacular events have culminated in a growing government involvement in the economy through more regulation and a general growth in government activity.

After the Civil War, the economy grew dramatically. Rail lines stretched from coast to coast, and the oil, steel, mining, and agriculture industries flourished. The early 1900s saw the rise of consumerism as automobiles, appliances, and electricity became common in households.

The Great Depression brought misery to the country as unemployment reached 25%, and more than 10,000 banks failed, wiping out the savings of many families. President Roosevelt's New Deal, including the National Recovery Administration, the Works Progress Administration, and many other pieces of legislation, helped to employ people and reduce the impact of the Depression. But, the buildup for World War II is credited with pulling the economy out of the Depression.

The Great Depression changed America's view of the role of government in economic affairs as Congress passed the Employment Act of 1946, making maximum employment, production, and purchasing power the responsibility of the government. This view of the government's role in the economy still predominates today.

The stagflation of the 1970s turned Americans away from government intervention in the economy and back toward markets. This approach seemed to work well because from the early 1980s until just recently, the economy enjoyed relative price stability, low unemployment, and steady growth. The recent financial crisis and recession has Americans debating again just how big government's role should be in regulating business and stimulating the economy.

## STEP 4          Consider These Hints, Tips, and Reminders

1. Pay attention to the links between the first section, which describes the requirements for efficient markets, and the second section, which analyzes market failures. The list is the same!
   - Accurate information
   - Protected property rights
   - Enforceable private contracts
   - No externalities
   - Competitive markets

   Most government programs fit into these five categories. When any of these elements are absent, the market does not provide the socially optimal level of output or pricing.

2. Keep in mind that market failure does not mean the market does nothing (with the exception of pure public goods); it simply provides a less than socially optimal result.

3. Profits drive markets (and individuals and corporations) to provide the products we take for granted. Higher profits act as signals that consumers want more of that commodity or service.

4. Markets are rationing devices. They separate us by how much we want a given product or service and ration out those who are unwilling (or unable) to pay the equilibrium market price.

5. Consumer surplus is just the difference between what you would have been willing to pay and market price. This is a benefit the market conveys to all of us. Anytime you "get a deal" on some product, you have received a consumer surplus.

6. Similarly, producer surplus is simply the difference between the price a firm would be willing to provide a product for and equilibrium market price. When gold-mining firms see the market price of gold rise (maybe because some event has created uncertainty in the world), they receive a producer surplus on each ounce of gold they sell.

## Do the Homework for Chapter 4
## Market Efficiency, Market Failure, and Government

## STEP 5

Instructor _____ Time _____ Student _____

**Use the answer key below to record your answers to these homework questions.**

1. _____     6. _____     11. _____     16. _____
2. _____     7. _____     12. _____     17. _____
3. _____     8. _____     13. _____     18. _____
4. _____     9. _____     14. _____     19. _____
5. _____     10. _____    15. _____     20. _____

1. Which of the following conditions is *not* necessary for markets to be efficient?
   a. Good information must be widely available.
   b. Everyone must get their fair share of the fruits of the market.
   c. Externalities (spillovers) are minimal.
   d. Competition must prevail.

2. Businesses, corporations, and other producers all want to charge high prices for the products they produce and sell. Why is it that they seldom are able to do this?
   a. High prices scare away other firms.
   b. Market shortages push prices down.
   c. Competition from other firms drives down prices.
   d. Their patents expire.

3. Which of the following is *not* a characteristic of competitive markets?
   a. The market has many buyers and sellers.
   b. The market is open to entry and exit by firms.
   c. Products in these markets have close substitutes.
   d. Extensive government regulations ensure that firms act competitively.

4. Market failure occurs when
   a. one firm gets a competitive advantage over the others in the market.
   b. the market completely collapses.
   c. asymmetric information makes trading difficult.
   d. consumers fail to purchase a product from an industry.

5. Which of the following is an example of a public good?
   a. airline travel
   b. the light from a lighthouse
   c. ferry boat
   d. bicycle

6. If one firm is able to capture the entire market for a product or service, what will most likely happen in this market?
   a. Market efficiency is enhanced.
   b. This firm will increase spending on research and development to improve the quality of the product.
   c. Consumers will stop buying the product.
   d. The price of the product will rise.

7. A good that is nonrival in consumption means that
   a. everyone wants to buy and consume this product.
   b. no one is interested in this product.
   c. many people can consume the good simultaneously.
   d. two companies cooperate to produce and sell this product.

8. An example of an external cost or negative spillover is
   a. pollution caused by steel factories.
   b. a lighthouse.
   c. national defense and homeland security.
   d. immunization efforts in Africa.

9. A private market that creates negative spillovers or external costs will
   a. produce that output where all costs are built into the price.

b. produce too much of the good at too low a price.

c. voluntarily reduce output to the socially optimal level.

d. collapse because no consumers will be willing to purchase the product.

10. Curbing monopoly or extensive monopoly power might require
    a. vigorous enforcement of antitrust laws.
    b. blocking mergers of large firms that control significant portions of a market.
    c. breaking up monopoly firms into smaller businesses.
    d. all of the above.

---

Use Figure HW-1 to answer questions 11–15. Remember, quantity is given in thousands.

11. Consumer surplus equals:

12. Producer surplus equals:

13. Assume that there are negative externalities of $10 per unit of the product. What is the socially optimal output?

14. If the government puts a price floor on this product at $40 per unit, by how much does consumer surplus decline?

15. If the government puts a price ceiling on this product at $10 per unit, how much will be produced and sold in the market?

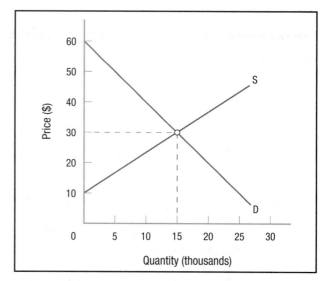

**HW-1**

---

16. The financial panic of 1907 led Congress to pass the Federal Reserve Act in 1913, creating the Federal Reserve in order to
    a. keep the federal government from spending more than it receives in taxes.
    b. help bankers get larger bonuses.
    c. regulate banks and the money supply.
    d. keep inflation above 10% a year.

17. During the Great Depression of the 1930s
    a. over 10,000 banks failed.
    b. unemployment reached 25%.
    c. Congress put tariffs on imported goods.
    d. all of the above
    e. none of the above

18. The Great Depression of the 1930s ended because
    a. people started investing in the stock market again.
    b. of government spending on military armaments for World War II.

c. big tax cuts were enacted in 1933.

d. gold was discovered in California.

19. Stagflation refers to a
    a. business cycle with periodic booms and busts.
    b. growing economy with little unemployment.
    c. deep recession like the Great Depression.
    d. financial panic caused by mortgage defaults.
    e. period of high unemployment and high inflation.

20. The economic history of the United States is represented by
    a. constant market failures.
    b. little government regulation of the economy.
    c. short periods of government intervention in the economy followed by long periods of market failure.
    d. periods when markets failed, followed by periods of growing government intervention in the economy.
    e. one long, steady period of uninterrupted economic growth.

| | Use the ExamPrep to Get Ready for Exams | **STEP 6** |

This sheet (front and back) is designed to help you prepare for your exams. The chapter has been boiled down to its key concepts. You are asked to answer questions, define terms, draw graphs, and, if you wish, add summaries of class notes.

## Markets and Efficiency

Describe the following five institutional requirements for efficient markets and describe why they are important.

1. Widely available accurate information:


2. Well protected property rights:


3. Contracts enforced:


4. No externalities:


5. Competitive markets:


Describe the reasons for the overall efficiency of markets:

## Market Failures

Define and describe the following reasons for market failure.

### Asymmetric Information

Adverse selection:


Moral hazard:

### Public Goods

Nonrivalry:


Nonexclusive:


Free rider:

### Contract Enforcement

Explain why enforcing contracts is necessary:

## Externalities

Use the grid at right to diagram external costs and benefits. Begin with the private market supply and demand curves labeled $S_p$ and $D_p$.

External costs: Draw the new supply curve $S_1$ that includes negative spillovers. List the implications for efficient markets:

External benefits: Draw the new demand curve $D_1$ that includes positive externalities. List the implications for efficient markets:

## Monopoly Power

Explain the harm from monopoly and the importance of competitive markets:

# Additional Study Help Chapterwide Practice Questions

## Matching

Match the description with the corresponding term.

___ 1. Property rights
___ 2. Asymmetric information
___ 3. Adverse selection
___ 4. Moral hazard
___ 5. Public goods
___ 6. Externalities

a. Occurs when products of different qualities are sold at a single price due to asymmetric information.
b. Both nonrival and nonexclusive goods. They give rise to the free rider problem.
c. A market failure caused when one party has better information than another.
d. Costs or benefits of economic activity that are not borne by the consumer or producer.
e. Occurs when insurance causes people to change their behavior in a detrimental way.
f. Clear ownership of possessions. They foster an incentive not to waste.

## Fill-In

Circle the word(s) in parentheses that complete the sentence.

1. The difference between what firms are willing to provide products for and market prices is (consumer, producer) _____ surplus, whereas the difference between what people would pay for a product and market price is (consumer, producer) _____ surplus.

2. Markets require (accurate, asymmetric, efficient) _____ information for efficient operation, but often (accurate, asymmetric, efficient) _____ information is a reality as one party has superior information over the other party.

3. When some contract or arrangement changes the economic incentives we face, economists refer to this as (adverse selection, moral hazard) _____, and when products of different qualities are sold at the same price because of asymmetric information, we refer to this as (adverse selection, moral hazard) _____.

4. A product consumed by others without reducing the benefits to other consumers is referred to as a (public good, free rider) _____.

5. Pollution is an example of an external (benefit, cost) _____, while education represents an external (benefit, cost) _____. If everyone owns an asset, it is a (monopoly, common property resource, public good) _____, but when one firm controls the market for a resource, it is a (monopoly, common property resource, public good) _____.

## True-False

Circle the correct answer.

T / F   1. As messy as markets are, they are far more efficient at allocating resources than are systems of central planning.

T / F   2. An efficient market requires that accurate information be made available to both buyers and sellers.

T / F   3. Informal property rights tend to be more economically efficient than formal property rights because they involve less paperwork.

T / F   4. The larger the scale on which business operates, the more important it is that the legal system strictly enforces contract obligations.

T / F   5. Market failure implies that a market has completely collapsed, or ceased to exist as a market.

T / F   6. Market failure can result both from sellers knowing more about a product than the typical buyer and from buyers knowing more about a product than the typical seller.

T / F   7. The problem of moral hazard occurs when an insurance company provides incentives for behavior it is trying to discourage.

T / F   8. Public goods give rise to the free rider problem.

T / F   9. Informal contract enforcement tends to work best when contracts are small and the parties to them have long been acquainted with one another.

T / F   10. Markets tend to overproduce goods with external benefits and underproduce goods with external costs.

T / F   11. In theory, a "free market" should be one in which the government rarely intervenes, but in actual practice, the government often takes active steps to promote competition and guard against the rise of monopolies.

## Multiple Choice

Circle the correct answer.

1. Which of the following is *not* one of the requirements for an efficient market?
   a. The market is dominated by just one or two major firms.
   b. Private contracts are strictly enforced.
   c. Spillover effects from other economic actors are limited.
   d. Property rights are protected.

2. One of the requirements for an efficient market is that accurate information be made widely available. For which of the following products are informational requirements most difficult to satisfy?
   a. corn
   b. bricks
   c. prescription drugs
   d. paper towels

3. A villager is unable to use his family home as collateral for securing a small business loan because a legal title has never been issued for the house. Which requirement for an efficient market is not being met in this case?
   a. Accurate information is widely available.
   b. Private contracts are well enforced.
   c. Spillover effects from other economic factors are limited.
   d. Property rights are protected.

4. A small window-washing firm sues one of its clients for nonpayment. The court ultimately compels the client to pay, but only after a legal process that lasts three years and costs the window-washing firms thousands of dollars in legal fees. Which requirement for an efficient market is not being met in this case?
   a. Competition prevails.
   b. Private contracts are well enforced.
   c. Spillover effects are limited.
   d. Property rights are protected.

5. A chemical company earns tremendous profits producing antifreeze, but the runoff from the production process begins killing fish in the local river. Which requirement for an efficient market is not being met in this case?
   a. Competition prevails.
   b. Private contracts are well enforced.
   c. Spillover effects from other economic factors are limited.
   d. Property rights are protected.

6. When economists say the market rations goods to consumers, this means
   a. the government has issued ration coupons, which consumers can use to purchase the goods they most need.
   b. market discipline is forcing producers to offer high-quality goods for sale at relatively low prices.
   c. lawmakers have placed legal limits on the quantities of certain goods that individual consumers can purchase.
   d. individual consumers have limited resources with which to purchase goods, so each consumer must decide which goods are most important to him or her.

7. Tobacco companies once promoted cigarettes as part of a healthy lifestyle, even after their own studies had shown that smoking causes lung cancer. What sort of market failure did this represent?
   a. asymmetric information
   b. adverse selection
   c. moral hazard
   d. the overproduction of negative externalities

8. An insurance company starts insuring businesses against the loss of data due to computer viruses, but this just leads firms to stop purchasing virus protection software. What sort of market failure does this represent?
   a. asymmetric information
   b. adverse selection
   c. moral hazard
   d. the free rider problem

9. A health insurance company begins offering free dental care as part of its basic insurance plan, but this just leads to a disproportionately large number of people with severe dental problems signing up for its plan. What sort of market failure does this represent?
   a. asymmetric information
   b. adverse selection
   c. moral hazard
   d. the overproduction of negative externalities

10. What sort of market failure did George Akerlof find to be most responsible for the low market price of used cars?
    a. asymmetric information
    b. adverse selection
    c. moral hazard
    d. the free rider problem

11. Normally, public goods are
    a. both exclusive and rival.
    b. exclusive, but nonrival.

c. rival, but nonexclusive.

d. both nonexclusive and nonrival.

12. Which of the following is an example of a public good?

a. automobiles

b. auto repair services

c. highways

d. bumper stickers

13. Which of the following is an example of a private good?

a. Super Bowl tickets

b. National Public Radio

c. the emergency broadcast system

d. homeland security precautions

14. A musician releases a new CD in stores, but an Internet service allows users to download the CD for free. What sort of market failure problem does this represent?

a. asymmetric information

b. adverse selection

c. moral hazard

d. the free rider problem

15. What is the most likely effect of a single firm achieving monopoly status in its industry?

a. Prices rise.

b. Product quality goes up.

c. Market efficiency increases.

d. The firm's profit margin declines.

## Essay-Problem

Answer in the space provided.

The questions below can be challenging. Don't get upset if your answers are not always the same as those we suggest. Use our answers as a way to see if you are in the ballpark. More importantly, use these questions and their answers to see the types of adjustments you must make when applying supply and demand analysis to real markets.

1. What is the essence of markets?

2. Does market failure always require some government solution?

3. Sears has the motto "Satisfaction Guaranteed or Your Money Back." Is it in Sears' interest to accept returns with no questions asked? How does this motto overcome information problems?

4. Why do small businesses cultivate a "good name" (good reputation)?

5. An acquaintance said that the most important thing for him in buying an automobile was a warranty, such as "7 years–70,000 miles." How do warranties encourage you to buy? How might warranties cause problems for consumers?

6. Radio broadcasts are public goods. People with automobile radios, for example, cannot be prevented from listening to radio stations, and my listening to one station does not prevent you from listening to it. Yet, most radio stations are private, not public. What solves the public goods problem here, and can it be used to solve other public good problems? (Hint: Break down the radio broadcast into its various segments. If it is a music station, do you hear music every moment? If it is a talk station, do you hear talk every moment?)

7. In some developing countries, land has been seized from large landowners by the government. This land is then parceled out to small farmers, but title to the land is kept by the government. Farmers are given low rents for set periods of time. Based on what you read in this chapter, what problems do you foresee with this arrangement?

8. If left on their own, why can we expect private companies to generate pollution?

## What's Next

With this and the last chapter under your belt, you now have a good feel for how markets work. You have seen what is needed to make sure markets work efficiently, and what can be done to overcome market failure. Also, you have seen how the beneficial effects of markets can be overthrown if government steps in and institutes the wrong policies.

## Answers to Chapterwide Practice Questions

### Matching

| | | |
|---|---|---|
| 1. f | 3. a | 5. b |
| 2. c | 4. e | 6. d |

### Fill-In

1. producer, consumer
2. accurate, asymmetric
3. moral hazard, adverse selection
4. public good
5. cost, benefit, common property resource, monopoly

### True-False

| | | | |
|---|---|---|---|
| 1. T | 4. T | 7. T | 10. F |
| 2. T | 5. F | 8. T | 11. T |
| 3. F | 6. T | 9. T | |

### Multiple Choice

| | | | |
|---|---|---|---|
| 1. a | 5. c | 9. b | 13. a |
| 2. c | 6. d | 10. a | 14. d |
| 3. d | 7. a | 11. d | 15. a |
| 4. b | 8. c | 12. c | |

### Essay-Problem

1. They bring buyers and sellers together.
2. No. Market failure may be quite mild, or can be overcome in other ways. Consider the lemons problem discussed in the chapter. A government solution is not necessary. The lemons problem will be overcome, for the most part, by used car dealers providing warranties or guarantees, buyers checking *Consumer Reports* or bringing mechanics to inspect vehicles of interest, and private sellers going to great lengths to document the quality of their cars.
3. By using such a motto, Sears in effect says to its customers: Do not worry about the products; do not spend an inordinate amount of time researching products; buy what you want in the full knowledge that if things do not work out the way you expected,

you will not have to pay for the product. This encourages buying, and it mitigates the information problem that all consumers face when purchasing any product. Of course, there is always the possibility of abuse on the part of customers. For example, Nordstrom's, which has a similar policy, was once approached by a man who wanted to return tires that dissatisfied him. Nordstrom's gave the man a credit. The problem was: Nordstrom's does not sell tires. So the man was abusing Nordstrom's. Such action occurs infrequently enough that stores such as Sears and Nordstrom's continue with their product guarantees.

4. A good name solves information problems and contracting problems. There are many small businesses. How do you choose which one to use? A good name keeps you from spending time hunting for information. For small tasks such as hiring a plumber for an emergency, a good reputation means you can proceed informally, rather than with a detailed contract. Solving these information and contracting problems means lower transaction costs, which encourages you to engage in some transactions that you might otherwise avoid.

5. A warranty is a signal that a manufacturer stands behind its product. It assures you that if there are problems that fall within the warranty's terms, they will be taken care of at minimal cost. That is the good side of warranties. A problem may arise, for example, if an auto manufacturer knows its car does not come up to the standards of other cars but is willing to bear the possible costs of repairs as an inducement to get you to buy. The value of your time is also a cost of warranties: How many times do you want to take your car to the dealer for repairs? So a response to the acquaintance can be: Do you want a car that has a good warranty and you know is a good car, so you will not be spending so much time at the dealership, or do you want a great warranty with a car of unknown quality that may have you at the dealership again and again? This is one reason people look at the frequency of repair records in *Consumer Reports.*

6. Advertisements fund private radio stations, solving the public goods problem in this instance. Can advertising be used in other cases? Would advertisements in public parks work? How about letting a restaurant open in a small section of parkland and using the rent and tax revenue for park upkeep? The point is, the public good problem may be solvable in some cases by having private ventures bear the costs.

7. By keeping title in its hands, the government takes away the incentives small farm owners would have not to waste resources. If there was any doubt that the government would not renew leases, this would provide an incentive to waste the land, squeezing out of it whatever one could. Ownership brings about a long-term view.

8. Pollution is a negative externality, caused by private firms not bearing the true cost of business. It costs money to clean up pollution, and if one private firm incurs these costs, its price may not be competitive in the market. People buying the product in Arizona may not care that the firm has a clean production process in Maine. Once a private firm is forced to bear this cost, say, by a government regulatory agency, the private firm will either produce less, thereby decreasing pollution, or produce the same amount but clean up the pollution. The private company will seek to minimize the additional cost it now has to bear. But all firms must now meet the same pollution control standards, so being competitive is not an issue.

# Elasticity 5

Russ Schelpman/Corbis

## Elasticity Is an Important Summary Measure of Demand and Supply

Elasticity is an important extension of supply and demand concepts. In the previous chapters, we saw that when price changes, quantity demanded and quantity supplied change as well. But by how much? The answer to this is given in a simple number that economists call "elasticity." Elasticity is the change in one variable caused by the change in another variable. You will see that this simple concept of elasticity provides a tremendous amount of information.

| This Is What You Need to Know | STEP 1 |
| --- | --- |

**After studying this chapter you should be able to**

■ Understand the concept of elasticity and why percentages are used to measure it.

■ Describe the difference between elastic and inelastic demand.

■ Compute price elasticities of supply and demand.

■ Use income elasticity of demand to define normal, inferior, and luxury goods.

■ Describe cross elasticity of demand and use this concept to define substitutes and complements.

■ Describe the relationship between total revenue and price elasticity of demand.

■ Describe the determinants of elasticity of demand and supply.

113

- Use the concept of price elasticity of supply to measure the relationship between quantity supplied and changes in product price.

- Describe the time periods economists use to study elasticity, and describe the variables that companies can change during these periods.

- Describe the relationship between elasticity and the burden and incidence of taxes.

## STEP 2          Review the Key Terms

**Price elasticity of demand:** A measure of the responsiveness of quantity demanded to a change in price, equal to the percentage change in quantity demanded divided by the percentage change in price.

**Elastic demand:** The absolute value of the price elasticity of demand is greater than 1. Elastic demands are very responsive to changes in price. The percentage change in quantity demanded is greater than the percentage change in price.

**Inelastic demand:** The absolute value of the price elasticity of demand is less than 1. Inelastic demands are not very responsive to changes in price. The percentage change in quantity demanded is less than the percentage change in price.

**Unitary elasticity of demand:** The absolute value of the price elasticity of demand is equal to 1. The percentage change in quantity demanded is just equal to the percentage change in price.

**Total revenue:** Price times quantity demanded (sold). If demand is elastic and price rises, quantity demanded falls off significantly and total revenue declines, and vice versa. If demand is inelastic and price rises, quantity demanded does not decline much and total revenue rises, and vice versa.

**Income elasticity of demand:** Measures how responsive quantity demanded is to changes in consumer income.

**Normal goods:** Goods that have positive income elasticities of less than 1. When consumer income grows, quantity demanded rises for normal goods, but less than the rise in income.

**Luxury goods:** Goods that have income elasticities greater than 1. When consumer income grows, quantity demanded of luxury goods rises more than the rise in income.

**Inferior goods:** Goods that have income elasticities that are negative. When consumer income grows, quantity demanded falls for inferior goods.

**Cross elasticity of demand:** Measures how responsive the quantity demanded of one good is to changes in the price of another good. Substitute goods have positive cross elasticities; complementary goods have negative cross elasticities.

**Substitutes:** Goods consumers substitute for one another depending on their relative prices, such as coffee and tea. Substitutes have a positive cross elasticity of demand.

**Complements:** Goods that are typically consumed together, such as coffee and sugar. Complements have a negative cross elasticity of demand.

**Price elasticity of supply:** A measure of the responsiveness of quantity supplied to changes in price. An elastic supply curve has elasticity greater than 1, whereas inelastic supplies have elasticities less than 1. Time is the most important determinant of the elasticity of supply.

**Elastic supply:** Price elasticity of supply is greater than 1. The percentage change in quantity supplied is greater than the percentage change in price.

**Inelastic supply:** Price elasticity of supply is less than 1. The percentage change in quantity supplied is less than the percentage change in price.

**Unitary elastic supply:** Price elasticity of supply is equal to 1. The percentage change in quantity supplied is equal to the percentage change in price.

**Market period:** Time period so short that the output and the number of firms are fixed.

**Short run:** Time period when plant capacity and the number of firms in the industry cannot change. Firms can employ more people, use overtime with existing employees, or hire part-time employees to produce more, but this is done in an existing plant.

**Long run:** Time period long enough for firms to alter their plant capacities and for the number of firms in the industry to change. Existing firms can expand or build new plants, or firms can enter or exit the industry.

**Incidence of taxation:** Refers to who bears the economic burden of a tax. The economic entity bearing the burden of a particular tax will depend on the price elasticities of demand and supply.

**Deadweight loss:** The loss in consumer and producer surplus due to inefficiency because some transactions cannot be made and therefore their value to society is lost.

## Work Through the Chapter Tutorials             STEP 3

# Elasticity of Demand

### Frequently Asked Questions

Q:  **What is price elasticity of demand?**
A:  Price elasticity of demand measures how sensitive the quantity demanded of a product is to price changes. Price elasticity of demand typically is expressed in absolute value terms. It is determined by dividing the percentage change in quantity demanded by the percentage change in price. Elasticity measures permit comparisons among products.

Q:  **What is the difference between elastic and inelastic demand curves?**
A:  When the absolute value of the price elasticity of demand is greater than 1, that product is said to have an elastic demand. Elastically demanded products have many substitutes, and their demand is quite sensitive to price changes. Foreign vacations and furniture have relatively elastic demand curves. When elasticity is less than 1, demand is inelastic. Quantity demanded is not very sensitive to price. Necessities like gasoline, prescription drugs, and tobacco have relatively inelastic demand curves. A value of elasticity equal to 1 is a unitary elastic curve, where the percentage change in quantity demanded is equal to the percentage change in price. Figure 1 on the next page has two demand curves: $D_1$ is relatively inelastic, and $D_2$ is relatively elastic.

Q:  **What are the determinants of elasticity?**
A:  There are four major determinants of elasticity. Elasticity is influenced by the availability of substitute products, the percentage of income spent on the product, whether the product is a necessity or a luxury good, and the length of time consumers have to adjust to price changes.

**FIGURE 1**

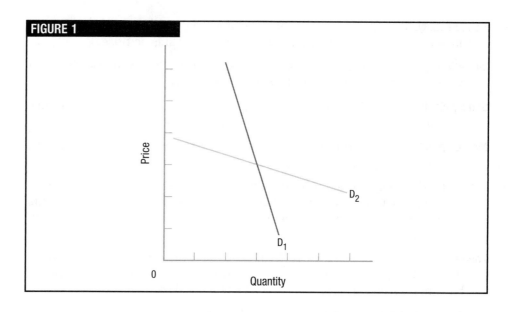

---

Q:  **How is elasticity computed?**

A:  To avoid the problem of getting two different elasticity calculations for the same price change whether price is rising or falling, we use the midpoint formula to compute elasticity:

$$E_d = \frac{Q_1 - Q_0}{(Q_1 + Q_0)/2} \div \frac{P_1 - P_0}{(P_1 + P_0)/2}$$

For example, in Figure 2, the elasticity between points $a$ and $b$ (price drops from \$25 to \$20) is

$$
\begin{aligned}
&= [(400 - 200)/300] \div [(20 - 25)/22.5] \\
&= 200/300 \div -5/22.5 \\
&= 0.67 \div -0.22 \\
&= -3.05 \\
&= |3.05|
\end{aligned}
$$

Q:  **Why does elasticity vary along a linear demand curve?**

A:  Along a linear (straight line) demand curve, elasticity varies from elastic at higher prices to inelastic at lower prices. When price is high, a 1-unit change in price is

**FIGURE 2**

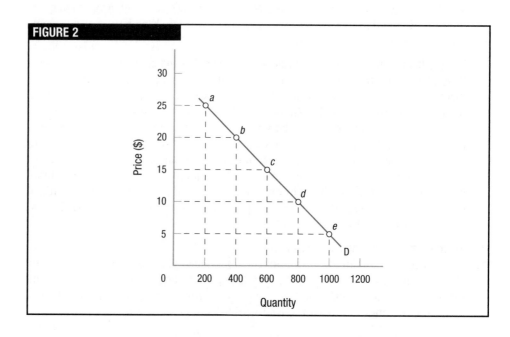

a small percentage change, but a big change in quantity demanded, and thus the demand is elastic. The opposite is true when price is low. In Figure 2, for example, between point *a* and point *b* demand is elastic, and it is inelastic between point *d* and point *e*. At point *c*, price elasticity of demand is unitary (1).

**Q:   How is total revenue affected by changing prices when demand is *inelastic*?**

**A:**   An inelastically demanded product may, for example, have more brand loyalty. Consequently, quantity demanded is less sensitive to price changes. So, when prices rise, total revenue rises, since quantity demanded falls off less than price increases. When price declines, total revenue falls since quantity sold grows at only a fraction of the price decline.

**Q:   How are total revenue and price related when demand is elastic?**

**A:**   An elastic demand means a price change can lead to large shifts in quantity demanded. Thus, when prices fall for an elastically demanded good, sales surge and total revenue rises. However, when price is raised, consumers find substitutes easily and sales plunge, resulting in lower total revenues.

**Q:   How are elasticity and total revenue related along a linear demand curve?**

**A:**   Figure 3 shows the relationship between price elasticity and total revenue along a straight line demand curve. Note how total revenue keeps rising as one moves down the demand curve (price falling) in the elastic range, and

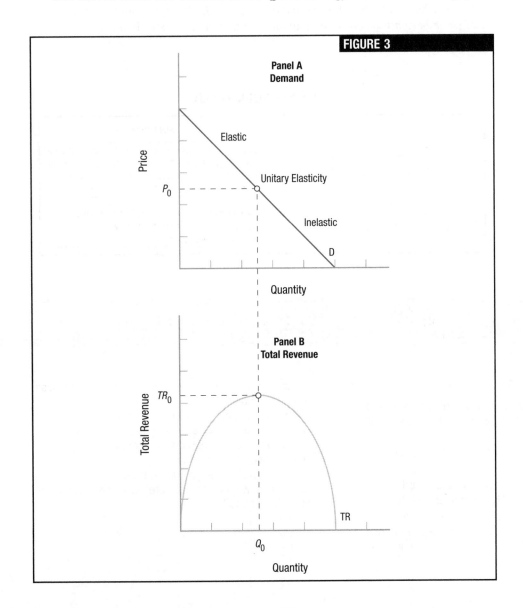

**FIGURE 3**

how total revenue falls as one moves down the demand curve in the inelastic range. Total revenue is maximized at the point of unitary elasticity.

Q:    What is income elasticity of demand?

A:    Income elasticity of demand measures how quantity demanded varies with consumer income. *Normal* goods have a positive income elasticity of demand but are less than 1. *Luxury* goods have income elasticities greater than 1. *Inferior* goods have negative income elasticities. As income rises, spending on luxury goods grows faster than income, while spending on inferior goods falls. When income rises, spending on normal goods rises, but at a pace that is less than the increase in income.

Q:    What is cross elasticity of demand?

A:    Cross elasticity of demand measures how responsive quantity demanded of one good is to changes in the price of another good. If cross elasticity of demand is positive, the two goods are *substitutes*. If negative, the two goods are *complements*.

## Key Point to Remember

When demand is inelastic ($E_d < 1$), a change in price leads to a *smaller percentage change* in quantity demanded. So when price *rises* total revenue *rises*, and vice versa. Alternatively, when demand is elastic ($E_d > 1$), a change in price leads to a *larger percentage change* in quantity demanded, and so when price *rises* total revenue *falls*, and vice versa.

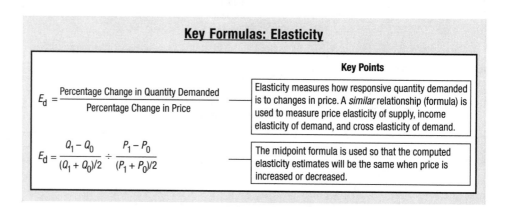

### Key Formulas: Elasticity

| | Key Points |
|---|---|
| $E_d = \dfrac{\text{Percentage Change in Quantity Demanded}}{\text{Percentage Change in Price}}$ | Elasticity measures how responsive quantity demanded is to changes in price. A *similar* relationship (formula) is used to measure price elasticity of supply, income elasticity of demand, and cross elasticity of demand. |
| $E_d = \dfrac{Q_1 - Q_0}{(Q_1 + Q_0)/2} \div \dfrac{P_1 - P_0}{(P_1 + P_0)/2}$ | The midpoint formula is used so that the computed elasticity estimates will be the same when price is increased or decreased. |

# Elasticity of Demand Quick Check

## Circle the Correct Answer

1. (T/F) If price elasticity of demand is low (inelastic), a small change in price will result in a relatively large change in quantity demanded.

2. (T/F) If demand is inelastic and the price of the product falls, total revenue will rise.

3. (T/F) If price elasticity of demand (expressed as an absolute value) is less than 1, demand is inelastic.

4. (T/F) If the demand is elastic and the price of the good rises, total revenue will rise because the change in quantity demanded is less than the change in price.

5. Which of the following is *not* a determinant of the elasticity of demand?
   a. the time period under consideration
   b. whether the good is a luxury or a necessity
   c. how easy it is to substitute other products
   d. the price of the product

6. If price drops from $8 to $4 and sales rise from 20 units to 40 units, what is the absolute value of the price elasticity of demand?
   a. 0.5
   b. 0.66
   c. 1
   d. 2

7. In Figure 4, the price elasticity of demand, expressed as an absolute value
   a. must be less than 1 at point *a*.
   b. must be less than 1 at point *b*.
   c. increases from point *b* to point *c*.
   d. must be greater than 1 at point *e*.

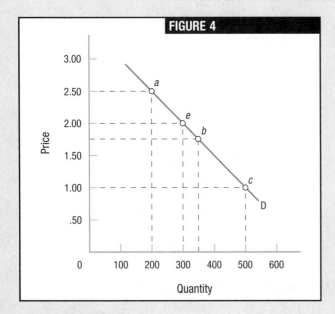

**FIGURE 4**

8. An income superior good is one for which income elasticity of demand $E_Y$ is
   a. $E_Y < 0$.
   b. $E_Y = 0$.
   c. $E_Y < 1$.
   d. $E_Y > 1$.

9. If price rises from $2.00 to $2.80 and quantity demanded falls from 160 to 80 units, what is the absolute value of the price elasticity of demand?
   a. 0.5
   b. 0.66
   c. 1
   d. 2

10. Using Figure 5, what is the elasticity of demand between points *a* and *b* (remember to express the answer in absolute value terms)?
    a. 0.85
    b. 1.0
    c. 1.75
    d. 2.2

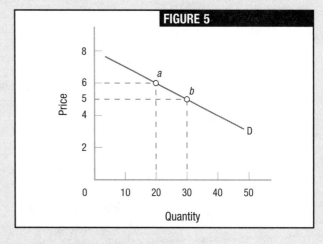

**FIGURE 5**

Score: _____

Answers: 1. F; 2. F; 3. T; 4. F; 5. d; 6. c; 7. d; 8. d; 9. d; 10. d

## If You Got 9 or 10 Correct

You have a good grasp of the concept of elasticity of demand, how it is calculated, the relationship between elasticity and total revenue, and the concepts of cross elasticity of demand and income elasticity of demand. These were not simple questions and that is a lot of material to absorb in one lesson. Congratulations. Go on to the next section, Elasticity of Supply.

## If You Didn't Get at Least 9 Correct

■ First note that the concept of elasticity and its computation are difficult and tedious. You need to keep a focus to get through this material.

■ Also, keep in mind that there is a lot of material in this section.

■ Go back and review the first part of the chapter in the text.

■ When you have completed this review, work through the solved problem below, then go to the next section, Elasticity of Supply.

## Solved Problem: Elasticity of Demand

The following data (see table) for gasoline sales and prices in the United States are from the U.S. Department of Energy. Prices are in dollars, and sales are in millions of gallons per day.

| Price | Sales (millions of gallons/day) |
|-------|-----------------------------------|
| 3.50  | 330 |
| 3.25  | 340 |
| 3.00  | 350 |
| 2.75  | 360 |
| 2.50  | 370 |
| 2.25  | 380 |
| 2.00  | 390 |
| 1.75  | 400 |
| 1.50  | 410 |
| 1.25  | 420 |
| 1.00  | 430 |

a. Compute the elasticity of demand when the price increases from $3.00 to $3.25.

b. Compute the elasticity of demand when the price increases from $1.25 to $1.50.

c. Why would the values be different?

d. When average gas prices are $1.50 a gallon, what does total revenue per day equal? What is total revenue when price is $3.00 a gallon? Is this consistent with your elasticity estimates in questions a and b?

e. A prominent economist, N. Gregory Mankiw (*Wall Street Journal,* October 20, 2006, p. A12), suggested that the government increase gasoline taxes by $1.00 a gallon. He suggested this tax increase would be good for the environment, reduce road congestion, help the federal budget, and improve national security, among other reasons. Assume that the current price of gasoline is $2.00 a gallon and the government followed Professor Mankiw's advice, slapping on a $1.00 tax per gallon of gasoline. Further assume that this raised the price to $3.00 a gallon (the last section of the chapter looks at the impact of taxes and elasticity estimates). Using the data in the table, how much revenue would the government collect in a *year*?

f. Why might such a tax be good for the environment, reduce road congestion, help the federal budget, and improve national security?

## Solution-Discussion

a. The elasticity of demand when price rises from $3.00 to $3.25 is equal to the percentage change in quantity demanded divided by the percentage change in price. Using the midpoint formula:

$$E_d = [(350 - 340)/((350 + 340)/2)] \div [(3.00 - 3.25)/((3.00 + 3.25)/2)]$$
$$= (10/345) \div (-0.25/3.125) = 0.02899 \div 0.08 = |-0.36| = 0.36.$$

b. In a similar fashion to question a, the elasticity of demand when price rises from $1.25 to $1.50 is

$$E_d = [(420 - 410)/((420 + 410)/2)] \div [(1.25 - 1.50)/((1.25 + 1.50)/2)]$$
$$= (10/415) \div (-0.25/1.375) = 0.02410 \div 0.1818 = |-0.13| = 0.13.$$

c. First, the demand relationship shown in the table is a linear relationship (if you plot the line, you will see it is a straight line). And we know that elasticity varies over a linear demand curve. Second, when prices rise, we would expect to see the elasticity become more elastic and this is the case in the table. As prices rise, consumers buy less as they find other substitutes for gasoline. In the short run, quantity demanded drops off maybe at 2% for every rise in price of 10%. People take fewer trips and consolidate those trips to accomplish more. Some people may even move to public transportation, leaving their cars home. In the long run, people will purchase cars with higher gas mileage or substitute smaller cars for their existing SUVs.

d. At $1.50 a gallon, 410 million gallons a day are sold, so total revenue is equal to $1.50 × 410 = $615 million a day. At $3.00 a gallon, total revenue is $3.00 × 350 = $1,050 million a day. Yes, it is consistent. When demand is inelastic and price increases, total revenue will rise, since the percentage increase in price is greater than the percentage decrease in sales.

e. If the government put a $1.00 per gallon tax on gasoline and we assume that the price would rise to $3.00, tax revenue per day would be $1 × 350 = $350 million. Annual revenue would equal $350 million × 365 = $127.75 billion.

f. Burning gasoline is harmful to the environment, increasing pollution and potentially adding to global warming. Increasing the gasoline tax would reduce automobile travel, thereby reducing both environmental harm and road congestion. We saw in question e that substantial tax revenue can be collected. The national security argument is a little more nuanced in that since the United States consumes a substantial part of world oil production, our demand may be what keeps oil prices high, resulting in large flows of cash to the Middle East. Also, our dependence on oil leads to concern with sometimes incendiary Middle East politics.

Now that you have reviewed this section, the Elasticity of Supply section will be easier since you now have a better understanding of elasticity of demand. As you read the material in the next section you will see that supply closely parallels demand. ∎

# Elasticity of Supply

## Frequently Asked Questions

Q: **What is the price elasticity of supply, and how is it measured?**

A: The price elasticity of supply measures how sensitive the quantity of a product supplied is to changes in price for that product. Economists find the price elasticity of supply by taking the percentage change in the quantity supplied

and dividing it by the percentage change in price (essentially the same formula as that for the price elasticity of demand). The slope of the supply curve
is positive, so the price elasticity of supply is always positive.

**Q: How are elastic and inelastic supply curves defined?**

A: An elastic supply curve has a price elasticity of supply greater than 1. Elasticity for inelastic supply curves is less than 1, and for unitary supply curves is
equal to 1. Figure 6 shows three supply curves: $S_1$ is inelastic, $S_2$ is unitary elastic, and $S_3$ is elastic.

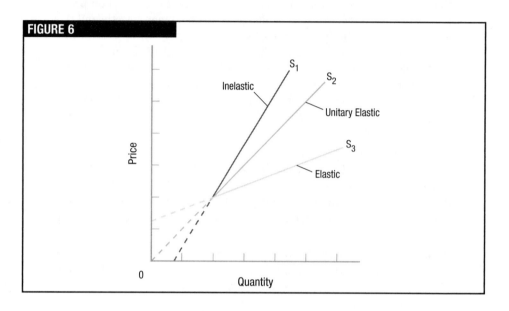

**FIGURE 6**

**Q: Why is time important in determining elasticity of supply?**

A: The market period, short run, and long run are the time periods economists
use to study elasticity. The market period, shown in Figure 7 as $S_{MP}$, is so short
that the output of firms is fixed (perfectly inelastic). The short-run supply curve
is shown as $S_{SR}$. In the short run, companies can change the amount of labor
and other variable factors to alter output, but physical plant is usually assumed
to be fixed. In the long run ($S_{LR}$), companies have time to build new production facilities and to enter or to exit the industry.

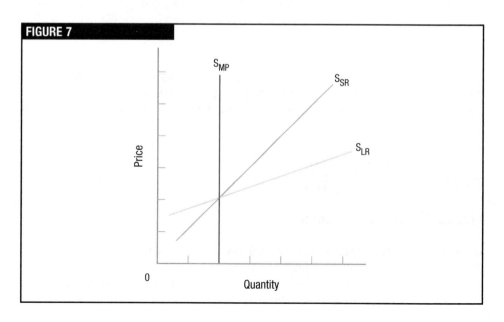

**FIGURE 7**

## Elasticity of Supply Quick Check

**Circle the Correct Answer**

1. (T/F) In the market period, the elasticity of supply is perfectly elastic.
2. (T/F) If a supply curve is linear and it intersects the quantity axis, the curve is inelastic.
3. (T/F) During the short run, plant capacity and the number of firms in an industry are fixed, but firms can adjust their output in response to market changes by adjusting the amount of inputs they employ.
4. The supply curve for the long run, $S_{LR}$, is
    a. relatively elastic.
    b. relatively inelastic.
    c. unitarily elastic.
    d. indeterminate.

5. If demand for Talking Elmo dolls suddenly increases because Sesame Street features Elmo more in its programs, what can suppliers do in the short run?
    a. Nothing.
    b. Increase supply to a small degree by using more labor and other variable inputs.
    c. Flood the market with additional dolls by building a new doll manufacturing plant.
    d. Increase supply greatly by converting a bicycle manufacturing plant into a doll plant.

Score: ____

Answers: 1. F; 2. T; 3. T; 4. a; 5. b

### If You Got All 5 Correct

Your knowledge of supply elasticity is solid. Go on to the next section that focuses on taxes and elasticity.

### If You Didn't Get All of Them Correct

These were relatively simple questions, so if you had trouble here, you probably haven't done well up to this point. Elasticity is not an easy concept to keep straight. It typically requires a little extra time and effort to get it down.

### Keep in Mind

- Elasticity of supply roughly follows the same structure as elasticity of demand.
- Computing elasticity of supply is done the same way as elasticity of demand, but since the supply curve is positively sloped, the resulting number is positive.
- The most important determinant of supply elasticity is time. When firms have a long time to adjust, the supply curve will be more *elastic*. As the adjustment time shortens, the supply curve becomes less elastic.

You might consider a quick review of the first two sections of the chapter at this point. The next section, Taxes and Elasticity, puts together both elasticity of demand and supply and assumes that you have a good feel for both concepts. After this review, continue on to the next section. ■

# Taxes and Elasticity

## Frequently Asked Questions

Q: **How does the elasticity of demand affect who actually pays a tax?**
A: Elasticity affects the burden and incidence of taxes. The more elastic the demand, the less a company can shift part of a tax to consumers in the form

of price increases. Consumers can readily substitute for an elastically demanded product when its price has increased due to taxes.

**Q: Why do consumers pay more of a tax when demand is inelastic?**

A:  An inelastically demanded product can absorb the increase in pcrice due to taxes without much impact on quantity demanded. In Figure 8, point $a$ represents a tax levied on a product with relatively inelastic demand. Note the larger increase in price compared to the smaller decrease in quantity demanded, and the ability suppliers have to shift most of this tax on to consumers because demand, $D_0$, is relatively inelastic.

**FIGURE 8**

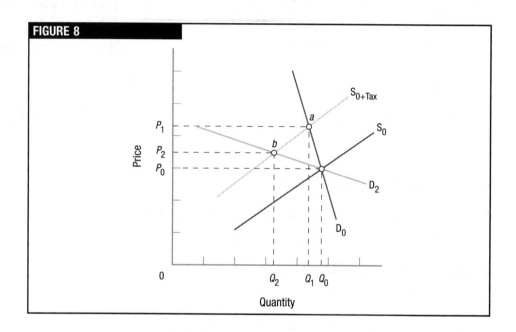

**Q: Why do sellers bear most of the tax burden when demand is relatively elastic?**

A:  When demand is relatively elastic, consumers have a lot of alternatives to the taxed product, so quantity demanded is highly sensitive to changes in price. Demand curve $D_2$ in Figure 8 is relatively elastic, and point $b$ shows the impact of the tax. Price rises very little, but quantity sold falls considerably to $Q_2$. In this case, firms (and their employees) bear the greater burden of this tax.

**Q: How does the elasticity of supply affect tax burdens?**

A:  The more inelastic the supply, the less consumers bear the burden of a tax. In Figure 9, the tax shifts the curve upward from $S_0$ to $S_{0+Tax}$. Price rises from $P_0$ to $P_1$ and the consumer's burden is relatively small. Firms bear some of the price increase, but the reduction in output is small. Contrast this with a perfectly elastic supply $S_2$ (the dashed supply curve) and its corresponding supply curve $S_{2+Tax}$ when the tax is applied. Consumers bear the full burden of the tax as price increases from $P_0$ to $P_2$. Notice that output falls to $Q_2$, so the firm bears the burden of lower output.

**Q: What is deadweight loss of taxes, and why is it important?**

A:  The deadweight loss of a tax is the loss of consumer and producer surplus over and above the tax revenue collected. We want to minimize deadweight losses because they represent inefficiencies associated with collecting taxes.

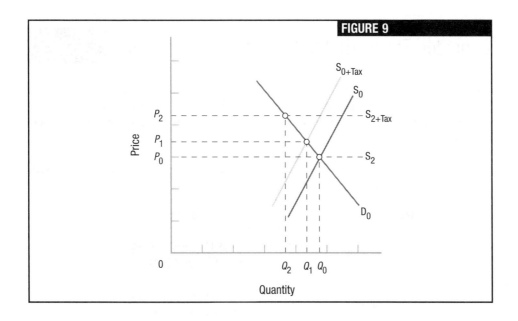

**FIGURE 9**

## Taxes and Elasticity Quick Check

### Circle the Correct Answer

1. (T/F) The more elastic the demand, the more the burden of an excise tax falls on producers.
2. (T/F) Where the supply is perfectly elastic, producers bear the greatest burden of an excise tax.
3. When an excise tax is placed on a product with relatively inelastic demand, which of the following occurs?
   a. Less revenue is collected than if the demand were elastic.
   b. Most of the tax is avoided through product substitution by consumers.
   c. Most of the tax is borne by the purchaser.
   d. Most of the tax is borne by the supplier.
4. If the excise tax on a product with relatively elastic demand is raised, sales of the product will
   a. rise.
   b. fall.
   c. remain constant.
   d. do any of the above; tax rates do not affect sales.
5. Excise taxes are usually placed on goods such as gasoline, cigarettes, and liquor because
   a. collection costs are lowest for these taxes.
   b. revenues collected are so small, ensuring that constituents will not be upset.
   c. government only taxes those products that are detrimental to public health.
   d. the demand for these products is relatively inelastic.

Score: ____

Answers: 1. T; 2. F; 3. c; 4. b; 5. d

You should have correctly answered all of these questions. If you didn't, continue on, but you will undoubtedly have to review this chapter again. As you read through the Hints, Tips, and Reminders that follow, if you are unable to understand the suggestions you will want to go back and review the entire chapter again. This is difficult (and sometimes tedious) stuff, but it will show up again in several more chapters. ■

## STEP 4          Consider These Hints, Tips, and Reminders

**1.** The basic idea of elasticity is how *responsive* quantity changes are to price changes; hence the general formula for elasticity is the percentage change in quantity (demanded, supplied, etc.) *divided by* percentage change in (price, income, etc.).

**2.** Keep in mind that as the table below shows, quantity is always the numerator of each elasticity equation.

| Elasticity | Equation |
|---|---|
| Price elasticity of demand | $\dfrac{\text{Percentage Change in } \textit{Quantity} \text{ Demanded}}{\text{Percentage Change in Price}}$ |
| Price elasticity of supply | $\dfrac{\text{Percentage Change in } \textit{Quantity} \text{ Supplied}}{\text{Percentage Change in Price}}$ |
| Income elasticity of demand | $\dfrac{\text{Percentage Change in } \textit{Quantity} \text{ Demanded}}{\text{Percentage Change in Income}}$ |
| Cross elasticity of demand | $\dfrac{\text{Percentage Change in } \textit{Quantity} \text{ Demanded of product a}}{\text{Percentage Change in Price of product b}}$ |

You should *always* be dividing something into quantity to determine the value of elasticity.

**3.** We use midpoints to keep elasticity estimates consistent whether price rises or falls. But keep in mind that if you are given the percentage changes for both quantity and price, you can compute elasticity directly from those values (percentage change in quantity demanded divided by percentage change in price). For example, a recent article in the *New York Times* cited a study by economist Christopher Knittel, who showed that between November 1975 and November 1980 when gasoline prices rose by 20%, consumers cut gas consumption by 6%.[1] But comparing a recent five-year period (March 2001 to March 2006), when gas prices rose by 20%, consumers only reduced their purchases of gasoline by 1%. In the earlier case, elasticity averaged 0.3 (6% ÷ 20%), while for 2006, the elasticity is much more inelastic at 0.05 (1% ÷ 20%). Why would this be the case? The author suggested that it might be due to longer commutes as a consequence of suburban sprawl, slower growth of mass transit over this period, and the fact that more two-earner households exist where earnings are high enough that gasoline prices have become a smaller portion of the household budget.

The important point here is that you will often be given these numbers (percentage changes) in newspaper and magazine articles, and they can quickly be converted to elasticities without resorting to midpoint calculations.

---

[1]Clifford Krauss, "Drivers Offer a Collective Ho-Hum as Gasoline Prices Soar," *New York Times,* March 20, 2007, p. C1.

| | | |
|---|---|---|
| | Do the Homework for Chapter 5 | **STEP 5** |
| | Elasticity | |

Instructor _____ Time _____ Student _____

---

**Use the answer key below to record your answers to these homework questions.**

1. _____   6. _____   11. _____   16. _____
2. _____   7. _____   12. _____   17. _____
3. _____   8. _____   13. _____   18. _____
4. _____   9. _____   14. _____   19. _____
5. _____   10. _____   15. _____   20. _____

---

Use the following paragraph to answer questions 1 and 2.

The *New York Times* (August 21, 2009) reported that "Starbucks was raising prices by up to 30 cents on some beverages to offset the drop in sales from the recession." A Starbucks spokeswoman explained, "The goal of it [the price increase] is really to continue to find ways to balance the value we're providing for our customers with the business responsibilities." The increases will go mostly to the already high-priced Frappuccinos and caramel macchiatos, but prices on small lattes and brewed coffees will remain the same or be slightly reduced.

1. If Starbucks is raising its prices on high-priced Frappuccinos and macchiatos they must think that these drinks have
   a. positively sloped demand curves.
   b. relatively elastic demands.
   c. lower costs and therefore higher profitability.
   d. relatively inelastic demands.

2. Starbucks has recently faced competition from McDonald's, which introduced "premium" coffees at its outlets. The reason(s) Starbucks didn't raise prices on its small lattes and brewed coffees is probably due to
   a. competition from McDonald's.
   b. relatively elastic demand for these coffees.
   c. the fact that raising prices on these coffees would have led to a big decline in revenues.
   d. all of the above
   e. none of the above

3. An elastic demand means that
   a. quantity demanded will decline rapidly when price falls.
   b. demand will rise dramatically in response to new product introductions.
   c. quantity demanded will drop dramatically in response to a rise in price.
   d. quantity demanded will hardly change when price rises.

4. Which of the following is *not* a determinant of elasticity of demand?
   a. the number of substitutes available for the product
   b. how much of the household budget is spent on the product
   c. the time period under consideration
   d. how hard it is to find the good in stores

Use Figure HW-1 to answer questions 5–7.

5. What is the absolute value of the price elasticity of demand for peaches between points $b$ and $c$ in the figure?
   a. 1.0
   b. 0.75
   c. 0.50
   d. 0.25

6. What is the absolute value of the price elasticity of demand for peaches between points $a$ and $b$ in the figure?
   a. 1.5
   b. 1.6
   c. 1.7
   d. 1.8

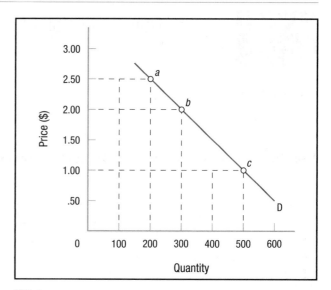

HW-1

7. When the price of peaches falls from $2.50 to $2.00 in the figure, total revenue will
   a. rise.
   b. fall.
   c. remain the same.
   d. There is no way to tell.

8. When demand is elastic and price increases
   a. quantity demanded will not decline substantially.
   b. total revenue will rise.
   c. total revenue will decline.
   d. consumers will find few substitutes for the product.

Use Figure HW-2 to answer questions 9 and 10.

9. When price increases from $6 to $10, total revenue will (rise, fall, remain unchanged).

10. The demand curve $D_0$ between $6 and $10 is
    a. relatively elastic.
    b. unitarily elastic.
    c. representative of a good that has lots of substitutes.
    d. relatively inelastic.

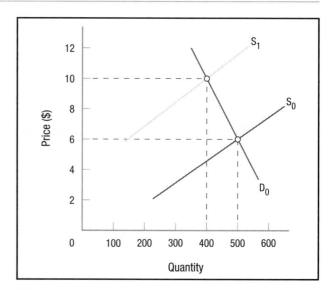

HW-2

11. The price elasticity of supply measures
    a. the responsiveness of quantity supplied to changes in price.
    b. how flexible households are to changes in product supplies.
    c. how rapidly changes in technology are reflected in lower prices.
    d. the percentage change in supply to a fixed percentage change in product price.

Use Figure HW-3 to answer question 12.

12. Which of the curves in Figure HW-3 represents an elastic supply curve?
    a. $S_1$
    b. $S_2$
    c. $S_3$

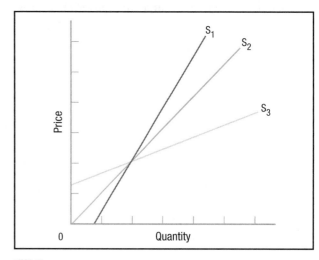

**HW-3**

Use the following paragraph to answer questions 13–15.

*Bized,* a British online newspaper (August 25, 2007), reported that a major European sugar refiner, Tale & Lyle, was going to increase the price of sugar because of the rising price of oil (energy is a big part of its refining costs—up to 40%). They expect to increase prices of refined sugar by 20%.

13. If the short-term price elasticity of demand for their sugar is –0.2, how far will sales of sugar decline from a 20% price increase?

14. Will sales revenue rise or fall?

15. Which of the following seems consistent with a short-term price elasticity of demand for sugar of –0.2?
    a. There are many cheap substitutes for sugar.
    b. Sugar is a small portion of the family budget.
    c. Sugar is an unhealthy product that leads to long-term health problems and therefore the demand is elastic.
    d. Consumer demand for sugar is so small that just a few customers will even notice a 20% price increase.

16. The supply curve for the long run is
    a. relatively elastic.
    b. relatively inelastic.
    c. unitary elastic.
    d. highly inelastic.

17. Chips and salsa
    a. are clearly inferior goods.
    b. have a positive cross elasticity of demand.
    c. sales are not affected by changes in price.
    d. have a negative cross elasticity of demand.

18. It has been noted that when the price of coffee rises by 20%, sales of tea rise by 8%. These two products
    a. are complements.
    b. have a cross elasticity of demand of 2.5.
    c. are normal inferior goods.
    d. have a cross elasticity of demand of 0.4.

Use Figure HW-4 to answer questions 19 and 20.

19. Assume a tax is levied and equilibrium moves from point $e$ to point $a$. In this instance, the largest burden of the tax falls on which of the following?
    a. businesses
    b. workers
    c. consumers
    d. government, because tax revenues are small

20. Given the tax, how large are government revenues?

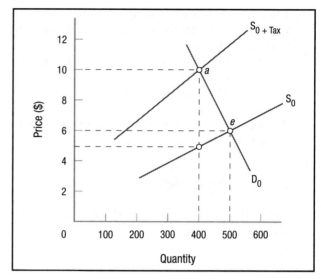

**HW-4**

| | Use the ExamPrep to Get Ready for Exams | **STEP 6** |
|---|---|---|

This sheet (front and back) is designed to help you prepare for your exams. The chapter has been boiled down to its key concepts. You are asked to answer questions, define terms, draw graphs, and, if you wish, add summaries of class notes.

## Elasticity of Demand

Define the general concept of elasticity of demand:

General formula for elasticity:

Describe the following.
Perfectly elastic demand curve:

Perfectly inelastic demand curve:

Unitary elastic demand curve:

In the grid below, draw the following:

■ A perfectly elastic demand curve
■ A perfectly inelastic demand curve
■ A relatively elastic demand curve
■ A relatively inelastic demand curve

List the determinants of elasticity of demand:

Give the midpoint formula for computing elasticity:

### Elasticity and Total Revenue

Complete the table below, describing the relationship among total revenue, price changes, and elasticity by indicating what happens to total revenue.

| | Change in Total Revenue | |
| --- | --- | --- |
| **Elasticity** | **Price Increases** | **Price Decreases** |
| Elastic | | |
| Inelastic | | |
| Unitary | | |

## Other Elasticities of Demand

Income elasticity of demand
List the formula:

Define normal goods:

Define luxury goods:

Define inferior goods:

Cross elasticity of demand
List the formula:

Define substitute goods:

Define complements:

## Elasticity of Supply

List the formula for price elasticity of supply:

Define the following.
Elastic:

Inelastic:

Unitary elastic:

List the three time periods for supply and their relative elasticity:

### Taxes and Elasticity

Fill in the following table with an approximation of who bears the highest excise tax burden (sellers or buyers).

| | **Demand Inelastic** | **Demand Elastic** |
| --- | --- | --- |
| Supply inelastic | | |
| Supply elastic | | |

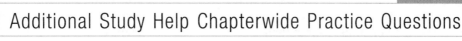

## Additional Study Help Chapterwide Practice Questions

## Matching

Match the description with the corresponding term.

___ 1. Price elasticity of demand
___ 2. Elastic demand
___ 3. Inelastic demand
___ 4. Unitary elasticity of demand
___ 5. Normal goods
___ 6. Inferior goods
___ 7. Cross elasticity of demand
___ 8. Substitutes
___ 9. Complements
___ 10. Price elasticity of supply
___ 11. Market period
___ 12. Short run
___ 13. Long run

a. A measure of how responsive the quantity demanded of one good is to the change in the price of another. It is defined as the percentage change in the quantity demanded of product a over the percentage change in the price of product b.

b. A length of time so short that firms have no ability to change their production levels in response to changes in markets. Output is fixed during this period, as are input levels, plant sizes, and the number of firms.

c. Quantity demanded is unresponsive to price changes. A large change in price will cause only a small change in quantity sold.

d. A measure of how responsive quantity demanded is to changes in price defined as the percentage change in quantity demanded over the percentage change in price.

e. Goods and services that are consumed as a replacement for another if price increases. They have a positive cross elasticity of demand.

f. If the percentage change in quantity demanded is precisely equal to the percentage change in price.

g. Goods that are usually consumed together. Their cross elasticity of demand is less than 0.

h. A period of time long enough for firms to adjust their production levels in response to market changes by adjusting labor and other inputs, but not long enough for changes in plant capacity or the number of firms in an industry.

i. The quantity demanded is responsive to price changes. The absolute value of price elasticity of demand is greater than 1.

j. Goods that have positive income elasticities but are less than 1.

k. A measure of how responsive quantity supplied is to price changes for a given product. It is defined as the percentage change in quantity supplied over the percentage change in price.

l. Goods that have income elasticities that are negative.

m. Firms can change their plant capacity and enter or exit the industry during this time period. The supply curve is relatively elastic.

## Fill-In

Circle the word(s) in parentheses that complete the sentence.

1. Price elasticity of demand is a measure of how responsive (price, quantity demanded) _____ is to changes in (price, quantity demanded) _____. If the absolute value of elasticity is greater than 1, demand is (inelastic, elastic, unitarily elastic) _____, when it is equal to 1, demand is (inelastic, elastic, unitarily elastic) _____, and when it is less than 1, demand is (inelastic, elastic, unitarily elastic) _____.

2. The more substitutes available the more (inelastic, elastic) _____ is demand, and the smaller the fraction of household income spent on a product the more (inelastic, elastic) _____ is demand. The longer the time period consumers have to consider the purchase of a product, the more (inelastic, elastic) _____ is demand.

3. When elasticity is inelastic and price increases, total revenue will (rise, fall, remain the same) _____, and (rise, fall, remain the same) _____ when price falls. When elasticity is elastic and price increases, total revenue will (rise, fall, remain the same) _____, and (rise, fall, remain the same) _____ when price falls.

4. When a product has an income elasticity coefficient greater than 1, it is a (normal, inferior, luxury) _____ good, and when its income elasticity is less than 1 but greater than 0, it is a (normal, inferior, luxury) _____ good, but if its income elasticity is less than 0, it is a (normal, inferior, luxury) _____ good.

5. When cross elasticity is greater than 0, the two goods are (substitutes, complements) _____. When cross elasticity is negative, the two goods are (substitutes, complements) _____.

6. When the price elasticity of supply is greater than 1, supply is (elastic, inelastic) ——————, and when the price elasticity of supply is less than 1, supply is (elastic, inelastic) ——————. The primary determinate of elasticity of supply is (price, quantity, time) ——————. The (market period, short run, long run) —————— is long enough for firms to change all variables; the (market period, short run, long run) —————— period restricts output and the number of firms in the industry; and the (market period, short run, long run) —————— allows firms to change the amount of labor and raw materials to adjust their output to changing market conditions.

7. When demand is (elastic, inelastic) ——————, consumers bear much of the burden of excise taxation, and when supply is (elastic, inelastic) ——————, consumers still tend to bear a higher burden of the excise taxes.

## True-False

Circle the correct answer.

T / F    1. If price elasticity of demand is high (elastic), a small change in price will result in a relatively large change in quantity demanded.

T / F    2. If price elasticity of demand (expressed as an absolute value) is less than 1, demand is inelastic.

T / F    3. A perfectly elastic demand curve is vertical.

T / F    4. If the price of computer desks rises by 9% and sales fall by 6%, price elasticity of demand is −1.5.

T / F    5. Income elasticity of demand is greater than 1 for a normal good.

T / F    6. Products are complements if their cross elasticity of demand is greater than 0.

T / F    7. If price elasticity of demand is unitary, a 10% rise in price will result in a 10% rise in total revenue.

T / F    8. If the demand for a product is elastic, a decline in its price will result in an increase in total revenue.

T / F    9. The more substitutes a product has, the more elastic demand for it will be.

T / F    10. Firms with elastically demanded products experience dramatic changes in sales in response to price changes.

T / F    11. Restaurants might offer a "buy one, get one free" deal because of the relatively high elasticity of demand in their industry.

T / F    12. All linear demand curves have an upper portion that is inelastic and a lower part that is elastic.

T / F    13. Changing brands is more likely to occur when a product's price is high, and when a product has fewer substitutes, its elasticity of demand will be higher.

T / F    14. In general, the smaller the proportion of consumers' income spent on a product, the higher the elasticity of demand.

T / F    15. If a supply curve is linear and it intersects the quantity axis, the curve is inelastic.

T / F    16. During the market period, plant capacity and the number of firms in an industry are fixed, but firms can adjust their output in response to market changes by adjusting the amount of inputs they employ.

T / F    17. The main determinant of the price elasticity of supply is time.

T / F    18. Most excise taxes are levied on goods with relatively inelastic demand curves.

T / F    19. If an excise tax is placed on a good with perfectly inelastic demand, the full burden of the tax will fall on consumers in the form of higher prices.

## Multiple Choice

Circle the correct answer.

1. In general, elasticity is a measure of
   a. consumer tastes and preferences.
   b. the responsiveness of one variable to changes in another.
   c. input price levels in different industries.
   d. worker productivity.

2. If a small rise in price causes a relatively large decrease in the quantity demanded of a product, the product's demand is
   a. relatively elastic.
   b. unitary elastic.
   c. relatively inelastic.
   d. perfectly inelastic.

3. Price elasticity of demand is defined as
   a. percentage change in quantity demanded over percentage change in price.
   b. percentage change in quantity supplied over percentage change in quantity demanded.
   c. absolute change in quantity demanded (number of units) over absolute change in price (dollars).
   d. percentage change in quantity demanded over the percentage change in income.

4. 1f the price of laptop computers drops by 4% and sales go up 2%, what is the price elasticity of demand for laptops expressed as an absolute value?
   a. 0.5
   b. 1
   c. 2
   d. 4

5. If the price of bananas rises from $0.84/lb to $1.05/lb, what is the percentage change in the price of bananas?
   a. −21%
   b. 21%
   c. 25%
   d. 84%

6. If the price of a certain sports car rises from $20,000 to $22,000 and the quantity demanded consequently drops from 7,500 to 6,000, what is the sports car's price elasticity of demand, expressed as an absolute value?
   a. 1.0
   b. 1.5
   c. 2.0
   d. 2.3

7. If a demand curve is perfectly elastic, it is
   a. horizontal.
   b. linear and falling.
   c. falling, bowed in toward the origin.
   d. vertical.

8. If price rises from $1.00 to $1.40 and quantity demanded falls from 80 to 40 units, what is the price elasticity of demand, expressed as an absolute value?
   a. 1.0
   b. 1.5
   c. 2.0
   d. 2.5

9. If price drops from $400 to $200 and sales rise from 400 units to 800 units, what is the price elasticity of demand, expressed as an absolute value?
   a. 0.5
   b. 0.66
   c. 1
   d. 2

10. If quantity demanded changes by 25% and price changes by −20%, what is the elasticity of demand, expressed as an absolute value?
    a. 0.8
    b. 1.0
    c. 1.25
    d. 2

11. A normal good is one for which
    a. quantity demanded rises as income rises, but not as fast as the increase in income.
    b. quantity demanded rises as income increases, rising faster than the increase in income.
    c. quantity demanded falls as income rises.
    d. quantity demanded is unaffected by changes in incomes.

12. A luxury good is one for which income elasticity of demand $E_Y$ is
    a. $E_Y < 0$.
    b. $E_Y = 0$.
    c. $0 < E_Y < 1$.
    d. $E_Y > 1$.

13. If the cross elasticity of demand for two products is less than 0, the two products are
    a. substitutes.
    b. complements.
    c. unrelated.
    d. identical.

14. If the price of an inelastically demanded good goes up, total revenue will
    a. rise.
    b. remain constant.
    C. fall.
    d. be indeterminate without further information.

15. If the price of a good demanded with unitary elasticity falls, total revenue will
    a. rise.
    b. remain constant.
    c. fall.
    d. any of the above—indeterminate without further information.

16. On a linear demand curve, the portion of the curve where $P$ is low and $Q$ is high has an elasticity of demand that is
    a. high, or elastic.
    b. unitary.
    c. low, or inelastic.
    d. the same as when $P$ is high and $Q$ is low.

17. When consumers have time to adjust their consumption patterns, what can happen to the elasticity of demand?
    a. It becomes less elastic.
    b. It tends to be more elastic.

c. Anything can happen to elasticity of demand.

d. There will be no change.

18. In response to incremental increases in gasoline prices, production of smaller, more fuel-efficient cars might increase. This would be an example of
    a. the impact of arc elasticity on suppliers.
    b. proportion of income spent on a product.
    c. the impact of time period and substitutability on elasticity of demand.
    d. perfect elasticity.

19. Which statement is *not* true of the long run?
    a. Firms may decide to leave the industry if they perceive the market as unfavorable.
    b. New firms can enter the business.
    c. Existing firms can alter their production capacity.
    d. The supply curve in the long run is inelastic.

20. If price elasticity of supply is greater than 1, supply is
    a. elastic.
    b. inelastic.
    c. unitary.
    d. inexhaustible.

21. If a supply curve is elastic, it intersects
    a. the price axis.
    b. the quantity axis.
    c. the origin.
    d. none of the above

22. Plant capacity, the number of firms in an industry, and quantity of variable inputs employed are all fixed during the
    a. purchasing period.
    b. market period.
    c. short run.
    d. long run.

23. If an excise tax is levied on a product for which there is relatively inelastic demand, most of the tax burden will be shifted onto
    a. consumers.
    b. sellers.
    c. the government.
    d. workers.

24. Most excise taxes are levied on goods for which demand is
    a. perfectly elastic.
    b. relatively elastic.
    c. unitarily elastic.
    d. relatively inelastic.

25. For products with excise taxes levied on them, as elasticity of supply declines, the portion of the tax burden borne by sellers
    a. increases.

b. decreases.

c. falls to zero.

d. remains constant.

## Essay-Problem

Answer in the space provided.

The questions below are challenging. Don't get discouraged if your answers are not always the same as those we suggest. Use these as another way to assess your progress, but more important, to discover some of the subtleties surrounding the concept of elasticity.

1. The price elasticity of demand for newspapers is 0.1. With such an inelastic demand, should the *Wall Street Journal,* the premier U.S. business newspaper, make it a policy to raise its prices by at least 25 cents every year? Why or why not?

2. Consider two products—laptop computers and mainframe computers—and explain why elasticity is computed in percentage terms.

3. Consider three products: a cup of coffee, a cup of cappuccino, and a cup of cappuccino at Starbucks. Which one is relatively most price inelastic? Which one is relatively most price elastic?

4. Consider a sweater purchased at three different stores: Banana Republic, The Gap, and Old Navy. At which store would you expect the sweater to be most price elastic?

5. Is it always a good idea for firms to lower prices in an attempt to increase total revenue

6. Name three inferior goods.

7. Name two superior goods.

8. Why are economists so vague in defining the short run and the long run? Why not use a fixed amount of time, such as one year?

9. Why do governments consistently tax gasoline and cigarettes?

10. Why does the actual payer of an excise tax not always bear the tax burden?

## What's Next

Having completed this chapter, you now have a good understanding of the concept of elasticity. Often elasticity is intuitively grasped by simply keeping in mind which is changing the most (in percentage terms)—quantity or price. Elasticity estimates provide useful information that consumers, decision makers, and governments can use. Elasticity helps to explain why some people flee some products at the merest hint of a price increase, and yet stay with other products when a price increase is large.

This is a tough, dense, and challenging chapter. But understanding these concepts will be necessary in later chapters on market structures: competition, monopoly, and oligopoly. In the next chapter, we look at how people determine whether prices of products are too high or just right. We focus on what underlies the demand curve.

## Answers to Chapterwide Practice Questions

### Matching

| | | | |
|---|---|---|---|
| 1. d | 5. j | 8. e | 11. b |
| 2. i | 6. l | 9. g | 12. h |
| 3. c | 7. a | 10. k | 13. m |
| 4. f | | | |

### Fill-In

1. quantity demanded, price, elastic, unitary elastic, inelastic
2. elastic, inelastic, elastic
3. rise, fall, fall, rise
4. luxury, normal, inferior
5. substitutes, complements
6. elastic, inelastic, time, long run, market period, short run
7. inelastic, elastic

### True-False

| | | | |
|---|---|---|---|
| 1. T | 6. F | 11. T | 16. F |
| 2. T | 7. F | 12. F | 17. T |
| 3. F | 8. T | 13. F | 18. T |
| 4. F | 9. T | 14. F | 19. T |
| 5. F | 10. T | 15. T | |

### Multiple Choice

| | | | |
|---|---|---|---|
| 1. b | 8. c | 14. a | 20. a |
| 2. a | 9. c | 15. b | 21. a |
| 3. a | 10. c | 16. c | 22. b |
| 4. a | 11. a | 17. b | 23. a |
| 5. c | 12. d | 18. c | 24. d |
| 6. d | 13. b | 19. d | 25. a |
| 7. a | | | |

## Essay-Problem

1. Although price elasticity of demand for newspapers in general is highly inelastic, we have to look at the possibility of substitutes for a specialized newspaper like the *Wall Street Journal.* Eventually, readers of the *Wall Street Journal* will question whether the premium price is worth it, and they will look at substitutes such as the *New York Times,* which has a large business section, though not as extensive as the *Wall Street Journal*'s. Furthermore, as the *New York Times* senses discontent, it will increase its business coverage. A price increase would increase total revenue in the short run, but might backfire in the long run. And continual price increases would exacerbate the problem. Additionally, newspapers in general—like gasoline—have an inelastic demand, but specific brands have more elastic demands.

2. Laptops sell for $1,000, and mainframes can sell for hundreds of thousands of dollars. A small change in the price of mainframes may be more than the total cost of a laptop. If we are going to compare the relative changes, we need a number that allows for this huge difference in price. Elasticity, measured in percentage terms, lets us directly compare changes in differently priced products.

3. The cup of coffee is the most price inelastic—we are more likely to do without cappuccino than coffee altogether, since cappuccino is more expensive. As to whether cappuccino or Starbucks cappuccino is more price elastic, that depends on the relative prices of the two: Starbucks cappuccino is likely to be more expensive than grocery store cappuccino, but it might be less expensive than a fancy restaurant's cappuccino.

4. We would expect the sweater would be most expensive at Banana Republic, since the stores—all part of The Gap empire—can be placed on the price spectrum from (most expensive to least expensive) Banana Republic to The Gap to Old Navy. Therefore, we would expect the sweater at Banana Republic to be most price elastic. But we could be wrong: It is possible that the demand curve for all three stores is similar, and more substitutes are available on the low end rather than the high end, so it may be that the Old Navy sweater is most price elastic of the three.

5. No. Take a look at Figure 4 in the text again. In the elastic range, lowering price will increase total revenue. But if the price is in the inelastic range and the firm lowers the price, total revenue actually will fall. This is why it is important for firms to estimate the elasticity for their products.

6. Beans, ramen noodles, hot dogs. The key thing here is to consider goods you buy when budgets are very tight, but that you would avoid if you had more money.

7. Coach handbags and Burberry scarves.

8. Economists use, for example, the ability to change plant capacity to determine the long run, but industries differ in the amount of time needed to change plant capacity. A computer chip plant may take years to build, so a one-year short-run–long-run limitation would be incorrect for this industry. In other industries, actual building may not take long, but, say, obtaining the necessary environmental clearance may take years. Therefore, the definition must fit the particular situation and so must remain adjustable.

9. Governments might put forward the "sin tax" argument for taxing something such as cigarettes ("they are bad for you") as a way of obtaining popular support for such a tax, but it is a little harder to make that argument for gasoline. The answer is that gasoline and cigarettes have relatively inelastic demands, so increases in the tax have little effect on quantity demanded, which means that in the short run at least, tax revenues will be substantial and reasonably predictable.

10. Here is where elasticity's usefulness as a concept can be seen. Even though a tax might be levied on a producer of a good and so paid by the producer, if price elasticity of demand is relatively inelastic, this tax can be shifted to the consumer in the form of higher prices. So the producer might pay the tax to the government, then recoup almost all of the payment by obtaining higher prices from consumers.

# Consumer Choice and Demand 6

## The Important Logic of Consumer Choice

Supply and demand analysis is based on the premise that consumers and producers make rational decisions about what they want and what they will produce. This chapter looks at the choices that we as consumers make, and the next chapter focuses on producers. You will see how the two major theories for understanding how consumers make choices will give you a better sense of what demand really is and how you go about making product selections every day.

| This Is What You Need to Know | STEP 1 |
| --- | --- |

### After studying this chapter you should be able to

- Use a budget line to determine the constraints on consumer choices.
- Describe the difference between total and marginal utility.
- Describe the law of diminishing marginal utility.
- Understand consumer surplus.
- Use marginal utility analysis to derive demand curves.

## STEP 2 — Review the Key Terms

**Marginal utility analysis:** A theoretical framework underlying consumer decision making. This approach assumes that satisfaction can be measured and that consumers maximize satisfaction when the marginal utilities per dollar are equal for all products and services.

**Budget line:** Graphically illustrates the possible combinations of two goods that can be purchased with a given income, given the prices of both products.

**Utility:** A hypothetical measure of consumer satisfaction.

**Total utility:** The total satisfaction that a person receives from consuming a given amount of goods and services.

**Marginal utility:** The satisfaction received from consuming an additional unit of a given product or service.

**Law of diminishing marginal utility:** As we consume more of a given product, the added satisfaction we get from consuming an additional unit declines.

**Utility maximizing rule:** Utility is maximized where the marginal utility per dollar is equal for all products, or $MU_a/P_a = MU_b/P_b = \ldots = MU_n/P_n$.

**Consumer surplus:** The difference between what consumers are willing to pay and what they actually pay for a product in the market.

## STEP 3 — Work Through the Chapter Tutorials

# Marginal Utility Analysis

### Frequently Asked Questions

**Q:  What is the budget line, and why is it important for consumer decisions?**

**A:** Because consumer budgets are limited, consumption decisions often require making tradeoffs. More of one good can be purchased only if less of another is bought. The budget line shown in Figure 1 graphically represents both this outer limit on consumption decisions and the various combinations of goods that can be purchased with this given level of income, in this case two goods (pizza and wall climbing).

**Q:  What is utility?**

**A:** The *utility* of a product is a hypothetical measure of how much satisfaction a consumer derives from the product. Though it can't be measured directly like weight or length, economists estimate the utility of various products at different levels of consumption to understand consumer preference and predict consumer behavior. The standard unit of utility is the *util*.

**Q:  How are total utility and marginal utility defined?**

**A:** *Total utility* is the entire amount of satisfaction a consumer derives from consuming some product; it is equal to the sum of the utility derived from the

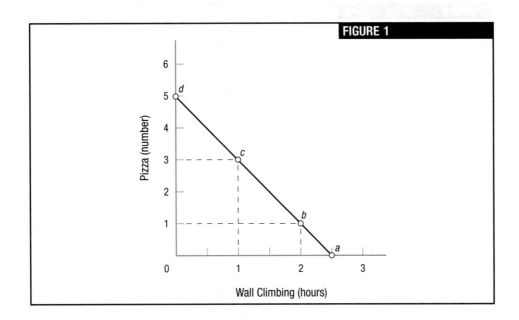

consumption of each individual unit of this product. *Marginal utility* is the amount of utility derived from consuming one more unit of a given product. As a person consumes more units of a product, marginal utility will change. Consuming the fifth unit of a product may lead to a different increase in total utility than did consuming the third unit. Figure 2 on the next page graphs total utility and marginal utility for two particular goods. Note how total utility keeps rising but marginal utility falls.

**Q:  What is the law of diminishing marginal utility?**
A:  The *law of diminishing marginal utility* states that as more units of any product are consumed, marginal utility will decline. Panel B of Figure 2 shows this law of diminishing marginal utility.

**Q:  How does marginal utility help us understand consumer decision making?**
A:  Marginal utility analysis provides a theoretical framework that economists use to understand how consumers make their consumption decisions among different products at varying price levels.

**Q:  How do consumers maximize their satisfaction with their limited income?**
A:  Marginal utility analysis reasons that consumers try to maximize utility within limited budgets by adjusting their spending to the point where the marginal utility derived from the last dollar spent on any product is equal to the marginal utility from the last dollar spent on other products. So for products $a$, $b$, $c$, through $n$, the consumer utility maximizing condition is

$$\frac{MU_a}{P_a} = \frac{MU_b}{P_b} = \frac{MU_c}{P_c} = \cdots = \frac{MU_n}{P_n}$$

In reality, the applicability of marginal utility theory is restricted. It assumes consumers can measure utility accurately and perform complex calculations of utility in their heads. Despite this drawback, marginal utility theory provides economists with a reasonable approach to how consumers make decisions about consumption choices with limited budgets.

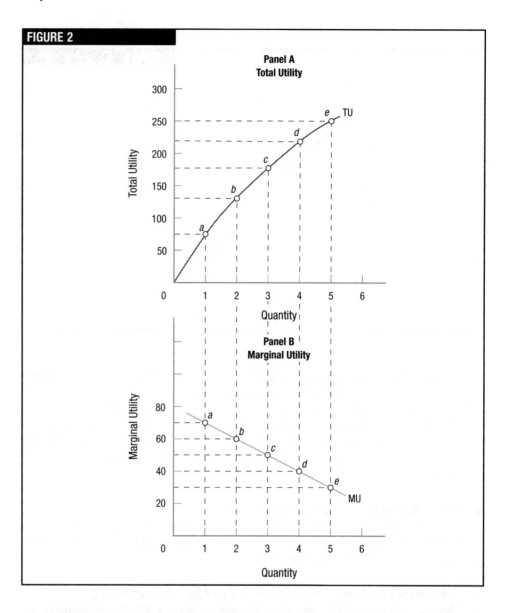

**FIGURE 2**

Panel A
Total Utility

Panel B
Marginal Utility

# Marginal Utility Analysis Quick Check

## Circle the Correct Answer

1. (T/F) A consumer's budget line with two products graphs the consumer's budget and the market supply of the two products.

2. (T/F) The law of diminishing marginal utility states that marginal utility falls as more units of a product are consumed.

3. (T/F) Economists believe that utility is readily observable and measurable.

4. (T/F) Marginal utility is the satisfaction a consumer derives from an additional unit of some product consumed.

5. If the utility derived from consuming the first unit is 12; from the second unit, 10; from the third unit, 8; from the fourth unit, 6; and from the fifth unit, 4; then the total utility derived from consuming 4 units is
   a. 6.
   b. 4.
   c. 36.
   d. 40.

6. Using marginal utility analysis, consumers maximize their satisfaction when they
   a. are able to get much more of one product than another.
   b. are able to get credit and spend more than their current income.
   c. are completely satiated.
   d. spend their income in such a way that the marginal utilities per dollar are equal for all products.

Complete the table below and use it to answer questions 7 and 8.

7. Assume a $20 food budget, spent in $4 increments. Bread costs $4 a loaf, and cereal costs $4 a box. Utility will be maximized by consuming which of the following?
   a. 1 loaf of bread and 2 boxes of cereal
   b. 2 loaves of bread and 3 boxes of cereal
   c. 3 loaves of bread and 2 boxes of cereal
   d. 4 loaves of bread and 1 box of cereal
8. The marginal utility per dollar for 3 boxes of cereal is
   a. 2.5.
   b. 5.0.
   c. 7.5.
   d. 10.0.
9. Marginal utility analysis assumes
   a. consumers make similar choices.
   b. consumers will consume products only when marginal utility rises; they will shun products when marginal utility falls.

c. consumers try to maximize utility within limited budgets by adjusting their spending to the point where the utility derived from the last dollar spent on any product is equal to the utility from the last dollar spent on other products.
d. marginal utility is generally the same for each unit consumed.

10. Total utility is which of the following?
    a. the utility a consumer receives from consuming a given number of units of the product
    b. the sum of the marginal utilities for a given number of units of the product
    c. generally grows at a diminishing rate as more of a given product is consumed
    d. all of the above

Score: ____

### Total and Marginal Utility for Bread and Cereal

| | Bread | | | | Cereal | | | |
|---|---|---|---|---|---|---|---|---|
| (1) | (2) | (3) | (4) | | (5) | (6) | (7) | (8) |
| Quantity (loaves of bread) | Total Utility | Marginal Utility | Marginal Utility per Dollar (price = $4) | | Quantity (boxes of cereal) | Total Utility | Marginal Utility | Marginal utility per Dollar (price = $4) |
| 0 | 0 | ____ | ____ | | 0 | 0 | ____ | ____ |
| 1 | 70 | ____ | ____ | | 1 | 50 | ____ | ____ |
| 2 | 125 | ____ | ____ | | 2 | 90 | ____ | ____ |
| 3 | 165 | ____ | ____ | | 3 | 120 | ____ | ____ |
| 4 | 190 | ____ | ____ | | 4 | 140 | ____ | ____ |
| 5 | 200 | ____ | ____ | | 5 | 150 | ____ | ____ |

## If You Got 9 or 10 Correct

You have a good grasp of the basics of marginal utility analysis. This is an important step in using the logic of utility analysis that follows in the next section.

## If You Didn't Get at Least 9 Correct

■ Go back and reread the first part of the chapter on the basics of marginal utility analysis.
■ Take a few moments and look back at the questions you missed in the quiz. Some of these are difficult questions. They really test your knowledge of marginal utility analysis. Be sure you can answer them correctly before you go on.

## Keep in Mind

One of the most important conclusions from marginal utility analysis is that utility (or consumer satisfaction) is maximized when the marginal utilities per dollar are equal for all products. Thus, if the price of one product rises, that product's ratio of marginal utility to price ($MU/P$) is now smaller, and consumers will now purchase less of that product. This makes marginal utility analysis consistent with the law of demand (quantity demanded is inversely related to prices). And further, this is how we derive demand curves with marginal utility analysis, discussed in the next section. ■

---

### Core Equation: Utility Maximizing Equation

$$\frac{MU_a}{P_a} = \frac{MU_b}{P_b} = \frac{MU_c}{P_c} = \ldots = \frac{MU_n}{P_n}$$

---

### Solved Problem: Utility Maximization

Here we solve question 7 in the Quick Check on the previous pages. You were asked to complete the table and solve where utility was maximized, given a $20 food budget spent in $4 increments, where both a loaf of bread and a box of cereal cost $4 each. The table is completed below.

| Bread | | | | Cereal | | | |
|---|---|---|---|---|---|---|---|
| (1) Quantity (loaves of bread) | (2) Total Utility | (3) Marginal Utility | (4) Marginal Utility per Dollar (price = $4) | (5) Quantity (boxes of cereal) | (6) Total Utility | (7) Marginal Utility | (8) Marginal Utility per Dollar (price = $4) |
| 0 | 0 | — | — | 0 | 0 | — | — |
| 1 | 70 | 70 | 17.5 | 1 | 50 | 50 | 12.5 |
| 2 | 125 | 55 | 13.8 | 2 | 90 | 40 | 10 |
| 3 | 165 | 40 | 10 | 3 | 120 | 30 | 7.5 |
| 4 | 190 | 25 | 6.25 | 4 | 140 | 20 | 5 |
| 5 | 200 | 10 | 2.5 | 5 | 150 | 10 | 2.5 |

### Solution-Discussion

Columns 4 and 8 ($MU/\$$ for each good) are where the decisions are made. Consumers make decisions at the margin! Your first $4 will be spent on bread (17.5 > 12.5). The second $4 will again be spent on bread (again, 13.8 > 12.5), but the third $4 will go to cereal, because the marginal utility per dollar has dropped to 10 for bread. The last two $4 expenditures will be for both bread and cereal since both the third loaf of bread and the second box of cereal have a $MU/\$$ ratio of 10.

So, the solution is 3 loaves of bread and 2 boxes of cereal.

Now, how does the utility-maximizing combination change when the price of cereal drops to $2 a box?

### Discussion

The marginal utility per dollar figures in column 8 now double since the cost of cereal has been cut in half. Write these new figures out to the side of column 8. The first $4 will be spent on cereal, then 1 loaf of bread, then another loaf of bread, then 2 boxes of cereal, and finally another loaf of bread and another box of cereal. The new expenditure combination will be 3 loaves of bread and 4 boxes of cereal. Note that as the price of cereal fell, this consumer purchased more cereal, consistent with the law of demand.

It is time to move on, but know that you will have to go over this section again. As you progress through the next section, Using Marginal Utility Analysis, which builds on this section, you may see how everything comes together. If not, review the marginal utility section carefully, and ask yourself if this is how you make choices between goods and services. Just how do you make the decision about whether to go to a movie or spend the time studying economics?

# Using Marginal Utility Analysis

## Frequently Asked Questions

Q:  What is consumer surplus, and how is it computed?

A:  *Consumer surplus* is the difference between what consumers are willing to pay for a product and what they must actually pay for the product in the market. Figure 3 depicts this, where the equilibrium price is $20 per hour, and consumer surplus is the area in the shaded triangle *fdb*.

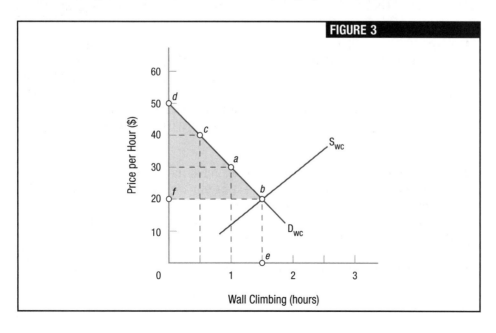

FIGURE 3

## Using Marginal Utility Analysis Quick Check

1. (T/F) Demand curves derived from marginal utility analysis are *not* consistent with the law of demand.
2. (T/F) To derive a demand curve using marginal utility analysis, you have to be concerned with the total utility derived from each product per dollar.
3. Consumer surplus is
   a. the extra utility from consuming one more unit of the product.
   b. the difference between total and marginal utility.
   c. the difference between the price consumers are willing to buy a good for and the price in the market.
   d. the difference between the price consumers are willing to buy a good for and the good's marginal utility to the consumer.
4. If the price of one good falls, marginal utility analysis concludes that
   a. consumers will continue to make the same choices as before the price change.
   b. consumers will consume more of the products where prices are the same because they are more valuable now.

   c. consumers will try to maximize utility within limited budgets by buying more of the product that has fallen in price.
   d. consumers will ignore the price change because all that matters is the size of marginal utility from consuming a particular product.
5. What is a serious critique of marginal utility theory?
   a. It has limited ability to explain how consumers make choices.
   b. It has been refuted by the behavioral economists.
   c. Consumer demand curves cannot be derived using marginal utility analysis.
   d. A basic assumption is that consumers can measure the utility of all products they consume.

Score: ____

Answers: 1. F; 2. F; 3. c; 4. c; 5. d

You should have scored 4 or 5 correct in this exercise. If you didn't, you will probably have to review this chapter again. Take a few moments and look at the Hints, Tips, and Reminders that follow. ■

---

## STEP 4          Consider These Hints, Tips, and Reminders

**1.** Treat the budget line as similar to the linear production possibilities frontier (PPF) we looked at in Chapter 2. Along (and on) the budget line, you are spending all of your income on some mix of the two goods. You can't spend beyond the budget constraint, and at points inside you are spending less than your total income (saving some). Keep in mind that your total income divided by the price of a product represents the most of one product you can buy, and these are the end points of the budget line.

**2.** This chapter really brings home the "thinking at the margin" concept discussed in Chapter 1. How do you decide to eat or buy *one more* piece of pizza? The answer is that you weigh the benefits against the costs, or *MU/P*. Marginal utility is the benefit and price is the cost. And most important, you do this kind of calculation for each additional piece you eat or buy.

**3.** So, each step in the consumer maximizing equation,

$$MU_a/P_a = MU_b/P_b = \ldots = MU_n/P_n$$

is really a series of incremental steps. The simple story is that you purchase that product first where *MU/P* is the highest, and then proceed to purchase that product with the highest ratio next, and so on until your budget is exhausted. Don't let the equation throw you; it is a simple "getting the *most* for your money" process.

**4.** Computing consumer surplus can often appear daunting, but it is really very easy. First, let's remind ourselves that consumer surplus is the amount above market price we would be willing to pay for a product and is equal to the area under the demand curve but above market price (the shaded area in Figure 4). The actual calculation of consumer surplus is straightforward if we remember one simple trick shown in the figure. If market price is $10 (point *e*) and 8 units are purchased, consumer surplus can be computed as follows: The shaded triangle (consumer surplus) is equal to *one-half* of the dashed rectangle, and that rectangle is equal to ($30 − $10) × 8 = $20 × 8 = $160. Thus, consumer surplus is equal to one-half of $160 or $80.

FIGURE 4

## Do the Homework for Chapter 6
## Consumer Choice and Demand

Instructor _____ Time _____ Student _____

**Use the answer key below to record your answers to these homework questions.**

1. _____     6. _____     11. _____     16. _____
2. _____     7. _____     12. _____     17. _____
3. _____     8. _____     13. _____     18. _____
4. _____     9. _____     14. _____     19. _____
5. _____    10. _____     15. _____     20. _____

1. Utility theory, or utilitarianism, developed by Jeremy Bentham
   a. looks at which products people purchase and then uses this information to determine how prices are determined.
   b. argues that utility or satisfaction cannot be measured accurately enough to be useful in analyzing consumer decisions.
   c. uses indifference curves to explain how consumers would maximize their satisfaction.
   d. developed a theory of consumer choice based on allocating limited resources to maximize happiness (utility).

2. The budget line or constraint shows
   a. the amount of money you have to spend if that raise is forthcoming.
   b. the amount of money you have to spend after retirement savings are deducted.
   c. a couple of combinations of goods and services that can be purchased, given prices and expected future income after you graduate.
   d. the possible purchasing combinations of two goods, given your limited income.

Use Figure HW-1 to answer questions 3 and 4.

3. Assume the budget line or constraint shown in the figure represents your weekly budget. If pizzas go for $5 each, what is your weekly budget?

4. Assume the budget line or constraint shown in the figure represents your weekly budget. If pizzas go for $5 each, how much must music downloads cost?

**HW-1**

5. The law of diminishing marginal utility states that
   a. satisfaction for consuming more of a good is often low and then rises as more and more units of that good are consumed.
   b. total utility will drop as soon as you consume the second unit of a product.
   c. utility can be measured.
   d. the gains to total utility from consuming additional units of a product declines.

6. To maximize their total utility, consumers should
   a. allocate their budget between goods so that the marginal utilities per dollar are equal for the last units purchased.
   b. spend their money so that each product has the same total utility as all others.
   c. buy the amount of each good up to the point where the diminishing marginal utility sets in.
   d. allocate their budget between goods so that the total utilities per dollar are just equal for the last units purchased.

7. The difference between what you are willing to pay for a product and what you must actually pay is called:

8. Marginal utility
   a. equals total utility for the last unit consumed.
   b. rises with every unit of the product consumed.
   c. remains unchanged with every unit of the product consumed.
   d. diminishes with every unit of the product consumed.

Use the table at the right to answer questions 9–12.

9. What is the marginal utility of the fourth pound of oranges?

10. Assume you have $8 to spend, trail mix and oranges each cost $4 per pound, and you can only buy these commodities in 1-pound increments. What mix of these goods would you purchase to maximize utility?
    pound(s) of trail mix
    pound(s) of oranges

11. Assume you have $20 to spend, trail mix and oranges each cost $4 per pound, and you can only buy these commodities in 1-pound increments. What mix of these goods would you purchase to maximize utility?
    pound(s) of trail mix
    pound(s) of oranges

12. Assume you have $20 to spend, trail mix and oranges each cost $4 per pound, and you can only buy these commodities in 1-pound increments. What will be the maximum total utility possible given these limitations?

| Trail Mix | | Oranges | |
|---|---|---|---|
| Quantity (pounds) | Total Utility | Quantity (pounds) | Total Utility |
| 0 | 0 | 0 | 0 |
| 1 | 140 | 1 | 100 |
| 2 | 250 | 2 | 180 |
| 3 | 330 | 3 | 240 |
| 4 | 380 | 4 | 280 |
| 5 | 400 | 5 | 300 |

Use Figure HW-2 to answer questions 13 and 14.

13. When market supply is equal to $S_0$, consumer surplus is equal to:

14. An increase in resource cost results in supply declining from $S_0$ to $S_1$. By how much has consumer surplus been *reduced*?

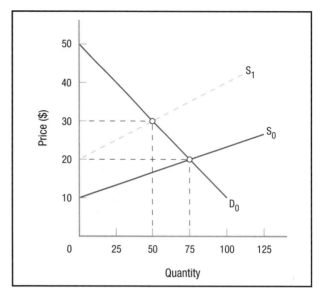

**HW-2**

15. Marginal utility helps explain how consumers select goods and services to purchase, but it faces which of the following criticisms?
    a. Consumers usually buy more than two goods.
    b. Marginal utility analysis is judged to be too elegant and logical.
    c. It assumes that consumers are able to measure the utility they get from the products they consume.
    d. It doesn't help explain consumer surplus.

Note to Student: There are 15 questions in this homework assignment.

| | Use the ExamPrep to Get Ready for Exams | **STEP 6** |

This sheet (front and back) is designed to help you prepare for your exams. The chapter has been boiled down to its key concepts. You are asked to answer questions, define terms, draw graphs, and, if you wish, add summaries of class notes.

## Marginal Utility Analysis

Define the following terms.
Utility:


Marginal utility:


Describe the law of diminishing marginal utility:


Describe the process of maximizing utility and the simple equation used to describe the utility maximization process:


## Consumer Surplus

Use the grid below to illustrate consumer surplus:

Describe the concept of consumer surplus:


Describe some of the problems and limitations of marginal utility analysis:

# Additional Study Help Chapterwide Practice Questions

## Matching

Match the description with the corresponding term.

___ 1. Budget line
___ 2. Utility
___ 3. Total utility
___ 4. Marginal utility
___ 5. Law of diminishing marginal utility
___ 6. Marginal utility analysis

a. The amount of utility derived from consuming one more unit of a product.
b. Shows the different combinations of goods that can be purchased at a given level of income.
c. As more of any product is consumed, marginal utility declines.
d. A hypothetical measure of consumer satisfaction.
e. The entire satisfaction a consumer derives from consuming some product.
f. This framework for understanding consumer choices assumes consumers try to maximize the utility they receive on their limited budgets, by adjusting their spending to the point where the utility derived from the last dollar spent on any product is equal to the utility from the last dollar spent on other products.

## Fill-In

Circle the word(s) in parentheses that complete the sentence.

1. The total satisfaction people receive from products and services is called (total, marginal, average) _____ utility, and the satisfaction received from consuming one more unit of the product is called (total, marginal, average) _____. The law of diminishing marginal utility implies that (total, marginal, average) _____ utility will decline.

2. Consumers maximize utility by purchasing goods up to the point where the marginal utility per dollar is (highest, equal, lowest) _____ for all goods.

3. Consumer surplus grows as prices (rise, fall, remain the same) _____, and it will (rise, fall, remain the same) _____ when prices rise.

## True-False

Circle the correct answer.

T / F  1. A budget line graphically represents the various combinations of two goods a consumer can afford on a particular budget.

T / F  2. A rise in income will push a consumer's budget line out and to the right.

T / F  3. Utility is something that is easily measured, like weight or length.

T / F  4. If a consumer purchases 5 units of a product, her marginal utility is the utility she derives from consuming all 5 units.

T / F  5. If a consumer prefers peaches to bananas, he can be sure to maximize his total utility by devoting his entire fruit budget to peaches, and none to bananas.

T / F  6. The law of diminishing marginal utility suggests that the consumer surplus from each additional purchase will eventually disappear as ever more units of some good are consumed.

T / F  7. Consumers can be expected to maximize their utility by spending each dollar of their limited budgets on the goods that provide them with the highest marginal utility per dollar.

## Multiple Choice

Circle the correct answer.

1. To economists, utility is
   a. a readily observable and measurable property of consumer goods.
   b. equivalent to a product's equilibrium price.
   c. a hypothetical measure of consumer satisfaction.
   d. a measure of the energy costs going into the production of a particular good.

2. Total utility is:
   a. the satisfaction a consumer derives from the last unit of some product consumed.
   b. the satisfaction a consumer derives from all of the units of some product consumed.

c. the satisfaction a consumer derives from receiving a consumer surplus.

d. something that doesn't change for each successive unit consumed.

3. Marginal utility is
   a. the satisfaction a consumer derives from an additional unit of some product consumed.
   b. the satisfaction a consumer derives from all of the units of some product consumed.
   c. equivalent to consumer surplus.
   d. something that is constant for each unit consumed.

4. Marginal utility
   a. diminishes with every additional unit consumed.
   b. rises indefinitely with every unit consumed.
   c. remains constant for each unit consumed.
   d. is of little use to economists in understanding consumer behavior, since it cannot be precisely measured.

Questions 5–9 refer to the table below. Complete the table. Assume that you have a $10 budget, and music downloads and poor boy sandwiches cost $2 each.

5. How will you spend your $10 budget to maximize utility?
   a. 4 music downloads and 1 poor boy sandwich
   b. 3 music downloads and 2 poor boy sandwiches
   c. 2 music downloads and 3 poor boy sandwiches
   d. 1 music download and 4 poor boy sandwiches

6. What is the marginal utility for the third music download?
   a. 10
   b. 20
   c. 30
   d. 40

7. What is the marginal utility per dollar for the fourth poor boy sandwich?
   a. 5
   b. 10

c. 15
d. 20

8. If the price of poor boy sandwiches doubles to $4, how many will you purchase to maximize utility?
   a. 1
   b. 2
   c. 3
   d. none

9. If the price of music downloads drops to $1 (poor boy sandwiches are still $2), how many music downloads will you purchase?
   a. 1
   b. 2
   c. 3
   d. 4

10. The difference between what consumers are willing to pay for a product and what they must actually pay for the product in the market is known as which of the following?
    a. the indifference curve
    b. marginal utility
    c. consumer surplus
    d. optimal consumer choice

11. If you are willing to spend $20 to purchase your first CD, but CDs cost only $15 each, your consumer surplus on that first CD is
    a. $5.
    b. $15.
    c. $20.
    d. unknowable without further information.

12. Assume that you are willing to spend $25 to purchase your first CD, $20 to purchase the second, and $15 for the third. The market price for CDs is $15 each. Thus, your consumer surplus on your purchase of three CDs is
    a. $5.
    b. $10.
    c. $15.
    d. $20.

**Total and Marginal Utility for Music Downloads and Poor Boy Sandwiches**

| Music Downloads | | | | Poor Boy Sandwiches | | | |
|---|---|---|---|---|---|---|---|
| (1) Quantity (downloads) | (2) Total Utility | (3) Marginal Utility | (4) Marginal Utility per Dollar (price = $2) | (5) Quantity (poor boy sandwiches) | (6) Total Utility | (7) Marginal Utility | (8) Marginal Utility per Dollar (price = $2) |
| 0 | 0 | ____ | ____ | 0 | 0 | ____ | ____ |
| 1 | 80 | ____ | ____ | 1 | 50 | ____ | ____ |
| 2 | 140 | ____ | ____ | 2 | 90 | ____ | ____ |
| 3 | 180 | ____ | ____ | 3 | 120 | ____ | ____ |
| 4 | 200 | ____ | ____ | 4 | 140 | ____ | ____ |
| 5 | 210 | ____ | ____ | 5 | 150 | ____ | ____ |

13. Which of the following assumptions does marginal utility analysis *not* make?
    a. Consumers will seek to maximize their utility in making their purchasing decisions.
    b. All consumers have similar tastes and preferences.
    c. Consumers are able to accurately measure utility.
    d. Consumers are able to perform complex computations regarding utility in their heads.

14. Why is marginal utility theory not entirely satisfactory?
    a. It doesn't seem to fit actual consumer behavior.
    b. It assumes that consumers can measure the utility of consumption.
    c. It isn't helpful in understanding consumer choices.
    d. Its conclusions are contradicted by the law of demand.

## Essay-Problem

Answer in the space provided.

The questions below can be challenging but are designed to improve your understanding of consumer choice. Don't get discouraged if your answers are not always the same as those we suggest. Use these as another way to assess your progress, but more important, to discover and learn some of the subtleties surrounding consumer choice and demand.

1. What is the essence of consumer choice theory?

2. Do young children follow the law of diminishing marginal utility?

3. Can marginal utility ever be negative?

4. The Cabbage Patch Kids were a hot toy and some parents reportedly flew to London to obtain the doll. Considering this doll fad, do you think there ever could be consumer surplus more than twice the price of a product?

5. Why are dollars a good proxy for utils?

6. To use marginal utility theory, do we have to assume that people act rationally all of the time?

7. Is the thought of people with internal utility calculators so silly that we should abandon marginal utility analysis?

## What's Next

This chapter gives you a good understanding of what lies behind demand: consumers making rational decisions about how particular products add to their satisfaction. In the next chapter, we look at what lies behind supply, with how producers decide how much of any product to provide to the market. We saw that the assumptions behind marginal utility analysis are a little far-fetched. This does not, however, negate the usefulness of the analysis. Just be aware of what demand analysis rests on.

## Answers to Chapterwide Practice Questions

### Matching

| | | |
|---|---|---|
| 1. b | 3. e | 5. c |
| 2. d | 4. a | 6. f |

## Fill-In

1. total, marginal, marginal
2. equal
3. fall, fall

## True-False

| | | | |
|---|---|---|---|
| 1. T | 3. F | 5. F | 7. T |
| 2. T | 4. F | 6. T | |

## Multiple Choice

| | | | |
|---|---|---|---|
| 1. c | 3. a | 4. a | 5. b |
| 2. b | | | |

### Total and Marginal Utility for Music Downloads and Poor Boy Sandwiches

| Music Downloads | | | | Poor Boy Sandwiches | | | |
|---|---|---|---|---|---|---|---|
| (1) | (2) | (3) | (4) Marginal Utility per Dollar (price = $2) | (5) | (6) | (7) | (8) Marginal Utility per Dollar (price = $2) |
| Quantity (downloads) | Total Utility | Marginal Utility | | Quantity (poor boy sandwiches) | Total Utility | Marginal Utility | |
| 0 | 0 | — | — | 0 | 0 | — | — |
| 1 | 80 | 80 | 40 | 1 | 50 | 50 | 25 |
| 2 | 140 | 60 | 30 | 2 | 90 | 40 | 20 |
| 3 | 180 | 40 | 20 | 3 | 120 | 30 | 15 |
| 4 | 200 | 20 | 10 | 4 | 140 | 20 | 10 |
| 5 | 210 | 10 | 5 | 5 | 150 | 10 | 5 |

| | | | |
|---|---|---|---|
| 6. d | 9. d | 11. a | 13. b |
| 7. b | 10. c | 12. c | 14. b |
| 8. a | | | |

## Essay-Problem

1. Consumers make product choices in some rational way.
2. Even children follow the law of diminishing marginal utility, though the number of times they may say "more" leads one to think that marginal utility falls slower than it would with an adult. Just how many times can one watch the *Bambi* movie without getting bored?
3. Yes. Consider eating ice cream on a hot day. The first ice cream may be wonderful. So may the second. Eventually (possibly after the 15th cone), if ice cream makes you violently sick, total utility will have gone down at that point, so marginal utility for that unit will be negative.
4. Yes. To calculate consumer surplus in this case, the cost of the airfare has to be added in to the actual price paid for a Cabbage Patch Kid doll; this puts consumer surplus many times greater than the doll. There is no defined limit to how high consumer surplus may be.
5. We normally think of utility in terms of goods purchased. Since the purchase price is given in dollars, we can think of a dollar as equal to 1 util (we could also think of $1 = 100 utils rather than 1 util, but this is just a case of scale).
6. No. People act irrationally every day. But they do not act irrationally a large part of the time, so marginal utility analysis is useful as a conceptual device.
7. No. As silly as this aspect of marginal utility analysis may appear, the general usefulness of the analysis remains. The theory has strong predictive power as to how consumers make choices. We may be bothered by the thought of people as calculators; this should spur economists to come up with better theories, not abandon theories that are useful.

# Appendix:
# Indifference Curve
# Analysis

## The Important Logic of Consumer Choice

Marginal utility analysis requires that utility be measured and that marginal utility per dollar be computed for each product. Indifference curve analysis only assumes that consumers can distinguish between bundles of goods and services and select those they prefer. With this analysis, satisfaction (or utility) does not have to be explicitly measured.

| This Is What You Need to Know | STEP 1 |
| --- | --- |

**After studying this appendix you should be able to**

- Understand the properties of indifference curves and preference maps.

- Use indifference curves to derive demand curves and measure income and substitution effects.

| Review the Key Terms | STEP 2 |
| --- | --- |

**Indifference curve:** Shows all the combinations of two goods where the consumer is indifferent (gets the same level of satisfaction).

**Indifference map:** An infinite set of indifference curves where each curve represents a different level of utility or satisfaction.

**Income effect:** When higher prices essentially reduce consumer income, the quantity demanded for normal goods falls.

**Substitution effect:** When the price of one good rises, consumers will substitute other goods for that good, so the quantity demanded for the higher priced good falls.

## STEP 3     Work Through the Appendix Tutorial

### Frequently Asked Questions

Q:  **What are indifference curves?**

A:  *Indifference curve analysis* seeks to avoid the problems with measurement faced by marginal utility analysis. The *indifference curve* graphically represents all the combinations of two products that provide the same level of satisfaction to consumers. The indifference curve identifies a set of possible consumption combinations that leaves the consumer indifferent (equally satisfied).

Q:  **How are indifference curves used to determine consumer purchases?**

A:  Indifference curve analysis helps economists understand how consumers allocate their limited budgets among diverse goods. Figure APX-1 has three indifference curves superimposed over a budget line, with two products considered. Note that the optimum point is where the budget line is just tangent at one point to an indifference curve.

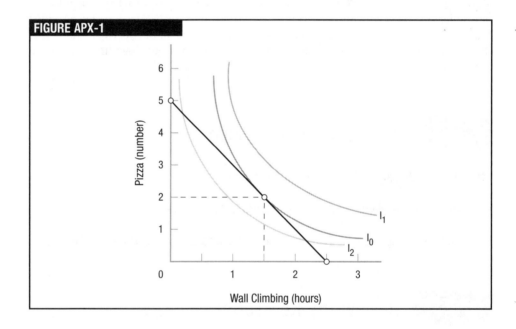

**FIGURE APX-1**

Q:  **Why use indifference curve analysis?**

A:  Indifference curve analysis leads to the same theoretical conclusions as marginal utility analysis but is subject to fewer restrictive assumptions. It does not require that consumers measure utility or calculate marginal utility per dollar, but only that consumers be able to decide which bundles of goods they would prefer to consume under varying circumstances.

Q:  **What is the income effect of a price change?**

A:  The *income effect* is a change in quantity demanded that comes as a result of a change in income due to a change in price. When the price of some regularly purchased good rises, this leaves consumers with less money to spend buying goods of all sorts. The rise in price therefore effectively reduces consumer income, resulting in a drop in quantity demanded for most normal goods.

Q:  **What is the substitution effect?**

A:  When the price of some good rises, quantity demanded for the good will typically fall as consumers begin purchasing cheaper substitute products; this is the
*substitution effect.* Note that when the price of a product rises, quantity
demanded for it will typically fall, partially due to the income effect and partially due to the substitution effect; indifference curve analysis helps us determine how much of this drop in demand is due to each effect.

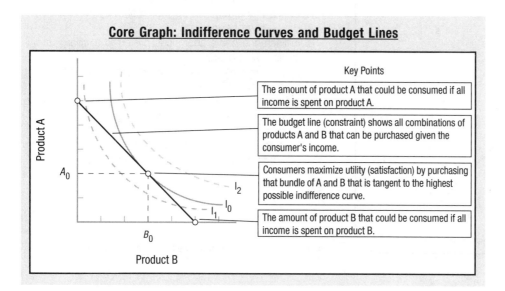

## Core Graph: Indifference Curves and Budget Lines

Key Points

The amount of product A that could be consumed if all income is spent on product A.

The budget line (constraint) shows all combinations of products A and B that can be purchased given the consumer's income.

Consumers maximize utility (satisfaction) by purchasing that bundle of A and B that is tangent to the highest possible indifference curve.

The amount of product B that could be consumed if all income is spent on product B.

# Indifference Curve Analysis Quick Check

## Circle the Correct Answer

1. (T/F) Indifference curve analysis assumes that people
can choose between different bundles of goods without
calculating the total utility of each bundle.

2. (T/F) Because of the law of diminishing marginal utility,
indifference curves are *not* straight lines.

3. (T/F) Consumer satisfaction is maximized where two
indifference curves intersect.

4. To maximize satisfaction on a limited budget, consumers
must make choices
   a. at the point where two indifference curves intersect.
   b. on the indifference curve that cuts the budget line
   twice.
   c. on the indifference curve that is tangent to the
   budget line.
   d. anywhere on indifference curves that are above the
   budget line.

5. If the price of heating oil rises during the winter, consumers will purchase less of other goods because of
   a. the substitution effect.
   b. the income effect.
   c. the law of diminishing marginal utility.
   d. changes in tastes and preferences.

6. If the price of J. Crew sweaters goes up, and consumers
purchase fewer J. Crew sweaters and more Gap
sweaters, this is an example of
   a. the substitution effect.
   b. the income effect.
   c. the law of diminishing marginal utility.
   d. changes in tastes and preferences.

7. An indifference curve is
   a. concave (bowed out) to the origin because of the law
   of diminishing marginal utility.
   b. concave to the origin because of the law of indifference curves.

c. convex (bowed in) to the origin because of the law of diminishing marginal utility.

d. convex to the origin because of the law of substitution.

Use Figure APX-2 to answer question 8.

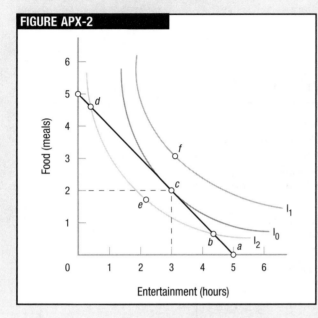

**FIGURE APX-2**

8. Satisfaction for this consumer would be maximized
   a. anywhere on indifference curve $I_1$.
   b. at either point b or point d on $I_2$.
   c. at point c on $I_0$.
   d. anywhere on the budget line.
9. If the price of gasoline goes up and you take an airplane to Disney World rather than drive, this would be an example of
   a. the income effect.
   b. the substitution effect.
   c. the law of diminishing marginal utility.
   d. the law of supply.
10. Indifference curve analysis is preferred to marginal utility analysis because
    a. it is easier to draw indifference curves than to fill in marginal utility tables.
    b. it deals with bundles of goods while marginal utility analysis can only deal with two goods.
    c. it is more scientific.
    d. it does not require that consumers measure utility for innumerable possible consumption choices.

Score: _____

## If You Got 9 or 10 Correct

You have mastered a tough concept. Indifference curve analysis is the modern method of determining consumer preferences, deriving demand curves, and analyzing many different issues involving decision making.

## If You Didn't Get at Least 9 Correct

Take a moment to go back and review the Appendix at the end of this chapter. Pay particular attention to the uniqueness of indifference curves and how, combined with the budget line, consumer choice is determined. Finally, spend a few moments and review those questions you missed to make sure you know why you missed them. Missing questions can be helpful—you won't make that same mistake again! ∎

## STEP 4    Consider These Hints, Tips, and Reminders

1. Keep in mind that indifference curve analysis essentially leads us to the same conclusions as marginal utility analysis without the restrictive assumptions that consumers can actually measure utility.

2. The other advantage of indifference curves is that the concept is easily applied to many other areas as the terrorist example suggests. The indifference concept is more widely applicable than marginal utility.

## Do the Homework for Chapter 6 Appendix Indifference Curve Analysis

**STEP 5**

Instructor _____ Time _____ Student _____

**Use the answer key below to record your answers to these homework questions.**

1. _____  6. _____  11. _____  16. _____
2. _____  7. _____  12. _____  17. _____
3. _____  8. _____  13. _____  18. _____
4. _____  9. _____  14. _____  19. _____
5. _____  10. _____  15. _____  20. _____

1. Which of the following is *not* a property of indifference curves?
   a. They slope upward and to the right.
   b. They are subject to the law of diminishing marginal utility.
   c. They have a negative slope.
   d. They are convex (bowed in) to the origin.

Use Figure HW APX-1 to answer questions 2–4.

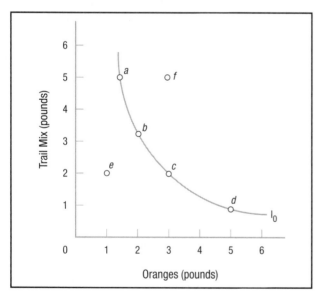

**HW APX-1**

2. Looking at indifference curve $I_0$, what can we say about points $a$ and $d$?
   a. Neither is very desirable to the consumer.
   b. The consumer would rather be at point $b$ than at points $d$ or $a$.

c. The consumer is indifferent between the two bundles of commodities.
   d. The consumer would prefer to be at point $e$ rather than at point $a$ or $d$.

3. What can we say about point $e$?
   a. It is preferred to points $a$ and $d$.
   b. All points on $I_0$ are preferred to point $e$.
   c. It is preferred to all other points noted in the figure.
   d. The consumer will select point $e$ over point $f$.

4. What can we say about point $f$?
   a. It is preferred to points $a$ and $d$.
   b. All points on $I_0$ are preferred to point $f$.
   c. It is not preferred to all other points on $I_0$.
   d. The consumer will select point $e$ over point $f$.

5. Indifference curves are used to
   a. measure total utility of two bundles of goods.
   b. derive demand curves.
   c. determine why consumers prefer luxury goods to necessities.
   d. evaluate marketing campaigns for expensive products and services.

6. Maximizing satisfaction using indifference curves requires that consumers
   a. measure utility and purchase where the marginal utility per dollar is maximized.
   b. focus their consumption on that one good that provides the highest level of satisfaction.
   c. find that point where two indifference curves intersect.
   d. select that combination of goods that is on the highest possible indifference curve given the consumer's budget constraint.

7. If the price of oil jumps from $50 a barrel to $100 and consumers reduce their purchases of many other goods, this would be an example of
   a. the substitution effect.
   b. the income effect.
   c. the budget effect.
   d. the indifference curve effect.

8. If the price of oil jumps from $50 a barrel to $100 and consumers take fewer long distance vacations, this would be an example of
   a. the substitution effect.
   b. the income effect.
   c. the budget effect.
   d. the indifference curve effect.

9. Indifference curve analysis is generally preferred to marginal utility analysis because
   a. consumers measure utility and purchase where the marginal utility per dollar is maximized.
   b. it does not require that consumers actually measure utility.
   c. it is easier to understand intuitively.
   d. it is newer analysis than marginal utility analysis.

10. Indifference curves do not cross because
   a. at the point where they cross, consumer income cannot be determined.
   b. each point on any indifference curve represents different levels of income.
   c. marginal utility cannot be measured at this point.
   d. each indifference curve represents different levels of satisfaction, and the point where they cross would be inconsistent with this assumption.

Note to Student: There are 10 questions in this homework assignment.

| | Use the ExamPrep to Get Ready for Exams | **STEP 6** |

This sheet (front and back) is designed to help you prepare for your exams. The chapter has been boiled down to its key concepts. You are asked to answer questions, define terms, draw graphs, and, if you wish, add summaries of class notes.

## Indifference Curve Analysis

Describe an indifference curve:

Describe the properties of indifference curves:

## Deriving a Demand Curve

Use the blank grids to illustrate the following:

- Draw a budget line in panel A for two products.

- In panel A, draw an indifference map of three indifference curves.

- Show the optimal consumer choice between these two goods.

- Set up panel B with output of the good on the horizontal axis and its price on the vertical axis of panel B. (Hint: This should be the good on the horizontal axis of panel A.)

- Transfer the optimal consumer choice (both price and output) to panel B.

- Now change the price of the product shown in panel B and shift the budget line in panel A.

- Show the new consumer equilibrium.

- Show that new point in panel B. Connect the points. You now have the demand curve.

**Panel A**

**Panel B**

## Income and Substitution Effects

Describe the substitution effect:


Describe the income effect:

## Additional Study Help Appendix Practice Questions

### True-False

Circle the correct answer.

T / F    1. Two indifference curves for the same set of products will never intersect.

T / F    2. To say that a consumer is at a point of indifference between two bundles of goods means that she does not really want to purchase either bundle.

T / F    3. Indifference curves are bowed-in, or convex toward the origin, due to the law of diminishing marginal utility.

T / F    4. Maximizing satisfaction on limited income requires purchasing some bundle of goods on the highest possible indifference curve given your limited income.

T / F    5. A rise in the price of an essential consumer good such as food effectively reduces consumer incomes.

### Multiple Choice

Circle the correct answer.

1. An indifference curve shows
   a. the quantity of a product a consumer would demand at various price levels.
   b. all combinations of two products that provide consumers with the same level of satisfaction.
   c. the level of supply at which producers are indifferent to whether or not they supply any additional units of a product.
   d. the level of spending at which consumers are indifferent to whether or not they purchase any more products.

2. An indifference curve has
   a. a positive slope and is convex to the origin.
   b. a positive slope and is concave to the origin.
   c. a negative slope and is convex to the origin.
   d. a negative slope and is concave to the origin.

3. Indifference curves can be used to derive
   a. measurements of total utility.
   b. demand curves.
   c. predictions regarding consumer incomes.
   d. supply curves.

4. A preference map contains
   a. a set of demand curves reflecting different levels of consumer income.
   b. a set of indifference curves that intersect at strategic points.
   c. a set of indifference curves representing different levels of satisfaction.
   d. a set of supply curves representing the producer preference for supplying various goods at different price levels.

5. Maximizing satisfaction on a limited budget requires
   a. selecting a point on the highest possible indifference curve, given a limited budget.
   b. selecting a point where two indifference curves cross.
   c. selecting one of two goods.
   d. selecting more of one good in exchange for more of another.

6. If consumers cut back on their purchases of many different goods because the price of heating oil has gone up, this behavior would be an example of the
   a. substitution effect.
   b. energy effect.
   c. environmental effect.
   d. income effect.

7. If consumers purchase fewer cucumbers and more tomatoes because the price of cucumbers has gone up, this would be an example of
   a. the substitution effect.
   b. consumer preference for red vegetables.
   c. the income effect.
   d. the complementary goods effect.

Use Figure MC APX-1 to answer questions 8 and 9.

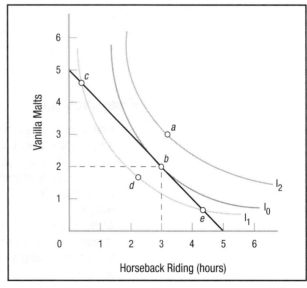

**MC APX-1**

8. What level of satisfaction *cannot* be achieved with this budget line and these indifference curves?
   a. point *d*
   b. point *c*
   c. point *e*
   d. point *a*

9. With a limited budget, satisfaction will be maximized at
   a. point *e*.
   b. point *a*.
   c. point *b*.
   d. point *d*.

## Essay-Problem

Answer in the space provided.

The questions below apply the indifference curve analysis of consumer choice. Your answers may not always be the same as those we suggest, but they should be in the same ballpark.

1. In comparing vacation A to vacation B, why would indifference curve analysis be preferred to marginal utility analysis?

2. When might the income effect predominate over the substitution effect?

3. Is the substitution effect the same for all products?

---

## Answers to Appendix Practice Questions

### True-False

| | | |
|---|---|---|
| 1. T | 3. T | 5. T |
| 2. F | 4. T | |

### Multiple Choice

| | | |
|---|---|---|
| 1. b | 4. c | 7. a |
| 2. c | 5. a | 8. d |
| 3. b | 6. d | 9. c |

### Essay-Problem

1. Indifference curve analysis would be easier because people would simply have to decide if bundle A (vacation A) would give more satisfaction than bundle B (vacation B). With marginal utility analysis, some attempt would have to be made to calculate utility for the various aspects of each vacation.
2. The income effect might dominate when the item in question is a large portion of one's budget.
3. As we saw in the previous chapter, products with inelastic demand have few substitutes, at least in the short run. Health care is one of these. We would expect the substitution effect to be weaker with inelastically demanded products than with elastically demanded products.

# Production and Cost

## Production and Cost Are Behind Decisions About Supply

Having looked in the last chapter at what lies behind demand curves by examining how consumers make choices, in this chapter we turn to what lies behind supply curves by examining how producers decide what to produce. It is important to understand why firms exist and how they determine their costs, in both the short run and the long run.

After studying this chapter you should be able to

- Describe the nature of firms and markets.

- Describe the nature of economic costs and profits.

- Differentiate between the short run and long run.

- Describe the nature of short-run production, total product, marginal product, and average product.

- Differentiate between increasing, constant, and decreasing returns.

- Describe the nature of short-run costs, fixed costs, variable costs, average costs, and marginal costs.

■ Use graphs to show the relationship between short-run average fixed cost, average variable cost, average total cost, and marginal cost curves.

■ Describe long-run costs.

■ Describe the reasons for economies and diseconomies of scale.

## STEP 2          Review the Key Terms

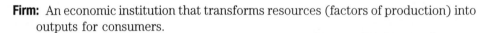

**Firm:** An economic institution that transforms resources (factors of production) into outputs for consumers.

**Sole proprietor:** A type of business structure composed of a single owner who supervises and manages the business and is subject to unlimited liability.

**Partnership:** Similar to a sole proprietorship, but involves more than one owner who shares the management of the business. Partnerships are also subject to unlimited liability.

**Corporation:** A business structure that has most of the legal rights of individuals, and in addition, the corporation can issue stock to raise capital. Stockholders' liability is limited to the value of their stock.

**Profit:** Equal to the difference between total revenue and total cost.

**Revenue:** Equal to price per unit times quantity sold.

**Economic costs:** The sum of explicit and implicit costs.

**Explicit costs:** Those expenses paid directly to another economic entity, including wages, lease payments, taxes, and utilities.

**Implicit costs:** The opportunity costs of using resources that belong to the firm, including depreciation, depletion of business assets, and the opportunity cost of the firm's capital employed in the business.

**Sunk costs:** Those costs that have been incurred and cannot be recovered, including, for example, funds spent on existing technology that have become obsolete and past advertising that has run in the media.

**Economic profits:** Profits in excess of normal profits. These are profits in excess of both explicit and implicit costs.

**Normal profits:** The return on capital necessary to keep investors satisfied and keep capital in the business over the long run.

**Short run:** A period of time over which at least one factor of production (resource) is fixed, or cannot be changed.

**Long run:** A period of time sufficient for firms to adjust all factors of production, including plant capacity.

**Production:** The process of turning inputs into outputs.

**Marginal product:** The change in output that results from a change in labor ($\Delta Q/\Delta L$).

**Average product:** Output per worker, found by dividing total output by the number of workers employed to produce that output ($Q/L$).

**Increasing marginal returns:** A new worker hired adds more to total output than the previous worker hired, so that both average and marginal products are rising.

**Diminishing marginal returns:** An additional worker adds to total output, but at a diminishing rate.

**Fixed costs:** Costs that do not change as a firm's output expands or contracts, often called overhead. These include items such as lease payments, administrative expenses, property taxes, and insurance.

**Variable costs:** Costs that vary with output fluctuations, including expenses such as labor and material costs.

**Average fixed cost:** Equal to total fixed cost divided by output (TFC/Q).

**Average variable cost:** Equal to total variable cost divided by output (TVC/Q).

**Average total cost:** Equal to total cost divided by output (TC/Q). Average total cost is also equal to AFC + AVC.

**Marginal cost:** The change in total costs arising from the production of additional units of output ($\Delta TC/\Delta Q$). Since fixed costs do not change with output, marginal costs are the change in variable costs associated with additional production ($\Delta TVC/\Delta Q$).

**Long-run average total cost (LRATC):** In the long run, firms can adjust their plant sizes so LRATC is the lowest unit cost at which any particular output can be produced in the long run.

**Economies of scale:** As a firm's output increases, its LRATC tends to decline. This results from specialization of labor and management, and potentially a better use of capital and complementary production techniques.

**Constant returns to scale:** A range of output where average total costs are relatively constant. Fast-food restaurants and movie theatres are examples.

**Diseconomies of scale:** A range of output where average total costs tend to increase. Firms often become so big that management becomes bureaucratic and unable to efficiently control its operations.

**Economies of scope:** By producing a number of products that are interdependent, firms are able to produce and market these goods at lower costs.

---

## Work Through the Chapter Tutorials | STEP 3

# Firms, Profits, and Economic Costs

## Frequently Asked Questions

Q:  **What are firms and what do they do?**
A:  Firms produce the goods and services we consume. Firms are economic institutions that transform inputs (factors of production) into outputs (products and services).

Q:  **How are entrepreneurs grouped?**
A:  Entrepreneurs are organized into three basic business structures: sole proprietorships, partnerships, and corporations.

Q:  **What is a sole proprietorship?**
A:  A sole proprietorship is composed of one owner who usually supervises the business's operation. Sole proprietorships are easily established and managed, but proprietors are limited in their ability to raise capital and their personal assets are subject to unlimited liability.

Q: **What is a partnership, and how does it differ from a sole proprietorship?**
A: A partnership is similar to a sole proprietorship, except that it has more than one owner. Partnerships can raise capital more easily and spread around the management responsibilities, but as with sole proprietors, partners are subject to unlimited liability for the entire partnership.

Q: **What is a corporation, and how does it differ from sole proprietorships and partnerships?**
A: Corporations are the premier form of business organization in most of the world. Corporations possess most of the legal rights of individuals, and they are able to issue stock to raise capital. Most significantly, the liability of individual owners (stockholders) is limited to the amount they have invested in the stock.

Q: **How are profits defined, and how do they relate to the goals of firms?**
A: Profits are the difference between total revenue and total cost. Firms are assumed to seek to maximize their profits. Although other assumptions about the goals of firms are possible, profit maximization is the typical assumption economists use.

Q: **How are economic costs defined?**
A: Economic costs are separated into explicit (out-of-pocket) and implicit (opportunity) costs. Explicit costs are paid to some other entity. They include wages, lease expenses, taxes, and so on. Implicit costs are not directly paid to others. These costs include the depreciation and depletion of company assets, as well as the cost of the capital the firm employs.

Q: **What are normal profits?**
A: Economists define a normal return as the return on capital that keeps investors willing to invest their capital in an industry over the long run. Firms earning just this level of profit are said to be earning normal profits. Firms earning more than this are earning economic profits, and firms earning less are suffering economic losses.

Q: **How are the short and long run defined?**
A: The short run is a period of time during which at least one factor of production is fixed, usually plant capacity. Firms can vary output in the short run by hiring more labor or changing other variable factors. In the long run, firms are able to vary all factors, including plant size. Moreover, existing firms can leave the industry, and new firms can enter.

# Firms, Profits, and Economic Costs Quick Check

## Circle the Correct Answer

1. (T/F) Firms transform inputs and outputs into goods and services for consumers.
2. (T/F) Total revenue is the difference between the amount of money a firm receives from the sale of its products and its total costs.
3. (T/F) Total revenue equals number of units sold times price per unit.
4. (T/F) Depreciation is an explicit cost.
5. Which of the following is *not* an explicit cost in your new business?
   a. rent
   b. insurance
   c. the amount of wages you pay yourself
   d. the amount of wages you give up if you quit your old job to start your new business
6. A normal rate of return on capital is
   a. a return that generates economic profits in excess of zero.
   b. the same for every business and industry.
   c. a profit just sufficient to keep investors satisfied and thus to keep capital in a business over the long run.
   d. okay in the short run but not okay in the long run.
7. Which of the following factors of production is usually assumed to be fixed in the short run?
   a. quantity of raw materials purchased

b. number of workers employed
c. number of shifts a factory operates
d. plant size

8. Economic profits are equal to
   a. total revenue minus explicit costs.
   b. total revenue minus explicit and implicit costs.
   c. total revenue minus implicit costs.
   d. total revenue minus capital costs.

9. Opportunity costs
   a. do not have to be considered in figuring profit.
   b. are explicit costs.
   c. are implicit costs.
   d. are zero when economic profits are normal.

10. The long run is usually the longest, in terms of actual months and years, for
    a. small, family-run businesses.
    b. firms that use labor-intensive production methods.
    c. large corporations that operate massive factories.
    d. industries capable of making quick adjustments to changes in market demand.

Score: ____

Answers: 1. F; 2. F; 3. T; 4. F; 5. d; 6. c; 7. d; 8. b; 9. c; 10. c

## If You Got 9 or 10 Correct

You have a good understanding of the nature of firms, entrepreneurs, profits, implicit and explicit costs, and the short run versus the long run. These are the basic concepts underlying production and cost. These are also the easiest ideas presented in the chapter. Go on to the next section, Production in the Short Run, and get ready for a little more of a challenge.

## If You Didn't Get at Least 9 Correct

You need to do a few things. These are relatively intuitive concepts, so first take a moment and reread the list of terms you need to know. That may be enough to cement these concepts in your mind. If not, reread the first section of the chapter, and go back and make sure you know why you missed the questions you did. As you work through the next section, Production in the Short Run (a little harder section), this material should become clearer.

But before you move on, take a piece of paper, define explicit and implicit costs, and list three examples of each. Now define normal profits, think of an example of some small business earning economic profits, then have costs increase sufficiently to cause the firm to earn only normal profits. Keeping these four concepts straight will make the remaining material in the chapter a lot easier. ■

# Production in the Short Run

## Frequently Asked Questions

Q: **How are average and marginal products defined?**

A: In the short run, firms can vary the output they produce by varying their labor inputs. The total product curve relates labor inputs to outputs. Marginal product is the change in output resulting from a change in labor input ($\Delta Q/\Delta L$). Marginal product is thus the change in output associated with hiring one additional worker. Average product or output per worker is equal to total output divided by labor input ($Q/L$).

Q:   **What do typical marginal and average product curves look like?**

A:   Figure 1 graphs total, average, and marginal product for a hypothetical
     firm. Note that the marginal product curve cuts the average product curve
     at its maximum point (point *b*); once marginal product (the output from
     one additional worker) is less than average product, it pulls the average
     down (see the movement from point *b* to *c*). Marginal returns diminish
     between points *a* and *c* and negative returns occur after 12 workers are hired
     (point *c*).

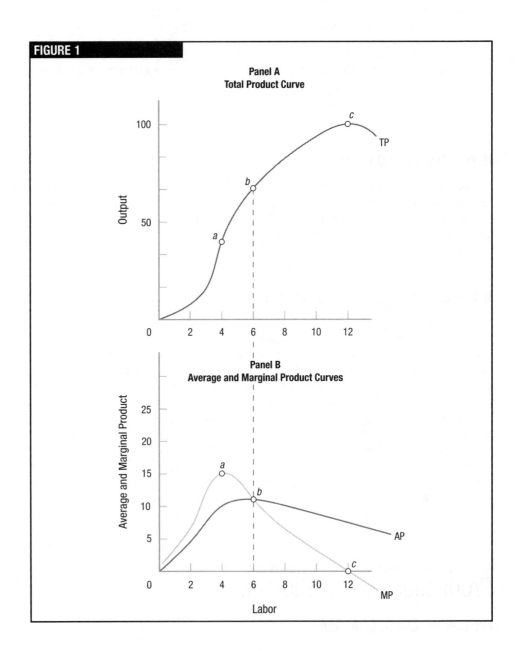

FIGURE 1

Panel A
Total Product Curve

Panel B
Average and Marginal Product Curves

Q:   **What are increasing and decreasing returns?**

A:   Typical production functions exhibit both increasing and decreasing returns.
     When increasing returns are present, each additional worker adds more to total
     output than previous workers. This can occur because of specialization. All pro-
     duction is eventually subject to the law of diminishing returns, whereby addi-
     tional workers add less and less to total output.

# Production in the Short Run Quick Check

## Circle the Correct Answer

1. (T/F) Hiring additional workers invariably leads to increases in total output.
2. (T/F) When marginal product is at a maximum, average product will always be at a maximum.
3. If hiring an additional worker yields a negative marginal return, this means that
   a. hiring the additional worker will still raise total output, but at a diminishing rate.
   b. hiring the additional worker will actually reduce total output.
   c. hiring the additional worker will increase average product.
   d. the additional worker will be paid a lower wage than other employees.

Use Figure 2 to answer questions 4 and 5.
4. Going from eight workers to nine workers illustrates
   a. decreasing average returns.
   b. diminishing marginal returns.
   c. negative returns.
   d. increasing returns.
5. Rational firms would never hire more than how many workers?
   a. 8          c. 22
   b. 12         d. indeterminate

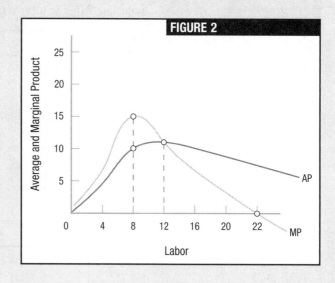

FIGURE 2

Score: ____

Answers: 1. F; 2. F; 3. b; 4. b; 5. c

## If You Got All 5 Correct

Short-run production is not a problem for you. This is relatively difficult material with its average and marginal product curves and the law of diminishing returns. Move on to the next section, Costs of Production, which builds on this section.

## If You Didn't Get All of Them Correct

You should review this section. First, reread the text. Then keep the following in mind and work through the solved problem on the next page.

## Key Point to Remember

Remember that in the short run, at least one factor of production is fixed (usually capital or plant size). Therefore, output varies directly with labor input. *Average product* is average output per worker, or Q/L. If 10 workers can produce 200 units of output, then average product is 20. *Marginal product* is the extra output the firm produces when one more worker is hired. So, if 10 workers can produce 200 units, the firm hires a new worker (the 11th), and total output rises to 225, then marginal product is 25 ($\Delta Q = 25$, $\Delta L = 1$, so $\Delta Q / \Delta L = 25/1 = 25$).

Don't make this material harder than it is. It is really quite straightforward. Take some time and review the solved problem below. It will help you a lot when you get to the next section, Costs of Production.

## Solved Problem: Production in the Short Run

Complete the following table, and graph average product and marginal product in the grid provided. Try to complete this before looking at the solution. After you have completed this review, move on to Final Check.

| L | Q | MP | AP |
|---|---|----|----|
| 0 | 0 | | |
| 1 | 14 | | |
| 2 | 30 | | |
| 3 | 50 | | |
| 4 | 80 | | |
| 5 | 108 | | |
| 6 | 130 | | |
| 7 | 150 | | |
| 8 | 168 | | |
| 9 | 180 | | |

## Solution-Discussion

Values for marginal and average product are shown in the table below. Notice that both marginal and average product initially increase, then marginal product declines until both are roughly equal when 6 units of output are produced, and then both continue to decline.

| L | Q | MP | AP |
|---|---|----|----|
| 0 | 0 | — | — |
| 1 | 14 | 14 | 14.00 |
| 2 | 30 | 16 | 15.00 |
| 3 | 50 | 20 | 16.66 |
| 4 | 80 | 30 | 20.00 |
| 5 | 108 | 28 | 21.60 |
| 6 | 130 | 22 | 21.66 |
| 7 | 150 | 20 | 21.42 |
| 8 | 168 | 18 | 21.00 |
| 9 | 180 | 12 | 20.00 |

Both marginal and average product are shown in Figure 3.

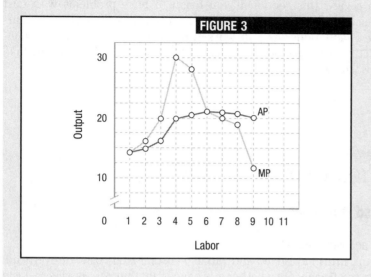

1. (T/F) Marginal product is the change in output that results from hiring one additional worker.
2. (T/F) Total product equals average product plus marginal product.

Use Figure 4 to answer questions 3 and 4.

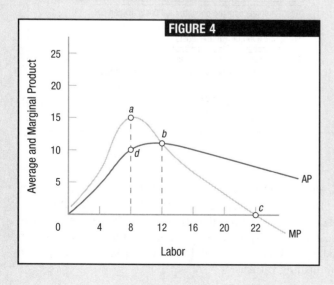

# Production in the Short Run Final Check

3. Should the firm hire more than eight workers?
   a. No, because that is where production is maximized.
   b. No, because after that the firm will face diminishing returns.
   c. No, because after that the firm faces negative returns.
   d. Yes, because average and marginal product are still positive.
4. After which point will there be negative returns?
   a. *a*
   b. *b*
   c. *c*
   d. *d*
5. Which of the following is true?
   a. Average product will be at its maximum when marginal product is at its maximum.
   b. Average product will be at its maximum when marginal product is zero.
   c. Average product will be at its maximum when marginal product equals average product.
   d. Average product never reaches a maximum.

Score: _____

Answers: 1. T; 2. F; 3. d; 4. c; 5. c

You should not have missed any in this quiz. Average and marginal product are the underlying concepts for the cost curves in the next section. Continue on, but you may have to review this section if you begin to have problems with cost curves. The next section on costs, however, gives you further practice with marginal and average calculations. As you work through these problems, the concepts from production may take hold. This is fundamental material that may take a little time to absorb. ∎

# Costs of Production

## Frequently Asked Questions

Q: **What are fixed and variable costs?**

A: In the short run, firms have fixed and variable costs. Fixed costs, or overhead, are those costs the firm incurs whether it produces anything or not. These costs include administrative overhead, lease payments, and insurance. Variable costs are those costs that vary with output, such as wages, utilities, and raw materials costs. Total costs are equal to total fixed costs plus total variable costs (TC = TFC + TVC).

Q: **How are average total costs, average fixed costs, and average variable costs computed?**

A: *Average total cost* (ATC) represents total cost per unit of production, or TC/Q. *Average fixed cost* (AFC) is equal to TFC/Q, and *average variable cost* (AVC) is equal to TVC/Q. Consequently, ATC = AFC + AVC.

### Core Equations: Cost Equations

**Key Points**

TC = TFC + TVC — Total costs are split into fixed and variable costs. Fixed costs do not vary with output, variable costs do.

ATC = TC/Q = AFC + AVC — Average total costs are equal to total costs divided by ouptut which is also equal to the sum of average fixed costs and average variable costs.

MC = ΔTC/ΔQ = ΔTVC/ΔQ — Marginal cost is equal to the change in total costs associated with a change in output. Since fixed costs are fixed and do not change when output changes, marginal cost is also equal to a change in total variable costs divided by the change in output.

Q: **What do typical ATC, AFC, and AVC curves look like when graphed?**

A: Figure 5 graphs average total cost, average fixed cost, and average variable cost. Note that average fixed cost declines continuously as output increases, because this fixed amount of cost is being spread over larger quantities of output. In contrast, average variable cost and average total cost first decrease, then increase because of diminishing returns.

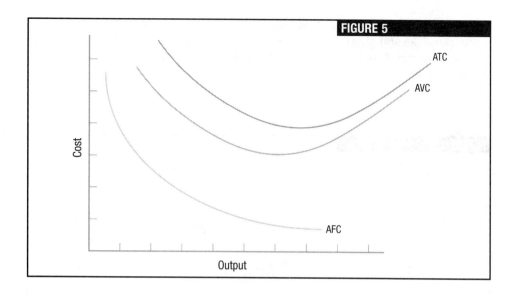

FIGURE 5

**Q: How are marginal costs defined and graphed?**

A: Marginal cost (MC) is the change in total costs associated with producing one additional unit. Since fixed costs do not change in the short run ($\Delta$TFC = 0), marginal cost is equal to the change in variable costs when one additional unit is produced; hence, MC = $\Delta$TVC/$\Delta$Q. Figure 6 graphs marginal cost along with average variable cost and average total cost. Note that marginal costs cut the average variable cost curve and the average total cost curve at their minimum points.

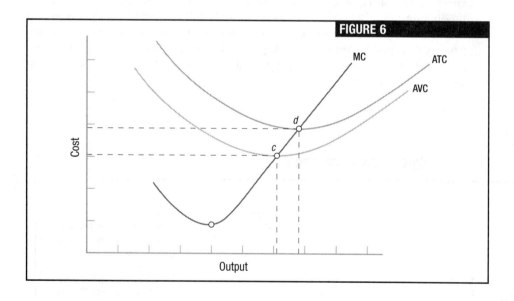

FIGURE 6

**Q: How is the long-run average total cost curve (LRATC) determined?**

A: In the long run, all factors of production are variable, and firms can enter or leave the industry. The long-run average total cost curve (LRATC) represents the lowest unit costs (ATC) for any specific output level in the long run. Figure 7 graphs the long-run average total cost curve as the minimum parts of several short-run average cost curves, using the assumption that in the long run, firms will build plants of the size best fitting the levels of output desired.

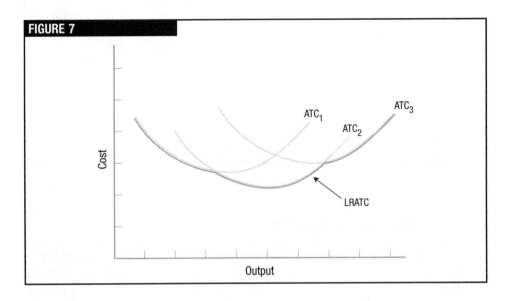

**FIGURE 7**

**Q:** Why do firms face economies and diseconomies of scale?

**A:** Economies of scale associated with larger firm size result from such factors as specialization in labor and management. As a firm grows, the average cost of production falls. Eventually, however, a firm will encounter diseconomies of scale when its size becomes so large that efficient management becomes impossible. At this point, average costs begin to rise. Today, advanced computer and communications technologies have radically increased the size of firms that can be efficiently managed.

## Core Graph: Measuring Costs

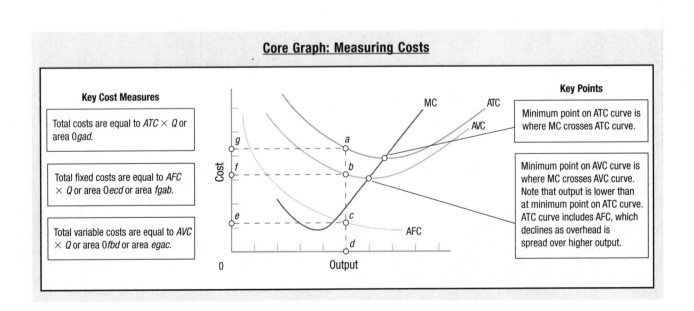

**Key Cost Measures**

Total costs are equal to $ATC \times Q$ or area $0gad$.

Total fixed costs are equal to $AFC \times Q$ or area $0ecd$ or area $fgab$.

Total variable costs are equal to $AVC \times Q$ or area $0fbd$ or area $egac$.

**Key Points**

Minimum point on ATC curve is where MC crosses ATC curve.

Minimum point on AVC curve is where MC crosses AVC curve. Note that output is lower than at minimum point on ATC curve. ATC curve includes AFC, which declines as overhead is spread over higher output.

# Costs of Production Quick Check

### Circle the Correct Answer

1. (T/F) Fixed costs include insurance and rent.
2. (T/F) Average variable costs equal average total costs minus average fixed costs.
3. In Figure 8, at what point will average variable cost exactly equal the cost of hiring one additional worker?
   a. *c*
   b. *d*
   c. cannot tell because average fixed costs are not included
   d. at the minimum point of the marginal cost curve
4. A firm's long-run average total costs (LRATC) curve is formed by combining a number of curves that represent:
   a. the firm's average total costs at various times, plant size being held constant.
   b. the firm's average variable cost, average fixed cost, and marginal cost.
   c. the firm's total product, average product, and marginal product.
   d. the firm's short-run average total costs for a variety of different plant sizes.
5. Diseconomies of scale result when
   a. fixed costs are large.
   b. a firm shrinks so much that individual workers must perform multiple tasks.
   c. a firm grows so large that it becomes difficult to manage in an efficient manner.
   d. a firm grows large enough that it can purchase advanced machinery.

Score: ____

Answers: 1. T; 2. T; 3. a; 4. d; 5. c

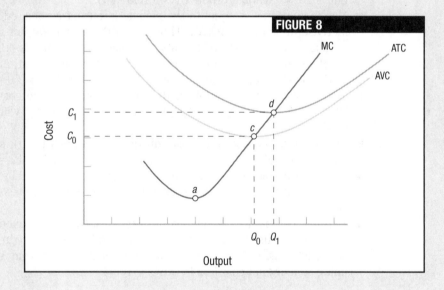

**FIGURE 8**

### If You Got All 5 Correct

Short-run and long-run costs are not a problem for you. You might find the Hints, Tips, and Reminders in the next section useful.

### If You Didn't Get All of Them Correct

You will need to review this section again. Even though this is difficult material, it is essential that you understand costs of production and cost curves to be able to master the concepts of profit maximization and market structure analysis that follow in the next few chapters. Review this section in the text and be sure to work the material in the Chapterwide Practice Questions section. When you have completed this work, study carefully the solved problem below. First, work the problem on your own, then read through the answer and the description of how each cost was determined. When you are done, take the short Final Quiz after this solved problem.

## Solved Problem: Costs of Production

Complete the table below assuming that fixed costs are $1,500 and wages are $100 per worker.

| L | Q | MP | AP | TVC | TC | ATC | AVC | MC |
|---|---|----|----|----|----|-----|-----|-----|
| 0 | — | ___ | ___ | ___ | ___ | ___ | ___ | ___ |
| 1 | 5 | ___ | ___ | ___ | ___ | ___ | ___ | ___ |
| 2 | 12 | ___ | ___ | ___ | ___ | ___ | ___ | ___ |
| 3 | 18 | ___ | ___ | ___ | ___ | ___ | ___ | ___ |
| 4 | 22 | ___ | ___ | ___ | ___ | ___ | ___ | ___ |
| 5 | 25 | ___ | ___ | ___ | ___ | ___ | ___ | ___ |

## Solution-Discussion

The table below shows the answers. Keep in mind the following:

- Average product is equal to Q/L, so when three workers are hired, output is 18, so average product is 6 ($18/3 = 6$).
- Marginal product is equal to the change in output associated with an increase in labor, or $\Delta Q/\Delta L$. Thus, when the fourth worker is hired, output grows from 18 to 22 units, and marginal product is 4.
- Total variable cost in this case is just equal to labor cost, and each worker costs 100, so when five workers are hired, TVC = 500.
- Total cost is equal to total fixed cost plus total variable cost (TC = TFC + TVC). Fixed cost is 1,500, so adding 1,500 to TVC will give us total cost.
- Average total cost is total costs divided by output (TC/Q), so when output is equal to 12, total cost is 1,700, so AVC = $1,700/12 = 141.7$.
- Average variable cost is equal to total variable cost divided by output. Thus, when output is equal to 22, total variable cost is 400, so AVC = $400/22 = 18.2$.
- Marginal cost is just the change in total cost (but since fixed cost is fixed, we can use total variable cost) divided by the change in output. When labor goes from 3 to 4 units, output increases from 18 to 22 units, so marginal cost is $\Delta TVC/\Delta Q = 100/4 = 25$.

| L | Q | MP | AP | TVC | TC | ATC | AVC | MC |
|---|---|----|----|-----|------|------|------|------|
| 0 | — | — | — | — | 1500 | — | — | — |
| 1 | 5 | 5 | 5 | 100 | 1600 | 320.0 | 20.0 | 20.0 |
| 2 | 12 | 7 | 6 | 200 | 1700 | 141.7 | 16.7 | 14.3 |
| 3 | 18 | 6 | 6 | 300 | 1800 | 100.0 | 16.7 | 16.7 |
| 4 | 22 | 4 | 5.4 | 400 | 1900 | 86.4 | 18.2 | 25.0 |
| 5 | 25 | 3 | 5 | 500 | 2000 | 80.0 | 20.0 | 33.3 |

If the firm has three workers, total cost is $1,800.00. If the firm can sell the 18 units of output it produces for $100.00 each, revenue to the firm is also $1,800.00, so the firm breaks even (earns a normal profit—remember that the cost curves include opportunity costs).

Now complete the Final Check section on the following page.

# Costs of Production Final Check

1. (T/F) Fixed cost is considered fixed in the short run but not in the long run.
2. Average cost, or cost per unit of output (TC/Q), is equal to
   a. TFC + TVC
   b. TFC/Q + TVC/Q
   c. TC − TFC/Q
   d. PVC + PDQ
3. Which curve is *not* typically bowl-shaped?
   a. the average total cost curve
   b. the average fixed cost curve
   c. the short-run average cost curve
   d. the average variable cost curve
4. In Figure 9, output in the range from $Q_0$ to $Q_1$ is considered
   a. economies of scale.
   b. constant returns to scale.

   c. diseconomies of scale.
   d. an example of the law of diminishing returns.
5. Marginal cost
   a. crosses through the minimum point of the total cost curve.
   b. crosses through the minimum point of the ATC curve before crossing through the minimum point of the AVC curve.
   c. doesn't cross through the minimum point of the AFC curve.
   d. is equal to the change in average fixed costs divided by the change in output.

Score: ____

**Answers: 1. T; 2. b; 3. b; 4. b; 5. c**

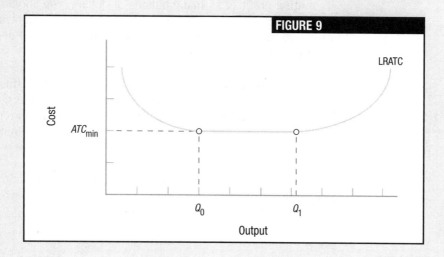

**FIGURE 9**

You shouldn't miss any in this exercise. If you did, this is a sign that you are still having trouble with the material in this chapter. If you have consistently had problems with this chapter, start at the beginning, reread the text, and work through the material again to this point. Since cost and production are so fundamental to much of the rest of the book, you will want to make sure you have these concepts down pat. ■

# Consider These Hints, Tips, and Reminders          STEP 4

**1.** Sunk costs can often be a difficult concept to grasp. Because you have already spent money on some activity and the money cannot be recovered, this spending is sunk and should have no impact on future decisions. This takes a little getting used to. Money spent on a cell phone last year should not affect your decision to buy a new phone that is many times better for less money.

2. Don't let the distinction between economic and accounting costs fool you. Accounting costs focus on those costs that are essentially out of pocket; costs for which you pay cash or for which you write checks. Economic costs include accounting costs plus opportunity costs.

   When you start a business, two opportunity costs are nearly always present. First, you quit a job (you were working, weren't you?), so you have given up that salary and benefits. Second, you put some of your savings (capital) into the business that could have earned interest in the bank. Adding these two opportunity costs to the explicit costs of running your business represents your economic costs. You will not earn an economic profit until all economic costs are covered. Note that your firm will earn a normal profit if the business *just* covers your economic costs.

3. The cost curves that economists draw include opportunity costs and therefore represent economic costs. Thus, when economists assume that total costs are equal to *X*, this *X* includes a reasonable return on the firm's capital invested in the business.

   So when you see some report that says Company ABC earned an obscene accounting profit of so many billions of dollars, you should ask yourself, How much capital does this firm have invested, and after subtracting a reasonable return on their capital, how big is the resulting profit? Keep in mind that any profit that remains is "economic profit."

4. The most important cost curves you learned about in this chapter are ATC, AVC, and MC. You will see and use these curves in the next three chapters. You need to be able to draw the curves fairly precisely, so remember: Both ATC and AVC are bowl-shaped, and MC passes through the minimum points on both curves.

5. The best way to draw the ATC, AVC, and MC curves is to draw a positively sloped MC curve first, then draw the ATC and AVC curves. Figure 10 shows step by step how to construct the curves.

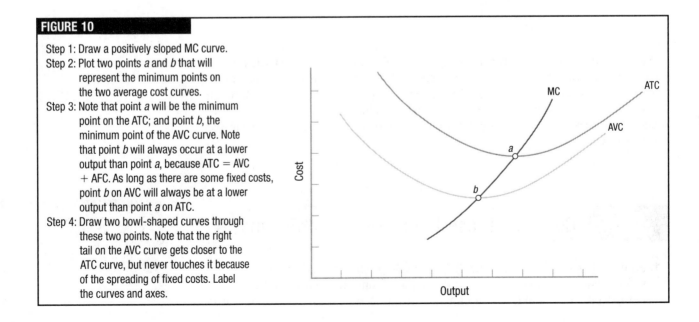

**FIGURE 10**

Step 1: Draw a positively sloped MC curve.
Step 2: Plot two points *a* and *b* that will represent the minimum points on the two average cost curves.
Step 3: Note that point *a* will be the minimum point on the ATC; and point *b*, the minimum point of the AVC curve. Note that point *b* will always occur at a lower output than point *a*, because ATC = AVC + AFC. As long as there are some fixed costs, point *b* on AVC will always be at a lower output than point *a* on ATC.
Step 4: Draw two bowl-shaped curves through these two points. Note that the right tail on the AVC curve gets closer to the ATC curve, but never touches it because of the spreading of fixed costs. Label the curves and axes.

**6.** You will need to become proficient with computing TVC from AVC and TC from ATC. Since AVC = TVC/Q, the relationship is straightforward: TVC = AVC × Q. Similarly, ATC = TC/Q, so TC = ATC × Q.

This is shown graphically in Figure 11. For three different points $a$, $b$, and $c$ on the AVC curve, TVC is just equal to AVC × Q. For point $a$, this is $C_2 \times Q_2$ which is equal to the shaded area. For point $b$, TVC would be $C_1 \times Q_1$, and for point $c$ it would be $C_3 \times Q_3$. Note these areas are not shaded. The exact same process applies for ATC and TC.

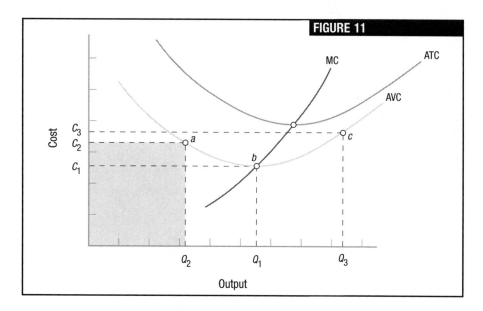

**FIGURE 11**

## Do the Homework for Chapter 7
## Production and Cost

### STEP 5

Instructor _____ Time _____ Student _____

**Use the answer key below to record your answers to these homework questions.**

1. _____    6. _____    11. _____    16. _____
2. _____    7. _____    12. _____    17. _____
3. _____    8. _____    13. _____    18. _____
4. _____    9. _____    14. _____    19. _____
5. _____    10. _____    15. _____    20. _____

1. Economic costs for the entrepreneur include
   a. rent on buildings.
   b. utility and communications bills.
   c. interest income forgone on the capital in the business.
   d. all of the above.

2. Which of the following costs are usually assumed to be fixed?
   a. leases on buildings
   b. utility bills
   c. wages and salaries
   d. all of the above

3. Which of the following differentiates the short run from the long run?
   a. the time it takes the firm to hire another CEO
   b. one factor of production is variable
   c. the rate at which firms can vary labor
   d. one factor of production is fixed

4. Total profits are defined as
   a. the difference between total costs and variable costs.
   b. what is left over after variable costs are subtracted from total revenues.
   c. the difference between total revenues and total costs.
   d. fixed costs plus variable costs plus implicit costs.

5. Normal profits are
   a. explicit costs plus implicit costs.
   b. necessary to keep investors willing to put capital into a firm.
   c. a rate of return on capital just equal to the average for the industry.
   d. zero as reported to the Internal Revenue Service.

6. The long run is defined by the fact that
   a. firms inevitably earn losses.
   b. firms continue to change production techniques to earn economic profits.
   c. firms are able to vary all of the factors of production.
   d. the plant capacity of firms is fixed.

7. Subtracting total costs from total revenues yields
   a. fixed costs.
   b. variable costs.
   c. the rate of return to the firm.
   d. profit.

Use Figure HW-1 to answer questions 8–11.

8. At which point will a new unit of labor hired add the most to total output of the firm?

9. At which point will each worker produce the most output?

10. Point *a* to point *e* on the marginal product (MP) curve illustrates
    a. the law of increasing returns.
    b. constant returns to scale.
    c. the law of diminishing returns.
    d. falling average product.

11. When 12 units of labor are hired, which of the following is *not* true?
    a. Marginal product is higher than average product.
    b. Marginal product is declining.
    c. Average product is equal to marginal product.
    d. Average product is at its maximum.

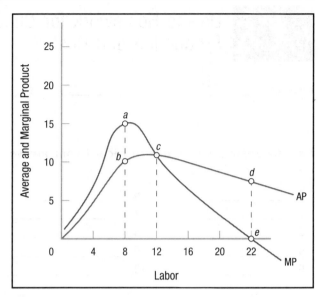

**HW-1**

12. Marginal cost equals the change in
    a. average total costs divided by the change in output.
    b. total variable costs divided by the change in output.
    c. total fixed costs divided by the change in output.
    d. total costs minus the change in fixed costs.

Use Figure HW-2 to answer questions 13–16.

13. At output 120, total fixed costs are equal to:

14. At output 120, total variable costs are equal to:

15. At output 120, total costs are equal to:

16. At output 120, marginal cost is equal to:

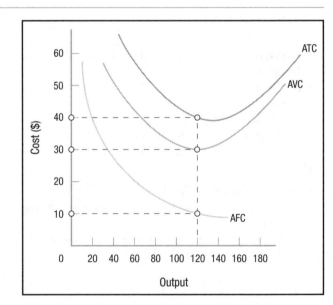

**HW-2**

17. When the average total cost curve is rising, the marginal cost curve will be

    a. falling.

    b. above the average total cost curve.

    c. rising slower than the average variable cost curve.

    d. rising slower than the average total cost curve.

18. Which of the following helps generate economies of scale as firms grow larger?

    a. A growing rift between management and workers.

    b. The inability of large firms to efficiently use their natural resources.

    c. Larger firms are able to purchase and implement more advanced equipment.

    d. The labor force becomes too large to efficiently manage.

19. When firms become so large that they are difficult to manage in an efficient manner, this is an example of _____ of scale.

20. The firm's long-run average total cost curve is derived from

    a. the short-run marginal cost curves of the firm.

    b. the summation of the firm's average variable cost and average fixed cost curves.

    c. the firm's short-run average cost curves for different plant sizes.

    d. a combination of the firm's short-run average variable cost and average total cost

| | Use the ExamPrep to Get Ready for Exams | **STEP 6** |
|---|---|---|

This sheet (front and back) is designed to help you prepare for your exams. The chapter has been boiled down to its key concepts. You are asked to answer questions, define terms, draw graphs, and, if you wish, add summaries of class notes.

## Firms

Define each of the following terms.

Firm:

Sole proprietor:

Partnership:

Corporation:

Profit:

Explicit costs:

Normal profit:

Economic profit:

Short run:

Long run:

## Production in the Short Run

Use the grids at right to illustrate the following:

■ Draw a total product curve in panel A.

■ In panel B, draw marginal and average product curves.

■ Label the areas of increasing returns, diminishing returns, and negative returns.

**Panel A**

**Panel B**

## Costs of Production

### Short-Run Costs

Define the following (use formulas where appropriate).

Fixed costs:

Variable costs:

Average fixed costs:

Average variable costs:

Average total costs:

Marginal costs:


Use the grid below to illustrate the following short-run curves.

Average fixed costs
Average variable costs
Average total costs
Marginal costs

(Hint: Keep in mind that the minimum point on the AVC curve comes at a lower output than the minimum point on the ATC curve. Also, the marginal cost curve goes through both minimum points)

### Long-Run Costs

Describe the long-run average total cost curve:

Describe economies and diseconomies of scale:

Describe the role technology plays in reducing long-run average cost:

## Additional Study Help Chapterwide Practice Questions

### Matching

Match the description with the corresponding term.

___ 1. Firms
___ 2. Revenue
___ 3. Economic costs
___ 4. Explicit costs
___ 5. Implicit costs
___ 6. Economic profits
___ 7. Normal profits
___ 8. Short run
___ 9. Long run
___ 10. Production
___ 11. Average product
___ 12. Marginal product
___ 13. Fixed costs
___ 14. Variable costs
___ 15. Marginal costs
___ 16. Economies of scale
___ 17. Diseconomies of scale
___ 18. Constant returns to scale

a. Costs a firm pays in the course of doing business, including both explicit and implicit costs.
b. The time period over which one production factor, usually plant capacity, is fixed.
c. A firm's output per unit of labor input.
d. Costs that change with the level of production.
e. The profit level where revenue exceeds both implicit and explicit costs.
f. Costs that do not change with the level of production in the short run.
g. A range of production output where long-run average total costs remain the same.
h. The range of production output where long-run average total cost goes up as output goes up.
i. The minimum level of profits necessary to keep investors willing to put capital in a firm.
j. A time period over which all production variables can change, including plant capacity and number of firms in the market.
k. Institutions or organizations that produce goods and services by transforming inputs into outputs.
l. The money a firm actually pays out while doing business.
m. A firm's output.
n. The amount of additional output created by adding one additional worker.
o. The opportunity costs of doing business.
p. The cost to a firm to produce one more unit of output.

q. The money a firm brings in from selling its goods or services.
r. The range of production output where long-run average total cost goes down as output goes up.

### Fill-In

Circle the word(s) in parentheses that complete the sentence.

1. The risks associated with production are assumed by (labor, capital, entrepreneurs) _____.

2. Price times units sold is equal to (explicit costs, total revenue, implicit costs, sunk costs, normal profits, economic profits) _____. Out-of-pocket expenses are (explicit costs, total revenue, implicit costs, sunk costs, normal profits, economic profits) _____, but opportunity costs are (explicit costs, total revenue, implicit costs, sunk costs, normal profits, economic profits) _____. Profits that just equal a normal rate of return are equal to (explicit costs, total revenue, implicit costs, sunk costs, normal profits, economic profits) _____, while profits in excess of a normal return are called (explicit costs, total revenue, implicit costs, sunk costs, normal profits, economic profits) _____.

3. Total output divided by number of workers is equal to (marginal, average, total) _____ product, while the change in total output divided by the change in the number of employees is equal to (marginal, average, total) _____ product.

4. Costs that do not change in the short run are called (fixed, variable, average, marginal) _____ costs. Labor and wages are an example of (fixed, variable, average, marginal) _____ costs. When additional labor is hired and costs change, this change in costs represents (fixed, variable, average, marginal) _____ costs, whereas cost per unit represents (fixed, variable, average, marginal) _____ costs.

5. As output increases, marginal cost first passes through the minimum point on the (average total, average variable) _____ cost curve, then passes through the minimum point on the (average total, average variable) _____ cost curve.

6. When long-run average total costs are rising, firms are encountering (economies, diseconomies) _____ of scale, and when long-run average total costs are falling, firms are facing (economies, diseconomies) _____ of scale.

## True-False

Circle the correct answer.

T / F  1. Firms located in areas with high labor costs tend to use labor-intensive production methods.

T / F  2. A firm's primary goal is to maximize its profits.

T / F  3. Explicit costs include all out-of-pocket expenses.

T / F  4. Total revenue is the amount of money a firm receives from the sale of its products or services.

T / F  5. Investors will remove capital from a firm earning zero economic profit.

T / F  6. In the short run, plant capacity is generally assumed to be fixed.

T / F  7. In the long run, all factors of production may vary, but the number of firms remains fixed.

T /F  8. Marginal product remains the same no matter what the level of output.

T / F  9. Marginal product is the change in profit that results from adding one additional worker.

T / F  10. The law of diminishing returns states that at some point additional workers will no longer improve output.

T / F  11. In the long run, all costs are fixed.

T / F  12. Variable costs include wages and expenditures for raw materials.

T / F  13. Average total cost is equal to average fixed cost minus average variable cost.

T / F  14. Marginal cost equals change in total fixed costs over change in output plus change in total variable costs over change in output.

T / F  15. The marginal cost curve will always intersect the maximum points of both the average variable cost curve and the average total cost curve.

T / F  16. Firms encounter constant returns to scale indefinitely as they grow in size.

T / F  17. Diseconomies of scale is caused by inefficiency once a firm grows past a certain point.

## Multiple Choice

Circle the correct answer.

1. Firms
   a. operate in only one market.
   b. produce goods and services.
   c. try to achieve zero profits.
   d. transform products into inputs.

2. Firms use low-technology, labor-intensive production methods in areas where
   a. labor is scarce and expensive.
   b. technology is advanced and inexpensive.
   c. labor is plentiful and cheap.
   d. product inputs are expensive.

3. The difference between a firm's total revenue and its total cost is
   a. profit.
   b. operating margin.
   c. marginal income.
   d. marginal return.

4. As a rule, firms try to maximize
   a. sales.
   b. market share.
   c. customer satisfaction.
   d. profits.

5. Number of units sold times price per unit equals
   a. marginal revenue.
   b. net profit.
   c. total revenue.
   d. gross profit.

6. A firm's out-of-pocket expenses are
   a. explicit costs.
   b. implicit costs.
   c. marginal costs.
   d. fixed costs.

7. Which of the following is an explicit cost?
   a. opportunity costs
   b. the cost of capital
   c. depreciation
   d. wages

8. An implicit cost
   a. is a direct out-of-pocket expense.
   b. is an opportunity cost of doing business.
   c. is a onetime expense.
   d. is offset by explicit costs.

9. To keep investors willing to put capital into a firm, that firm must
   a. earn more than zero economic profit.
   b. earn more than normal economic profit.
   c. earn zero economic profit.
   d. have a positive marginal profit.

10. Zero economic profit is considered
    a. a normal profit.
    b. a sign of a failing firm.
    c. an excess profit.
    d. insufficient profit.

11. Total revenue minus explicit and implicit costs equals
    a. economic profit or loss.
    b. zero profit.
    c. normal economic profit.
    d. marginal profit.

12. The number of firms in an industry can change
    a. only in the long run.
    b. in the short run if there is a market shortage.
    c. in the short run if there is a market surplus.
    d. only in the short run.

13. The change in output from adding one additional worker is
    a. marginal product.
    b. total product.
    c. marginal profit.
    d. total income.

14. Total output divided by the number of workers employed equals
    a. marginal product.
    b. marginal return.
    c. total product.
    d. average product.

15. When hiring one more worker increases output by an amount less than the average output of existing workers, hiring this additional worker will
    a. decrease average productivity.
    b. decrease total productivity.
    c. increase average productivity.
    d. have no effect on productivity.

16. If hiring an additional worker actually reduces total output, this is an example of
    a. increasing returns.
    b. positive marginal return.
    c. negative marginal return.
    d. diseconomies of scale.

Use Figure MC-1 to answer questions 17 and 18.

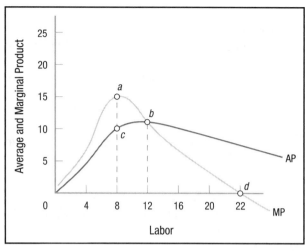

**MC-1**

17. Going from 15 workers to 16 workers illustrates
    a. constant return.
    b. decreasing returns.
    c. increasing returns.
    d. economy of scale.

18. At which point are workers, on average, producing the most output?
    a. *a*
    b. *b*
    c. *c*
    d. *d*

19. In the short run, total cost equals
    a. total fixed cost.
    b. total variable cost.
    c. total variable cost minus total fixed cost.
    d. total variable cost plus total fixed cost.

20. Which of the following is typically regarded as a fixed cost?
    a. shipping costs
    b. insurance payments
    c. raw material costs
    d. wages

21. Change in output does *not* cause changes in
    a. variable cost.
    b. average fixed cost.
    c. marginal cost.
    d. total fixed cost.

22. TFC/Q + TVC/Q is the formula for
    a. average total cost.
    b. marginal cost.

c. total cost.

d. variable cost.

23. Marginal cost equals
    a. change in total variable cost divided by change in total fixed cost.
    b. change in total variable cost divided by change in quantity.
    c. change in total fixed cost divided by change in quantity.
    d. change in total variable cost minus change in total fixed cost.

24. If a firm can produce 100 DVDs for $100 and 200 DVDs for $150, what is the marginal cost per DVD of the additional 100 DVDs?
    a. $1.00
    b. $0.75
    c. $0.50
    d. $0.25

25. The long-run average total cost (LRATC) curve is able to portray the lowest unit cost at which any specific output can be produced in the long run because
    a. fixed costs are stable in the long run.
    b. it takes into account changes in plant size.
    c. it ignores changes in plant size.
    d. it ignores changes in variable costs.

26. A firm's long-run average total cost (LRATC) curve shows
    a. the lowest unit cost for any level of output.
    b. the highest unit cost for any level of output.
    c. the marginal cost for any level of output.
    d. the variable cost for any level of output.

27. When a firm grows so large that it becomes difficult to manage in an efficient manner, this is an example of
    a. economies of scale.
    b. constant returns to scale.
    c. diseconomies of scale.
    d. increasing returns to scale.

Use Figure MC-2 to answer questions 28 and 29.

28. $ATC_1$, $ATC_2$, and $ATC_3$ represent different levels of output in relation to
    a. worker productivity.
    b. demand.
    c. cost.
    d. plant size.

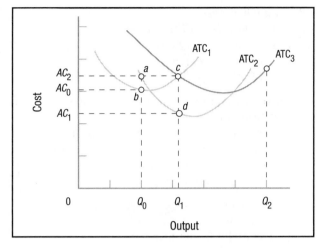

**MC-2**

29. If you wanted to produce output $Q_1$, you would operate which plant size?
    a. plant 1 associated with $ATC_1$
    b. plant 2 associated with $ATC_2$
    c. plant 3 associated with $ATC_3$
    d. plant 1 associated with $ATC_1$, but add more capital

## Essay-Problem

Answer in the space provided.

Learning and applying cost and production concepts can be challenging. Don't get discouraged if your answers below are not always the same as those we suggest. Use these as guidelines, but more important, to help you learn some of the difficult issues surrounding firms, production, and costs.

1. Why are entrepreneurs important for any economy?

2. Was profit maximization the goal of Enron?

3. To get a porch built on your house, you have to apply for a permit, go before the local zoning board and explain your request, and hire a contractor to do the work. Why is appearing before the zoning board an implicit cost in this case?

4. If interest rates go up, will existing normal profits be sufficient to keep investors in the firm happy?

5. Why is it important for small businesses to have an accurate estimate of fixed costs?

6. In the short run, why is marginal cost so much more important for average variable cost than for average fixed cost?

7. Will the LRATC curve for an oil refinery be bumpy or smooth?

8. Hotrod Skateboards manufactures skateboards. It has the following costs:

   wages
   rent
   wheels
   boards
   paint
   insurance

   Which of these are fixed costs, and which are variable costs?

9. Would you categorize the personal computer industry as operating under economies of scale, constant returns to scale, or diseconomies of scale?

10. Fill in the following table.

| Number of Workers | Total Product | Marginal Product | Average Product |
|---|---|---|---|
| 50 | 100 | _____ | _____ |
| 55 | 120 | _____ | _____ |
| 60 | 150 | _____ | _____ |
| 65 | 200 | _____ | _____ |
| 70 | 225 | _____ | _____ |
| 75 | 235 | _____ | _____ |
| 80 | 240 | _____ | _____ |

11. Complete the following production and cost table. Plot the ATC, AVC, and MC curves in Figure EP-1.

| L | Q | MP | AP | TFC | TVC | TC | AFC | ATC | AVC | MC |
|---|---|---|---|---|---|---|---|---|---|---|
| 0 | 0 | __ | __ | __ | __ | __ | __ | __ | __ | __ |
| 1 | 7 | __ | __ | __ | __ | __ | __ | __ | __ | __ |
| 2 | 15 | __ | __ | __ | __ | __ | __ | __ | __ | __ |
| 3 | 25 | __ | __ | __ | __ | __ | __ | __ | __ | __ |
| 4 | 40 | __ | __ | __ | __ | __ | __ | __ | __ | __ |
| 5 | 54 | __ | __ | __ | __ | __ | __ | __ | __ | __ |
| 6 | 65 | __ | __ | __ | __ | __ | __ | __ | __ | __ |
| 7 | 75 | __ | __ | __ | __ | __ | __ | __ | __ | __ |
| 8 | 84 | __ | __ | __ | __ | __ | __ | __ | __ | __ |
| 9 | 90 | __ | __ | __ | __ | __ | __ | __ | __ | __ |
| 10 | 95 | __ | __ | 2000 | 20000 | __ | __ | __ | __ | __ |

EP-1

12. Use Figure EP-2 to answer the following questions.

    a. What output level has the lowest average variable cost?

    b. At what point is marginal cost equal to average variable cost?

    c. Minimum average total cost is equal to _____.

    d. Why is the minimum point on ATC at 35 units greater than the minimum point on the AVC curve at 30 units?

    e. Why does the marginal cost curve cross through the minimum points on the ATC and AVC curves?

EP-2

## What's Next

You now should have a good understanding of what lies behind supply curves. Firms seek out profitable business opportunities. Once they gauge a business need, they have to determine how they are going to produce the good or service, then determine the cost. With this information in hand, they can determine if there is a profit to be made.

In the next chapter, we look at competitive markets and see the forces that shape supply and demand in these markets. In that chapter, we give the assumption of profit maximization a much clearer analytical base.

## Answers to Chapterwide Practice Questions

### Matching

| | | | |
|---|---|---|---|
| 1. k | 6. e | 11. c | 15. p |
| 2. q | 7. i | 12. n | 16. r |
| 3. a | 8. b | 13. f | 17. h |
| 4. l | 9. j | 14. d | 18. g |
| 5. o | 10. m | | |

### Fill-In

1. entrepreneurs
2. total revenue, explicit costs, implicit costs, normal profits, economic profits
3. average, marginal
4. fixed, variable, marginal, average
5. average variable, average total
6. diseconomies, economies

### True-False

| | | | |
|---|---|---|---|
| 1. F | 6. T | 10. F | 14. F |
| 2. T | 7. F | 11. F | 15. F |
| 3. T | 8. F | 12. T | 16. F |
| 4. T | 9. F | 13. F | 17. T |
| 5. F | | | |

### Multiple Choice

| | | | |
|---|---|---|---|
| 1. b | 9. c | 16. c | 23. b |
| 2. c | 10. a | 17. b | 24. c |
| 3. a | 11. a | 18. b | 25. b |
| 4. d | 12. a | 19. d | 26. a |
| 5. c | 13. a | 20. b | 27. c |
| 6. a | 14. d | 21. d | 28. d |
| 7. d | 15. a | 22. a | 29. b |
| 8. b | | | |

## Essay-Problem

1. Entrepreneurs see new business opportunities by finding unmet market needs. Meeting these needs helps economies to grow.

2. Yes. The problem was that this goal conflicted with the goals of some of the officers of the corporation, who sought to profit at Enron's expense. This sorry episode shows that profit maximization may indeed be the goal of the firm, but it may not be the goal of all of the members of that firm: This is the point at which trouble begins. The profit maximization assumption does not mean companies do *anything* to make higher profits. Economists limit this assumption to lawful behavior. Keep in mind that long-run profit concerns mean not doing things in the short run (illegal or unethical behavior) that threaten the long-run viability of the firm.

3. It is not an explicit cost because you do not pay yourself anything to go before the board. It is an opportunity cost and so should be included in the total costing for the project because you could have done other things with your time. Now, if your alternative was to play golf, then the opportunity cost may be low. But if you had to take time off from work, the cost is the wages forgone, or the personal day taken.

4. No. Economists link normal profits to the cost of capital. If interest rates go up, the cost of capital will go up. Therefore, what previously was considered normal profits will have to increase to meet the new cost of capital rate. Think of it this way: If you could get 5% interest from the bank, the cost of capital would have to be at least this rate to get you to invest your money in something else; when the interest rate the bank pays you goes up, you will need a higher rate from an investment to even consider taking the money out of the bank and investing it in an enterprise.

5. In the short run, fixed costs—rent, insurance—are fixed. Small businesses often have widely fluctuating sales and, therefore, fluctuating income. Fixed costs are the minimum a small business has to pay each month (often called "the nut"). Without accurate estimates of what these fixed costs are, small businesses owners may be surprised to find that they do not have the cash to pay these costs at various times of the year.

6. In the short run, fixed costs are fixed. Marginal costs have no bearing on fixed costs.

7. The LRATC is constructed by combining the ATC curves for a firm for different plant sizes, with the lowest possible production costs at every possible level of production. An oil-refining firm may have only a few different options for the size of its refineries, with the building of new refineries requiring investments of hundreds of millions of dollars. With only a few options for plant size being realistically available, any change in plant size can be expected to have a major impact on average costs, thus resulting in a bumpy LRATC curve for this firm.

8. Fixed: rent, insurance. Variable: wages, wheels, boards, paint.

9. Because the price of personal computers has fallen consistently over the years and is still falling, we would expect the industry as a whole to be operating under economies of scale. Individual companies, however, could be operating at any one of the three places on the LRATC.

10.

| Number of Workers | Total Product | Marginal Product | Average Product |
|---|---|---|---|
| 50 | 100 | — | 2.00 |
| 55 | 120 | 4 | 2.18 |
| 60 | 150 | 6 | 2.50 |
| 65 | 200 | 10 | 3.08 |
| 70 | 225 | 5 | 3.21 |
| 75 | 235 | 2 | 3.13 |
| 80 | 240 | 1 | 3.00 |

11. See the following table and Figure EPA-1.

| L | Q | MP | AP | TFC | TVC | TC | AFC | ATC | AVC | MC |
|---|---|----|----|-----|-----|----|----|----|----|----|
| 0 | 0 | 0 | — | 2000 | 0 | 2000 | — | — | — | — |
| 1 | 7 | 7 | 7 | 2000 | 2000 | 4000 | 285.71 | 571.43 | 285.71 | 285.71 |
| 2 | 15 | 8 | 7.50 | 2000 | 4000 | 6000 | 133.33 | 400.00 | 266.67 | 250.00 |
| 3 | 25 | 10 | 8.33 | 2000 | 6000 | 8000 | 80.00 | 320.00 | 240.00 | 200.00 |
| 4 | 40 | 15 | 10.00 | 2000 | 8000 | 10000 | 50.00 | 250.00 | 200.00 | 133.33 |
| 5 | 54 | 14 | 10.80 | 2000 | 10000 | 12000 | 37.04 | 222.22 | 185.19 | 142.86 |
| 6 | 65 | 11 | 10.83 | 2000 | 12000 | 14000 | 30.77 | 215.38 | 184.62 | 181.82 |
| 7 | 75 | 10 | 10.71 | 2000 | 14000 | 16000 | 26.67 | 213.33 | 186.67 | 200.00 |
| 8 | 84 | 9 | 10.50 | 2000 | 16000 | 18000 | 23.81 | 214.29 | 190.48 | 222.22 |
| 9 | 90 | 6 | 10.00 | 2000 | 18000 | 20000 | 22.22 | 222.22 | 200.00 | 333.33 |
| 10 | 95 | 5 | 9.50 | 2000 | 20000 | 22000 | 21.05 | 231.58 | 210.53 | 400.00 |

EPA-1

12. a. 30
   b. *c*
   c. $8
   d. Because fixed costs are included in ATC. This spreading of overhead means that ATC reaches a minimum after AVC.
   e. Marginal cost is the cost to produce one more unit of output. If MC is less than ATC, then ATC must fall (adding a smaller number to the average will bring the average down). Similarly, if MC is higher than ATC, ATC must be rising (again, adding a larger number to the average will increase the average). Only when MC = ATC is ATC at its minimum. The same analysis applies to AVC.

# Competition

## The Competitive Market Model Is a Cornerstone of Microeconomics

If supply and demand is the foundation of economics, the analysis of market structure is a close second. It is here where you will see how firms put together the profit equation of revenues minus costs. You looked at production and costs in the last chapter. Here, we start putting some of these ideas to work when we bring in revenues and show how costs help determine what a firm will produce. Pay special attention to the market model discussed in this chapter—competition—because what you learn here will make it much easier to understand other market structures in the following chapters.

| This Is What You Need to Know | STEP 1 |
| --- | --- |

**After studying this chapter you should be able to**

- Name the primary market structures and describe their characteristics.

- Define a competitive market and the assumptions that underlie it.

- Distinguish the differences between competitive markets in the short run and the long run.

- Analyze the conditions for profit maximization, loss minimization, and plant shutdown for a firm.

- Derive the firm's short-run supply curve.

■ Use the short-run competitive model to determine long-run equilibrium.

■ Describe why competition is in the public interest.

## STEP 2            Review the Key Terms

**Market structure analysis:** By observing a few industry characteristics such as number of firms in the industry or the level of barriers to entry, economists can use this information to predict pricing and output behavior of the firm in the industry.

**Competition:** Exists when there are many relatively small buyers and sellers, a standardized product, with good information to both buyers and sellers, and no barriers to entry or exit.

**Price taker:** Individual firms in competitive markets get their prices from the market since they are so small they cannot influence market price. For this reason, competitive firms are price takers and can produce and sell all the output they produce at market-determined prices.

**Marginal revenue:** The change in total revenue from selling an additional unit of output. Since competitive firms are price takers, P = MR for competitive firms.

**Profit maximizing rule:** Firms maximize profit by producing output where MR = MC. No other level of output produces higher profits.

**Normal profits:** Equal to zero economic profits; where P = ATC.

**Shutdown point:** When price in the short run falls below the minimum point on the AVC curve, the firm will minimize losses by closing its doors and stopping production. Since P < AVC, the firm's variable costs are not covered, so by shutting the plant, losses are reduced to fixed costs.

**Short-run supply curve:** The marginal cost curve above the minimum point on the average variable cost curve.

**Productive efficiency:** Goods and services are produced and sold to consumers at their lowest resource (opportunity) cost.

**Allocative efficiency:** The mix of goods and services produced are just what society desires. The price that consumers pay is equal to marginal cost and is also equal to the least average total cost.

**Increasing cost industry:** An industry that in the long run faces higher prices and costs as industry output expands. Industry expansion puts upward pressure on resources (inputs), causing higher costs in the long run.

**Decreasing cost industry:** An industry that in the long run faces lower prices and costs as industry output expands. Typically the result of technological advances.

**Constant cost industry:** An industry that in the long run faces roughly the same prices and costs as industry output expands. Some industries can virtually clone their operations in other areas without putting undue pressure on resource prices, resulting in constant operating costs as they expand in the long run.

| | Work Through the Chapter Tutorials | **STEP 3** |

# Market Structure Analysis

## Frequently Asked Questions

**Q: What is market structure analysis, and why is it useful?**

A:  Market structure analysis is used by economists to categorize industries by looking at a few key characteristics. Once categorized, an industry's behavior in
pricing and output can be predicted.

**Q: What are the basic market structures, and how are they defined?**

A:  Economists have identified four basic market structures: competition, monopolistic competition, oligopoly, and monopoly. They are defined by the following
factors: the number of firms in the industry, the nature of the product produced, the extent of barriers to entry and exit, and the degree to which individual firms can control prices.

**Q: What are the main characteristics of the competitive market structure?**

A:  The competitive market structure assumes, first, a market with many buyers
and sellers, none large enough to influence product prices. Second, it assumes
that a homogeneous or standardized product is produced. Third, it assumes all
buyers and sellers have all relevant information about prices and product quality. Fourth, barriers to entry and exit are insignificant.

**Q: What does it mean to say that competitive firms are price takers?**

A:  Competitive firms are price takers because they cannot significantly alter the
sales price of their products. Product prices are determined in broad markets.
Figure 1 depicts a competitive market, and the firm faces a horizontal demand
curve—the firm cannot affect the price; it can only accept it.

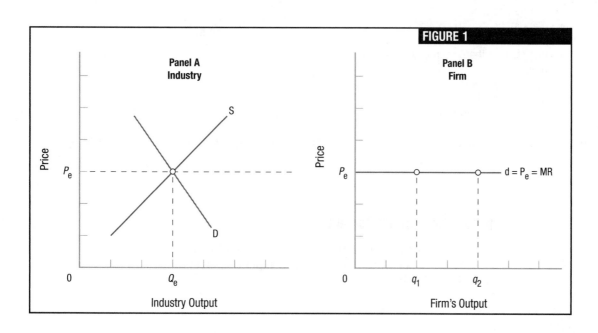

Q: **How is the short run defined?**

A: In the short run, at least one factor of production (usually plant capacity) is fixed. Also in the short run, firms cannot enter or exit the industry.

Q: **How is the long run defined?**

A: In the long run, all factors of production are variable, with short-run profit levels inducing entry or exit.

## Keep in Mind

Market structure analysis is a way to look at definable characteristics of an industry. Based on this assessment, one can predict industry pricing and output behavior. Competitive firms are price takers and have to accept market prices as given.

# Market Structure Analysis Quick Check

## Circle the Correct Answer

1. (T/F) Monopolies have substantial control over price.
2. (T/F) Competitive markets have homogeneous products.
3. (T/F) All markets have roughly the same number of buyers and sellers.
4. (T/F) In the short run, plant size and the number of firms in the industry are regarded as fixed.
5. Airlines represent what market structure?
   a. competition
   b. monopolistic competition
   c. oligopoly
   d. monopoly
6. Competitive markets
   a. are usually dominated by one or two large firms.
   b. have many sellers but often have few buyers.
   c. set up effective barriers to entry.
   d. put individual sellers in the position of price takers.
7. In a competitive market, a firm
   a. will sell its product for less than the market price in the hope of increasing sales.
   b. will try to influence government in the hope of getting the price raised.
   c. will try to maximize its profit by setting its sales price above the market price.
   d. will accept the market price as a given.

8. Competitive markets are characterized by
   a. many buyers and sellers, of varying sizes ranging from small to large.
   b. easy entry and exit from the industry in the short run.
   c. little opportunity to make profits in the short run.
   d. buyers and sellers having all the information they need about prices and product quality to make informed decisions.
9. Individual firms in competitive markets face horizontal demand curves. This means that any individual firm
   a. is a price maker.
   b. is a price taker.
   c. is not concerned with price.
   d. has a bowl-shaped marginal revenue curve.
10. Corn farming is an example of
    a. competitive markets.
    b. monopolistically competitive markets.
    c. oligopolistic markets.
    d. monopoly markets.

Score: ____

**Answers: 1. T; 2. T; 3. F; 4. T; 5. c; 6. d; 7. d; 8. d; 9. b; 10. a**

## If You Got 9 or 10 Correct

You have a good grasp of the general concept of market structure, and more particularly of the characteristics of the competitive model. Go on to the next section, Short-Run Decisions.

## If You Didn't Get at Least 9 Correct

Do a careful review of this introductory material because it is the foundation for this chapter and the next two chapters. First, be sure you can list the four major market structures. Second, jot down the main characteristics of the competitive market model. Finally, list the difference between the short run and the long run—this difference becomes important at the end of the chapter. Continue on, but be prepared to review this section again. Working through the next section, Short-Run Decisions will probably help you to see why it is important to understand the assumptions of competitive markets. ■

# Competition: Short-Run Decisions

## Frequently Asked Questions

Q:  **How is marginal revenue defined, and how is it related to market price for a competitive firm?**

A:  Total revenue equals price per unit times quantity sold (TR = $p \times q$). Marginal revenue is equal to the change in total revenue that comes from producing an added unit of the product (MR = $\Delta$TR/$\Delta q$). In a competitive market, a firm can sell all it wants at the market price, so marginal revenue is equal to market price for the competitive firm.

Q:  **How will a competitive firm maximize its profits?**

A:  Firms will maximize their profits by selling a level of output at which marginal revenue is just equal to marginal cost (MR = MC). For the competitive firm, this translates into MR = MC = P. In the short run, a firm can earn economic profits, normal profits, or economic losses, depending on a product's market price.

Q:  **How do average total costs determine profits for the competitive firm in the short run?**

A:  If price is above the minimum point on the ATC curve, a firm will earn economic profits in the short run. If price is just equal to the minimum point on the ATC curve, the firm will earn normal profits. If price should fall below the minimum ATC, the firm will earn economic losses.

Q:  **Why is the minimum point on the AVC curve known as the shutdown point?**

A:  If price falls below the minimum point on the AVC curve, the firm will shut down and incur a loss equal to its fixed costs, since firms will not operate if they cannot cover their variable costs.

Q:  **What is the short-run supply curve for the competitive firm?**

A:  The short-run supply curve for the competitive firm is the marginal cost curve above the minimum point on the AVC curve.

Q:  **At what price will a competitive firm in the short run earn economic profits? Normal profits? Losses?**

A:  Figure 2 on the next page shows the short-run supply curve for a competitive firm. It also shows the profit possibilities discussed above. The competitive firm will earn economic profits with a price above $P_1$ (above point $b$), normal profits at a price of $P_1$ (at point $b$), and it will lose money at a price below $P_1$. The firm will remain in business in the short run at prices between $P_0$ and $P_1$ even though losses are incurred because variable costs will be

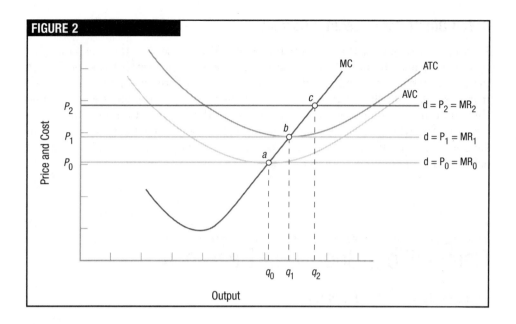

**FIGURE 2**

covered and some revenue will be available to pay fixed costs. Below a price of $P_0$, the firm will shut down because it will not be able to cover all of its variable costs, much less any of its fixed costs.

### Key Point to Remember

Competitive firms are price takers so MR = P. Competitive firms (and firms in all of the market structures you will study) maximize profits by producing output where MR = MC. Thus, competitive firms maximize profits where P = MR = MC.

## Core Equation: Profit Maximization

| | Key Idea |
|---|---|
| MR = MC | Firms (competitive and others) maximize profit by producing output where MR = MC. For firms in competitive markets, this means producing where P = MR = MC. |

## Competition: Short-Run Decisions Quick Check

### Circle the Correct Answer

1. (T/F) If a company earns an additional $1,500 in revenue by selling 10 additional units, its marginal revenue is $1,500.

2. (T/F) A firm in a competitive market will maximize its profits by producing a level of output where marginal revenue equals marginal cost.

3. (T/F) If a company earns $3,000 in revenue, hires an additional worker for $100 in wages and then earns a total of $3,500 in revenue, its marginal revenue is $400.

4. (T/F) A firm in a competitive market will always want to produce as much output as it can because it will maximize its profits.

5. If a competitive firm produces at the point where the marginal cost curve intersects the average total cost curve at its minimum point, the firm will earn
   a. economic profits.
   b. normal profits.
   c. no profits.
   d. a short-run loss.

6. Should the competitive firm keep producing even if it faces short-run losses if it is producing at a point on the marginal cost curve that is above the minimum point of its average variable cost curve?
   a. Yes, because it is producing normal profits at this point.
   b. Yes, because it is still producing more than zero economic profits at this point.
   c. Yes, because it still covers its variable costs and has some revenue to pay for fixed costs.
   d. No, it should never incur losses.

7. For a competitive firm, the portion of the marginal cost (MC) curve that exists above the minimum point on the average variable cost (AVC) curve is actually the firm's
   a. short-run demand curve.
   b. long-run demand curve.
   c. average total costs curve.
   d. short-run supply curve.

8. If a competitive firm produces at the point where the marginal cost curve intersects the average variable cost curve at its minimum point, the firm will
   a. earn economic profits.
   b. earn normal profits.
   c. have a short-run loss, but it will just cover its variable costs.
   d. have a short-run loss, but it will not cover its variable costs.

9. A competitive firm seeking to minimize its losses in the short run should shut down its plant as soon as
   a. it suffers economic losses.
   b. profits drop to zero.
   c. losses exceed normal profits.
   d. losses exceed total fixed costs.

10. The short-run supply curve for the competitive firm is a portion of
    a. the average total cost (ATC) curve.
    b. the average variable cost (AVC) curve.
    c. the average fixed cost (AFC) curve.
    d. the marginal cost (MC) curve.

Score: ____

**Answers: 1. F; 2. T; 3. F; 4. F; 5. b; 6. c; 7. d; 8. c; 9. d; 10. d**

## If You Got 9 or 10 Correct

You have been able to pick up some relatively difficult material, including an understanding of the profit possibilities for the competitive firm in the short run and the derivation of the competitive firm's short-run supply curve. You can move on to Competition: Long-Run Adjustments, the last section in this chapter. However, because of the importance of the competitive model, we suggest you do a quick review of the solved problem below. This review should be worth it.

## If You Didn't Get at Least 9 Correct

Don't get upset—this is tough material. A patient review will be worth it. Reflect on the role played by profit maximizing and when and why the firm would shut the plant.

Next, put this reflection to work by looking again at the figures in this section. Be sure you know the relationship between price, the average total costs curve, and profits. Read the caption to each figure and make sure you see why each figure is different and what ideas are conveyed. This approach to marginal decision making (profits are maximized by equating MR and MC) will show up continually in upcoming chapters. Take a moment to study the Solved Problem on the next page.

## Solved Problem: Short-Run Competitive Decisions

Figure 3 represents a firm in a competitive industry. Answer the following questions:

a. At what price will this firm shut down and produce no output at all?

b. If the market sets a price of $10 a unit, how much output will this firm produce? Will it make an economic profit? If so, roughly how much?

c. If market price falls to $8 a unit, how much output will the firm produce? Will it make a profit? If so, roughly how much?

d. If market price is $7 a unit, how much will the firm produce? Again, will it make a profit? How much?

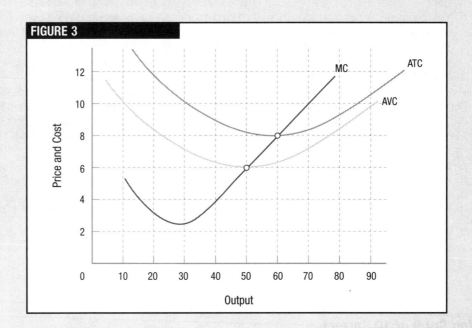

**FIGURE 3**

## Solution-Discussion

a. The minimum point on the AVC curve is at $6 a unit. At a price below $6, the firm is unable to cover its variable costs, and losses exceed fixed costs, so the firm is better off closing its doors.

b. At $10 a unit, the firm will produce 70 units of output. Because price is above ATC, the firm will earn an economic profit. Profit per unit is roughly $1.50 a unit (P − ATC at an output of 70), so total economic profit is roughly $105 ($1.50 × 70 = $105).

c. At a price of $8, the firm will produce 60 units. This is the minimum point on the ATC curve, so the firm's TR = TC, and therefore it earns a normal profit.

d. At $7 a unit, the firm equates MR and MC at roughly 55 units of output. This price is below ATC but above AVC, so the firm is earning a loss. Because P > AVC, the firm is able to pay its variable costs and contribute to overhead (fixed costs), so by producing 55 units it is minimizing losses (losses are smaller than fixed costs and are roughly $55).

**Hint:** To see the answers for each of these questions, draw a horizontal line at the price and see where it intersects the MC curve.

## Keep in Mind

The approach contained in short-run competitive decision making is too important for future chapters for you to have only partial knowledge. You owe it to yourself to make sure you understand this material thoroughly. The approach is used over and over again throughout economics.

Examine the figures again, and be sure you know how profit is determined in the short run for the competitive firm. Take a little time and draw your own graph for ATC, AVC, and MC. Draw a horizontal line for price, outline the profit maximizing output, and shade in profit (or loss). Do not continue on until you are confident you understand how to determine profits and costs and can show and describe a situation in which the firm is just earning normal profits. As the Core Graph below shows, you only need *two* points on the standard cost curve graph to be able to show the following situations:

- Economic profits
- Normal profits
- Economic losses, but the firm keeps operating
- Economic losses exceeding fixed costs, so the firm shuts down

**Core Graph: Short-Run Competitive Markets**

**Key Points**

When P > ATC, firms earn economic profits.

When P = ATC, firms earn normal profits.

If $AVC_{min} < P < ATC_{min}$, firms produce where MR = MC, but earn economic losses less than total fixed costs (TFC).

If $P < AVC_{min}$, firms shut down and suffer economic losses equal to total fixed costs (TFC).

Once you have these concepts down, continue on. The next section on long-run adjustments in competitive markets provides perspective on these short-run competitive decisions. ∎

# Competition: Long-Run Adjustments

## Frequently Asked Questions

Q:  How is the long run defined?

A:  In the long run, all factors of production are variable, including the ability to exit or enter an industry.

Q:  How are profits and losses long-run signals to other firms?

A:  When the firms in an industry earn economic profits in the short run, this attracts new firms to the industry, reducing product price until firms are just earning normal profits. A corresponding adjustment occurs when the firms in an industry suffer short-term economic losses: Some firms leave the industry, thus raising prices until the remaining firms are again earning normal returns.

**Q: How do competitive markets serve the public interest?**

A: Competitive markets serve the public interest by ensuring that firms price their products at their marginal cost, which also equals $LRATC_{min}$. Therefore, the quantity of products consumers want is provided at the lowest possible opportunity cost ($LRATC_{min}$). This is shown in Figure 4.

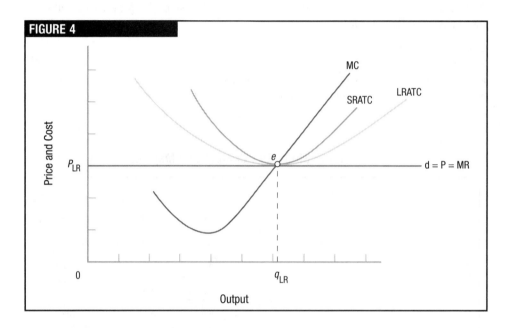

**FIGURE 4**

**Q: What are increasing cost, decreasing cost, and constant cost industries?**

A: An industry may be an increasing cost industry (average total costs increase in the long run as more output is produced), a decreasing cost industry (average total costs decrease in the long run as more output is produced), or a constant cost industry (average total costs remain constant in the long run even as output is increased) depending on the industry's precise structure, the current state of technology, and the degree of economies and diseconomies of scale.

### Core Equation: Competitive Market Efficiencies

| | Key Idea |
|---|---|
| $P = MR = MC = SRATC_{min} = LRATC_{min}$ | Economists consider competitive markets the benchmark by which all other market structures are compared. Consumers get those products they value the most (as determined by price) at the lowest possible resource or opportunity cost: $MC = SRATC_{min} = LRATC_{min}$. |

## Key Point to Remember

Entry and exit are unrestricted in competitive markets. As a result, short-run profits and losses act as signals to existing firms and potential entrants. In the long run, economic profits encourage entry and economic losses encourage exit by existing firms. These dynamic movements ensure that firms in competitive markets only earn normal (zero economic) profits in the long run. Economists find the long-run dynamics of competitive markets a thing of beauty. The analysis shows why competitive markets are the standard by which other market structures are compared.

---

# Competition: Long-Run Adjustments Quick Check

## Circle the Correct Answer

1. (T/F) In the long run, competitive markets are both productively and allocatively efficient.
2. (T/F) In an increasing cost industry, expansion leads to upward pressure on inputs such as raw materials, leading to higher prices and costs.
3. What will happen in the long run in Figure 5?
   a. Short-run profits will encourage more firms to enter the market, and they will earn economic profits.
   b. Short-run profits will encourage more firms to enter the market, and they will earn normal profits.
   c. Short-run losses will encourage some firms to leave the market, and the remaining firms will earn economic profits.
   d. Short-run losses will encourage some firms to leave the market, and the remaining firms will earn normal profits.

4. In the long run, the individual competitive firm in Figure 5 will earn
   a. economic profits equal to $(MC \times P_0) - (ATC \times P_L)$.
   b. economic profits equal to $0P_0aq_0$.
   c. economic losses.
   d. zero economic profits.
5. When a competitive market is in long-run equilibrium, price (P) is *not* equal to which of the following terms?
   a. MC
   b. $LRATC_{min}$
   c. MR
   d. $SRATC_{min}$

Score: _____

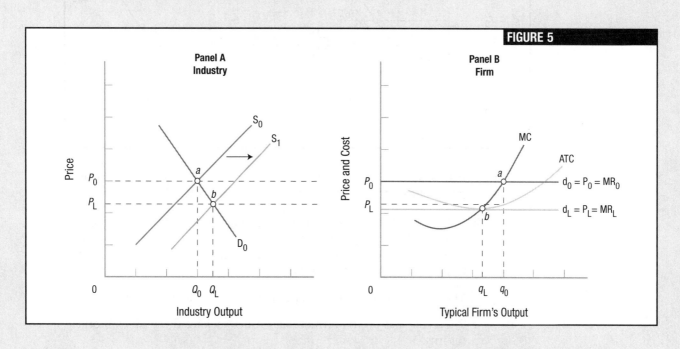

**FIGURE 5**

Panel A
Industry

Panel B
Firm

### If You Got All 5 Questions Correct

You seem to have the analysis down pat. Just in case you got lucky with this quick quiz, take a few moments and work through the next section, Outlining the Transition from Short Run to Long Run in Competitive Markets.

### If You Didn't Get All of Them Correct

Keep in mind that long-run adjustments in competitive markets can be some of the more difficult material to absorb in the book. It may take you several attempts to really master this material. For both short-run economic profits and losses, the transition to the long run is really stylistic analysis. In the following we break the story down into its parts. Work through this material and it should help you to get the process straight.

### Outlining the Transition from Short Run to Long Run in Competitive Markets

The transition of competitive markets from short-run to long-run equilibrium can be thought of as stylistic analysis with a series of steps. We will do this for both short-run economic profits and short-run economic losses. As you work through this section, make sure you understand the reasons for each step before you move on.

**Short-Run Economic Profits to Long-Run Normal Profits**

1. In the short run, firms earn *economic profits* and profit maximizing output is found at point *a* in Figure 6 where P = MR = MC.

2. Notice that at point *a*, the firm is producing beyond the *minimum* point on the ATC curve (point *b*). Also note that the AVC curve (grayed out) is there for reference in the short run, but it is not crucial when the firm is earning economic profits.

3. The shaded area in the short run is equal to economic profits.

4. The economic profits attract *new* firms seeking these above normal returns.

5. As new firms enter the industry, supply *expands* and price *falls*.

6. As price declines, individual firm output *falls* and economic profits *decline*.

7. Once entry is sufficient to reduce price to $P_{LR}$ (point $b$), only *normal profits* are earned and the incentive for new firms to enter no longer exists.

8. In long-run equilibrium (point $b$), P = MC = SRATC$_{min}$ = LRATC$_{min}$. Consumers get the product at the lowest possible opportunity (resource) cost.

## Short-Run Economic Losses to Long-Run Normal Profits

**FIGURE 7**

1. In the short run, firms earn *economic losses*, and loss-minimizing output is found at point $a$ in Figure 7 where P = MR = MC. Losses are smaller than fixed costs because price is above the AVC curve. So, the firm continues to produce.

2. Notice that at point $a$, the firm is producing *less* output than that associated with the *minimum* point on the ATC curve (point $b$).

3. The shaded area in the short run is equal to economic losses.

4. These economic losses lead some existing firms to *leave* the industry.

5. As these firms exit the industry, supply *falls* and price *rises*.

6. As price increases, individual firm output *grows* and economic losses *decline*.

7. Once exit is sufficient to raise price to $P_{LR}$ (point $b$), *normal profits* are earned and the incentive for firms to leave the industry no longer exists.

8. In long-run equilibrium (point $b$), P = MC = SRATC$_{min}$ = LRATC$_{min}$. Consumers get the product at the lowest possible opportunity (resource) cost.

At this point you should understand how profits and losses work as signals and why competitive markets are so efficient. Now see how you do on the questions that follow.

# Competition: Long-Run Adjustments Final Check

## Circle the Correct Answer

1. (T/F) In the long run, the price of finished goods will drop in constant cost industries.
2. Competitive markets are efficient because
   a. $P = MC = LRAVC_{min}$
   b. $P = MC = LRAFC_{min}$
   c. $P = MC = LRATC_{min}$
   d. $P = MC = LRTR_{min}$
3. What will happen in the long run in Figure 8?
   a. Short-run profits will encourage more firms to enter the market, and they will earn economic profits.
   b. Short-run profits will encourage more firms to enter the market, and they will earn normal profits.
   c. Short-run losses will encourage some firms to leave the market, and the remaining firms will earn economic profits.
   d. Short-run losses will encourage some firms to leave the market, and the remaining firms will earn normal profits.

4. In the long run, the individual competitive firm in Figure 6 will
   a. earn economic profits.
   b. earn normal profits.
   c. earn zero profits.
   d. incur economic losses.
5. When a competitive market is in long-run equilibrium, price (P) is equal to which of the following terms?
   a. MR
   b. $LRATC_{min}$
   c. MC
   d. all of the above

Score: _____

Answers: 1. F; 2. c; 3. d; 4. b; 5. d.

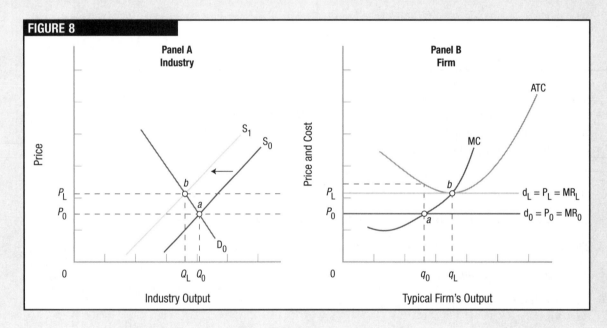

FIGURE 8

Panel A
Industry

Panel B
Firm

You should have gotten all of these correct. If not, you should review this material one more time. ∎

| | Consider These Hints, Tips, and Reminders | **STEP 4** |

**1.** What you must take away from this chapter:

- Profits are maximized by producing output where MR = MC.
- In the short run,
  - ☐ If P > ATC, the firm makes an economic profit.
  - ☐ If P < ATC, the firm makes losses.
  - ☐ If AVC < P < ATC, the firm produces output but makes losses.
  - ☐ If P < AVC, the firm shuts down and minimizes losses (losses equal fixed costs).
- In the long run,
  - ☐ Short-run economic profits encourage entry, and short-run losses result in exit by some existing firms.
  - ☐ Entry and exit drive profits to normal levels.
- Competitive markets are the benchmark to which all other market structures are compared. Competitive markets serve the public interest because consumers get what they want at the lowest price; P = MC = $SRATC_{min}$ = $LRATC_{min}$.

**2.** Market structure analysis is a very powerful analytic approach. You look at the industry's characteristics and forecast how its firms will determine price and output. This may seem straightforward when markets are competitive, but it gets a little more complex when other market structures are considered. Keep in mind that profits are maximized when MR = MC. This will be how you analyze all other market structures as well.

| | |
|---|---|
| ███ | Do the Homework for Chapter 8<br>Competition |

# STEP 5

Instructor _____ Time _____ Student _____

**Use the answer key below to record your answers to these homework questions.**

| | | | |
|---|---|---|---|
| 1. _____ | 6. _____ | 11. _____ | 16. _____ |
| 2. _____ | 7. _____ | 12. _____ | 17. _____ |
| 3. _____ | 8. _____ | 13. _____ | 18. _____ |
| 4. _____ | 9. _____ | 14. _____ | 19. _____ |
| 5. _____ | 10. _____ | 15. _____ | 20. _____ |

1. Which of the following is not an assumption of competitive markets?
   a. homogeneous products in this market
   b. a large number of buyers and sellers
   c. barriers to entry or exit
   d. good knowledge by both buyers and sellers

2. Which of the following markets is likely to be the most competitive?
   a. cable television
   b. automobile and truck manufacturing
   c. oil refining
   d. farm commodities

3. In a competitive market, firms will
   a. reduce their prices to increase their market share.
   b. advertise the uniqueness of their products.
   c. produce at the lowest possible cost to maximize per unit profits.
   d. generally accept the market price as a given.

4. The demand curve facing a competitive firm is
   a. upward sloping.
   b. highly inelastic.
   c. horizontal.
   d. downward sloping.

Use Figure HW-1 to answer questions 5–15.

5. If the demand curve facing the competitive firm in the figure is $d_2$, the competitive price will be:

6. f the demand curve facing the competitive firm in the figure is $d_2$, profits earned by this firm will be:

7. If the demand curve facing the competitive firm in the figure is $d_2$, total variable costs for this firm will be:

8. If the demand curve facing the competitive firm in the figure is $d_2$, total costs for this firm will be:

9. If the demand curve facing the competitive firm in the figure is $d_2$, total profits for this firm will be:

10. If the price falls below _____, the firm will shut down.

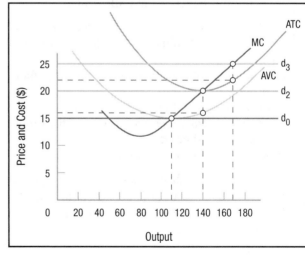

**HW-1**

11. If this firm represents the typical firm in the industry, long-run equilibrium price will be:

12. If this firm is producing 140 units of output, average fixed cost will be:

13. If in the short run the equilibrium price for the industry is $17, what will happen in this industry in the long run?
    a. Short-run profits will encourage more firms to enter the market, and industry output will expand.
    b. Short-run profits will discourage new firms from entering, since the competitive pressures are so intense.
    c. Short-run losses will encourage some firms to leave the industry, and industry and individual firm output will decline.
    d. Short-run losses will encourage some firms to leave the industry, and industry output will decline, but the remaining firms will earn normal profits.

14. If the short-run equilibrium price for the industry is $25, what will happen in this industry in the long run?
    a. Short-run profits will encourage more firms to enter the market, and industry output will expand, but individual firm output and profit will decline.
    b. Short-run profits will discourage new firms from entering, since the competitive pressures are so intense.
    c. Short-run profits will encourage new firms to enter the industry, but the intense competition will cause industry and individual firm output to decline.
    d. Short-run losses will encourage some firms to leave the industry, and industry output will decline, but the remaining firms will earn normal profits.

15. The short-run supply curve for this firm will be the marginal cost curve above a price of
    a. $10.
    c. $15.
    c. $20.
    d. There is no supply curve for this firm.

16. For a competitive firm in the short run, if marginal revenue is greater than marginal costs, then the firm should
    a. shut the plant and move the capital into a more profitable industry.
    b. decrease production until MR = MC.
    c. not do anything because if MR > MC, profits must be maximized.
    d. increase production until MR = MC.

17. For a competitive firm in the short run, if marginal revenue is less than marginal costs, then the firm should
    a. shut the plant and move the capital into a more profitable industry.
    b. decrease production until MR = MC.
    c. not do anything because if MR > MC, profits must be maximized.
    d. increase production until MR = MC.

18. For a competitive firm, if marginal revenue equals marginal cost which equals average total cost, and this is just equal to average revenue or price, then the firm is

    a. making economic profits.
    b. making such large losses that it needs to close the firm.
    c. making normal profits.
    d. not producing enough output to make a profit.

19. The most important reason that competitive firms only earn normal profits in the long run is because
    a. supply cannot exceed demand.
    b. of easy entry and exit into and out of the industry.
    c. corporate income taxes reduce profits to zero.
    d. fixed costs are extremely low for most industries.

20. To maximize profits, a competitive firm
    a. produces where average total costs are minimized.
    b. sets a price that maximizes total revenue.
    c. produces an output where marginal revenue is just equal to total costs.
    d. produces an output where marginal revenue is just equal to marginal costs.

| | **Use the ExamPrep to Get Ready for Exams** | **STEP 6** |

This sheet (front and back) is designed to help you prepare for your exams. The chapter has been boiled down to its key concepts. You are asked to answer questions, define terms, draw graphs, and, if you wish, add summaries of class notes.

## Market Structure Analysis

List the characteristics of each market structure in the following table.

| Competition | Monopolistic Competition | Oligopoly | Monopoly |
|---|---|---|---|
| | | | |
| | | | |
| | | | |
| | | | |
| | | | |

## Competition: Short-Run Decisions

Define marginal revenue:

Why is marginal revenue a straight line at the market price for the competitive firm?

## Profit Maximizing Output

Use the grid below to draw the following short-run cost curves:

- Average variable costs
- Average total costs
- Marginal costs

(Hint: Keep in mind that the minimum point on the AVC curve comes at a lower output than the minimum point on the ATC curve. Also, the marginal cost curve goes through both minimum points.)

Draw in a demand curve for this firm that is above the minimum point on the ATC curve and label it $d_{profits}$. Now cross-hatch in total profits and label the area "profits."

Draw in a demand curve for this firm that is just equal to the minimum point on the ATC curve and label it $d_{normal\ profits}$. Indicate the point where the firm earns economic profits. Does this firm earn a profit at all? Explain:

## Loss Minimizing Output

Use the grid below to draw the following short-run cost curves:

■ Average variable costs
■ Average total costs
■ Marginal costs

(Hint: Keep in mind that the minimum point on the AVC curve comes at a lower output than the minimum point on the ATC curve. Also, the marginal cost curve goes through both minimum points.)

Draw in a demand curve for this firm that is below the minimum point on the ATC curve and label it $d_{losses}$. Now cross-hatch in total losses and label the area "losses." Why does the firm continue to operate if it incurs losses?

Use the two figures you have drawn to explain why the marginal cost curve above the minimum point on the AVC curve is the firm's supply curve.

## Competition: Long-Run Adjustments

Explain what happens in a competitive industry in the long run when firms are earning economic profits in the short run.

Explain what happens in a competitive industry in the long run when firms are earning economic losses in the short run.

Why in both instances do firms only earn normal profits in the long run?

Explain why the competitive market is the ideal market structure.

# Additional Study Help Chapterwide Practice Questions

## Matching

Match the description with the corresponding term.

___ 1. Market structure
___ 2. Competitive markets
___ 3. Profit maximization
___ 4. Shutdown point
___ 5. Increasing cost industry
___ 6. Decreasing cost industry
___ 7. Constant cost industry

a. Losses exceed total fixed costs and revenues are not even enough to cover variable costs.

b. An industry that expands in the long run without enjoying economies or suffering diseconomies.

c. According to this principle, firms will continue to produce and sell output until marginal revenue, the change in total revenue that results from the sale of one more unit of the product, equals marginal cost.

d. When the firms in an industry expand or new firms enter it, added demands push up the price of raw materials and labor. These diseconomies cause costs to increase.

e. Economists categorize industries as competitive, monopolistically competitive, oligopolistic, or monopolistic.

f. An industry that enjoys economies as it expands, thus reducing average production costs.

g. Many buyers and sellers but none large enough to influence product prices, homogeneous products, complete information for buyers and sellers, no barriers to entry or exit, and thus no long term economic profits.

## Fill-In

Circle the word(s) in parentheses that complete the sentence.

1. When just a few firms that are mutually interdependent control an industry, the industry is representative of a(n) (competition, monopolistic competition, oligopoly, monopoly) _____ market structure. When many firms exist in an industry with standardized products, the industry represents (competition, monopolistic competition, oligopoly, monopoly) _____ market structure. A one-firm industry is a(n) (oligopoly, monopoly) _____.

2. An important assumption of competitive markets is (differentiated products, no barriers to entry or exit) _____, while for monopolistically competitive markets, an important assumption is (differentiated products, no barriers to entry or exit) _____.

3. For the competitive firm, marginal revenue is equal to (profit, price, output) _____, and profit maximizing output is found where marginal revenue equals (price, marginal cost) _____.

4. When market price is greater than the minimum of average total costs, the firm earns (normal profits, economic profits, economic losses) _____. If market price falls below the minimum of average total costs, but average variable costs are covered, the firm earns (normal profits, economic profits, economic losses) _____; but when average variable costs cannot be covered, the firm (closes its doors, minimizes losses by producing and selling some output where MR = MC) _____. When market price is just equal to the minimum of average total costs, the firm can expect to earn (normal profits, economic profits, economic losses) _____.

5. Short-term (normal profits, economic profits, economic losses) _____ attract firms into the industry, resulting in (normal profits, economic profits, economic losses) _____ over the long run. Short-term (normal profits, economic profits, economic losses) _____ cause the industry to contract, causing market price to (rise, fall, remain the same) _____, and ultimately lead to (normal profits, economic profits, economic losses) _____ over the long run.

6. Competitive industries exhibit (allocative, productive) _____ efficiency because products are produced at the lowest opportunity cost and also achieve (allocative, productive) _____ efficiency because consumers get the products they want at marginal cost.

## True-False

Circle the correct answer.

T / F   1. Competitive markets have virtually no barriers to entry or exit.

T / F    2. The individual firms in an oligopoly have little control over the price of their products.

T / F    3. In a competitive market, an individual firm's demand curve is vertical.

T / F    4. If a company earns an additional $700 in revenue by selling 5 additional units, its marginal revenue is $140.

T / F    5. If a bicycle company in a competitive market finds it can sell as many mountain bikes as it produces at $400 each, it will definitely want to produce and sell as many mountain bikes as it can.

T / F    6. A firm in a competitive market will maximize its profits by producing a level of output where marginal revenue equals marginal cost.

T / F    7. A firm that is earning zero economic profits is not earning any profits at all.

T / F    8. As soon as a firm begins to suffer economic losses, it can be expected to shut down its production facilities.

T / F    9. To minimize losses, a competitive firm will shut down its plant once prices fall below the minimum point on the average variable costs curve.

T / F    10. A competitive firm's short-run supply curve is the marginal cost curve above the minimum point on the average variable costs curve.

T / F    11. In a competitive market, individual firms may earn economic profits in the short run, but they will earn zero economic profits in the long run.

T / F    12. If the individual firms in a competitive market are earning normal profits, this will draw new firms into the market in the long run.

T / F    13. Competitive markets are both productively and allocatively efficient.

T / F    14. Easy entry and exit ensure that only normal profits are earned by competitive firms in the long run.

T / F    15. A decreasing cost industry enjoys certain economies as it expands its output, thereby reducing the price of finished products.

## Multiple Choice

Circle the correct answer.

1. In what way do competitive markets, as described by Adam Smith, resemble the realm of biological life, as described by Charles Darwin?
   a. Money is essential for determining the courses of both.
   b. In both, minor adjustments take thousands of years to complete.
   c. The best place to observe both is the Galapagos Islands.
   d. In both, only the most efficient survive.

2. What does market structure analysis allow economists to do?
   a. Predict the long-range viability of various products.
   b. Predict the pricing and production behavior of firms in various industries.
   c. Understand the physical layout of stores and other marketplaces.
   d. Predict consumer behavior in various markets.

3. Which of the following factors are not relevant to determining the market structure of a particular industry?
   a. the size of the industry in terms of total revenues
   b. the extent of barriers to market exit and entry
   c. the extent to which individual sellers can control prices
   d. the number of firms in the industry

4. The benchmark for comparing other market structures is which of the following?
   a. competition
   b. monopolistic competition
   c. oligopoly
   d. monopoly

5. Which market structure features many buyers and sellers, differentiated products, no barriers to entry or exit, no long-run economic profits, and some control over price on the part of individual sellers?
   a. competition
   b. monopolistic competition
   c. oligopoly
   d. monopoly

6. Which market structure features few firms, mutually dependent decision making, substantial barriers to entry, the potential for long-run economic profits, and shared market power, with considerable control over price on the part of individual sellers?
   a. competition
   b. monopolistic competition
   c. oligopoly
   d. monopoly

7. Which of the following is not assumed of competitive markets?
   a. The market contains many buyers and sellers.
   b. Firms have no potential for long-term economic profits.
   c. Individual sellers have some control over market prices.
   d. Homogeneous products are offered for sale.

8. Which of the following is *not* assumed of monopolies?
   a. Firms have no potential for long-run economic profits.
   b. The industry contains only one firm.
   c. There are major and effective barriers to market entry.
   d. The individual firm has substantial control over the price of its products.

9. An individual firm is a price taker if
   a. it has some control over the sales price of its product.
   b. it has complete control over the sales price of its product.
   c. market prices are irrelevant to its production decisions.
   d. it has little choice but to sell its product at the established market price.

10. The individual firms in a competitive market produce goods that are
    a. highly differentiated.
    b. moderately differentiated.
    c. homogeneous, or standardized.
    d. typically of low quality.

11. In a competitive market, a firm
    a. can be expected to sell its product for less than the market price.
    b. could conceivably sell its product for less than the market price, but would normally have no reason to do so.
    c. can maximize its profit by setting its sales price above the market price.
    d. will rarely pay attention to the market price in setting the price of its own product.

12. Why are the individual firms in a competitive market price takers?
    a. The industry has so many firms, and each is so small, that none have much control over the price of their products.
    b. The managers in such firms rarely have time to figure out their own prices, so they just go with the prices the market sets.
    c. The industry has so few firms, and each is so large, that none of them has much control over the price of their products.

d. High barriers to entering or exiting the market force individual firms to accept the market price.

13. Which of the following industries is least likely to be in a competitive market structure?
    a. soybeans
    b. semiconductors
    c. military aircraft
    d. sheet metal

14. Why do firms in competitive markets have little control over the price of their products?
    a. The government regulates the prices of such firms.
    b. Competitive markets are dominated by one or two giant corporations, which largely determine product price.
    c. There are so many small firms in competitive markets that none can have much influence over product price.
    d. High exit barriers prevent such firms from leaving the market.

15. In the short run, which factors are usually regarded as fixed?
    a. number of workers employed and the quantity of raw materials purchased
    b. plant size and the number of firms in the industry
    c. number of workers employed and the number of shifts the plant operates
    d. total costs and total revenues

16. Marginal revenue is equal to
    a. change in revenue over change in quantity sold.
    b. price per unit times quantity sold.
    c. change in revenue over change in price.
    d. total revenue over quantity sold.

17. For firms in competitive industries, marginal revenue is equivalent to
    a. total revenue.
    b. change in quantity sold.
    c. profit per unit.
    d. price per unit.

18. If price is above the minimum point on a firm's ATC curve in the short run, the firm will
    a. incur economic losses.
    b. earn normal profits.
    c. earn economic profits.
    d. be producing at a level of output in which MC exceeds MR.

19. In Figure MC-1, if the firm were to expand its production from 84 to 87 units of output, it would be
    a. operating at a level of optimal productive efficiency.

b. reducing its profits by producing where marginal cost exceeds price.

c. increasing its profits by producing and selling more units.

d. realizing economies of scale by increasing its output.

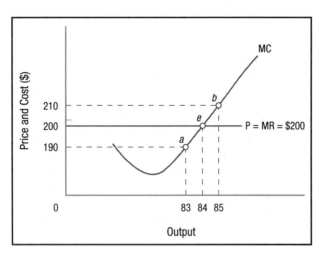

**MC-1**

20. In a competitive industry, a profit maximizing firm will continue producing and selling output until
   a. marginal revenue equals average cost.
   b. total revenue equals marginal cost.
   c. marginal revenue equals marginal cost.
   d. average cost exceeds marginal revenue.

21. When a competitive firm is earning normal economic profits
   a. it is earning zero economic profits.
   b. other firms can be expected to enter the industry.
   c. existing firms can be expected to leave the industry.
   d. it is earning economic profits greater than zero.

22. A competitive firm seeking to minimize its losses in the short run should shut down its plant as soon as
   a. it begins suffering economic losses.
   b. total losses exceed total variable costs.
   c. total losses exceed total fixed costs.
   d. profit per unit falls below zero.

23. For a competitive firm, what does the marginal cost (MC) curve above the minimum point on the average variable costs (AVC) curve represent?
   a. the firm's short-run supply curve
   b. the firm's long-run demand curve
   c. the firm's average variable costs curve
   d. the firm's short-run demand curve

Use Figure MC-2 to answer questions 24–28. Figure MC-2 portrays the cost curves for a competitive firm in the short run.

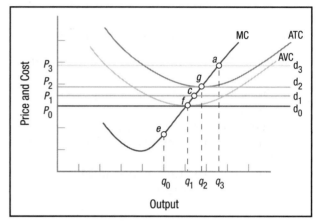

**MC-2**

24. If the market price is $P_3$ and the firm produces $q_3$ units of output, the firm will
   a. earn economic profits.
   b. earn normal profits.
   c. incur a loss, though not enough to shut down.
   d. incur a loss greater than fixed costs, so it will shut down.

25. If the market price is $P_2$ and the firm produces $q_2$ units, the firm will
   a. earn economic profits.
   b. earn normal profits.
   c. incur a loss.
   d. incur a loss equal to fixed costs.

26. If the market price is $P_0$ and the firm produces $q_1$ units, the firm will be at the point of
   a. economic profits.
   b. normal profits.
   c. zero economic profits.
   d. shutdown.

27. Competitive firms will never produce at point
   a. $g$.
   b. $a$.
   c. $f$.
   d. $e$.

28. At point $c$, firms will
   a. reap a normal profit.
   b. face a loss but continue producing because some fixed costs are covered.

c. face a loss and shut down because variable costs are not covered.

d. face a loss and shut down because competitive firms should never incur a loss.

29. If the firms in an industry are earning economic profits, what happens in the long run?
a. Some existing firms will exit the industry.
b. New firms can be expected to enter the industry.
c. There will be no pressure for firms to either enter or exit the industry.
d. Total revenues in the industry can be expected to fall.

30. If the firms in an industry are earning economic losses, what happens in the long run?
a. Some existing firms can be expected to exit the industry.
b. New firms can be expected to enter the industry.
c. There will be no pressure for firms either to enter or to exit the industry.
d. Total revenues in the industry can be expected to rise.

31. In the long run, the firms in a competitive industry can be expected to
a. suffer economic losses.
b. earn economic profits.
c. set their prices above market prices.
d. earn normal profits.

32. If a large number of firms, having suffered economic losses, exit a competitive market, which of the following would we *not* expect to take place?
a. a shift to the left of the industry supply curve
b. the establishment of a new equilibrium at a higher level of output
c. a reduction of the losses suffered by firms remaining in the market
d. the establishment of a new equilibrium at a higher price level

33. What does productive efficiency mean?
a. The market allocates the production of various goods in accord with consumer wants.
b. A market contains the minimum number of producers feasible.
c. Goods are produced and sold to consumers at their lowest possible opportunity cost.
d. The market allocates the production of various goods in accord with government directives.

34. What does allocative efficiency mean?
a. A market allocates the production of various goods in accord with consumer wants.

b. The market contains the minimum number of producers feasible.
c. Goods are produced and sold to consumers at their lowest possible opportunity cost.
d. The market allocates the production of various goods in accord with government directives.

35. When a competitive market is in long-run equilibrium, price (P) is *not* equal to which of the following terms?
a. MC
b. $LRATC_{min}$
c. MR
d. TC

36. In a competitive market, the most efficient level of production occurs when
a. P = MR
b. MR = AVC
c. $MC = LRATC_{min}$
d. all of the above

37. In an increasing cost industry,
a. as the industry expands, the price of necessary inputs falls.
b. as the industry expands, the price of necessary inputs rises.
c. as the industry expands, the price of its finished goods falls.
d. industry size does not affect the price of inputs or of its finished goods.

38. In a constant cost industry,
a. as the industry expands, the price of necessary inputs falls.
b. as the industry expands, the price of necessary inputs rises.
c. as the industry expands, the price of its finished goods falls.
d. industry size does not affect the price of inputs or of its finished goods.

39. Which of the following factors does *not* affect whether an industry is an increasing cost, constant cost, or decreasing cost industry?
a. consumer demand for the industry's products
b. the nature of economies of scale
c. the extent of diseconomies of scale
d. the current state of technology

## Essay-Problem

Answer in the space provided.

The questions below are challenging. Don't get discouraged if your answers are not always the same as those we suggest. Use these as another way to assess your progress, but more important, to learn more about the competitive model.

1. Why do economists put industries into market structure categories?

2. Why does the competitive model require that there are many buyers and many sellers?

3. Why is the demand curve horizontal for a firm in a competitive market?

4. Why are costs so important for a competitive firm?

5. The profit maximizing rule for a competitive firm is to produce until marginal revenue equals marginal cost. What would happen if the competitive firm produced where marginal cost was lower than marginal revenue? Marginal cost was higher than marginal revenue?

6. In the long run, why are economic profits signals?

7. Why are competitive markets in the public interest?

8. Give an example of an increasing cost industry and a decreasing cost industry, and explain why they are so.

9. Do firms like to be in competitive markets?

10. In the long run, competitive markets squeeze out economic profits. Can any competitive firm hope to generate economic profits in the long run, or is it just dreaming?

## What's Next

This chapter gave you an introduction to market structure, how competitive markets determine output in the short and long runs, and why economists use the competitive model as a measuring stick for all other market structures. Now you can go on to these other market structures and see why they do not achieve the production and allocative efficiencies of competitive markets.

## Answers to Chapterwide Practice Questions

### Matching

1. e     3. c     5. d     7. b
2. g     4. a     6. f

### Fill-In

1. oligopoly, competition, monopoly
2. no barriers to entry or exit, differentiated products
3. price, marginal cost
4. economic profits, economic losses, closes its doors, normal profits
5. economic profits, normal profits, economic losses, rise, normal profits
6. productive, allocative

### True-False

1. T     5. F     9. T      13. T
2. F     6. T     10. T     14. T
3. F     7. F     11. T     15. T
4. T     8. F     12. F

### Multiple Choice

1. d     11. b     21. a     31. d
2. b     12. a     22. c     32. b
3. a     13. c     23. a     33. c
4. a     14. c     24. a     34. a
5. b     15. b     25. b     35. d
6. c     16. a     26. d     36. c
7. c     17. d     27. d     37. b
8. a     18. c     28. b     38. d
9. d     19. b     29. b     39. a
10. c    20. c     30. a

## Essay-Problem

1. Grouping industries into a few categories allows economists to predict the pricing and production behavior of firms in that industry.

2. The competitive model requires that buyers and sellers be price takers: No one consumer or firm has any power to influence the price. This requirement of the model is best met when there are many buyers and many sellers. We will see in later chapters what happens when a buyer or seller has some pricing power.

3. A horizontal demand curve means that the firm is a price taker. It must simply accept the established market price, at which price it is assumed the firm can sell as much of its product as it wants. If the individual firm were to try setting its price above the market price, consumers would not buy anything from it, since other firms are offering the same product at the lower market price. Conceivably, the firm could set its price below the market price, but it would have no reason to do so, since it can sell all the product it wants at the higher market price.

4. The profit equation is: profit = total revenues minus total costs. In competitive markets, firms have no power to set the prices that determine revenues. All they can do is adjust output to maximize profits.

5. If marginal cost was lower than marginal revenue, the firm could continue to hire more workers (variable inputs) and still come out ahead. The amount paid out to the additional worker is less than the amount added to revenues, so profit will rise. If marginal cost was higher than marginal revenue, the cost of each additional worker would be greater than the additional revenue brought in, so profits would fall; the firm would be worse off than if it did nothing more.

6. Economic profits tell firms outside the industry that there are profit possibilities greater than the opportunity cost of capital. Economic profits attract new market entrants the way honey attracts bees.

7. The competitive market is productively efficient. Products are produced and sold to consumers at their lowest possible opportunity cost. Competitive markets are also allocatively efficient. If output falls below equilibrium, marginal cost is less than price. Consumers place a higher value on that product than it costs to produce. Therefore, society will be better off if more of it is in the market. If output is above equilibrium, marginal cost exceeds price, and we will be better off if those resources are used to produce another product more highly valued by society. But competitive markets ensure that equilibrium is at the most efficient point.

8. In an increasing cost industry, as total industry output rises, the average total costs of production similarly rise, thereby raising the price of the finished products. Industries depending on very specialized forms of labor known only to a few people—many sorts of indigenous artwork, for instance—fit into this category. This sort of specialized labor is in such short supply that its price will rise dramatically if the demand for some form of indigenous art should rise, thus driving up the average costs of production.

    In a decreasing costs industry, as total industry output rises, average total costs of production will fall. This is because the industry begins to realize economies of scale as it increases its total output. The semiconductor industry is a good example of a decreasing cost industry: As the demand for semiconductors has soared, new methods for producing them inexpensively come into play, thus decreasing the average total costs of semiconductors. Most manufacturing processes exhibit economies of scale.

9. In general, no. Firms in competitive markets have no power over price; to be profitable, all they can do is produce the profit maximizing output and only earn normal returns in the long run. Firms would prefer to have some pricing power and be under less cost pressure and have the opportunity to earn economic profits longer.

10. In reality, firms might generate long-run economic profits if they continually are the low-cost producer. Prospects are not great for a firm to be able to do this over the long run, but it can happen. Our competitive model has such restrictive assumptions that economic profits are not possible in the long run.

# Monopoly 9

AP Photo/Jens Meyer, file

## If Competition Serves the Public Interest, Why Do Firms Want to Be Monopolies?

Monopoly is the other extreme on the market structure spectrum, opposite from the competitive market ideal. You will put to work what you have learned in the previous chapter on competitive markets to analyze monopoly markets. Unlike competitive firms, which are price takers, monopolists are *price makers*. Their monopoly power allows monopolists to adjust their output in ways that give them significant control over product price. You will see that while competitive markets are in the public interest, monopolies definitely are not. The chapter will show you what can be done to alleviate this situation.

| This Is What You Need to Know | STEP 1 |
|---|---|

**After studying this chapter you should be able to**

■ Describe the characteristics of a monopoly and monopoly power.

■ Describe the ways in which monopoly power is maintained.

■ Use monopoly market analysis to determine the equilibrium level of output and price for a monopoly.

■ Describe the differences between monopoly and competition.

- Describe the different forms of price discrimination.
- Describe the different approaches to regulating a natural monopoly.
- Relate the history and purpose of antitrust legislation to monopoly analysis.
- Apply concentration ratios and the Herfindahl-Hirshman index to analyze the likelihood of regulation in a given market.
- Describe the conditions of a contestable market and its significance.

## STEP 2     Review the Key Terms

**Monopoly:** A one-firm industry with no close product substitutes and with substantial barriers to entry.

**Monopoly power:** A firm with monopoly power has some control over price.

**Economies of scale:** As the firm expands in size, average total costs decline.

**Rent seeking:** Resources expended to protect a monopoly position. These are used for such activities as lobbying, extending patents, and restricting the number of licenses permitted.

**X-inefficiency:** Protected from competitive pressures, monopolies do not have to act efficiently. Spending on corporate jets, travel, and other perks of business represent x-inefficiency.

**Price discrimination:** Charging different consumer groups different prices for the same product.

**Natural monopoly:** Large economies of scale mean that the minimum efficient scale of operations is roughly equal to market demand.

**Marginal cost pricing rule:** Regulators would prefer to have natural monopolists price where P = MC, but this would result in losses (long term) because ATC > MC. Thus, regulators often must use an average cost pricing rule.

**Average cost pricing rule:** Requires a regulated monopolist to produce and sell output where price equals average total costs. This permits the regulated monopolist to earn a normal return on investment over the long term and so remain in business.

**Rate of return regulation:** Permits product pricing that allows the firm to earn a normal return on capital invested in the firm.

**Price caps:** Maximum price at which a regulated firm can sell its product. They are often flexible enough to allow for changing cost conditions.

**Antitrust law:** Laws designed to maintain competition and prevent monopolies from developing.

**Concentration ratio:** The share of industry shipments or sales accounted for by the top four or eight firms.

**Herfindahl-Hirshman index (HHI):** A way of measuring industry concentration, equal to the sum of the squares of market shares for all firms in the industry.

**Contestable markets:** Markets that look monopolistic but have entry costs so low that the sheer threat of entry keeps prices low.

**Network externalities:** Markets in which the network becomes more valuable as more people are connected to the network.

| Work Through the Chapter Tutorials | STEP 3 |

# Monopoly Markets

## Frequently Asked Questions

**Q: How are monopolies defined?**

A: For economists, a monopoly is defined by three key characteristics. First, the market has just one seller; the monopolistic firm *is* the industry. Second, no close substitutes exist for the monopolist's product, so consumers cannot easily substitute other products for the product sold by the monopolist. Third, significant barriers to entry keep other firms from entering the industry. This means the monopolist faces no competition, even in the long run.

**Q: For the monopolist, how are price and output linked?**

A: Monopoly power is the degree to which a firm can control the price of its product by adjusting output. Competitive firms are price takers, meaning that they have no monopoly power; the prices for their products are determined by competitive markets. Monopolists, in contrast, are price makers. They enjoy considerable monopoly power and much freedom in deciding what to charge for their products.

**Q: Where does monopoly power come from?**

A: Monopoly power is caused by significant barriers to entry.

**Q: Why are economies of scale a barrier to entry?**

A: The economies of scale in an industry can be so large that demand will support only one firm in what economists would refer to as a "natural monopoly." Utilities have traditionally been considered natural monopolists because of the high fixed costs associated with power plants.

**Q: Can control over an important production input be a barrier to entry?**

A: If a firm owns or has control over an important input into the production process, that firm can keep potential rivals out of the market.

**Q: Can government provide barriers to entry?**

A: Government provides some barriers to market entry. For instance, it may grant a franchise to a firm, giving permission to provide specific goods or services, while prohibiting others from doing so. Patents protect firms and individuals that invent new products and processes. Copyrights give firms or individuals the exclusive right to produce intellectual products for a long period of time.

**Q: How is product price determined in a monopolistic market?**

A: Because the monopolist constitutes the entire industry, it faces a downward sloping demand curve. Product price is determined in a monopoly by how much the monopolist wishes to produce. This contrasts with the competitive firm, which can sell all it wishes, but only at the market determined price.

**Q: How does a monopolist maximize profit?**

A: Like the competitive firm, the monopolist maximizes its profit at output where MR = MC. This is shown in Figure 1. Because of the monopolist's downward sloping demand curve, marginal revenue is less than price. To determine the monopolist's profit maximizing price, extend a vertical line through the point where MR = MC (point $e$) to the demand curve (point $a$). This intersection determines the price ($P_M$) to be found on the vertical axis. The monopolist's profit equals the difference between this price and average total costs ($a - b$), multiplied by the number of units sold ($Q_M$).

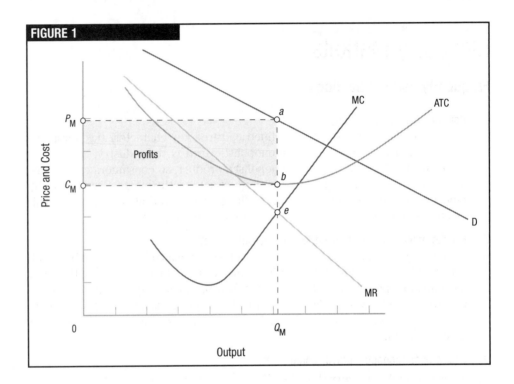

**FIGURE 1**

**Q: Do monopolists always make economic profits?**

A: Monopolies are not guaranteed economic profits. If a monopolist's profit maximizing price is lower than its average total costs, it will suffer a loss. Just like competitive firms, as long as price exceeds average variable costs, the monopolist will minimize its losses in the short run by continuing to produce. But if price should fall below average variable costs, the monopolist will shut down. If these losses persist, the monopolist will exit the industry in the long run.

**Q: How does monopoly output and price compare to competitive markets?**

A: Monopoly output is lower and monopoly price is higher. Monopolies earn economic profits by reducing consumer surplus.

**Q: What is the deadweight loss from monopoly?**

A: The loss to society from monopoly output and pricing is known as deadweight loss, or welfare loss. This is shown as area $cab$ in Figure 2.

**Q: What is rent-seeking behavior?**

A: To maintain their advantageous position, monopolists engage in rent-seeking behavior. They undertake a variety of activities to avoid competition, such

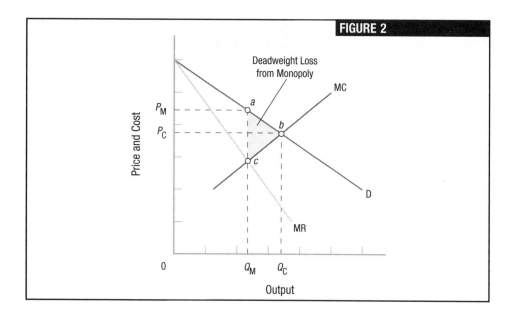

**FIGURE 2**

Deadweight Loss from Monopoly

as hiring lawyers and lobbyists to obtain favorable treatment, such as tariff protection from Congress. All these activities are inefficient, in that they shift resources from one group to another without producing a useful good or service, and so rent seeking represents an added loss to society from monopoly.

**Q:**    What is x-inefficiency?

**A:**    Some economists argue that monopolies do not operate efficiently because they are protected from competitive pressures; this is known as x-inefficiency. Management can offer itself perks, for instance, without worrying about whether costs are kept at efficient levels.

## Key Points to Remember

- A monopolist *is* the industry, there are no good substitutes for the monopolist's product, and substantial barriers to entry exist.
- Because monopoly demand is downward sloping, MR < P.
- Monopolies are price makers and maximize profits by producing where MR = MC, but set price off the demand curve.
- Monopolies sell less output at higher prices than competitive markets.

## Monopoly Markets Quick Check

### Circle the Correct Answer

1. (T/F) Monopolists are price makers, not price takers.
2. (T/F) A natural monopoly can arise in an industry when economies of scale are so large that demand will support only a single firm.
3. (T/F) For a firm to have monopoly power, it must have nearly complete control over the price at which it sells its product.
4. (T/F) For the monopolist, MR = P.

5. Which of the following is true for a monopoly?
   a. D = MR
   b. P = MR
   c. P < MR
   d. P > MR

6. What determines the price at which a monopolist can sell its product?
   a. rules imposed by government regulatory agencies
   b. the price set by competitors
   c. the level of output at which the monopolist decides it wants to produce
   d. the monopolist's ability to earn a profit by selling at any price

7. In Figure 3, area $P_CP_Mac$ represents
   a. x-inefficiency.
   b. the maximum amount of rent-seeking behavior we might expect from this monopoly.
   c. the deadweight loss from monopoly.
   d. normal profits for the monopolist.

8. The profit maximizing output for the monopolist is found where
   a. MR = MC.
   b. MR = ATC.
   c. MR = P.
   d. ATC = P.

9. Which of the following is *not* an example of rent-seeking behavior?
   a. increasing management salaries and perks
   b. lobbying Congress for laws limiting imports
   c. hiring lawyers to extend patent protection
   d. securing a government franchise

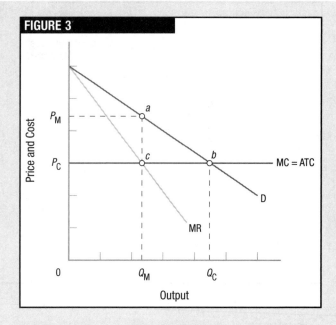

**FIGURE 3**

10. Which one of the following is *not* correct?
    a. Monopolists are price makers; competitive firms are price takers.
    b. Monopolists produce less at higher prices than competitive firms.
    c. Monopolists tend to be inefficient because they do not face the same market pressures as competitive firms.
    d. Monopolists never lose money, while competitive firms may do so.

Score: ____

Answers: 1. T; 2. T; 3. F; 4. F; 5. d; 6. c; 7. b; 8. a; 9. a; 10. d

## If You Got 9 or 10 Correct

You have a good start on monopoly. The important concepts are monopoly pricing and output decisions and the differences between monopoly and competition. Make sure you get this and then go on to the next section. There is a lot to learn in this first section, so an extra review might be helpful.

## If You Didn't Get at Least 9 Correct

Don't worry. This is tough material. Take it slowly through this section again. List the differences between the monopoly and the competitive models. Review each figure again. Pay particular attention to how monopolies set price and output for their market. Work through the solved problem below to make sure you understand these concepts. Once you finish this review, go to the next section, Monopoly Market Issues.

## Solved Problem: Monopoly Price, Output, and Profits

The market in Figure 4 is controlled by one firm with the demand and cost curves shown.

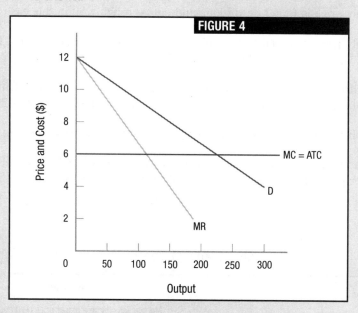

FIGURE 4

a. What would be the profit maximizing output and price?

b. How large are economic profits?

### Solution-Discussion

a. Profits are maximized by producing output where MR = MC. In this case, output is equal to 115 (point $c$ in Figure 5), and the price is found on the demand curve at $9 (point $a$).

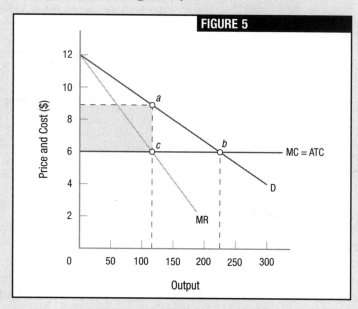

FIGURE 5

b. Profit is equal to the shaded area in Figure 5, and is equal to (P − ATC) times output. Price is $9, average total cost (ATC) is $6, and output is equal to 115 units, so profit = ($9 − $6) × 115 = $3 × 115 = $345.

## Keep in Mind

1. Monopolies (and all firms) maximize profit by producing where MR = MC (point *c* in Figure 5). Monopoly output is equal to roughly 115.

2. Monopoly price is found on the demand curve, roughly $9 in this case.

3. Monopoly profit is equal to the shaded area in Figure 5 and is equal to (P − ATC) × Q = ($9 − $6) × 115 = $3 × 115 = $345.

4. Competitive price and output are at point *b,* where P = ATC and economic profits equal zero (normal profits). Competitive price is $6 and output is 225.

5. Monopolists sell less output at higher prices than competitive markets.

6. The deadweight loss (consumer and producer surplus lost from lower output at higher prices from monopoly) is equal to triangle *abc.* ■

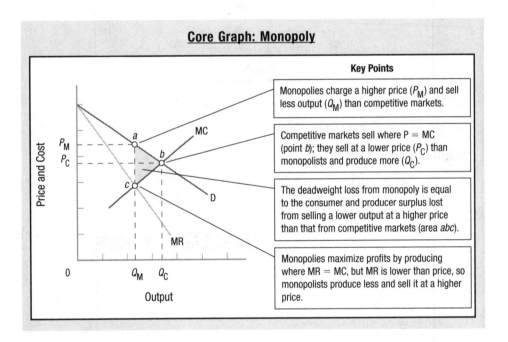

### Core Graph: Monopoly

**Key Points**

Monopolies charge a higher price ($P_M$) and sell less output ($Q_M$) than competitive markets.

Competitive markets sell where P = MC (point *b*); they sell at a lower price ($P_C$) than monopolists and produce more ($Q_C$).

The deadweight loss from monopoly is equal to the consumer and producer surplus lost from selling a lower output at a higher price than that from competitive markets (area *abc*).

Monopolies maximize profits by producing where MR = MC, but MR is lower than price, so monopolists produce less and sell it at a higher price.

# Monopoly Market Issues

## Frequently Asked Questions

**Q: What is price discrimination?**

A: When firms with monopoly power price discriminate, they charge different consumers different prices for the same product. The goal is to maximize profits by charging each customer (or group) as much as each is willing to pay.

**Q: What is needed for successful price discrimination?**

A: Several conditions are required for successful price discrimination. First, sellers must have some monopoly power, or some control over price. Second, sellers must be able to separate the market into different consumer groups based on their elasticities of demand. Third, sellers must be able to prevent arbitrage; that is, it must be impossible or prohibitively expensive for low-price buyers to resell to higher-price buyers.

Q: **What is first-degree price discrimination?**

A: First-degree (or perfect) price discrimination involves charging each customer the maximum price each is willing to pay. This is exemplified by the flea market, where sellers and buyers haggle and barter for each product.

Q: **What is second-degree price discrimination?**

A: Second-degree price discrimination involves charging different customers different prices based on the quantities of the product they purchase. Many firms charge a high price for the first units of a product sold to a customer, but then offer a bulk discount on the sale of added units.

Q: **What is third-degree price discrimination?**

A: The most common form of price discrimination is third-degree price discrimination. This involves charging different groups of people different prices, as when airlines set different ticket prices for business travelers and vacationers.

Q: **What causes a natural monopoly, and what can be done about this?**

A: A natural monopoly exists when economies of scale are so large that the minimum efficient scale of operation is roughly equal to market demand. In such cases, policymakers employ a variety of measures to prevent natural monopolists from abusing their positions of market dominance.

Q: **What is a marginal cost regulatory pricing rule?**

A: A marginal cost pricing rule requires the monopolist to set its price where P = MC, the profit maximizing rule in competitive markets. But, because this price is often below the monopolist's average total costs, losses result, equal to distance *dc* per unit in Figure 6. For the monopoly to remain in business, it must be heavily subsidized by the government. For this reason, this approach is seldom used.

Q: **What is an average cost regulatory pricing rule?**

A: An average cost pricing rule requires the monopolist to produce and sell at the level where demand equals average total costs (point *b* in Figure 6). The result is that the firm earns a normal return. Consumers do lose something, in that they must pay a higher price for a lower output than they would under competitive conditions. Still, the normal profits keep the firm in business, and the losses to consumers are significantly less than if the firm were left unregulated.

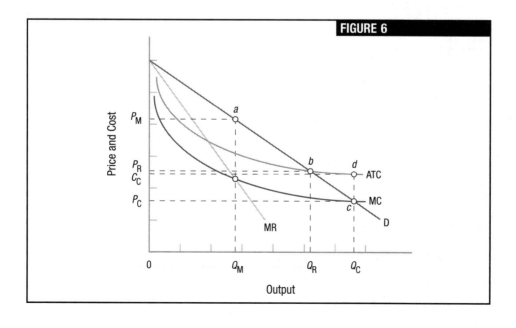

**FIGURE 6**

Q: Why do regulators use rate of return or price caps to regulate natural monopolies, and what are they?

A: In practice, estimating demand and cost curves is extremely difficult, so regulators often abandon the theoretical regulatory strategies noted above and turn to rate of return or price cap regulation. Rate of return regulation allows the monopolist to price its product in such a way that it can earn a normal return on capital invested. Price caps place maximum limits on the prices firms can charge for products.

## Key Point to Remember

Price discrimination occurs when firms with monopoly power can group its customers with different elasticities of demand and charge different prices for the same product. Firms do this because it increases profits. Note that firms do not have to be monopolists, but they must have some control over price. We see price discrimination everyday in airline tickets, hotel prices, and movie tickets.

This is relatively tough material, but you should have answered most of the questions correctly. The issues of price discrimination and regulating natural monopolies show how broadly the analysis of monopoly can be applied. You can use this analysis to answer subtle questions about firms and industries with monopoly power, even if they are not pure monopolists.

Concerns about monopoly power and monopoly were behind the European Union's half-billion-dollar fine of Microsoft in 2004 and the requirements that it split the Windows operating system into several different versions (bare bones and expanded) and not add additional functions without EU permission. Microsoft appealed both the fine and the new regulations. A similar situation again plagued Microsoft in Europe with its introduction of Windows Vista in early 2007. European regulators again required multiple versions to exclude specific functions.

## Monopoly Market Issues Quick Check

### Circle the Correct Answer

1. (T/F) For price discrimination to be successful, it must be very difficult for low-price buyers to resell to higher-price buyers.
2. (T/F) Regulators have trouble determining actual demand and cost curves.
3. (T/F) To price discriminate successfully, sellers must be able to separate the market into different consumer groups based on their elasticities of demand.
4. Which of the following is an example of first-degree price discrimination?
   a. Early Bird discounts given to people who have dinner before 6 P.M.
   b. half-price discounts for children going to movies
   c. a bulk discount for electricity after the purchase of a certain fixed amount
   d. an owner of a rare Pez dispenser who offers it for sale on eBay
5. In Figure 7, the MC and ATC curves decline continually because
   a. MC and ATC curves for a monopoly, unlike competitive firms, are never bowl-shaped.

FIGURE 7

b. natural monopolies enjoy economies of scale.

c. natural monopolies can price discriminate.

d. natural monopolies are not as efficient as competitive firms, and so always face declining cost curves rather than bowl-shaped ones.

6. In Figure 7, if the government mandates a marginal cost pricing rule,

a. the monopolist would produce at point *b*.

b. the monopolist would face a loss of *dc* per unit and ultimately would shut down.

c. the monopolist would earn a normal profit.

d. the monopolist would *not* produce at the socially optimal point.

7. What type of price discrimination occurs when a hotel in Key West, Florida, increases its prices between January 1 and April 1?

a. First-degree price discrimination.

b. Second-degree price discrimination.

c. Third-degree price discrimination.

d. None of the above; this is not an example of price discrimination.

8. What type of price discrimination occurs when customers are charged one rate for the first 100 kilowatt-hours of energy used in one month and another rate for the next 100 kilowatt-hours?

a. First-degree price discrimination.

b. Second-degree price discrimination.

c. Third-degree price discrimination.

d. None of the above; this is not an example of price discrimination.

9. What happens when the government imposes rate of return regulation on a natural monopolist?

a. The monopolist will see its economies of scale evaporate.

b. The monopolist will suffer economic losses unless it is publicly subsidized.

c. The monopolist is prohibited from selling its product above a stipulated maximum price.

d. The monopolist will be able to earn a normal rate of return on capital invested.

10. When government uses rate of return to regulate a natural monopoly, which one of the following does *not* occur?

a. Monopolists try to include as many expenses as possible under the category "legitimate business expenses."

b. Regulatory commissions wind up having large staffs to consider the monopolist's attempts to include every expense as a business expense.

c. Monopolists take regulatory commissions to court.

d. Monopolists appear before the regulatory commission every few months to have price increases approved.

Score: _____

**Answers: 1. T; 2. T; 3. T; 4. d; 5. b; 6. b; 7. c; 8. d; 9. d; 10. d**

## If You Got 9 or 10 Correct

Go on to the Antitrust Policy section, which focuses on the policies designed to eliminate monopolies and prevent attempts to monopolize.

## If You Didn't Get at Least 9 Correct

We suggest you review this section once more. The material is tough, but the review will be useful. Do the normal stuff like rereading the section and reworking the quiz to be sure you know why you missed the questions you did.

## Keep in Mind

■ Firms price discriminate (sell the same product to different customers at different prices) because it is *profitable* to do so. Ask yourself why few new-car dealerships have a meaningful posted price on their cars. Most retailers post their prices and sell at those posted prices. Car dealers (and their sales staff) operate in a way to get you to pay the highest price you are willing to pay rather than do without the car. You are negotiating against both the salesperson and the manager in back. Your job as a buyer is to find the dealer's lowest price at which it is willing to sell the car. Auto purchases are a classic example of first-degree or perfect price discrimination.

■ Price discrimination requires that arbitrage not be possible. If low-cost buyers can sell to higher-cost buyers, price discrimination will fail (everyone will pay a low price). Along the borders of Mexico and Canada, people with large prescription drug bills routinely cross the border to purchase low-cost medicines. American pharmaceutical manufacturers sell the same drugs more cheaply in both countries.

Since most people do not live on the border, the few Americans who buy medications outside the United States are not a serious problem for drug companies. However, with Internet pharmacies from both countries now selling low-priced prescriptions, big pharma's multiprice model is in jeopardy. Ask yourself who stands to lose and who will benefit if pharmaceutical firms cannot price discriminate.

■ The answer to the question just posed is complex, but as a beginning, consider that since price discrimination leads to higher revenue and profits for drug companies, eliminating multiple prices will lead to lower prices in the United States and to higher prices elsewhere, but reduced profits and revenues for the companies. This could ultimately lead to reduced research and development and fewer drug breakthroughs in the future.

■ Regulation is tricky and complex and, where possible, should be avoided. Both airlines and trucking are more robust industries since deregulation. In both, output has expanded and real prices have fallen. The only calls for re-regulation come from the industry itself, for reasons George Stigler outlined several decades ago.

Continue on, but be prepared to review this section and the section on monopoly again. The next section, Antitrust Policy, discusses the major policies and laws used by the federal government to eliminate monopolies and, more important, to keep them from forming in the first place. ■

# Antitrust Policy

## Frequently Asked Questions

Q:  What are the major antitrust laws?
A:  Since 1890, the U.S. Congress has passed a series of major statutes that form the core of the country's antitrust laws. These include the Sherman Act (1890), the Clayton Act (1914), the Federal Trade Commission Act (1914), the Robinson-Patman Act (1936), and the Celler-Kefauver Antimerger Act (1950).

Q:  What was the purpose of the early antitrust laws?
A:  The early antitrust Acts were passed with the intention of promoting the equitable distribution of wealth and protecting small businesses against predatory monopolies. The intensity of antitrust enforcement has varied with presidential administrations and courts over the past century.

Q:  What is the purpose of antitrust policy today?
A:  There is general agreement among economists and judges that some antitrust regulation is needed, and that its basic purpose is to prevent the inefficiencies associated with significant monopoly power.

Q:  How is market concentration measured?
A:  Economists have developed several means of measuring market concentration. The most widely used of these, the $n$-firm concentration ratio, reports the share of industry sales accounted for by the $n$ largest firms. Typically, the four- and eight-firm concentration ratios are reported.

Q:  What is the Herfindahl-Hirshman index, and how is it defined?
A:  The Herfindahl-Hirshman index (HHI) is the principal measure of concentration used by the U.S. Justice Department to evaluate mergers and judge monopoly power. The HHI is defined by the equation: HHI $= (S_1)^2 + (S_2)^2 + (S_3)^2 + \ldots + (S_n)^2$ where $S_1, S_2, \ldots S_n$ are the percentage market shares of each firm in the industry. By squaring market shares, the HHI gives greater weight to those firms with large market shares.

**Q: What are contestable markets?**

A: Contestable markets are those with entry costs so low that firms can enter or leave the industry rapidly. If a firm is earning economic profits, new firms will enter the market until returns have been driven back down to normal levels. The sheer threat of entry therefore keeps prices in contestable markets low, even if the market is now a monopoly. Monopoly firms in potentially contestable markets must, moreover, avoid x-inefficiency, since they always need to be ready for the possibility of facing competition.

# Antitrust Policy Quick Check

## Circle the Correct Answer

1. (T/F) Antitrust legislation began, among other reasons, as a way to protect the country against "robber barons."
2. (T/F) Contestable markets have low entry costs.
3. (T/F) The Sherman Act, the first major piece of antitrust legislation, was passed in 1914.
4. (T/F) Lawmakers who passed the early antitrust legislation were mainly concerned with improving the allocative efficiency of the marketplace.
5. Antitrust cases can be filed by all of the following *except*
   a. the Antitrust Division of the Department of Justice.
   b. the Federal Trade Commission.
   c. lawyers for private plaintiffs.
   d. the monopolist itself.
6. If an industry contains four firms with market shares of 40, 25, 20, and 15%, respectively, its Herfindahl-Hirshman index is which of the following?
   a. 100
   b. 10,000
   c. 2,850
   d. 7,150
7. Which one of these features does *not* tend to make monopolies in the "new economy" transitory?
   a. Much of what the new economy produces is intellectual property, which tends to be easy to clone.
   b. Easy entry and exit.
   c. Modest capital requirements.
   d. Low rates of innovation.

8. Which one of the following has *not* been a rationale for antitrust legislation?
   a. protecting small businesses from the predatory practices of monopolies
   b. protecting consumers from market concentration, with the expectation that market concentration will lead to more monopoly pricing power
   c. prohibiting price discrimination
   d. forcing monopolists to follow the P = MC rule
9. If an industry contains four firms with market shares of 35, 25, 25, and 15, respectively, its Herfindahl-Hirshman index would classify it as being
   a. unconcentrated.
   b. moderately concentrated.
   c. highly concentrated.
   d. monopolistic.
10. If the price charged by a monopolist is close to what would be charged by a competitive firm, it is likely that
    a. the monopolist cannot price discriminate.
    b. the market is contestable.
    c. the monopolist is public spirited.
    d. the monopolist is a price taker in this particular market.

Score: _____

Answers: 1. T; 2. T; 3. F; 4. F; 5. d; 6. c; 7. d; 8. d; 9. c; 10. b

## If You Got 9 or 10 Correct

Move on to Step 4 and study the Hints, Tips, and Reminders.

## If You Didn't Get at Least 9 Correct

This is not difficult material. If you didn't get nine or more correct, this is not good! You are clearly focused on something other than economics. Work through the Hints, Tips, and Reminders in the next section. Maybe something there will get you on the right track. If you still are having problems, you may want to start again from the beginning of this chapter, proceeding slowly. Some of the early material in the chapter can be tough. ■

# STEP 4          Consider These Hints, Tips, and Reminders

1. Keep in mind that a monopoly is a one-firm industry, so the downward sloping industry demand is the monopoly firm's demand, not horizontal like the competitive firm. This means that marginal revenue (MR) lies below price on the demand curve.

2. When drawing graphs for a monopoly, use this simple trick to draw the MR curve. First draw a straight-line demand curve beginning somewhere on the vertical or price axis (point $a$ in Figure 8) with a negative slope (remember the law of demand?). To put in the marginal revenue curve, split the distance from a point on the demand curve (point $c$) at a relatively low price ($P_0$). This results in point $b$. Remember that distance $P_0b$ = distance $bc$. Now connect a straight line from the beginning of the demand curve (point $a$) through this new point $b$. This is the MR curve that bisects the linear demand curve. This simple technique of bisecting the linear demand curve to get an accurate MR curve will make drawing monopoly graphs easier.

**FIGURE 8**

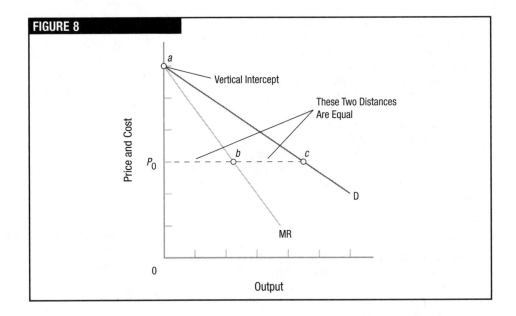

3. This chapter focuses on monopoly—a one-firm industry. Pure monopolies are rare and represent what we would prefer to avoid. Every firm, however, strives for a monopoly position but most only obtain some *monopoly power*. This may come from location, superior product, and so on. The issue eventually comes down to how much monopoly power is too much, and that is the focus of antitrust laws.

4. Why do firms price discriminate? Because they make more profit! Therefore, firms that can separate customers into different groups with different elasticities of demand will price discriminate. Firms are not being *nice* to seniors, students, or flyers who book 14 days in advance and stay over a weekend. Firms do this to make money.

5. Another technique to simplify your graphs is to use a horizontal ATC curve so that the curve represents MC as well. In the same way that P = MR for a horizontal demand curve (competitive model), MC = ATC when the ATC curve is horizontal. This simplifies your graph by reducing the number of distinct points you have to consider.

## Do the Homework for Chapter 9
## Monopoly

**STEP 5**

Instructor _____ Time _____ Student _____

**Use the answer key below to record your answers to these homework questions.**

1. _____
2. _____
3. _____
4. _____
5. _____

6. _____
7. _____
8. _____
9. _____
10. _____

11. _____
12. _____
13. _____
14. _____
15. _____

16. _____
17. _____
18. _____
19. _____
20. _____

1. Which of the following is *not* an assumption of monopoly markets?
   a. homogeneous products in this market
   b. no close substitutes for the seller's product
   c. barriers to entry or exit
   d. one seller in the market

2. The monopolist's demand curve will be
   a. upward sloping.
   b. smaller than the market itself.
   c. downward sloping.
   d. horizontal at the market set price.

3. A monopolist maximizes profit by producing an output where
   a. marginal revenue is equal to price.
   b. average total costs are equal to average revenue.
   c. marginal revenue is equal to price.
   d. marginal revenue is equal to marginal cost.

Use Figure HW-1 to answer questions 4–7.

4. The monopolist maximizes profit by producing at what output level?

5. What is the profit maximizing price for this monopolist?

6. What is the total profit of this profit maximizing monopolist?

7. What are the total costs for this profit maximizing monopolist?

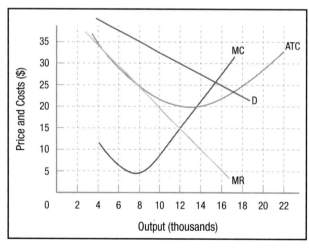

**HW-1**

8. Profits for the profit maximizing monopolist will equal
   a. marginal costs times output.
   b. price minus average total costs, times output.
   c. zero economic profits most of the time.
   d. price minus marginal costs, times output.

Use Figure HW-2 to answer questions 9–11.

9. Area *cab* is called
   a. monopoly profit.
   b. profit margin.
   c. normal profits.
   d. deadweight loss of monopoly.

10. In this figure,
    a. a monopoly would produce output $Q_1$ and sell it for $P_1$.
    b. a competitive firm would produce at point *b*.
    c. even a competitive firm would earn economic profits in the long run.
    d. monopoly profits would equal area *cab*.

11. This monopolist will
    a. earn monopoly profits equal to area *cab*.
    b. produce and sell $Q_0$ units at price $P_0$.
    c. produce and sell $Q_1$ units at price $P_2$.
    d. earn monopoly profits equal to area $P_2P_1ac$.

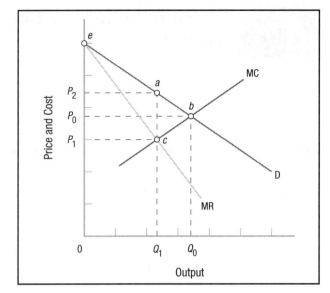

**HW-2**

Use Figure HW-3 to answer questions 12–14.

12. This monopoly will
    a. earn monopoly profits equal to area *cab*.
    b. produce and sell $Q_0$ units at price $P_0$.
    c. produce and sell $Q_1$ units at price $P_1$.
    d. earn monopoly profits equal to area $P_0P_1ab$.

13. This monopoly will
    a. earn monopoly profits equal to area $P_0P_1ac$.
    b. produce and sell $Q_0$ units at price $P_0$.
    c. produce and sell $Q_1$ units at price $P_0$.
    d. earn monopoly profits equal to area $P_0P_1ab$.

14. A competitive firm will
    a. earn economic profits equal to area $P_0P_1ac$.
    b. produce and sell $Q_0$ units at price $P_0$.
    c. produce and sell $Q_1$ units at price $P_0$.
    d. earn economic profits equal to area $P_0P_1ab$.

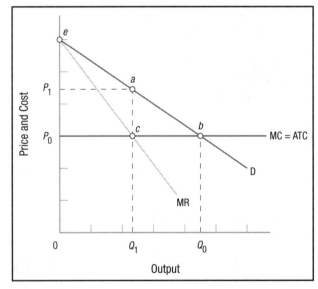

**HW-3**

15. Which of the following is an example of rent-seeking behavior?
    a. fees paid to lawyers for copyright and trademark services
    b. fees paid to public relations firms and advertising agencies to market a brand
    c. fees paid to lobbyists for extensions on tariffs
    d. fees paid to lawyers for drafting contracts

16. When a firm is able to perfectly price discriminate,
    a. it can separate its customers into a few groups and charge different prices to each of these groups.
    b. it is able to provide quantity discounts to some customers.
    c. it can vary the product just slightly enough to convince customers that the higher price is worth it.
    d. it can charge each customer just what they are willing to pay for the product.

17. When a firm is able to use second-degree price discrimination,
    a. it can separate its customers into a few groups and charge different prices to each of these groups.
    b. it is able to provide quantity discounts to some customers.
    c. it can vary the product just slightly enough to convince customers that the higher price is worth it.
    d. it can charge each customer just what they are willing to pay for the product.

18. When a firm is able to use third-degree price discrimination,
    a. it can separate its customers into a few groups and charge different prices to each of these groups.
    b. it is able to provide quantity discounts to some customers.
    c. it can vary the product just slightly enough to convince customers that the higher price is worth it.
    d. it can charge each customer just what they are willing to pay for the product.

19. Concentration ratios measure
    a. the degree to which an industry is concentrated in one regional location such as Silicon Valley.
    b. the percentage of an industry's sales controlled by the largest firm.
    c. the share of industry sales accounted for by the industry's largest few firms.
    d. how concentrated patents are in the industry.

20. The Herfindahl-Hirshman index
    a. measures the degree to which an industry is concentrated in one regional location such as Silicon Valley.
    b. is the percentage of an industry's sales controlled by the largest firm.
    c. is the share of industry sales accounted for by the industry's largest few firms.
    d. is the measure used by the Justice Department to approve or disapprove mergers.

| Use the ExamPrep to Get Ready for Exams | STEP 6 |
|---|---|

This sheet (front and back) is designed to help you prepare for your exams. The chapter has been boiled down to its key concepts. You are asked to answer questions, define terms, draw graphs, and, if you wish, add summaries of class notes.

## Monopoly Markets

List the key characteristics of a monopoly market:

List the main sources of monopoly power:

## Monopoly Pricing and Output Decisions

Describe why marginal revenue is less than price for a monopolist:

Use the grid below to draw the following:

- Average total costs
- Marginal costs

(Hint: Keep in mind that the marginal cost curve goes through the minimum point of the ATC curve.)

Now draw in a demand and marginal revenue curve for a monopolist. (Hint: Remember that the marginal revenue curve bisects [splits] a linear demand curve.)

Show the profit maximizing output and price, and shade in and label profit.

Show the price and output that a competitive industry would produce.

Discuss why monopolies are less efficient than competition.

## Monopoly Market Issues

### Price Discrimination

Discuss the three forms of price discrimination:

Why do firms price discriminate?

### Regulating the Natural Monopolist

Define a natural monopoly:

Describe the marginal cost pricing rule and why it is seldom used:

Describe the average cost pricing rule:

Discuss the complications of implementing regulations:

## Antitrust Policy

Describe the major antitrust laws:

Describe the following tools that economists use to define the relevant market.

Concentration ratios:

Herfindahl-Hirshman index (HHI):

List the merger guidelines from the Justice Department using the HHI:

Discuss the concept of contestable markets and its usefulness:

## Additional Study Help Chapterwide Practice Questions

### Matching

Match the description with the corresponding term.

___  1. Economies of scale
___  2. Monopoly
___  3. Rent seeking
___  4. Price discrimination
___  5. Contestable markets
___  6. Marginal cost pricing rule
___  7. Average cost pricing rule
___  8. Concentration ratios
___  9. Herfindahl-Hirshman index (HHI)

a. A measure of industry concentration equal to the sum of the percentage market shares squared of each firm in the industry.

b. When monopolists devote resources to protecting their monopoly position.

c. The result when increases in output reduce the average costs of production.

d. Markets with entry costs so low that firms can enter or leave the industry rapidly.

e. Charging different customers different prices for the same product.

f. A regulatory mandate compelling a monopolist to produce and sell at levels of output and price where price equals average total costs.

g. A regulatory mandate compelling a monopolist to sell its product at levels of output and price where price equals the marginal cost of production.

h. A measure of the degree to which an industry's production and sales are primarily in the hands of a few firms.

i. A market with just one seller, no close substitutes for the firm's product, and significant barriers to entry.

### Fill-In

Circle the word(s) in parentheses that complete the sentence.

1. A monopolist is (the industry, a factor of production) _____. Monopolies often have (the best technology, high-quality products, a patent) _____.

2. For the monopolist, price is (below, greater than, equal to) _____ marginal revenue, and profits are maximized when marginal cost is (below, greater than, equal to) _____ marginal revenue.

3. When comparing monopoly price and output with competitive prices and output, monopoly price is (higher than, lower than, about the same as) _____ those in competitive markets, and monopoly output is (higher, lower, about the same) _____.

4. Monopoly behavior designed to reduce competitive pressures through lobbying for special circumstances is called (x-inefficiency, rent seeking) _____, and when monopolists aren't as attentive to levels of costs, economists refer to this as (x-inefficiency, rent seeking) _____.

5. When firms can charge customers the maximum amount they would be willing to pay, economists refer to this as (perfect, second-degree, third-degree) _____ price discrimination. When customers are split into groups and are charged different prices, this is an example of (perfect, second-degree, third-degree) _____ price discrimination; and finally, when customers are charged different prices for different blocks of consumption, (perfect, second-degree, third-degree) _____ price discrimination is present.

6. The share of an industry's sales accounted for by the four largest firms is a (contestable market, concentration ratio, Herfindahl-Hirshman index) _____, while the sum of the market shares squared is the (contestable market, concentration ratio, Herfindahl-Hirshman index) _____.
When prices in an industry approach competitive levels because entry is easy, economists refer to this as a (contestable market, concentration ratio, Herfindahl-Hirshman index) _____.

### True-False

Circle the correct answer.

T / F   1. Monopolists are price takers.

T / F   2. Monopoly power implies that a firm has some control over the price at which its product sells.

T / F   3. A natural monopoly is an industry with economies of scale so large that demand will support only a single firm.

T / F   4. For the monopolist, marginal revenue is greater than price.

T / F  5. For the monopolist, profit maximizing output is at that level where marginal revenue equals average total costs.

T / F  6. Deadweight loss is the loss to society that comes about as a result of a monopoly market.

T / F  7. Because monopolists do not get bogged down in competition, they tend to operate more efficiently than competitive firms.

T / F  8. First-degree price discrimination involves charging different groups of consumers different prices.

T / F  9. Pricing movie tickets differently for children, adults, and seniors is an example of third-degree price discrimination.

T / F  10. If everything else is equal, prices will be lower in a contestable market than in a noncontestable market.

T / F  11. Contestable markets often require more regulatory oversight than other markets.

T / F  12. If regulators require a natural monopolist to sell its output for a price equal to the firm's average total costs, the firm will suffer economic losses and require government subsidies to stay in business.

T / F  13. Rate of return regulation allows monopolists to price their products such that they can earn a normal rate of return on the capital they invest.

T / F  14. In the early 1900s, most policymakers who supported antitrust legislation did so because they wanted to ensure the allocative efficiency of the marketplace.

T / F  15. Antitrust cases can be filed by the Antitrust Division of the Department of Justice, the Federal Trade Commission (FTC), state attorneys general, and lawyers for private plaintiffs.

T / F  16. The Herfindahl-Hirshman index measures market concentration by adding together the squares of the market shares of all the firms in a particular industry.

T / F  17. The HHI is inconsistent with our intuitive notions about market power.

T / F  18. Monopolies are often transitory in the "new economy."

## Multiple Choice

Circle the correct answer.

1. Which of the following is *not* a defining characteristic of monopolies?
   a. No close substitutes for the seller's product.
   b. Significant barriers to market entry.
   c. Sellers are price makers.
   d. Many sellers in the market.

2. Monopoly power is
   a. a market containing just one seller.
   b. the power a firm has to control price by adjusting output.
   c. a market containing numerous sellers.
   d. the power the government has to regulate monopolies.

3. Which of the following statements concerning monopoly power is most accurate?
   a. Most firms have some monopoly power, though true monopolists enjoy the most such power.
   b. Only firms that are true monopolies enjoy any monopoly power.
   c. Monopoly power is a market structure that contains a single seller, has no close substitutes, and has high entry barriers.
   d. Most firms have some monopoly power, though competitive firms enjoy the most such power.

4. Which of the following is *not* a typical source of monopoly power?
   a. patents
   b. economies of scale
   c. control over a significant factor of production
   d. product homogeneity

5. Which of the following industries would *not* traditionally be a natural monopoly?
   a. electric power
   b. waste treatment
   c. baked goods
   d. local telephone service

6. A natural monopoly is an industry
   a. with economies of scale so large that a single firm encompasses the market.
   b. that could support multiple firms, but is limited to a single firm by government mandate.
   c. that contains only a single firm at the moment, but is highly contestable.
   d. that is rarely regulated in this country.

7. What does a government franchise do?
   a. It provides the inventor of a new product or process with protection against competition for a limited period of time.

b. It grants a particular firm permission to provide a specific good or service, while prohibiting other firms from doing so.

c. It grants the author of a piece of intellectual property the exclusive right to reproduce that product for a certain period of time.

d. It gives government regulators the power to appropriate specified products for public consumption.

8. What is the typical length of a patent in the United States?
   a. 6 months
   b. 5 years
   c. 20 years
   d. 50 years

9. Which of the following will be true for an unregulated monopoly?
   a. P < MR
   b. P = MR
   c. P > MR
   d. D = MR

10. A monopolist's demand curve will be
    a. relatively more inelastic than for competition.
    b. the industry's demand curve.
    c. downward sloping.
    d. all of the above.

11. What determines the price at which a monopolist can sell its product?
    a. The price at which other firms in the industry are selling their products.
    b. The level of output at which the monopolist decides it wants to produce.
    c. Rules imposed by government regulatory agencies.
    d. Nothing—the monopolist can earn a profit by selling at any price.

12. The profit maximizing output for the monopolist is found where?
    a. MR = P
    b. ATC = P
    c. MR = MC
    d. MR = ATC

13. The profit maximizing monopolist will earn profits equal to which of the following?
    a. (P − ATC) × Q
    b. (P − MC) × Q
    c. (ATC − MR) × Q
    d. (ATC − MC) × Q

14. When will the profit maximizing monopolist shut down its plant?
    a. Never—monopolists can always earn economic profits, so they never have reason to shut down.

b. When marginal revenue drops below price.

c. When price drops below average total costs.

d. When price drops below average variable costs.

15. The profit maximizing monopolist will produce $Q_M$ units, as shown in Figure MC-1. Profit will be
    a. distance $ae$ times $Q_M$.
    b. distance $ab$ times $Q_M$.
    c. distance $be$ times $Q_M$.
    d. none of the above.

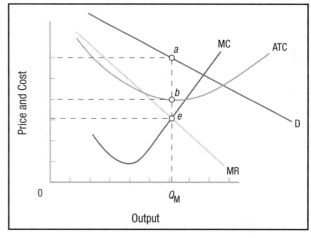

**MC-1**

16. Monopolists generally offer consumers _____ and _____ than competitive firms.
    a. lower output; lower prices
    b. lower output; higher prices
    c. higher output; lower prices
    d. higher output; higher prices

17. Which of the following is *not* an example of rent-seeking behavior?
    a. securing a patent extension
    b. lobbying Congress for a protective tariff
    c. running an advertisement touting the firm's product
    d. securing a government franchise

18. Rent seeking involves any behavior on the part of a monopolist that is intended to
    a. protect its monopoly position.
    b. generate a normal return.
    c. increase its customer base.
    d. improve efficiency so as to discourage potential competitors from entering the industry.

19. Monopolists tend to be x-inefficient because
    a. they often hold numerous patents.
    b. they produce at higher levels of output than competitive firms.
    c. they face such large economies of scale.
    d. they are not subjected to the pressures of the market.

20. In Figure MC-2, the deadweight loss from this monopolist is which of the following?
    a. $200
    b. $225
    c. $250
    d. $300

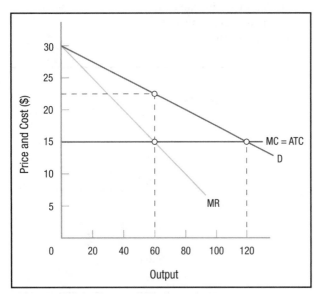

**MC-2**

21. In Figure MC-2, the monopoly profit earned by this monopolist is which of the following?
    a. $350
    b. $400
    c. $450
    d. $500

22. Which of the following is an example of first-degree price discrimination?
    a. movie tickets for children, adults, and seniors
    b. a garage sale
    c. a bulk discount for buying laundry detergent in large quantities
    d. airline rates that vary for all sorts of reasons

23. Which of the following is *not* among the conditions required for firms to be able to price discriminate successfully?
    a. Sellers must be able to separate the market into different consumer groups based on their elasticities of demand.
    b. Sellers must be able to prevent arbitrage.
    c. Sellers must have a patent to maintain their monopoly power.
    d. Sellers must have some monopoly power, or some control over price.

24. When a delivery company will ship packages at $2 per pound for the first 10 pounds, then at $1.50 per pound for every pound after that,

which sort of price discrimination is this an example of?
    a. First-degree price discrimination.
    b. Second-degree price discrimination.
    c. Third-degree price discrimination.
    d. None of the above; this is not an example of price discrimination.

25. What type of price discrimination occurs when a restaurant offers seniors a 10% discount?
    a. First-degree price discrimination.
    b. Second-degree price discrimination.
    c. Third-degree price discrimination.
    d. None of the above; this is not an example of price discrimination.

Figure MC-3 shows the demand and marginal revenue curves for a restaurant engaging in price discrimination. Use this figure to answer questions 26–28.

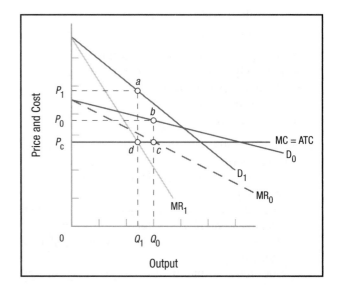

**MC-3**

26. Which point represents the price and quantity that the monopolist will supply for regular customers (those with the least elastic demand curve)?
    a. *a*
    b. *b*
    c. *c*
    d. *d*

27. Which point represents the price and quantity that the monopolist will supply for potential customers who need a discount as an inducement to buy from the restaurant?
    a. *a*
    b. *b*
    c. *c*
    d. *d*

28. Had the monopolist not price discriminated, it would have priced at $P_1$. What is the profit gained by offering a discount to nonregular customers (price discriminating)?
    a. $0P_0bQ_0$
    b. $P_CP_0bc$
    c. $P_CP_1ad - P_CP_0bc$
    d. $aQ_10P_1 - bQ_00P_0$

29. Contestable markets are those
    a. with low entry costs, such that new firms can enter the market rapidly.
    b. with a large number of firms selling homogeneous products.
    c. that tend to be among the most inefficient in the economy.
    d. that cannot support more than one firm in the industry.

30. What holds price to something close to a competitive level in a contestable market, even if that market should be a monopoly?
    a. the fact that the market contains numerous firms selling a homogeneous product
    b. the potential for other firms to enter the market and offer the monopolist some competition
    c. government-imposed price caps
    d. the weakness of consumer demand, which defines contestable markets

31. Which of the following are *not* among the questions a firm considering hit-and-run entry into a contestable market must ask itself?
    a. Can the firm earn a profit at the industry price after the firm has entered the market?
    b. Are the entry costs low enough to make market entry worthwhile?
    c. Can the firm make some sales quickly, before the established firm in the market has had a chance to respond?
    d. Can the firm earn a profit over the long run at the current industry price?

32. Which of the following is *not* among the traditional approaches to regulating a natural monopoly?
    a. Firms desiring a monopoly right must compete for it; the winner is offered a franchise stipulating certain price and output conditions that were contained in the original competitive bid.
    b. Monopolistic firms are publicly owned and thus ultimately subject to political control.
    c. The firm that can first establish market dominance is allowed to set price and output levels as it sees fit.
    d. Monopolistic firms are privately owned, but subject to government regulations, especially regarding pricing and output.

33. If the monopolist in Figure MC-4 were a private, unregulated firm, it would produce at what point?
    a. $a$
    b. $b$
    c. $c$
    d. $d$

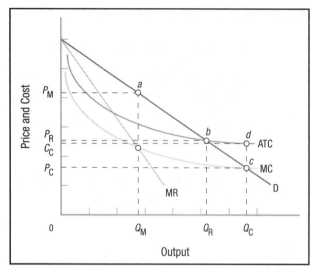

**MC-4**

34. What would happen if regulators invoked a $P = MC$ rule (the competitive market ideal) and forced the monopolist in Figure MC-4 to produce $Q_C$ units at price $P_C$?
    a. This is the best of all worlds for everyone because it is precisely the quantity demanded by the market at that price.
    b. The monopolist would earn normal profits at this point, just as a competitive firm would with a $P = MC$ rule.
    c. The monopolist would earn zero economic profits at this point, just as a competitive firm would with a $P = MC$ rule.
    d. The monopolist would face a loss of $cd$ per unit because price is lower than average total costs.

35. If regulators invoked an average cost pricing rule on the monopolist in Figure MC-4, which of the following would *not* happen?
    a. The monopolist would produce at point $b$ and earn a normal return.
    b. The monopolist would produce at point $d$.
    c. The monopolist would produce more than if left on its own, but less than the socially optimal amount.
    d. The monopolist would produce at a price less than if left on its own, but higher than the socially optimal price.

36. In what year did the Congress pass the Sherman Act, the first major piece of American antitrust legislation?
    a. 1866
    b. 1890
    c. 1914
    d. 1950

37. What was the purpose of the Robinson-Patman Act?
    a. It outlawed any combination or conspiracy in restraint of trade or commerce.
    b. It amended the Clayton Act in 1936 to prohibit price discrimination and to protect mom and pop stores.
    c. It closed a merger loophole in the Clayton Act.
    d. It established the Federal Trade Commission.

38. If an industry contains eight firms with market shares of 25, 18, 15, 12, 10, 10, 6, and 4, respectively, its four-firm concentration ratio is which of the following?
    a. 30
    b. 70
    c. 100
    d. 1,318

39. The Justice Department would classify an industry with an HHI of 1,345 as
    a. unconcentrated.
    b. moderately concentrated.
    c. highly concentrated.
    d. monopolistic.

40. These days, roughly what percent of all mergers are rapidly approved by the government?
    a. less than 2%
    b. 70%
    c. 50%
    d. 99%

## Essay-Problem

Answer in the space provided.

The questions in this section ask you to apply what you have learned and can be challenging. Use our answers as guides and as another way to assess your progress.

1. What is the difference between being a monopoly and having monopoly power?

2. What are the three primary sources of monopoly power? Describe each one.

3. Why is rent-seeking behavior such as lobbying inefficient from a public interest perspective?

4. Construct an argument in favor of monopoly.

5. What is a major benefit of price discrimination to the monopolist, and a major loss to consumers?

6. Why are price-discriminating monopolists more likely to offer senior discounts and child discounts than general discount coupons mailed to a prospective consumer group that has a high elasticity of demand for the product?

7. Why does the federal government continue to subsidize Amtrak?

8. George Stigler showed that regulators can be "captured" by the monopolies they are supposed to regulate and wind up helping them rather than promoting the public interest. How does this happen?

9. How can regulated monopolies possibly justify country club memberships for their managers as legitimate business expenses?

10. If the initial push for antitrust legislation over 100 years ago did not have allocative efficiency as its goal, how can it be said to have an economic rationale behind it?

11. The table below shows sales and market shares for the top 10 firms in the semiconductor industry.

| Company | Revenue (billions of dollars) | Market Share (%) |
| --- | --- | --- |
| Intel | 27.1 | 15.3 |
| Samsung Electronics | 10.5 | 5.9 |
| Renesas Technology | 7.9 | 4.5 |
| Texas Instruments | 7.4 | 4.2 |
| Toshiba | 7.4 | 4.1 |
| STMicroelectronics | 7.2 | 4.0 |
| Infineon Technologies | 6.9 | 3.9 |
| NEC Electronics | 6.3 | 3.6 |
| Motorola | 4.6 | 2.6 |
| Phillips Semiconductor | 4.5 | 2.5 |

a. What is the four-firm concentration ratio?
b. What is the eight-firm concentration ratio?
c. Assume these firms represent the entire industry, and these market shares represent the market shares for the entire industry (don't re-calculate market shares so they total 100%). What is the HHI for this industry?
d. Is this industry rather competitive or tending toward monopoly?
e. If Intel and Samsung wanted to merge, would they be permitted under the HHI guidelines?

## What's Next

By completing this chapter, you now have a good understanding of the two market structures at the extreme: the competitive model and monopoly. You have seen the public benefits from the competitive model and the problems that arise with monopolies. In the next chapter, we look at the two market structures between these two poles.

## Answers to Chapterwide Practice Questions

### Matching

1. c
2. i
3. b
4. e
5. d
6. g
7. f
8. h
9. a

### Fill-In

1. the industry, a patent
2. greater than, equal to

3. higher than, lower
4. rent seeking, x-inefficiency
5. perfect, third-degree, second-degree
6. concentration ratio, Herfindahl-Hirshman index, contestable market

## True-False

| | | | |
|---|---|---|---|
| 1. F | 6. T | 11. F | 16. T |
| 2. T | 7. F | 12. F | 17. F |
| 3. T | 8. F | 13. T | 18. T |
| 4. F | 9. T | 14. F | |
| 5. F | 10. T | 15. T | |

## Multiple Choice

| | | | |
|---|---|---|---|
| 1. d | 11. b | 21. c | 31. d |
| 2. b | 12. c | 22. b | 32. c |
| 3. a | 13. a | 23. c | 33. a |
| 4. d | 14. d | 24. b | 34. d |
| 5. c | 15. b | 25. c | 35. b |
| 6. a | 16. b | 26. a | 36. b |
| 7. b | 17. c | 27. b | 37. b |
| 8. c | 18. a | 28. b | 38. b |
| 9. c | 19. d | 29. a | 39. b |
| 10. d | 20. b | 30. b | 40. b |

## Essay-Problem

1. A monopoly is defined as a market containing a single seller where there are no close substitutes for the monopolist's product, and market entry is nearly impossible. Monopoly power, on the other hand, is the power a monopolist (or any firm) has to control the price of its product by virtue of its market strength. Nearly every firm has some monopoly power, in the sense that it often has some control over price. As markets approach competitive conditions, this control over price becomes minor; as markets approach the monopoly structure, control over price becomes more important.

2. The three primary sources of monopoly power are economies of scale, control over a significant factor of production, and legal mandates. Some industries have economies of scale so large that demand can support only a single firm in the industry. The investment necessary for other firms to enter the market would be so large that the entry of competitors into the industry is virtually impossible. When one firm has exclusive control over some key ingredient in a product's production, it can monopolize production of that product. For many years, Alcoa Aluminum monopolized the production of aluminum by controlling most of the world's supply of bauxite. In a similar way, De Beers controlled the supply of the world's diamonds for over half a century. Government patents, franchises, and copyrights all grant specific individuals or firms the exclusive right to produce certain products for an extended period of time.

3. Hiring lobbyists costs the firm resources that could be devoted to things that would better serve the rest of society, such as increased production or research and development of new products. The most a lobbyist does is maintain or increase a monopolist's position.

4. "My firm operates in an industry with extremely large economies of scale; thus it requires extremely large investments just to enter the industry. Given these high capital costs, demand in my industry will support only a single firm. If the industry were broken into multiple, smaller firms, none of them would survive. Furthermore, by investing in enormous—and enormously expensive—factories and machines, my firm is able

to offer consumers more output at a lower price than multiple firms could manage, each of them producing on a smaller, less efficient scale. Finally, with my firm's massive budget, I am able to make large investments in research and development, thus paving the way for even better, less expensive products down the road. If the industry were broken into smaller competitive firms, all of them having tight budgets, none of them would make these R&D investments, and thus new products would never be developed."

5. Monopolists (or firms with pricing power) benefit from price discrimination because they can charge different prices to different people, and so better capture what each person or group is willing to pay, leading to much greater profit possibilities than if only one price were charged. While consumers pay what they are willing to pay under price discrimination, and so, in this sense, they are not hurt, they do not get the consumer surplus that arises when only one price is available.

6. Seniors and children are easily identifiable groups. General discount coupons mailed to a prospective group may find their way into the hands of people with inelastic demand, either by accident or because acquaintances with highly elastic demand give them to people with inelastic demand. For price discrimination to work, the seller must clearly identify groups and prevent arbitrage between groups with elastic and inelastic demand.

7. The simplest answer is that the government believes it is in the public interest to subsidize this money-losing monopoly. Amtrak does face competition from the airlines for many locations on its routes, but it also goes to places not served by the airlines. Furthermore, its prices usually are lower than airline prices. And people in areas served by Amtrak can be very vocal politically about the need for its train service, while the general populace is affected by its subsidies only to a minor degree, and so it does not get worked up about the subsidy. These reasons explain why Amtrak is subsidized; they do not explain whether the subsidy makes good economic sense.

8. In a straightforward sense, regulators hear a monopolist's arguments over and over. Over time, regulators can tune these arguments out or become sympathetic to the problems faced by monopolists. The arguments can become sophisticated and clever. When the usual topics of conversation are a monopolist's problems, and where public input is lacking, it is not surprising that regulators become more conciliatory to monopolists. In a less favorable sense, regulators sometimes wind up in the private sector with higher-paying jobs, working for the very monopolist that they had regulated. Did expectations of a future job lead to more sympathetic behavior?

9. Two arguments usually are given. First, the firm claims that business is transacted at the country club: Just as a business meal eases business activities, so does playing golf at an exclusive country club. Second, the firm claims that this is simply a cost of hiring people, that the top people would not be attracted by low salaries or must have what their colleagues in the unregulated sectors have. Because regulators are open to public scrutiny, it is harder for firms to make these claims to regulators than to shareholders of a private firm.

10. There was a general sense that large firms wielded monopoly power, especially against small businesses. There was—and is—a general inclination to think that big firms have muscle that they are not shy about exercising. Bigness may not always be bad, but as we have seen in this chapter, big firms with monopoly power can be expected to use that power to some degree to increase profits. Consumers and society lose when this happens. Preventing these losses is a good rationale for antitrust policy.

11. a. 29.9
    b. 45.5
    c. 380.78
    d. competitive
    e. New HHI = 561.32. Yes, the merger would be allowed.

# Monopolistic Competition, Oligopoly, and Game Theory

# 10

## Competition, Monopoly: Now What Is in the Middle?

We have already analyzed competition and monopoly, which are market structure extremes. We now want to look at the two structures in the middle: monopolistic competition and oligopoly. This will round out our discussion of market structures. Furthermore, in looking at oligopoly, we look at game theory, an area of much ferment in economics because it is useful in exploring oligopolistic behavior.

| | This Is What You Need to Know | STEP 1 |
|---|---|---|

**After studying this chapter you should be able to**

- Describe product differentiation and its impact on the firm's demand curve.

- Describe short-run pricing and output decisions for monopolistically competitive firms.

- Describe the reasons why, in the long run, monopolistically competitive firms only earn normal profits.

- Compare the efficiency of monopolistic competition to competition.

- Describe and recognize oligopolistic industries.

- Describe cartels and the reasons for their instability.

- Describe the kinked demand curve model and why some economists feel prices are relatively stable in oligopoly industries.

- Describe the Prisoner's Dilemma and determine the outcome of other games using the approach of minimizing your maximum loss.

- Understand the nature of Nash equilibria and their importance to economists.

## STEP 2          Review the Key Terms

**Monopolistic competition:** Involves a large number of small firms and is similar to competition, with easy entry and exit, but unlike the competitive model, the firms have differentiated their products. This differentiation is either real or imagined by consumers.

**Product differentiation:** One firm's product is distinguished from another's through advertising, innovation, and location, and so on.

**Oligopoly:** A market with just a few firms dominating the industry where (1) each firm recognizes that it must consider its competitors' reactions when making its own decisions (mutual interdependence), and (2) there are significant barriers to entry into the market.

**Mutual interdependence:** When only a few firms constitute an industry, each firm must consider the reactions of its competitors to its decisions.

**Cartel:** An agreement between firms (or countries) in an industry to formally collude on price and output, then agree on the distribution of production.

**Kinked demand curve:** An oligopoly model that assumes that if a firm raises its price, competitors will not raise theirs; but if the firm lowers its price, all of its competitors will lower their price to match the reduction. This leads to a kink in the demand curve and relatively stable market prices.

**Game theory:** An approach to analyzing oligopoly behavior using mathematics and simulation by making different assumptions about the players, time involved, level of information, strategies, and other aspects of the game.

**Prisoner's Dilemma:** A noncooperative game where players cannot communicate or collaborate in making their decisions about whether to confess or not, which results in inferior outcomes for both players. Many oligopoly decisions can be framed as a Prisoner's Dilemma.

**Nash equilibrium:** An important proof that an $n$-person game where each player chooses his optimal strategy, given that all other players have done the same, has a solution. This was important because economists now knew that even complex models (or games) had an equilibrium, or solution.

**Static games:** One-off games (not repeated) where decisions by the players are made simultaneously and are irreversible.

**Dynamic games:** Sequential or repeated games where the players can adjust their actions based on the decisions of other players in the past.

**Predatory pricing:** Selling below cost to consumers in the short run, hoping to eliminate competitors so that prices can be raised in the longer run to earn economic profits.

**Trigger strategies:** Action is taken contingent on your opponent's past decisions.

**Tit-for-tat strategies:** Simple strategies that repeat the prior move of competitors. If your opponent lowers price, you do the same. This approach has the efficient quality that it rewards cooperation and punishes unfavorable strategies (defections).

## Work Through the Chapter Tutorials

# Monopolistic Competition

## Frequently Asked Questions

**Q: What are the key characteristics of monopolistic competition?**

A: Monopolistic competition assumes nearly the same characteristics as the competitive model, including a large number of small firms with insignificant market share and an absence of barriers to entry and exit, but the products sold by these firms are differentiated. Product differentiation is the key to this market structure. Products are similar, but consumers view them as different because of brand preference, physical location, inherent product differences, or many other factors.

**Q: How does product differentiation affect the demand curve?**

A: Product differences are often modest. Because of these differences, each firm nonetheless faces a downward sloping demand curve with an associated marginal revenue curve. Note, however, that this demand curve is highly elastic.

**Q: What is the short-run pricing and output for a monopolistically competitive firm?**

A: Monopolistically competitive pricing and output behavior in the short run looks a lot like that for a weak monopolist. Profit is maximized by selling an output where MR = MC. This is shown in Figure 1. Profits are maximized by selling $q_0$ units at $P_0$, and profits are equal to the shaded area.

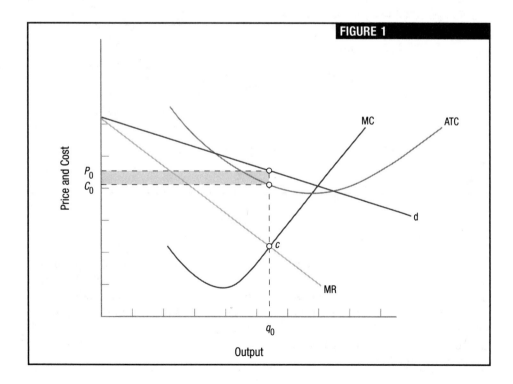

**FIGURE 1**

**Q:   What happens in the long run to the profits of the monopolistically competitive firm?**

**A:**   In the long run, easy entry and exit of other firms eliminates short-run profits or losses. If short-run profits exist, entry will reduce individual demand
curves until the demand curve is just tangent to the long-run average total cost
curve. If short-run losses are the rule, exit will expand the demand curve of
remaining firms until, again, the demand curve is just tangent to the long-run
ATC curve.

**Q:   What is the cost to consumers of product differentiation?**

**A:**   At long-run equilibrium, P = LRATC, and the firm earns normal profits.
Note that this output level is not equal to the minimum point on the LRATC
curve. This can be seen in Figure 2. Because the demand curve has a
negative slope, the tangent occurs at point *a*, an output level that is lower
than that needed to minimize costs (minimum point on the LRATC curve).
This represents the cost to consumers for product differentiation. The
immense selection of goods available does not come without costs. Costs
of advertising, rapid innovation, and "me too" copying are all included in
the price of the products we purchase. Figure 2 compares long-run equilibrium of monopolistic competition (point *a*) with the competitive model
(point *b*), and it shows that output is less and price is higher under monopolistic competition.

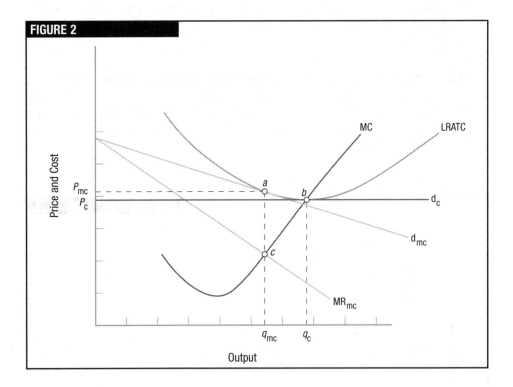

**FIGURE 2**

## Key Point to Remember

The key characteristic about monopolistic competition is *product differentiation*. This gives the firms some control over price (monopoly power). But entry
and exit are easy, so the economic profits from their limited monopoly power
is eliminated in the long run. Remember that product differentiation can come
from the firm's location, the nature of the product or service, or perceived differences from advertising (differences do not have to be real, just considered
different by consumers).

## Monopolistic Competition Quick Check

### Circle the Correct Answer

1. (T/F) Monopolistically competitive firms sell differentiated products.
2. (T/F) Because of product differentiation, the demand curve facing a monopolistically competitive firm will be relatively inelastic.
3. (T/F) In the short run, the monopolistically competitive firm will produce at the point where MR = MC.
4. In the short run, profit maximization for the monopolistically competitive firm will be similar to that for
   a. a monopolist, but will tend to be more.
   b. a monopolist, but will tend to be less.
   c. a competitive firm, but will tend to be more.
   d. a competitive firm, but will tend to be less.
5. In the long run, a monopolistically competitive firm will earn
   a. economic profits because of product differentiation.
   b. economic profits because of entry restrictions.
   c. normal profits because economic profits will attract new firms and there are no entry restrictions.
   d. normal profits because costs are high for monopolistically competitive firms.
6. In Figure 3, in the long run, the monopolistically competitive firm will
   a. produce at point b because it will earn normal profits only, just as the competitive firm does.
   b. produce at point b because it is at the minimum of the long-run ATC curve.

c. produce at point a because it faces a demand curve that is somewhat elastic due to its product differentiation.
d. produce at point a because its profit will be distance $ac$ times $q_{mc}$ units.

7. In the run long, the monopolistically competitive firm
   a. will produce more than the monopolist, but at a higher price because of product differentiation.
   b. will produce less than the competitive firm, but at a higher price.
   c. will produce less than the competitive firm, but at a lower price because it faces relatively elastic demand.
   d. will produce more than the competitive firm because it offers a differentiated product, rather than a standardized one.
8. In the long run, which one of the following will *not* happen for the monopolistically competitive firm?
   a. Economic profits will tend to evaporate because they will attract new entrants to the market because entry is easy.
   b. Quantity of output produced will be less than with competitive firms, and at a higher price.
   c. Short-run profits will be less than with a monopoly.
   d. Long-run output will be produced at the minimum of the long-run average total cost curve.
9. Which one of the following is *not* an example of a monopolistically competitive product?
   a. Coach handbags
   b. Armani suits

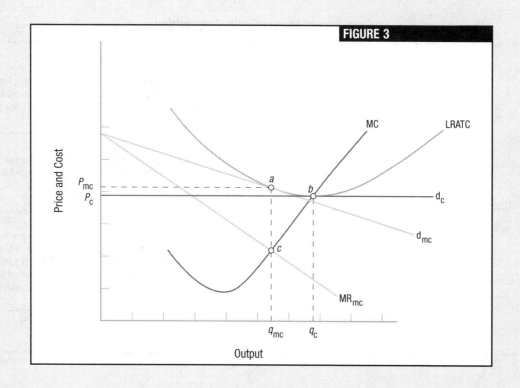

**FIGURE 3**

c. Burberry raincoats

d. Safeway brand salt

10. Monopolistic competition is similar to competition *except* for which one of the following?

a. Both have a large number of small firms.

b. Both face easy entry and exit to the market.

c. Both are price takers.

d. Both do not earn long-run economic profits.

Score: ____

## If You Got 9 or 10 Correct

You're solid on monopolistic competition. Go on to the next section, Oligopoly.

## If You Didn't Get at Least 9 Correct

Spend some time reviewing this material. If you understood competition and monopoly, you should have little trouble understanding monopolistic competition. Keep in mind that a monopolistically competitive firm prices like a monopolist (with little monopoly power) in the short run, but easy entry and exit reduces profits to zero (normal) in the long run.

Remember, monopolistic competition is essentially the same as the competitive model with product differentiation instead of homogeneous products. This means that consumers will have some brand loyalty that is absent in competitive markets with standardized products. The costs of differentiating products are the inefficiency associated with this market structure. These costs are relatively small and are considered the price we pay for innovation, advertising, and brand preference.

Monopolistic competition is quite close in market structure to the competitive model. In the next section, Oligopoly, you will look at a model that is significantly different from the three models you have studied so far. ■

**Core Graph: Monopolistic Competition**

**Key Points**

The demand curve for monopolistically competitive firms is not perfectly elastic at the market price, because product differentiation gives these firms a little monopoly power over pricing.

Long-run equilibrium for monopolistically competitive firms is where MR = MC, and LRATC is just tangent to their demand curve. In the long run, monopolistically competitive firms only earn normal profits.

Contrasting the monopolistically competitive firm with the long-run competitive equilibrium illustrates the inefficiency of monopolistic competition. Less is produced at a somewhat higher price. This inefficiency is partially offset by the benefits of product choice and the information content of brands.

# Oligopoly

## Frequently Asked Questions

Q: **What is an oligopoly?**

A: Oligopoly industries are those in which the market is controlled by just a few firms. What constitutes a few firms is not precisely defined. Oligopoly products can be the same or differentiated and barriers to entry are usually substantial. Because there are only a few firms, decisions by one firm are dependent on the decisions of other firms in the industry. Economists refer to this as mutual interdependence.

Q: **What are cartels?**

A: Cartels are illegal in the United States and the European Union, but are permitted in other parts of the world. Firms in a cartel collude and agree to set monopoly prices and share the market according to some formula. Cartels are inherently unstable because cheating is immensely profitable.

Q: **What is the kinked demand curve model of oligopoly?**

A: The kinked demand curve model of oligopoly answers the question of why oligopoly prices often appear stable. The model assumes that if the firm raises its price, competitors will not react and raise their price, but if the firm lowers its price, other firms will lower theirs in response. These *reactions* by competitors create a "kink" in the firm's demand curve and a discontinuity in the MR curve. This discontinuity permits marginal costs to vary considerably (between points *a* and *b* in Figure 4) before the firm will change its price. Study the kinked demand curve model of oligopoly in Figure 4 before going on to work the problems.

**FIGURE 4**

If the firm increases its price, rivals will *not* follow; they expect to gain market share.

Current price

If the firm lowers its price, all rivals will follow to retain their market share.

Discontinuity in MR creates a range where MC can vary, but price remains at $P_0$.

## Key Point to Remember

Oligopolies are industries with a *few* firms with fairly substantial barriers to entry. Because there are only a few firms, their decisions are *mutually interdependent*. When only a few firms compete, if one firm makes a decision that enhances its competitive advantage, the other firms will react to mitigate this competitive advantage.

# Oligopoly Quick Check

## Circle the Correct Answer

1. (T/F) Oligopoly firms can set prices without considering competitors because each firm is so large.
2. (T/F) There are only two oligopoly models: cartels and kinked demand curves.
3. (T/F) Oligopolies represent an industry having few firms and significant barriers to entry.
4. (T/F) Mutual interdependence in decision making between firms is the key characteristic of oligopolies.
5. Cartels are *not* found in the United States because
   a. they require many member firms, making them too large to police.
   b. there are too many incentives to cheat in our competitive economy.
   c. they require collusion, which is difficult to accomplish with a prying press corps.
   d. they are prohibited by law.
6. In Figure 5, if an oligopoly firm raises prices at any point to the left of point a on demand curve d, rival firms will
   a. have the same price increase because oligopolies are mutually interdependent.
   b. have the same price increase because they want to obtain the same economic profits.
   c. ignore the price increase because the first-moving firm will find that its price increase leads to reduced market share, with the other firms picking up new customers.
   d. ignore the price increase because rival firms' costs will be in between points b and c, not at either point.

7. The oligopolist in Figure 5 will price its product
   a. somewhere between $P_1$ and $P_2$ because it faces kinked demand.
   b. at $P_2$.
   c. at $P_1$.
   d. at $P_0$.
8. Cartels are inherently unstable because
   a. they are prevented by law.
   b. they require secrecy, which is very hard to achieve.
   c. the demand curve for their product is highly elastic.
   d. cheating is highly profitable.
9. In the kinked demand curve model, a lowering of price by one oligopoly firm will cause rivals to
   a. ignore the price decrease so as not to decrease profits.
   b. ignore the price decrease because demand is kinked.
   c. match the price decrease so as not to lose market share.
   d. match the price increase because demand is relatively inelastic.
10. In the kinked demand curve model, the profit maximizing point is which of the following?
   a. $MR = MC = P$
   b. $MR > MC = P$
   c. $MR = MC < P$
   d. $MR = MC > P$

Score: _____

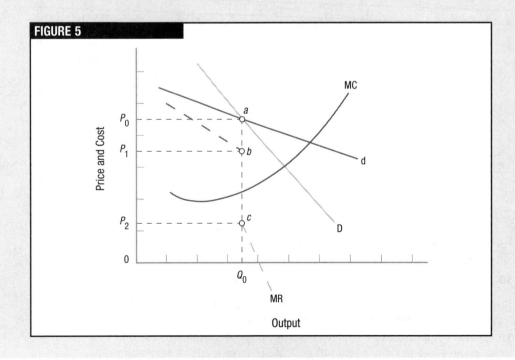

**FIGURE 5**

## If You Got 9 or 10 Correct

Oligopoly and the two models covered in the text (cartels and the kinked demand curve) are no problem for you. Go on to Game Theory, the last section in the chapter. You will find this section a little more challenging.

## If You Didn't Get at Least 9 Correct

Review the material carefully. Cartels probably will be easier to understand than the kinked demand curve. Do all the standard stuff: Reread the text and spend some time rereading the captions for the figures.

If you had trouble with monopolistic competition, sit down and, using the table below, list the attributes of both monopolistic competition and oligopoly and list some industries that fit those characteristics.

| Monopolistic Competition | | Oligopoly | |
|---|---|---|---|
| Characteristics | Examples | Characteristics | Examples |
| _____ | _____ | _____ | _____ |
| _____ | _____ | _____ | _____ |
| _____ | _____ | _____ | _____ |

Ask yourself how you would expect firms in these two market structures to differ. Keep in mind that monopolistic competition is closer to the competitive ideal and oligopoly is closer to monopoly.

Now take a few moments and work through the solved problem on the kinked demand curve model below.

## Solved Problem: Kinked Demand Curve

The data in the table below are for two different demand curves facing an oligopolist, where demand curve $D_0$ represents the firm's demand curve when its competitors will match their changes in price, and demand curve $D_1$ reflects demand when competitors do not follow the firm's price changes. Using these data, answer the questions below:

| P | $D_0$ | $D_1$ | $MR_1$ | $MR_0$ |
|---|---|---|---|---|
| 20 | 0 | 0 | 0 | 0 |
| 18 | 20 | 0 | 0 | 10 |
| 16 | 40 | 0 | 0 | 20 |
| 14 | 60 | 40 | 20 | 30 |
| 12 | 80 | 80 | 40 | 40 |
| 10 | 100 | 120 | 60 | 50 |
| 8 | 120 | 160 | 80 | 60 |
| 6 | 140 | 200 | 100 | 70 |
| 4 | 160 | 240 | 120 | 80 |
| 2 | 180 | 280 | 140 | 90 |
| 0 | 200 | 320 | 160 | 100 |

a. Use the grid that follows to plot the demand and marginal revenue curves. (Hint: The marginal revenue curves bisect each demand curve.)

b. At what price do the two demand curves cross? Assume this is the current price charged by the firm.

c. Now describe what happens if the firm raises or lowers its price. Darken the relevant portions of the demand curve facing the firm. Now darken the relevant portions of the marginal revenue curves.

d. Given the discontinuity in the marginal revenue curve, what is the range for marginal cost before the firm will change its price?

e. What behavioral implications does this model provide about oligopoly pricing behavior?

f. What is one criticism of this kinked demand curve model?

## Solution-Discussion

a. See Figure 6 on the following page.

b. $12. The curves cross at point *e*.

c. If the firm raises its price, competitors do not match the price increase, so the upper portion of $D_1$ above point *e* has been darkened. If the firm lowers its price, all competitors lower their price as well, thus, the lower portion of $D_0$ below point *e* has been darkened. The darkened portion of the two demand curves represents the demand curve facing our oligopolist.

d. Output for this firm will remain at 80 units as long as marginal cost is between roughly $4.50 and $8.00 ($MC_0$ and $MC_1$).

**FIGURE 6**

e. Prices tend to be relatively stable in oligopolistic industries where competitors react in the way formulated by this model. Another implication of this model is that there is a wide range of possible oligopoly models depending on the behavioral reaction of competitors. It does illustrate that the most important aspect of oligopolies is their mutual interdependence and the importance of how they react to their competitor's decisions.

f. A major shortcoming of the kinked demand curve model is that we really don't know how the $12 price was established in the first place. Why has the industry set that price as the initial equilibrium price and not some other price?

The kinked demand curve model usually requires a second viewing. After this, go on to the next section on game theory. ∎

## Game Theory

### Frequently Asked Questions

Q:  **What is the Prisoner's Dilemma?**

A:   The Prisoner's Dilemma is a noncooperative game where each player must anticipate whether the other is going to confess or not. Both would be better off by not confessing, but each will confess in the end. Both players end up minimizing their worst outcome, prison time. The Prisoner's Dilemma is applicable to many other areas, including business pricing, advertising, war, and research and development decisions.

**Q:  What important point did John Nash make about game theory?**

**A:**  John Nash, in a very short paper, showed that an $n$-person game, if each player chooses his optimal strategy given that all other players have done the same, has a solution. This was an important result that allowed economists to develop realistic but complex games of market interactions, because they knew a solution existed.

**Q:  How can the four key market structures be summarized?**

**A:**  At this point, you have covered the four market structures. The major characteristics are listed in the table below. Study the summary table before checking your understanding.

| | Competition | Monopolistic Competition | Oligopoly | Monopoly |
|---|---|---|---|---|
| Number of Firms | Many | Many | Few | One |
| Product | Homogeneous | Differentiated | Homogeneous or differentiated | Unique |
| Barriers to Entry or Exit? | No | No | Yes | Yes |
| Strategic Interdependence? | No | No | Yes | Not Applicable |
| Long-Run Price Decision? | P = ATC | P = ATC | P > ATC | P > ATC |
| Long-Run Profits? | Zero | Zero | Usually economic | Economic |
| Key Summary Characteristic | Price taker | Product differentiation | Mutual interdependence | One-firm industry |

# Game Theory Quick Check

## Circle the Correct Answer

1. (T/F) In the Prisoner's Dilemma, each participant chooses a strategy that leads to the highest possible outcome.
2. (T/F) John Nash proved that some complex games could have a solution, now known as a Nash equilibrium.
3. (T/F) In a Prisoner's Dilemma, prisoners communicate with each other to determine the best strategy to take.
4. (T/F) Game theory helps explain both market structures in the middle: oligopolies and monopolistically competitive firms.

Use the payoff matrix below to answer question 5. Assume that oligopolists A and B both charge $15 for the product and face roughly the same costs.

| | Firm B's Price | |
|---|---|---|
| **Firm A's Price** | **$15** | **$10** |
| $15 | $200,000,$200,000 | $100,000,$500,000 |
| $10 | $500,000,$100,000 | $150,000,$150,000 |

5. If firm A lowers its price to $10,
   a. it will gain $300,000 in profit.
   b. firm B will gain $300,000 in profit.
   c. firm B will match firm A's price, leading to lower profits for both.
   d. firm B will match firm A's price, and both will gain $150,000 in profit.

6. Which one of the following is *not* correct?
   a. Competitive firms are price takers.
   b. Monopolies are price makers.
   c. Oligopolies have some pricing power.
   d. Monopolistically competitive firms are price takers.

7. Which one of the following is *not* correct?
   a. Oligopolies are mutually interdependent.
   b. Monopolies enjoy significant barriers to entry.
   c. Monopolistically competitive firms have differentiated products.
   d. Competitive firms achieve long-run economic profits.

8. If one airline lowers its price, game theory suggests that
   a. the other airlines will do nothing.

b. the other airlines will do nothing because they are at a Nash equilibrium.

c. the other airlines will immediately do the same to minimize profits.

d. the other airlines will immediately do the same to minimize the effect of the first-moving airline on their profits.

9. Which one of the following is *not* correct?

a. Competitive firms produce only homogeneous products.

b. Oligopolies produce only homogeneous products.

c. Monopolies price at P > ATC in the long run.

d. Monopolistically competitive firms face no significant barriers to entry.

10. Which one of the following is *not* correct?

a. Monopolistically competitive firms are mutually interdependent.

b. Monopolies earn economic profits in the long run.

c. Oligopolies price at P > ATC in the long run.

d. Competitive firms maximize profit where MR = MC.

Score: ____

**Answers: 1. F; 2. T; 3. F; 4. F; 5. F; 6. d; 7. d; 8. d; 9. b; 10. a**

## If You Got 9 or 10 Correct

You have a good grasp of the basics of game theory and the essence of market structures. Spend a few moments with the Hints, Tips, and Reminders in the next step.

## If You Didn't Get at Least 9 Correct

Look back and make sure that you know why your answers were incorrect. Market structure analysis forces you to pull together this and the previous two chapters. It often takes a little time for the material to sink in, and students often need several attempts to really master this material.

If you had trouble with this chapter, now is the time to solve this problem.

## Keep in Mind

■ Product differentiation distinguishes monopolistic competition from competition. This leads to slight monopoly power and a highly elastic demand curve.

■ Short-run equilibrium for a monopolistically competitive firm looks like a weak monopolist.

■ In the long run, entry and exit eliminate economic profits or losses for a monopolistically competitive firm.

■ Oligopolies involve few firms that are mutually interdependent; their decisions are based on expected reactions by rivals. This makes oligopoly models numerous and complex.

■ The kinked demand curve model assumes that rivals will not follow price increases, but match price reductions. This leads to a gap in the marginal revenue curve that permits a range of cost conditions before the firm will change its price. This model predicts price stability in oligopolistic markets.

■ Game theory is another way of modeling oligopoly mutual interdependence.

If you get a handle on these items, you have the essence of the chapter down pat. Read through the Hints, Tips, and Reminders that follow. ■

# STEP 4          Consider These Hints, Tips, and Reminders

**1.** Here is something to keep in mind as you work through all of the market structure analysis and try to graph each market: The firm's cost curves are drawn
the same way for all market structures, only the demand and marginal revenue
curves change.
- Competition—horizontal at market price due to standardized product.
- Monopolistic competition—modestly downward sloping due to product differentiation.
- Oligopoly—more of a downward slope because of firm's size (maybe with a
kink) and more reflective of the industry if a cartel.
- Monopoly—the industry's demand curve.

**2.** Also keep in mind that monopolistic competition is closer to the competitive
model, and oligopoly is closer to monopoly (see the continuum below).

|--------|----------------------------------|----------|
Competition  Monopolistic                        Oligopoly    Monopoly
          Competition

## Do the Homework for Chapter 10
## Monopolistic Competition, Oligopoly, and Game Theory

### STEP 5

Instructor _____ Time _____ Student _____

**Use the answer key below to record your answers to these homework questions.**

1. _____    6. _____    11. _____    16. _____
2. _____    7. _____    12. _____    17. _____
3. _____    8. _____    13. _____    18. _____
4. _____    9. _____    14. _____    19. _____
5. _____    10. _____    15. _____    20. _____

1. Which of the following is *not* an assumption of monopolistically competitive markets?
   a. There are just a few firms.
   b. Each of the firms produce slightly differentiated products.
   c. Firms have some control over the price of their products.
   d. There are no significant barriers to entry into this market.

2. Monopolistic competitive markets are similar to competitive markets in that
   a. there are just a few firms.
   b. differentiated products are produced.
   c. the socially optimal level of output is produced in the long run.
   d. both earn normal profits in the long run.

3. A monopolistically competitive market is one in which
   a. only one firm produces a differentiated product.
   b. all firms sell the exact same product.
   c. many firms sell a slightly differentiated product.
   d. most firms sell the same products, and just a few are able to differentiate their products.

4. In the short run for monopolistically competitive firms,
   a. price is equal to marginal cost.
   b. the firm only earns normal profits.
   c. the firm's demand curve is horizontal.
   d. price is greater than marginal cost.

Use Figure HW-1 to answer questions 5–8.

5. In the long run, what is the profit maximizing price for this monopolistically competitive firm?

6. In the long run, what is the profit maximizing output for this monopolistically competitive firm?

7. In the long run, what is the total economic profit for this monopolistically competitive firm?

8. If this industry were a competitive industry, what would be the profit maximizing output?

HW-1

9. A major difference between a monopoly and an oligopoly is that
   a. oligopolies produce where price is greater than marginal cost.
   b. oligopolies are able to earn long-run economic profits.
   c. unlike monopolies, oligopolies produce the socially optimal level of output in the long run.
   d. oligopolies must consider the reactions of competitors to their policies.

10. Which of the following is *not* an assumption of oligopoly markets?
    a. There are substantial barriers to entry into oligopolistic markets.
    b. The products sold in oligopolistic markets are differentiated.
    c. There are only a few firms in an oligopolistic industry.
    d. Oligopolies must consider the reactions of competitors to their policies.

11. One reason that cartels are inherently unstable is that
    a. keeping track of who cheats in a cartel is simple with modern technology.
    b. there are no laws protecting cartel arrangements.
    c. rational individual firms have a tremendous incentive to cheat.
    d. there are few benefits in being a member of a cartel.

12. Oligopoly markets are different from monopolistically competitive markets in that
    a. there are substantial barriers to entry into oligopolistic markets.
    b. firms in oligopoly markets must consider the potential actions of their competitors and act strategically.
    c. there are only a few firms in an oligopolistic industry.
    d. all of the above.

13. Which of the following is an assumption of monopolistically competitive markets and not an assumption of oligopoly markets?
    a. There are substantial barriers to entry.
    b. The products sold are differentiated.
    c. There are only a few firms in the industry.
    d. Firms in the industry must consider the reactions of competitors to their policies.

14. Which of the following is the best example of an oligopolistic industry?
    a. California apple growers
    b. fitness club industry
    c. cigarettes
    d. Los Angeles restaurant market

15. When oligopolists are able to collude,
    a. both price and output usually rise.
    b. both price and output usually fall.
    c. price falls and output rises.
    d. price rises and output falls.

16. In which of the following industries is there a cartel?
    a. computer memory chips
    b. oil
    c. movies
    d. wheat

17. A cartel fixes price in order to
    a. increase the market share of the cartel itself.
    b. restrict entry into the cartel.
    c. eliminate competition.
    d. increase profits.

18. Modern game theory owes its origins to
    a. John Maynard Keynes.
    b. Adam Smith.
    c. John von Neumann.
    d. Milton Friedman.

Use the payoff matrix at right to answer questions 19 and 20.

19. In the payoff matrix, two possible pricing policies for firms A and B are shown, and the profit payoff to each firm (A, B) is shown in the table. If firm B sets its price at $30, what will firm A do?
    a. Nothing, because what firm B does has no impact on firm A.
    b. Set its price at $50 to keep profits at a maximum.
    c. Exit the business, since losses are inevitable.
    d. Set its price at $30.

| Firm A's Price | Firm B's Price | |
| --- | --- | --- |
| | **$50.00** | **$30.00** |
| $50.00 | $300,000, $300.000 | $150,000, $450,000 |
| $30.00 | $450,000, $150,000 | $200,000, $200,000 |

20. In the payoff matrix, two possible pricing policies for firms A and B are shown, and the profit payoff to each firm (A, B) is shown in the table. If the two firms are able to successfully collude, which of the following will happen?

a. Both will set their prices at $30.

b. Firm A will charge $50, and firm B will charge $30.

c. Firm A will charge $30, and firm B will charge $50.

d. Both will set their prices at $50.

| | Use the ExamPrep to Get Ready for Exams | **STEP 6** |

This sheet (front and back) is designed to help you prepare for your exams. The chapter has been boiled down to its key concepts. You are asked to answer questions, define terms, draw graphs, and, if you wish, add summaries of class notes.

## Monopolistic Competition

List the characteristics of monopolistic competition:

### Short-Run Price and Output under Monopolistic Competition

Use the grid below for the following:

Draw the following curves: Average total cost and marginal cost. (Hint: Keep in mind that the marginal cost curve goes through the minimum point of the ATC curve.)

Now draw in a demand and marginal revenue curve for a monopolistically competitive firm. (Hint: Remember that the marginal revenue curve bisects [splits] a linear demand curve and that the demand is highly elastic.)

In the figure show the profit maximizing output and price, and shade in and label profit. (Hint: This is essentially the same as for a monopolist, but demand is more elastic and economic profits are considerably smaller.)

### Long-Run Price and Output under Monopolistic Competition

Use the grid on the next page for the following:

Again, draw the following curves: Average total cost and marginal cost.

Now draw in a demand and marginal revenue curve for a monopolistically competitive firm.

Show the profit maximizing output and price in the long run. What kind of profits do these firms earn? Why?

Contrast the price and output that a monopolistically competitive industry would produce with that for a competitive firm.

Discuss why monopolistically competitive firms are less efficient than competitive firms.

## Oligopoly

List the characteristics of an oligopoly:

### Cartels

Describe cartels and their chances for long-run success:

### The Kinked Demand Curve Model

List the assumptions of the kinked demand curve model:

What happens when an oligopolistic firm raises its price?

Lowers its price?

Describe why prices are inherently stable in the kinked demand curve model:

## Game Theory

In the Prisoner's Dilemma (a noncooperative game), why will each prisoner confess?

Complete the table below.

**Summary of Market Structures**

|  | Competition | Monopolistic Competition | Oligopoly | Monopoly |
|---|---|---|---|---|
| Number of firms |  |  |  |  |
| Product |  |  |  |  |
| Barriers to entry or exit? |  |  |  |  |
| Strategic Interdependence? |  |  |  |  |
| Long-run price decision? |  |  |  |  |
| Long-run profits? |  |  |  |  |
| Key summary characteristic |  |  |  |  |

# Additional Study Help Chapterwide Practice Questions

## Matching

Match the description with the corresponding term.

___ 1. Monopolistic competition
___ 2. Product differentiation
___ 3. Oligopoly
___ 4. Mutual interdependence
___ 5. Cartel
___ 6. Kinked demand curve
___ 7. Game theory
___ 8. Prisoner's Dilemma
___ 9. Nash equilibrium

a. Caused by the reactions of competing firms to match price decreases but not follow price increases.
b. An industry containing a few firms.
c. A Nobel Prize was won for this analysis.
d. Something that makes consumers desire one product versus another.
e. Why decisions made independently are often different from those made collectively or collusively.
f. Many firms vying for the consumer's dollar through innovation and product differentiation.
g. Any rule-governed situation with a well-defined outcome, characterized by strategic interdependence.
h. The most important aspect of oligopolistic decision making.
i. An industry where the firms get together and agree to set price and output quotas and share the market.

## Fill-In

Circle the word(s) in parentheses that complete the sentence.

1. The most important characteristic of monopolistic competition that causes it to differ from competitive markets is (homogeneous, differentiated) _____ products. In the short run, both firms in monopolistic competition and competitive markets can earn (normal, economic) _____ profits, but in the long run both will end up earning (normal, economic) _____ profits.

2. Compared to competitive firms, monopolistically competitive firms produce (more, less, the same) _____ and charge a (higher, lower, the same) price. Both maximize profit where (P < MC, P = MC, MR = MC) _____.

3. Oligopoly industries involve (many, few, one) _____ firm(s) that have (few, many, no) _____ barriers to entry and are mutually (independent, interdependent) _____.

4. The kinked demand curve model assumes that if the firm increases its product price, the other firms in the industry (will, will not) _____ follow, but if the firm lowers its price other firms in the industry (will, will not) _____ follow. This model leads to (highly variable, stable) _____ prices.

5. The Prisoner's Dilemma is a (cooperative, non-cooperative) _____ game where ultimately, both will (confess, go free) _____. In static games, decisions are made (sequentially, simultaneously) _____, but with dynamic games, players' decisions occur (sequentially, simultaneously) _____.

## True-False

Circle the correct answer.

T / F    1. The source of market power for monopolistically competitive firms is their differentiated products.

T / F    2. The demand curve facing the firm in a monopolistically competitive environment is flat at the market price due to product differentiation.

T / F    3. Monopolistic competition is defined by a small number of firms selling differentiated products.

T / F    4. In the short run, the monopolistically competitive firm sets prices and output in a manner similar to a monopolist.

T / F    5. In the long run, the monopolistically competitive firm can earn economic profits, but not as many as a monopoly firm.

T / F    6. Oligopoly represents an industry with few firms with insignificant market power.

T / F    7. The key aspect of oligopolies is the mutual interdependence in decision making between firms.

T / F    8. Oligopolies typically earn normal profits.

T / F    9. In oligopoly markets, there are no significant barriers to entry.

T / F   10. Pricing models of oligopoly are easy to devise because there are so few firms to be concerned with in the construction of the model.

T / F   11. Game theory is used to analyze highly competitive markets.

T / F   12. The Prisoner's Dilemma is an unrealistic game.

T / F   13. Participants in Prisoner's Dilemma situations try to select a strategy that guarantees the highest possible outcome.

T / F   14. All game theory models result in stable and predictable outcomes.

T / F   15. John Nash's proof of a game theory equilibrium under certain circumstances set game theory back for decades.

## Multiple Choice

Circle the correct answer.

1. Monopolistic competition is *not* characterized by which of the following?
   a. a large number of sellers
   b. product differentiation
   c. downward sloping demand curve
   d. stable prices for the product

2. The demand for the monopolistically competitive firm's product is downward sloping because
   a. quantity demanded rises as price falls.
   b. these firms have immense market power and can charge whatever price they desire.
   c. of product differentiation.
   d. many firms competing for business increases the demand.

Use Figure MC-1 depicting a monopolistically competitive firm to answer questions 3–5.

3. What will be equilibrium output in the short run?
   a. 340 units
   b. 320 units
   c. 300 units
   d. no output

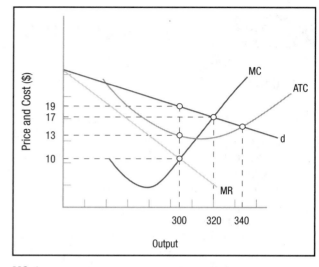

**MC-1**

4. In the short run, what will be the profit earned by this monopolistically competitive firm?
   a. $2,700
   b. $600
   c. zero
   d. $1,800

5. If demand declines in the long run such that output remains the same in long-run equilibrium as it was in the short run, what will be the price in the long run for the product?
   a. $19
   b. $17
   c. $13
   d. $10

6. In long-run equilibrium for monopolistically competitive firms, which of the following will hold?
   a. P = MC = MR  and  P = minimum  point  on LRATC curve
   b. P > MC = MR  and  P > minimum  point  on LRATC curve
   c. P > MC = MR  and  P = minimum  point  on LRATC curve
   d. P = MC = MR  and  P > minimum  point  on LRATC curve

7. In long-run equilibrium for monopolistically competitive firms,
   a. firms sell as much output as they can.
   b. firms differentiate their products by charging more than competitors.
   c. firms sell at the minimum point on the LRATC curve.
   d. firms earn a normal return like competitive firms.

Use Figure MC-2 to answer questions 8 and 9.

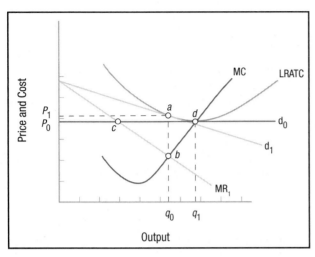

**MC-2**

8. Long-run equilibrium for the competitive firm is at point
   a. *a*.
   b. *b*.
   c. *c*.
   d. *d*.

9. Long-run equilibrium for the monopolistically competitive firm is at point(s)
   a. *a* and *b*.
   b. *b* and *c*.
   c. *c*.
   d. *d*.

10. Which of the following industries is a monopolistically competitive industry?
    a. automobiles
    b. cigarettes
    c. shoe stores
    d. computer microprocessor chips

11. The most important characteristic of oligopoly is
    a. numerous firms.
    b. insignificant barriers to entry.
    c. mutual interdependence.
    d. sticky or stable price structures.

12. A cartel or joint profit maximization oligopolist will maximize profits by setting
    a. MR = MC = P.
    b. MR > MC = P.
    c. MR = MC < P.
    d. MR = MC > P.

13. The essential characteristic of a cartel is
    a. the industry's demand curve is highly elastic.
    b. collusion between the members is necessary.
    c. the size of the market.
    d. how much profit each cartel member can make.

14. Which of the following industries or organizations operate as a cartel?
    a. steel industry
    b. Organization of Petroleum Exporting Countries (OPEC)
    c. automobile industry
    d. cigarette industry

15. Cartels are inherently unstable because
    a. cartels have too many members to police.
    b. buyers rebel at high prices, forcing demand to drop, causing the cartel to break up.
    c. politicians are able to pass laws prohibiting them.
    d. the incentives to cheat are too great.

16. The kinked demand curve model requires
    a. a lot of firms selling in the market.
    b. high barriers to entry and exit.
    c. different reactions to price changes from rivals.
    d. multiple marginal cost curves.

Use Figure MC-3 to answer questions 17–19.

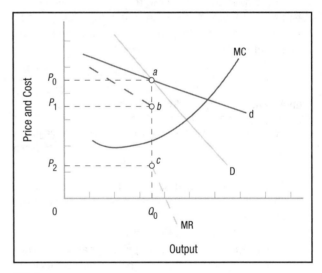

**MC-3**

17. Equilibrium price for the oligopolist pictured is
    a. $P_0$.
    b. $P_1$.
    c. $P_2$.
    d. somewhere between $P_1$ and $P_2$.

18. Demand curve d represents that demand curve where
    a. price is attractive to buyers.
    b. changes in prices are *not* followed by rivals.
    c. changes in prices are followed by rivals.
    d. demand is associated with cartel behavior.

19. Demand curve D represents that demand curve where
    a. price is unattractive to buyers.
    b. changes in prices are *not* followed by rivals.

c. changes in prices are followed by rivals.
d. demand is associated with cartel behavior.

20. Which of the following industries is *not* an oligopoly?
    a. cigarettes
    b. prescription drugs
    c. oil
    d. personal computers

21. Game theory is useful
    a. to keep mathematicians employed.
    b. to help economists understand how monopo-
       listically competitive firms set prices and
       outputs.
    c. to help economists understand how oligopo-
       lists make decisions involving mutual interde-
       pendence.
    d. to help economists see the differences be-
       tween monopolistically competitive firms and
       oligopolists.

Use the payoff matrix below to answer question 22.
Assume that firms A and B are currently charging $10
for the product and face roughly the same cost and
demand curves.

| Firm A's Price | Firm B's Price | |
| --- | --- | --- |
| | **$10** | **$8** |
| $10 | $200,000,$200,000 | $100,000,$500,000 |
| $8 | $500,000,$100,000 | $150,000,$150,000 |

22. Firm A is considering lowering its price to $8.
    Under which of the following circumstances would
    firm A lower its price?
    a. To beat firm B to the punch.
    b. It would never lower its price because all other
       profit opportunities, given its rival's reactions,
       are lower.
    c. If the pricing decisions shown in the diagram
       were irreversible and occurred simultaneously
       (essentially a Prisoner's Dilemma situation).
    d. If it found a way to improve its product.

## Essay-Problem

Answer in the space provided.

The following questions call for extended answers.
Your answers may not always be the same as those we
suggest. While your words will differ, the essence of
your answer should be similar. Use these as another
way to assess your progress in applying monopolistic
competition, oligopoly, game theory, and market
structure analysis in general.

1. What is the essence of monopolistically competitive markets?

2. Marketing people have said that "firms sell products, but people buy brands." Consider your local
   grocery, and explain whether the quotation is true.

3. What is the value of the Coca-Cola brand?

4. If cartels are inherently unstable, why legally ban
   them at all?

5. Why do auto companies give rebates rather than
   lower prices?

6. The kinked demand curve helps to explain the stability of prices for some oligopolies. Why is it useful
   in showing why oligopolists tend not to lower prices?

7. In the Prisoner's Dilemma, why must prisoners be
   kept apart from each other?

8. Of the four market structures, which is the best
   for society?

9. Of the four market structures, which one do firms
   *not* want to be in?

10. Why do monopolies and oligopolies tend to be reg-
    ulated rather than monopolistically competitive
    and competitive firms?

## What's Next

This and the previous two chapters focused on market structure. This analysis is a very important tool in the microeconomist's toolkit. This analysis helps us understand why firms act as they do, and all we really need to know are some key market characteristics. In the next chapter, we will put some of the basic market structure analysis to work when we look at resource markets, especially labor markets. Just keep in mind the general idea of market power and how it is derived.

## Answers to Chapterwide Practice Questions

### Matching

| | | |
|---|---|---|
| 1. f | 4. h | 7. g |
| 2. d | 5. i | 8. e |
| 3. b | 6. a | 9. c |

### Fill-In

1. differentiated, economic, normal
2. less, higher, MR = MC
3. few, many, interdependent
4. will not, will, stable
5. noncooperative, confess, simultaneously, sequentially

### True-False

| | | | |
|---|---|---|---|
| 1. T | 5. F | 9. F | 13. F |
| 2. F | 6. F | 10. F | 14. F |
| 3. F | 7. T | 11. F | 15. F |
| 4. T | 8. F | 12. F | |

### Multiple Choice

| | | | |
|---|---|---|---|
| 1. d | 5. c | 12. c | 19. c |
| 2. c | 6. b | 13. b | 20. d |
| 3. c | 7. d | 14. b | 21. c |
| 4. d ($19 − | 8. d | 15. d | 22. c |
| $13) × 300 = | 9. a | 16. c | |
| $6 × 300 = | 10. c | 17. a | |
| $1,800. | 11. c | 18. b | |

### Essay-Problem

1. Differentiated products.
2. It is mainly true because firms try to differentiate their products to gain some pricing power, and people become loyal to brands, but it is not true to the extent that people buy generic products. Do you buy generics for some products? What brand of milk do you buy? What brand of oranges or apples?

3. Because Coca-Cola is considered the most widely recognized brand in the world, its value must be huge. Consider the soft-drink dispensing machine at your school: How much extra would you pay for a Coca-Cola as compared to a grocery store house brand? Now multiply that by millions of servings a day, and you might get a sense of the value of the brand. Interestingly enough, Coca-Cola values its brand name at $1 on its corporate balance sheet, but you can bet that if it put the brand name up for sale, the asking price would be in the many billions of dollars.

4. Since there is no short-run or long-run benefit to consumers, but only to the cartel members, the existence of cartels is damaging to society. The only question is how damaging. Since this is so one-sided, banning cartels seems like the best solution.

5. The effect to the consumer is the same: Rebates *lead to* lower prices. There seems to be some perception by the auto companies that lowering the price will somehow damage the brand, while rebates are perceived as temporary things. Evidence for this has not been forthcoming. In addition, lowering sticker prices in bad years and increasing them in good ones would lead to the impression that auto companies were exploiting consumers with extremely high price increases. Everyone understands that rebates are temporary incentives to get you to buy now before they expire.

6. The kinked demand curve shows graphically that if one oligopoly firm lowers its price, it will gain market share at the expense of the others, so the others will rush to meet the price decrease—the end result being that everyone is worse off because price will be much less and the increase in quantity sold will be very small. So, no firm wants to undertake that action as long as it thinks others will follow suit.

7. If the prisoners could communicate, they might work out a deal in which none of them confesses because they would see that this is the best strategy for them combined. However, this combined strategy is not the best strategy for each individual when the individual does not know what the others will do.

8. The competitive model is the best for society in that it leads to both production and allocative efficiency.

9. Competitive markets, because firms have no pricing power. The competitive firm is under constant competitive pressure to lower costs. Firms would rather have less pressure on them. What is good for General Motors is not necessarily good for society.

10. The key factor is that barriers to entry exist with monopolies and oligopolies, and these barriers give them considerable market power, while barriers to entry are insignificant for monopolistically competitive firms and are nonexistent for competitive firms. Regulation thus seeks to mitigate the market power of monopolies and oligopolies.

# Theory of Input Markets 11

Illustration Works/Alamy

## From Products to Inputs

With this chapter, we turn our attention from product markets to input markets. Behind the production of goods and services lie workers, machinery, and plants. Most firms need employees and capital to operate. You will be able to bring some of your market analysis insights from the previous three chapters to this examination of input markets.

| This Is What You Need to Know | STEP 1 |
| --- | --- |

**After studying this chapter you should be able to**

■ Define and describe competitive labor markets.

■ Derive a supply curve for labor.

■ Describe the factors that can change labor supply.

■ Describe the factors that can change labor demand.

■ Determine the elasticity of demand for labor.

■ Derive the market demand for labor.

■ Describe monopoly and monopsony power and their impact on imperfect labor markets.

- Determine the present value of an investment.
- Compute the rate of return of an investment.
- Describe the impact of the supply of land on markets.
- Describe the impact of economic profits on entrepreneurs and markets.

---

## STEP 2             Review the Key Terms

**Supply of labor:** The amount of time an individual is willing to work at various wage rates.

**Substitution effect:** Higher wages mean that the value of work has increased, and the opportunity costs of leisure are higher, so work is substituted for leisure.

**Income effect:** Higher wages mean you can maintain the same standard of living by working fewer hours. The impact on labor supply is generally negative.

**Demand for labor:** Demand for labor is derived from the demand for the firm's product and the productivity of labor.

**Marginal physical product of labor:** The additional output a firm receives from employing an added unit of labor ($MPP_L = \Delta Q \div \Delta L$).

**Marginal revenue product:** The value of another worker to the firm is equal to the marginal physical product of labor ($MPP_L$) times marginal revenue (MR).

**Value of the marginal product:** The value of the marginal product of labor ($VMP_L$) is equal to price multiplied by the marginal physical product of labor, or $P \times MPP_L$.

**Elasticity of demand for labor:** The percentage change in the quantity of labor demanded divided by the percentage change in the wage rate.

**Monopsony:** A labor market with one employer.

**Monopolistic exploitation of labor:** When a firm has monopoly power in the product market, marginal revenue is less than price (MR < P) and the firm hires labor up to the point where $MRP_L$ = wage. Because $MRP_L$ is less than the $VMP_L$, workers are paid less than the value of their marginal product, and this difference is called monopolistic exploitation of labor.

**Marginal factor cost (MFC):** The added cost associated with hiring one more unit of labor. For competitive firms, it is equal to the wage; but for monopsonists, it is higher than the new wage (W) because all existing workers must be paid this higher new wage, making MFC > W.

**Monopsonistic exploitation of labor:** Because monopsonists hire less labor than competitive firms, and workers are paid less than the value of their marginal products, this difference is referred to as monopsonistic exploitation of labor.

**Capital:** All manufactured products that are used to produce goods and services.

**Present value:** The value of an investment (future stream of income) today. The higher the discount rate, the lower the present value today, and vice versa.

**Rate of return:** Uses the present value formula, but subtracts costs, then finds the interest rate (discount rate) at which this investment would break even.

**Rent:** The return to land as a factor of production. Sometimes called economic rent.

# Competitive Labor Supply

## Frequently Asked Questions

**Q: What are the characteristics of competitive labor markets?**

**A:** Competitive labor markets comprise firms that are price takers. They compete with other firms in the wider market for labor. Labor is assumed to be a homogeneous input: One unit of labor is just as productive as all others. Information about prices and wages is assumed to be widely available, and supply and demand interact to determine the equilibrium wage for the industry. Each firm then decides how much labor to purchase at the going wage rate.

**Q: What is the supply of labor, and why is the supply of labor curve backward bending?**

**A:** The supply of labor is the time an individual is willing to work (the labor the person is willing to supply) at various wage rates. The supply of labor is positively sloped because, at higher wages, workers will substitute work for leisure. However, when wages rise high enough, workers may elect more leisure over greater income, resulting in a backward bending supply of labor curve.

**Q: What causes the supply of labor curve to shift?**

**A:** Changes in wage rates will change the quantity of labor supplied or cause movements along the supply of labor curve. Demographic changes and changes in the nonmonetary aspects of a job, the wages for alternative jobs, and nonwage income will all shift the supply of labor curve. Such a shift might be precipitated, for instance, by a change in labor force participation rates, a reduction in the risk of a job, or a change in income from other sources.

## Keep in Mind

Competitive firms are price takers in both product and labor markets. They get the going wage for homogeneous labor from the market, then determine how many workers to hire. The supply of labor is determined by demographics, nonmonetary wage aspects of the job, wages for alternative jobs, and nonwage income of workers.

## Competitive Labor Supply Quick Check

### Circle the Correct Answer

1. (T/F) In competitive labor markets, workers are divided into two categories: substitute workers (one worker is similar to another) and income workers (workers who produce more than the average worker).

2. (T/F) The substitution effect for labor is always positive.

3. (T/F) In competitive markets, labor supply is derived from the demand for the firm's product and the productivity of labor.

4. (T/F) A backward bending supply of labor curve means that the income effect eventually will swamp the substitution effect.

5. At high wage rates, people who begin to choose leisure rather than more work are examples of

   a. the substitution effect.

   b. the income effect.

   c. the competitive labor markets effect.

   d. the consumer surplus effect.

6. The backward bending supply of labor curve means that at some point
   a. the cost of leisure is too great.
   b. income becomes too high and leisure is more attractive.
   c. the substitution effect will finally win out.
   d. people cannot work any more hours in the day.

7. Which of the following will not produce a shift in the supply of labor curve for a book-shelver's job at your school library?
   a. A new staff lounge is opened that includes a microwave.
   b. The admissions department miscalculated last year, and there are now 25% more entering students than projected.
   c. The campus food service just raised starting wages.
   d. The library just raised the wage rate for book-shelvers.

8. If the opportunity cost of leisure is too high,
   a. people will substitute work for leisure.
   b. people will substitute leisure for work.
   c. it will be overcome by the income effect.
   d. it will be overcome by the leisure effect.

9. An increase in the quantity supplied of labor for a particular job results from
   a. more women entering the labor force.
   b. more immigrants entering the country.
   c. an increase in safety regulations for the job.
   d. an increase in the wage rate for the job.

10. Which of the following will not produce an increase in the supply of labor curve?
   a. A new policy is instituted making job hours more flexible.
   b. An economic recession leads to a decline in demand for the product.
   c. Wages are increased.
   d. Other firms in the industry raise wages for their workers.

Score: ____

Answers: 1. F; 2. T; 3. F; 4. T; 5. b; 6. b; 7. d; 8. a; 9. d; 10. c

## If You Got 9 or 10 Correct

You can handle the concept of labor supply in competitive labor markets. Go on to the next section, Competitive Labor Demand.

## If You Didn't Get at Least 9 Correct

You should have answered most of these questions correctly. They are relatively easy. If not, review this material carefully and concentrate on how the competitive product model applies to input markets. You might review income and substitution effects of labor supply once more.

In any event, keep going, but be prepared to look at this section again. As you focus next on labor demand, you will begin to put the two together. Workers supply labor for one set of reasons, and firms demand labor for another set. Try to keep this perspective. ■

# Competitive Labor Demand

## Frequently Asked Questions

Q: Where does the demand for labor come from?
A: The demand for labor is a derived demand. It is derived from the productive capabilities of labor and the demand for the good or service produced. The demand for labor is equivalent to the marginal revenue product ($MRP_L$) curve. Marginal revenue product is equal to marginal physical product of labor times the product's marginal revenue.

**Q:  How is the competitive firm's demand for labor linked to the value of the marginal product of labor?**

**A:**  Because competitive firms are price takers, marginal revenue is equal to price. So, the competitive firm's demand for labor is equal to what economists call the value of the marginal product ($\text{VMP}_L$). The value of the marginal product is equal to marginal physical product times price ($\text{MPP}_L \times P$).

**Q:  How do changes in labor demand come about?**

**A:**  Since the demand for labor is a derived demand, changes in labor demand come about because of changes in labor productivity or changes in product demand. Anything that changes the price of a firm's product will change its labor demand. If new equipment is added and worker productivity increases, labor demand will rise. An increase in the cost of capital increases the demand for labor because labor-intensive production methods become more attractive to firms.

**Q:  What is the elasticity of demand for labor?**

**A:**  The elasticity of demand for labor is the percentage change in the quantity of labor demanded divided by the percentage change in the wage rate. An inelastic demand for labor is one where the absolute value of the elasticity is less than 1. An elastic demand is greater than 1. Elasticity of demand for labor is determined by the elasticity of demand for the product, the ease of input substitutability, and the size of labor's share in production costs.

**Q:  How do competitive firms determine how many workers to employ?**

**A:**  Figure 1 shows that competitive labor markets determine an equilibrium wage of $W_e$ (point $e$ in panel A). Then individual firms hire employees up to the point where equilibrium wage is equal to marginal revenue product (point $e$ in panel B). For competitive markets, the marginal revenue product of labor is equal to the value of the marginal product of labor ($\text{MRP}_L = \text{VMP}_L$) because $\text{MR} = \text{P}$.

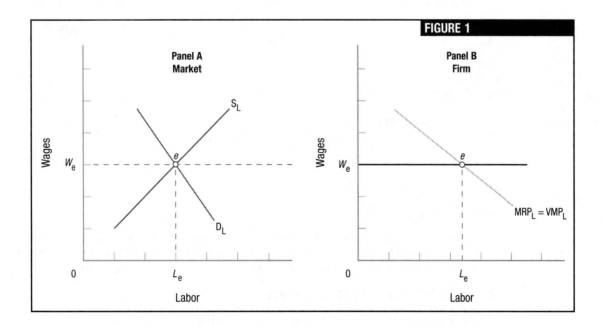

FIGURE 1

## Key Points to Remember

The demand for labor is a *derived* demand and is based on the demand for the product and the productivity of labor. The demand for labor is equal to the marginal revenue product of labor ($\text{MRP}_L$) and is defined as the marginal physical product of labor times marginal revenue (MPP$_L$ × MR). Remember, competitive firms are price takers so MR = P and, therefore, the competitive firm's demand for labor is also equal to MPP$_L$ × P = VMP$_L$. Competitive firms hire labor up to the point where VMP$_L$ = wage.

## Competitive Labor Demand Quick Check

### Circle the Correct Answer

1. (T/F) The competitive firm's demand for labor is derived from demand for the firm's products and the productive capabilities of labor.
2. (T/F) The marginal physical product of labor is equal to the quantity of physical units produced divided by the number of workers.
3. (T/F) For firms in competitive product markets, VMP$_L$ = MPP$_L$ × MR.
4. (T/F) Time is an important factor in the elasticity of demand for labor in competitive markets because, in the short run, firms may not be able to adjust to changing wages, but in the long run all production inputs can be adjusted.
5. For a competitive firm, which of the following is *not* true?
   a. MRP$_L$ = MPP$_L$ × MR
   b. MPP$_L$ = ΔQ/ΔL
   c. VMP$_L$ = MPP$_L$ × P
   d. MRP$_L$ = VMP$_L$/ΔQ
6. Which of the following will *not* lead to an increase in a particular firm's demand for labor?
   a. an increase in the demand for the firm's product
   b. an increase in the price of capital
   c. an increase in worker productivity
   d. an increase in the firm's wage rate
7. Which of the following does *not* influence the elasticity of demand for labor?
   a. the time firms have to adjust to changing wage rates
   b. ease of input substitutability
   c. nonmoney aspects of the job
   d. labor's share of total production costs
8. If the market supply of labor decreases (shifts to the left) individual firms will
   a. hire more workers to ensure they have enough to produce their products.
   b. outsource some work to India.
   c. see their demand for labor curve decline as well (shift inward to the left).
   d. hire fewer workers.
9. If the interest rate for loans rises in a competitive market, the firm's demand for labor will
   a. not be affected.
   b. decrease because the firm will have to cut back on workers to justify buying more expensive machinery.
   c. increase because the firm will substitute workers for capital.
   d. decrease as machines replace workers.
10. Which of the following influences the elasticity of demand for labor in the computer industry?
    a. wages in the automobile industry
    b. how quickly firms can adjust to changing wage rates
    c. demographic changes in the workforce
    d. the substitution effect of labor

Score: _____

**Answers: 1. T; 2. F; 3. T; 4. T; 5. d; 6. d; 7. c; 8. d; 9. c; 10. b**

## If You Got 9 or 10 Correct

You have successfully made it through some relatively difficult material. You might find it worthwhile to take a quick look at the solved problem below before you move on to the next section, Imperfect Labor Markets and Other Input Markets.

## If You Didn't Get at Least 9 Correct

Be patient in your review of the material. Remember that competitive firms are price takers in both the product and labor market.

Competitive firm labor decisions are the logical extension of the competitive profit maximization of producing output at the point were MR = MC. Since the productivity of labor was an important component of the firm's costs when we analyzed competitive product markets, it is only logical that it will be a prime determinant of just how many workers the firm hires to produce the profit maximizing output.

Overall markets for labor determine wages, and firms look at their production processes and determine the value of workers to them (the $MRP_L$), then simply hire workers if their $MRP_L \geq W$. This is really a simple concept. Don't make more of it than it is. These decisions are more complex in the next section when we consider monopoly (a single seller in the product market) and monopsony (one buyer of labor). The solved problem below will take you through all of these steps.

## Solved Problem: Competitive Labor Market

Consider the following Web site construction firm that is a competitor in both the labor and product markets. Wages are $200 a day, and its output sells for $10 a unit. Answer the following questions.

a. Complete the table below.

| Labor | Output | MPP$_L$ | MRP$_L$ = VMP$_L$ | Wage |
|-------|--------|---------|-------------------|------|
| 0 | 0 | ——— | ——— | ——— |
| 1 | 14 | ——— | ——— | ——— |
| 2 | 30 | ——— | ——— | ——— |
| 3 | 50 | ——— | ——— | ——— |
| 4 | 80 | ——— | ——— | ——— |
| 5 | 108 | ——— | ——— | ——— |
| 6 | 130 | ——— | ——— | ——— |
| 7 | 150 | ——— | ——— | ——— |
| 8 | 168 | ——— | ——— | ——— |
| 9 | 180 | ——— | ——— | ——— |

b. Graph the supply and demand for labor in the grid provided.

c. How many workers will this firm hire to maximize profits? How large are these profits?

## Solution-Discussion

a. See the table on the following page. Marginal physical product of labor ($MPP_L$) is the change in output from hiring another worker, marginal revenue product ($MRP_L$) is equal to the value of the marginal product

(VMP$_L$) because for the competitive price taker, P = MR. Wages (or the supply of labor facing the competitive firm) is assumed to be the wage rate, or $200.

| Labor | Output | MPP$_L$ | MRP$_L$ = VMP$_L$ | Wage |
|-------|--------|---------|-------------------|------|
| 0 | 0 | — | — | — |
| 1 | 14 | 14 | 140 | 200 |
| 2 | 30 | 16 | 160 | 200 |
| 3 | 50 | 20 | 200 | 200 |
| 4 | 80 | 30 | 300 | 200 |
| 5 | 108 | 28 | 280 | 200 |
| 6 | 130 | 22 | 220 | 200 |
| 7 | 150 | 20 | 200 | 200 |
| 8 | 168 | 18 | 180 | 200 |
| 9 | 180 | 12 | 120 | 200 |

b. See Figure 2 below.

**FIGURE 2**

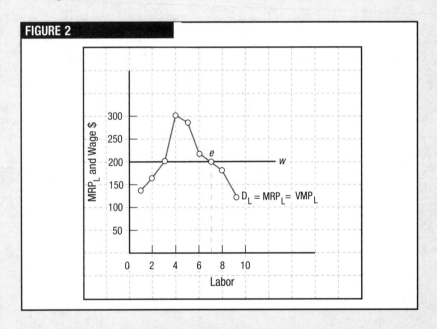

c. This firm will hire workers up to the point where MRP$_L$ = W. In this case, the firm hires seven workers for total costs of $1,400 ($200 × 7 = $1,400). Total revenue is equal to price times quantity sold, or $1,500 (150 × $10 = $1,500). So total profit is equal to $100 ($1,500 − $1,400 = $100).

Working through this solved problem should have clarified any questions you had about competitive labor markets and how firms decide how many workers to hire and at what wage rate. If not, you should review this section on labor demand. The next section starts by analyzing what happens in imperfect labor markets, so you will be using what you have learned about the supply and demand for labor in competitive markets. If you do not understand the material by this point, you will have real trouble in the next section.

Make sure you can write answers to the following questions for competitive markets.

- What determines the demand for labor?
- Why do competitive firms hire where $MRP_L = W$?
- What are the main determinants of the supply of labor?
- What factors cause the demand for labor to shift?
- What factors influence the elasticity of demand for labor?

Write your answers for these questions, then check them in the text. When you have confidence in your understanding, you will be ready to tackle Imperfect Labor Markets. ■

# Imperfect Labor Markets and Other Input Markets

## Frequently Asked Questions

**Q:   What is monopolistic exploitation of labor?**

**A:** If wages are determined in a competitive market, a firm will hire labor until $MRP_L = W$. But if the firm enjoys some monopoly power in the product market, marginal revenue product will be less than the value of the marginal product because $MR < P$. The difference between the value of the marginal product and marginal revenue product is known as monopolistic exploitation of labor.

**Q:   What is monopsonistic exploitation of labor?**

**A:** A monopsony is a market with a single buyer or employer. Marginal factor cost (MFC) is the added cost associated with hiring one more unit of labor. For the monopsonist, the MFC curve lies above the supply of labor curve, because the firm must increase the wages of all workers to attract added labor. If the monopsonist purchases labor from a competitive market, it hires labor up to the point where $MRP_L = MFC > W$. At this point, the value of labor's marginal product exceeds the wage rate; economists refer to this as monopsonistic exploitation of labor.

**Q:   How are imperfect labor market equilibria diagrammed?**

**A:** Figure 3 on the next page puts together a labor market consisting of a monopolist in the product market and a monopsonist in the input market. By bringing in monopoly and monopsony to our labor market analysis, we now have four possible product and labor market equilibria:
- *Competitive product market and competitive labor market:* Firms hire where $VMP_L = MRP_L = W$ (point $d$).
- *Monopoly product market and competitive labor market:* Firms hire where $VMP_L > MRP_L = W$ (point $c$), resulting in monopolistic exploitation ($VMP_L > W$) or ($W_2 - W_1$).
- *Competitive product market and monopsony labor market:* Firms hire where $W < MFC = VMP_L = MRP_L$ (point $b$), but pay the wage $W_1$ from the supply of labor curve (point $c$), resulting in monopsonistic exploitation ($VMP_L > W$) or ($W_2 - W_1$).

**FIGURE 3**

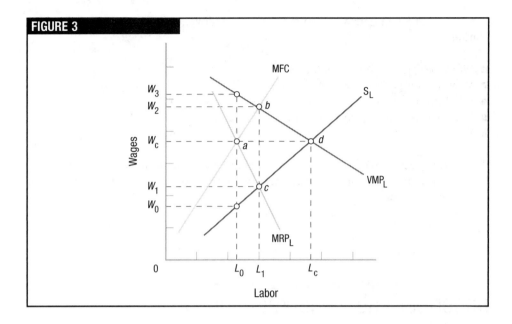

- *Monopoly product market and monopsony labor market:* Firms hire where $VMP_L > MRP_L = MFC > W$ (point $a$). Wages and employment are the lowest in this case ($W_0$ and $L_0$), and both monopolistic and monopsonistic exploitation exist ($W_3 - W_0$).

Note that in Figure 3 monopolistic and monopsonistic exploitation just happens to be the same ($W_2 - W_1$), but this is typically not be the case.

**Q:** What are capital markets, and what role do they play?

**A:** Capital includes all manufactured goods that are used to produce other goods and services. Capital markets are those markets where financial resources are available for the purchase of capital goods. The loanable funds market determines equilibrium interest rates for these funds. Firms look at their potential investment projects and borrow money to invest when the rate of return on a project is greater than or equal to the market interest rate.

**Q:** How do firms determine whether potential investments might be profitable?

**A:** Two approaches are used to determine whether investments are potentially profitable. The present value approach discounts projected future streams of income to determine their present value. This is then compared to the cost of the investment to determine whether it will be profitable. The rate of return approach uses the same present value formula but looks for the rate of return, or discount rate, where the potential income stream and investment costs will be just equal.

**Q:** What is land to an economist?

**A:** Land, to the economist, means land and other natural resources that are nearly fixed in supply, or inelastically supplied. Because the supply of land is fixed, the rent on land is determined by demand.

**Q:** How are entrepreneurship and profits linked?

**A:** Profits are rewards to entrepreneurs for combining the other inputs of production—land, labor, and capital—in ways that produce goods and services, and for assuming the risks associated with production. Economic profits are profits that exceed normal levels. They act as signals to other entrepreneurs and firms that consumers want more of the profitable product. These signals produce shifts in resources toward those goods that consumers want.

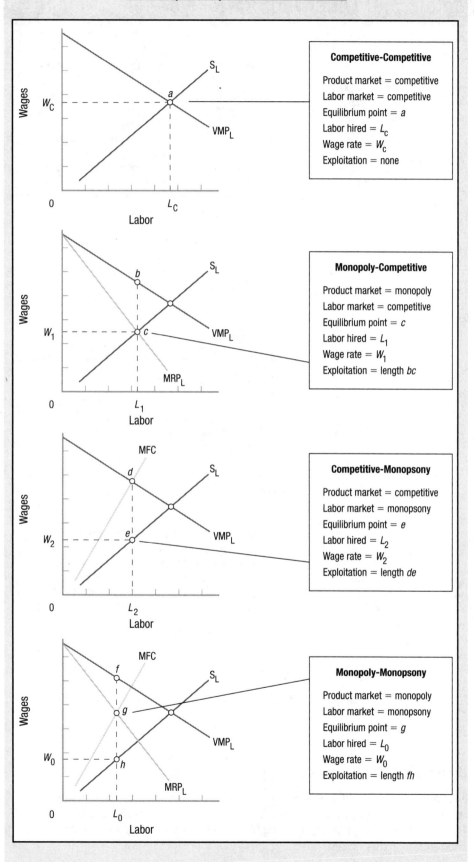

## Core Graphs: Imperfect Labor Markets

**Competitive-Competitive**

Product market = competitive
Labor market = competitive
Equilibrium point = $a$
Labor hired = $L_c$
Wage rate = $W_c$
Exploitation = none

**Monopoly-Competitive**

Product market = monopoly
Labor market = competitive
Equilibrium point = $c$
Labor hired = $L_1$
Wage rate = $W_1$
Exploitation = length $bc$

**Competitive-Monopsony**

Product market = competitive
Labor market = monopsony
Equilibrium point = $e$
Labor hired = $L_2$
Wage rate = $W_2$
Exploitation = length $de$

**Monopoly-Monopsony**

Product market = monopoly
Labor market = monopsony
Equilibrium point = $g$
Labor hired = $L_0$
Wage rate = $W_0$
Exploitation = length $fh$

# Imperfect Labor Markets and Other Input Markets Quick Check

## Circle the Correct Answer

1. (T/F) If a firm employs seven workers at $8 per hour, but it must offer $10 per hour to attract an eighth worker, the marginal factor cost of this eighth worker is $24.
2. (T/F) The present value of a payment next year of $750 will be less than $750.
3. (T/F) A market that has a single buyer is called a monopsony.
4. Distance $bc$ in Figure 4 is called
   a. monopolistic exploitation of labor.
   b. monopsonistic exploitation of labor.
   c. imperfect exploitation of labor.
   d. optimum exploitation of labor.

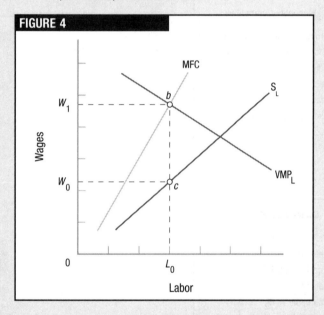

**FIGURE 4**

5. You have just retired and want to buy an annuity to make sure you have enough money to pay your annual expenses. You calculate that you need $25,000 per year, and that the market interest rate is 5%. How much will you pay for this annuity?
   a. $5,000
   b. $50,000
   c. $125,000
   d. $500,000

6. To economists, land is a natural resource with
   a. a supply curve that is horizontal.
   b. a relatively elastic supply curve.
   c. lots of trees.
   d. an absolutely inelastic supply curve.
7. Which of the following is *not* correct for a firm that has both monopoly and monopsony power?
   a. It will employ fewer workers than in competitive markets.
   b. It will pay workers less than in competitive markets.
   c. It will exploit workers both monopolistically and monopsonistically.
   d. It will employ fewer workers but at a wage higher than the market wage rate.
8. What is the present value of $1,000 received in three years if the interest rate is 6%?
   a. $1,191.02
   b. $ 839.63
   c. $ 869.71
   d. $1,180.00
9. For the rate of return approach, which one is *not* correct?
   a. The rate of return is also called the internal rate of return.
   b. The rate of return considers the cost of capital.
   c. The rate of return approach is superior to the present value approach.
   d. A risk premium adjusts the rate of return for risky projects.
10. For entrepreneurs, which one of the following is *not* correct?
   a. Profits reward entrepreneurs for combining labor, land, and capital to produce goods and services.
   b. Profits reward entrepreneurs for bearing risk.
   c. Economic profits signal entrepreneurs that consumers want more of the good or service.
   d. Economic profits signal entrepreneurs to shift resources to areas of lower demand to shore them up because there is money to be made there.

Score: ____

**Answers: 1. T; 2. T; 3. T; 4. b; 5. d; 6. d; 7. d; 8. b; 9. c; 10. d**

## If You Got 9 or 10 Correct

Nice job on some tough material. Even though you did well, you might want to work through the solved problem below. Also, take a few moments and check out the Hints, Tips, and Reminders; they might be helpful even though you seem to have a good grasp of this material.

## If You Didn't Get at Least 9 Correct

Don't give up the ship. Monopoly and monopsony in labor markets are difficult topics. It often takes students more than one attempt at this material to really master it. Take a quick look back at the core graphs and make sure you know why each equilibrium point has been selected.

Work through the solved problem below. This numerical example should help you see how market structure in both product and labor markets affects wages and the level of employment.

## Solved Problem: Imperfect Labor Markets

Using the data for labor, wage rates, marginal factor cost, value of the marginal product, and marginal revenue product in the table below, answer the questions that follow.

| Labor | Wage | MFC | VMP | MRP |
|-------|------|-----|-----|-----|
| 0 | 0 | 0 | 0 | 0 |
| 1 | 50 | 50 | 500 | 500 |
| 2 | 75 | 100 | 450 | 400 |
| 3 | 100 | 150 | 400 | 300 |
| 4 | 125 | 200 | 350 | 200 |
| 5 | 150 | 250 | 300 | 100 |
| 6 | 175 | 300 | 250 | 0 |
| 7 | 200 | 350 | 200 | −100 |
| 8 | 225 | 400 | 150 | −200 |
| 9 | 250 | 450 | 100 | −300 |

First, graph all four curves in the grid below.

a. Assume that both the product and labor markets are competitive. Label the equilibrium point *a*. How many employees will be hired? What is the level of labor exploitation in this situation?

b. Now assume that the product market is monopolistic and the labor market continues to be competitive. Label the new equilibrium point *b*. How many employees will be hired? What is the level of monopolistic exploitation in this situation?

c. Now assume that the product market is competitive and the labor market becomes monopsonistic. Label the new equilibrium point *c*. How many employees will be hired? What is the level of monopsonistic exploitation in this situation?

d. Now assume that the product market is monopolistic and the labor market becomes monopsonistic as well. Label the new equilibrium point *d*. How many employees will be hired? What is the total level of monopolistic and monopsonistic exploitation in this situation?

## Solution-Discussion

Figure 5 graphs all four curves.

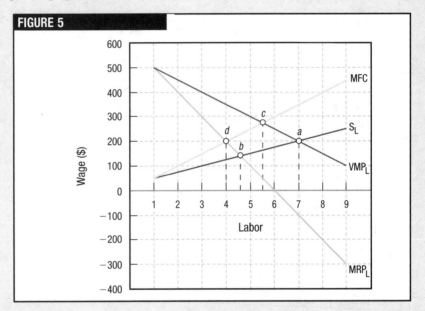

**FIGURE 5**

a. When both markets are competitive, equilibrium will be found where the supply of labor crosses the value of the marginal product of labor, or point *a* in the figure above. Since both markets are competitive, no exploitation occurs, and labor is paid its VMP.

b. When the product market becomes monopolistic, labor is hired where the supply of labor is equal to the marginal revenue product, point *b* in the figure above. Monopolistic firms are the market and they must lower price to get higher sales, so MR < P, and therefore $MRP_L < VMP_L$. Somewhere between four and five workers are hired and the monopolistic exploitation of labor is equal to $VMP_L$ − wage, or roughly 187.5 (325 − 137.5 = 187.5). The $VMP_L$ between four and five workers is 325, and the wage from the supply curve for between four and five workers is 137.5. This is equal to the vertical distance from point *b* to the $VMP_L$ curve in the figure above.

c. When the product market is competitive and the labor market becomes monopsonistic (one buyer of labor), labor is hired where the marginal factor cost (MFC) of labor is equal to the value of the marginal product, point *c* in the figure above. Monopsonistic firms are the only buyers of labor, and their MFC is higher than the supply of labor curve because they must pay everyone a higher wage when they want to hire another worker. Somewhere between five and six workers are hired and the monopsonistic exploitation of labor is equal to $VMP_L$ − wage, or roughly 112.5 (275 − 162.5 = 112.5). The $VMP_L$ between five and six workers is 275, and the wage from the supply curve for between five and six workers is 162.5. This is equal to the vertical distance from point $c$ on the $VMP_L$ curve to the wage rate on the supply of labor curve in the figure above.

d. When the product market is monopolistic and the labor market becomes monopsonistic (one buyer of labor), labor is hired where the marginal factor cost (MFC) of labor is equal to marginal revenue product, point $d$ in the figure above. Four workers are hired, and the sum of both monopsonistic and monopolistic exploitation of labor is equal to $VMP_L$ − wage, or equal to 225 (350 − 125 = 225). The $VMP_L$ for four workers is 350, and the wage from the supply curve for four workers is 125. This is equal to the vertical distance from the point on the $VMP_L$ curve above point $d$ to the wage rate on the supply of labor curve in the figure above.

Ideally, working through this solved problem with numbers will help you see how imperfect labor markets equilibrate. This is not easy material, but looking at the wages and employment levels for anything other than competitive markets illustrates why economists favor competitive markets both in product markets and in labor markets. Take a moment to look back at the Quick Check and figure out why you missed the question(s) you did, then spend some time with the Hints, Tips, and Reminders that follow. ■

---

## Consider These Hints, Tips, and Reminders          STEP 4

**1.** While not explicitly discussed in the chapter, there is a straightforward relationship among wages, the marginal productivity of labor, and the firm's marginal costs. To see the relationship among these three variables, remember that in competitive markets (we will just look at the competitive labor and product market combination), $VMP_L = P \times MPP_L = W$ is the profit maximization condition. This equation reduces to

$$P = W / MPP_L$$

Also, profit maximization requires that MR = P = MC. Substituting MC for P in the earlier equation yields

$$MC = W / MPP_L$$

Thus, the wage rate divided by the marginal physical product of labor is equal to marginal cost. So, for example, if wages are $200 a day and marginal physical product for the last person hired is 10 units a day, then marginal cost for each unit produced that day is $20. This is just common sense; you produced 10 units that sell for $200, so marginal cost to produce these units is $20 each.

2. Keep in mind that when we are computing marginal physical product for a unit of labor that is producing a particular product, computing $MPP_L$ is relatively easy. However, computing $MPP_L$ for work such as Web site design, research, and artwork is much more difficult and often virtually impossible unless the work is put up for sale via some form of auction market like eBay.

3. The hardest part in this chapter is hiring rules for various markets (competitive, monopoly, and monopsony). Try approaching each the following way:

   First, go to the competition-competition case where supply and demand cross. This will be the *highest* wage and employment combination of all the possibilities.

   Second, look at the monopoly-competition case. Ask yourself how monopolies differ from competitive markets. The answer is that marginal revenue is less than price because product demand is downward sloping, so $MRP_L < VMP_L$ and monopolies will hire fewer workers (and sell a smaller output—remember?).

   Third, assume that the competitive situation now becomes a competitive-monopsony. Now with a single buyer of labor, each additional unit of labor costs more than the wage rate because all other workers must be paid the new higher wage required to attract more labor. Higher labor costs again mean that fewer workers will be hired, so both wages and employment will be lower than in competitive markets.

   Fourth, when you combine monopoly and monopsony, firms will hire the fewest workers at the lowest wages, because employment is determined where $MRP_L = MFC_L$.

4. This chapter focused on labor markets, but the same conclusions would hold for other factor markets under competitive, monopoly, and monopsony conditions.

# Do the Homework for Chapter 11
## Theory of Input Markets

**STEP 5**

Instructor _____ Time _____ Student _____

**Use the answer key below to record your answers to these homework questions.**

1. _____    6. _____    11. _____    16. _____
2. _____    7. _____    12. _____    17. _____
3. _____    8. _____    13. _____    18. _____
4. _____    9. _____    14. _____    19. _____
5. _____   10. _____    15. _____    20. _____

1. Which of the following is *not* an assumption describing competitive labor markets?
   a. The firms operating in the market are operating in competitive markets.
   b. Labor is treated as a homogeneous commodity.
   c. Firms in the industry are able to increase their prices to meet the wage demands of their workers and unions.
   d. Information in the industry is accurate and widely available.

2. The backward bending supply curve of labor means that
   a. workers can always be induced to work more if the wage is high enough.
   b. the substitution effect is always dominant.
   c. worker hours in the day are limited.
   d. when income is sufficiently high, workers desire more leisure.

3. When wages rise and workers increase their hours of work
   a. the income effect is dominant.
   b. leisure time is less expensive, so workers will increase their hours of work.
   c. workers are substituting work for leisure since leisure now has a higher opportunity cost.
   d. the income effect implies that working more means they will earn higher incomes.

4. Which of the following factors will *not* change labor supply?
   a. an increase in interest rates that increase the interest income a worker receives from large bond holdings

   b. the wage rates that a competitive firm is paying for the same skills
   c. a change in immigration rates
   d. a change in wages offered by employers

5. The marginal revenue product is
   a. the marginal cost of hiring one more unit of labor.
   b. the revenue the firm receives from adding one more unit of labor.
   c. the additional labor required to produce one more unit of the product.
   d. the revenue the firm receives from selling one more unit of the product.

6. What is the difference between marginal revenue product and the value of the marginal product in competitive labor markets?
   a. The value of the marginal product is higher than marginal revenue product.
   b. The value of the marginal product is lower than marginal revenue product.
   c. Marginal revenue product is based on output, whereas the value of the marginal product is based on sales of the product.
   d. There is no difference because marginal revenue and price are equal.

7. If the demand for the product rises in a competitive market, the demand for labor in a competitive labor market will
   a. not change.
   b. rise until marginal revenue product just equals total variable costs.
   c. rise.
   d. fall.

8. In the table to the right, the marginal product of the second worker is
   a. 20.
   b. 15.
   c. 10.
   d. 5.

| Labor | Output |
| --- | --- |
| 0 | 0 |
| 1 | 25 |
| 2 | 45 |
| 3 | 60 |
| 4 | 70 |
| 5 | 75 |

9. In the table to the right, if the competitive price of the product is equal to $20, then the marginal revenue product of the fourth worker is
   a. $200.
   b. $150.
   c. $100.
   d. $50.

10. Which of the following will have the *least* impact on the demand for labor?
    a. a change in the price of the product
    b. a rise in worker productivity due to the introduction of computers in the production process
    c. a change in interest rates
    d. a change in the price of the product with a cross elasticity of demand equal to zero

Use Figure HW-1 to answer questions 11–13.

11. If the firm is a competitor in both the product and input markets, what would equilibrium employment equal?

12. If the firm is a competitor in the input market and a monopolist in the product market, what would equilibrium wage be?

13. If the firm is a competitor in the input market and a monopolist in the product market, what would monopolistic exploitation of each unit of labor equal?

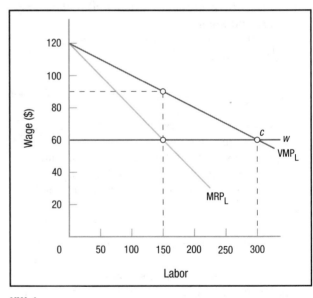

**HW-1**

Use Figure HW-2 to answer questions 14–16.

14. If the firm is a competitor in the product market and a monopsonist in the labor market, what would equilibrium employment be?

15. If the firm is a competitor in the product market and a monopsonist in the labor market, what would equilibrium wage be?

16. If the firm is a competitor in the product market and a monopsonist in the labor market, what would monopsonistic exploitation of each unit of labor equal?

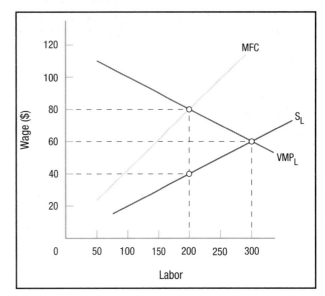

**HW-2**

17. Which of the following factors does *not* affect the elasticity of demand for labor?
    a. how elastic or inelastic the demand is for the product
    b. how difficult it is to substitute capital for labor
    c. how much the average worker earns weekly
    d. how large labor cost is as a percent of total costs

18. Marginal factor cost is
    a. how much more it costs the firm to produce an additional unit of the product.
    b. the additional cost of replacing a worker with a piece of equipment.
    c. how much more a monopolist must pay to retain good employees.
    d. the added cost of hiring one additional unit of labor.

19. When the supply of land is perfectly inelastic,
    a. rent is determined by how difficult it is to bring more land into productive use.
    b. rent depends entirely on the demand for land.
    c. taxing this land would lead to drastic cuts in the amount of land being used.
    d. rent depends entirely on the degree of regulation of business.

20. If an asset (like land) is expected to produce rent of $2,000.00 a year forever, and interest rates are currently 5%, then a rough approximation of the value of this asset is
    a. $10,000.
    b. $20,000.
    c. $40,000.
    d. $80,000.

| | Use the ExamPrep to Get Ready for Exams | STEP 6 |

This sheet (front and back) is designed to help you prepare for your exams. The chapter has been boiled down to its key concepts. You are asked to answer questions, define terms, draw graphs, and, if you wish, add summaries of class notes.

## Competitive Labor Supply

Describe the characteristics of competitive labor markets:

Describe the choices an individual makes when determining whether to supply labor to the market:

What is the shape of the individual's labor supply curve?

Describe the substitution effect:

Describe the income effect:

### Factors That Change Labor Supply

List the factors that can alter the supply of labor:

## Competitive Labor Demand

Define the following.

Marginal revenue product:

The value of the marginal product:

### Factors That Change Labor Demand

List the factors that can alter the demand for labor:

### Elasticity of Demand for Labor

Define the elasticity of demand for labor:

List the factors that can alter the elasticity of demand for labor:

### Competitive Labor Market Equilibrium

In the grid, diagram the competitive firm's labor market equilibrium. (Hint: Assume the overall market has set an equilibrium wage of $W_e$ for labor.)

## Imperfect Labor Markets and Other Input Markets

Define monopsony:

The table below summarizes the four market possibilities for imperfect labor markets (labor and product markets). Use the four grids below to graph and label each of these possibilities.

| Labor Market | Product Market | |
|---|---|---|
| | Competitive | Monopolist |
| Competitive | W = VMP | W = MRP < VMP |
| Monopsony | W < MFC = VMP | W < MFC = MRP < VMP |

## Capital Markets

Define the following.

Capital:

Capital markets:

Present value:

Rate of return:

## Land

Describe the concept of economic rent:

## Entrepreneurship

Describe the role of the entrepreneur:

What motivates entrepreneurs?

# Additional Study Help Chapterwide Practice Questions

## Matching

Match the description with the corresponding term.

___ 1. Supply of labor
___ 2. Income effect
___ 3. Substitution effect
___ 4. Demand for labor (derived demand)
___ 5. Marginal revenue product
___ 6. Value of the marginal product
___ 7. Elasticity of demand for labor
___ 8. Monopsony
___ 9. Exploitation of labor
___ 10. Present value
___ 11. Rate of return
___ 12. Rent
___ 13. Economic profit

a. Derived from consumer demand for a product and the productive capacities of labor.
b. The time a person is willing to spend or the amount of labor a person is willing to supply at various wage rates.
c. The above-normal reward entrepreneurs receive for combining land, labor, and capital to produce goods and services and for assuming the risks that come with producing goods and services.
d. The value of an added worker to a firm.
e. At high enough wage rates, people may conclude that they can earn enough to support their lifestyles by working fewer hours.
f. Defined as marginal physical product times price.
g. The tendency to replace work for leisure as wages rise.
h. A market with a single buyer or employer.
i. Evaluating investment proceeds by asking at what rate of interest the investment will break even.
j. The responsiveness of the quantity of labor demanded to changes in wages.
k. Workers are paid less than the value of their marginal product.
l. Measures how much future returns are worth today.
m. The return or income that flows to land as an input (factor) of production.

## Fill-In

Circle the word(s) in parentheses that complete the sentence.

1. The time an individual is willing to work is referred to as the (substitution effect, income effect, sup-

ply of labor) _____, and when higher wages lead to fewer hours worked, we know that the (substitution effect, income effect, supply of labor) _____ is at work, but when higher wages lead to more hours worked, then the (substitution effect, income effect, supply of labor) _____ must dominate.

2. Marginal revenue times the marginal physical product of labor is equal to (value of the marginal, marginal revenue) _____ product of labor. Competitive firms are price takers, meaning that they hire workers up to the point where the wage is equal to the (value of the marginal, marginal revenue) _____ product of labor.

3. Changes in the demand for labor are caused by a change in product demand and (changes in worker productivity, labor's share of production costs, nonwage income) _____. The elasticity of demand for labor is affected by the elasticity of demand for product and (changes in worker productivity, labor's share of production costs, nonwage income) _____.

4. Firms that are monopolies in the product market but face competition in labor markets hire labor where (W = VMP, W = MRP, W = MFC) _____. Firms that are competitive in both markets hire labor where (W = VMP, W = MRP, W = MFC) _____, but monopsonists in the labor market who are competitors in product markets hire labor where (W = VMP, W = MRP, W = MFC) _____.

5. When market interest rates rise, the present value of an annuity will (rise, fall, not change) _____. When a resource like land is fixed in supply, rent is determined by (cost, demand, present value) _____. Entrepreneurs are paid (rent, income, profit) _____ for combining factors to produce a product and for assuming the risk of the business.

## True-False

Circle the correct answer.

T / F 1. In a competitive labor market, firms will tightly control or even distort wage information so that workers rarely know what other workers are paid.

T / F 2. In a competitive labor market, labor is regarded as a homogeneous commodity—

one employee is assumed to be just as productive as another.

T / F   3. To the economist, *leisure* implies only those activities that are truly relaxing or enjoyable.

T / F   4. Industry labor supply curves are positively sloped.

T / F   5. When people begin to substitute leisure for the income that comes from work at very high wage rates, this is evidence of the substitution effect.

T / F   6. The more wages rise, the lower the opportunity cost of leisure.

T / F   7. Demographic changes in the workforce, such as an increased labor force participation rate among women, will cause shifts in the supply of labor curve rather than changes in the quantity of labor supplied.

T / F   8. The competitive firm's demand for labor is derived from the demand for the firm's products and the productivity of labor.

T / F   9. For firms in competitive labor markets, $VMP_L = MRP_L$.

T / F   10. A decline in the demand for a product will raise MRPL for the firm producing it.

T / F   11. The more difficult it is for a firm to substitute capital for labor, the more elastic will be its demand for labor.

T / F   12. The elasticity of demand for labor is more elastic in the short run than it is in the long run.

T / F   13. A monopsony is a market that contains only a single buyer.

T / F   14. A firm that is a monopolist in the product market will offer its workers a wage equal to the value of their marginal product.

T / F   15. The monopsonist will face a positively sloped supply curve for the input of which it is the only buyer.

T / F   16. If a firm employs five workers at $10 per hour, but it must offer $12 per hour to attract a sixth worker, the marginal factor cost of this sixth worker is $12.

T / F   17. A firm with both monopoly and monopsony power will hire more workers, but pay them a lower wage than would a competitive firm.

T / F   18. The present value of a payment of $500 next year will be worth something less than $500.

T / F   19. The rate of return approach to evaluating investments proceeds by asking at what rate of interest the investment would just break even.

T / F   20. The single-tax movement initiated by Henry George sought to derive all tax revenues from business profits.

## Multiple Choice

Circle the correct answer.

1. Which of the following is *not* true of a competitive labor market?
   a. Wage information is accurate and widely available.
   b. Its firms operate in competitive product markets.
   c. Wage rates reflect the monopsonistic exploitation of labor.
   d. Labor is regarded as a homogeneous commodity.

2. An individual's supply of labor curve will typically be
   a. downward sloping.
   b. upward sloping indefinitely.
   c. upward sloping until daily hours worked equals 24.
   d. upward sloping for some time, then bending backward at very high wage rates.

3. When people begin substituting leisure for the income from work at high wage rates, this is evidence of
   a. the substitution effect.
   b. the income effect.
   c. the monopsony effect.
   d. monopsonistic exploitation of labor.

4. When people choose to work more hours as wage rates rise, this is evidence of
   a. the substitution effect.
   b. the income effect.
   c. the labor-wage effect.
   d. monopsonistic exploitation of labor.

5. The substitution effect for labor is
   a. always positive.

b. initially positive, but becomes negative at very high wage rates.

c. always negative.

d. initially negative, but becomes positive at very high wage rates.

6. Which of the following will *not* produce a shift in the supply of labor curve for a particular job?

a. demographic changes in the workforce

b. a change in the nonmonetary aspects of the job, such as its pleasantness or riskiness

c. a change in the job's wage rate

d. a change in the wage rates of alternative jobs

7. If workers in the steel industry are given a raise, the supply of labor the iron industry faces can be expected to

a. grow.

b. remain about the same.

c. shrink.

d. do any of the above—the labor situations in the two industries are completely unrelated.

8. Which of the following would likely cause the supply of labor for a particular job to shrink?

a. New safety regulations are implemented, making the job less risky.

b. The wages for several alternative jobs are reduced.

c. Welfare payments for people who do not work are reduced.

d. Immigration laws are tightened, reducing population growth.

9. A competitive firm's demand for labor is derived from

a. demand for the firm's output and workers' income needs.

b. demand for the firm's output and the productive capabilities of its workers.

c. political pressures to reduce unemployment rates.

d. the supply of available labor and its productive capabilities.

10. The number of units of output produced by the last worker hired is labeled

a. marginal physical product of labor.

b. marginal revenue.

c. marginal revenue product of labor.

d. value of the marginal product.

11. Which of the following is *not* true for a competitive firm?

a. $VMP_L = MRP_L$

b. $MPP_L = VMP_L \times MR$

c. $MRP_L = MPP_L \times MR$

d. $MPP_L = \Delta Q / \Delta L$

12. Which of the following will *not* change a particular firm's demand for labor?

a. a change in the price of capital equipment

b. a change in demand for the firm's product

c. a change in worker productivity brought about by installing a new generation of machinery

d. a change in the wage rates unions will accept

13. If the price of capital drops (interest rates go down), a firm's demand for labor can be expected to

a. decline.

b. stay about the same.

c. increase.

d. any of the above—there is no relation between the cost of capital and the demand for labor.

14. Which of the following does *not* influence the elasticity of demand for labor?

a. labor's share of the total production costs

b. the elasticity of demand for the product

c. wage rates in alternative jobs

d. the ease of input substitutability

15. The market demand for labor in a competitive industry is found by

a. surveying all of the executives in the industry.

b. summing all wages paid in the industry.

c. summing the marginal revenue product of labor of all the firms in the industry.

d. summing the adjusted market demand curves of all of the firms in the industry.

16. If the elasticity of demand for toasters rises, the elasticity of demand for labor in the toaster manufacturing market can be expected to

a. rise.

b. remain about the same.

c. fall.

d. any of the above—elasticity of product demand and elasticity of demand for labor aren't related to each other.

Fill in the table below for a firm in a competitive labor market, where P = \$10 and W = \$100, then use it to answer questions 17 and 18.

| L | Q | MPP | P | MRP = VMP | W |
|---|----|-----|----|-----------|-----|
| 0 | 0  | 0   | 10 | 0         | 100 |
| 1 | 8  |     | 10 | _____     | 100 |
| 2 | 18 |     | 10 | _____     | 100 |
| 3 | 30 |     | 10 | _____     | 100 |
| 4 | 40 |     | 10 | _____     | 100 |
| 5 | 48 |     | 10 | _____     | 100 |
| 6 | 54 |     | 10 | _____     | 100 |

17. What is the equilibrium level of employment for the firm?

a. either two or four workers

b. three workers
c. four workers
d. six workers

18. What is the equilibrium level of employment for the firm if the wage rate falls to $80?
   a. four workers
   b. three workers
   c. five workers
   d. six workers

19. Monopsony power is defined as
   a. a market that has only a single seller.
   b. a market that has only a single buyer.
   c. the control a firm has over the price of its product.
   d. the control firms exercise over their workers.

20. A firm with a monopoly in the product market that buys labor in a competitive market can be expected to pay its workers
   a. something less than the prevailing market wage.
   b. the prevailing market wage.
   c. something more than the prevailing market wage.
   d. a wage equal to the value of the marginal product of labor.

21. Which of the following *least* fits the description of a monopsonist?
   a. the U.S. Postal Service
   b. a steel town's lone steel mill
   c. a fast-food restaurant
   d. the U.S. Air Force

22. Marginal factor cost (MFC) of labor is
   a. the amount it costs a firm to hire one more worker.
   b. the wage a firm must pay to the last worker hired.
   c. the difference between the wage of the last worker hired and that of previous workers.
   d. the cost to a firm of replacing a machine with a human worker.

23. Which of the following does *not* occur in cases of monopsonistic exploitation of labor?
   a. Labor is paid less than the value of it marginal product.
   b. The monopsonist offers a wage at the level where $S_L = VMP_L$.
   c. The monopsonist hires at a level where $MFC = VMP_L$.
   d. The monopsonist's demand for labor equals its $VMP_L$.

24. If the interest rate is 8%, what is the present value of an investment that promises to yield $500 annually forever?
   a. $62.50

b. $500
c. $4,000
d. $6,250

25. To economists, land is any natural resource that is
   a. elastically supplied.
   b. essentially unlimited.
   c. inelastically supplied.
   d. used in production.

26. Profits are the rewards to entrepreneurs for all *except* which one of the following?
   a. combining land, labor, and capital to produce goods and services
   b. assuming the risks of producing goods and services
   c. seeing market needs that others have not seen
   d. owning land

## Essay-Problem

Answer in the space provided.

The questions below can be challenging. Your answers may not always the same as those we suggest, but they should be close. Use these questions as another learning exercise for the material in this chapter.

1. What are the four inputs?

2. What assumption about competitive labor markets seems the most controversial?

3. Why is the opportunity cost of leisure important in determining the supply of labor?

4. At what point does the labor supply curve become backward bending?

5. Which is likely to have more monopsony power: the New York City school district or a much smaller rural school district in upstate New York?

6. Why would one use the rate of return approach rather than sticking with the present value approach?

7. Does land really have a vertical supply curve?

8. Is entrepreneurship more likely to be found in small companies or large corporations?

9. Why do interest rates affect the demand for labor?

10. Is the substitution effect the same for product markets and input markets?

## What's Next

This chapter has covered a lot of material. You now have a good understanding of what input markets are and how they work. In the same way that competitive product markets are the benchmark for market structures, competitive labor markets lead to the best results for workers. In competitive markets, individuals are paid the value of their marginal products. How productive you are determines your wages and your standard of living.

In the next chapter, we look at some specific aspects of labor markets, including investment in human capital (education and on-the-job training) that increase productivity and living standards. In addition, we examine economic discrimination and look at the history and impacts of unions and collective bargaining.

## Answers to Chapterwide Practice Questions

### Matching

| | | |
|---|---|---|
| 1. b | 6. f | 11. i |
| 2. e | 7. j | 12. m |
| 3. g | 8. h | 13. c |
| 4. a | 9. k | |
| 5. d | 10. l | |

### Fill-In

1. supply of labor, income effect, substitution effect
2. marginal revenue, value of the marginal
3. changes in worker productivity, labor's share of production costs
4. W = MRP, W = VMP, W = MFC
5. fall, demand, profit

## True-False

| | | | |
|---|---|---|---|
| 1. F | 6. F | 11. F | 16. F |
| 2. T | 7. T | 12. F | 17. F |
| 3. F | 8. T | 13. T | 18. T |
| 4. T | 9. T | 14. F | 19. T |
| 5. F | 10. F | 15. T | 20. F |

## Multiple Choice

| | | | |
|---|---|---|---|
| 1. c | 5. a | 9. b | 13. a |
| 2. d | 6. c | 10. a | 14. c |
| 3. b | 7. c | 11. b | 15. d |
| 4. a | 8. d | 12. d | |

16. a

| L | Q | MPP | P | MRP = VMP | W |
|---|---|---|---|---|---|
| 0 | 0 | 0 | 10 | 0 | 100 |
| 1 | 8 | 8 | 10 | 80 | 100 |
| 2 | 18 | 10 | 10 | 100 | 100 |
| 3 | 30 | 12 | 10 | 120 | 100 |
| 4 | 40 | 10 | 10 | 100 | 100 |
| 5 | 48 | 8 | 10 | 80 | 100 |
| 6 | 54 | 6 | 10 | 60 | 100 |

| | | |
|---|---|---|
| 17. c | 21. c | 25. c |
| 18. c | 22. a | 26. d |
| 19. b | 23. b | |
| 20. b | 24. d | |

## Essay-Problem

1. Labor, capital, land, and entrepreneurship.
2. Labor is considered a homogeneous commodity—one unit of labor is a perfect substitute for another.
3. For most people, the cost of leisure rises as the wage rate rises. Having fun costs more when the alternative—working—increases in value. Only those people who are fabulously rich might ignore the call of very high wages.
4. The simple answer is when the income effect swamps the substitution effect. The backward bending labor supply curve has been observed empirically. In general, it takes high levels of income before the income effect overpowers the substitution effect. But ultimately, it depends on each individual's preferences.
5. Most likely, the smaller rural school district will have more monopsony power because it faces no—or fewer—competitors in the immediate area. The New York City school district, though a large employer of labor, faces competition from suburban school districts.
6. The rate of return approach lets one compare projects of different sizes. A plant expansion might lead to a large income stream, whereas a product expansion might lead to a much smaller income stream. The present value of the first might be much larger than the second. But the second might be much more profitable; the rate of return approach would tell you this.

7. It is useful to think of it in this way. Yet, when housing prices rise spectacularly, this puts pressure on current landholders to improve their land. Landholders drain swampland or remove boulders so that they can sell this previously unused land to housing developers. However, there is an ultimate physical limit to land—you cannot squeeze 2 acres of land out of 1 acre.

8. Large corporations tend to be bureaucratic, whereas small companies tend to be more flexible. Large corporations can encourage entrepreneurship, but it is tough to do this. Thus, entrepreneurs tend to be driven out of large corporations and form their own companies.

9. Interest rates drive the cost of capital. When capital becomes more expensive, firms seek to substitute less-expensive labor for more-expensive capital. Specifically, if a firm finds that it has to increase production, but the cost of capital has made machinery much more expensive, it will try to hire more workers to meet its production needs.

10. No. In input markets such as labor, when the price (wage rate) rises, people substitute more hours of work. The substitution effect for labor is always positive. In product markets, the substitution effect is negative: When price falls, consumption rises.

# Labor Market Issues

# 12

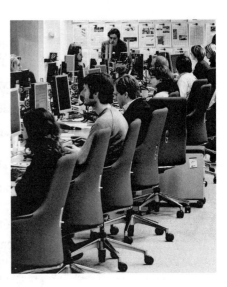

imagebroker/Alamy

## Everyone Is Affected by Labor Market Issues

In the last chapter, we looked at the theory of input markets. Now we want to look more closely at one particular input: labor markets. We will discuss such topics as the link between education and earnings, economic discrimination, and unions. You undoubtedly will have some personal interest in these topics.

| | This Is What You Need to Know | STEP 1 |
| --- | --- | --- |

**After studying this chapter you should be able to**

■ Describe the relationship between education and earnings.

■ Understand how the rate of return on a college degree is computed.

■ Know how market equilibrium levels for human capital are determined.

■ Understand the different theories of human capital.

■ Describe the difference between general and specific training.

■ Describe Becker's theory of economic discrimination.

■ Describe the concept of segmented labor markets and how they affect wage levels.

■ Describe federal laws and policies regarding discrimination.

- Describe the history, costs, and benefits of trade unions.
- Discuss the evolution of labor markets.

---

## STEP 2     Review the Key Terms

**Investment in human capital:** Investments such as education and on-the-job training that improve the productivity of human labor.

**Screening/signaling:** The argument that higher education simply lets employers know that the prospective employee is intelligent and trainable and has the discipline potentially to be a good employee.

**On-the-job training:** Training typically done by employers, ranging from suggestions at work to sophisticated seminars.

**General training:** Training that improves a worker's productivity in all firms.

**Specific training:** Training that improves a worker's productivity in a specific firm.

**Economic discrimination:** When workers of equal ability are paid different wages or in any other way discriminated against because of race, color, religion, gender, age, national origin, or disability.

**Segmented labor markets:** Labor markets split into separate parts. This leads to different wages paid to different sectors even though both markets are highly competitive.

**Secondary boycott:** Occurs when unions clash with one firm and put pressure on a neutral, second firm to enlist the help of the second firm to obtain the union's objectives with the original firm.

**Closed shop:** Workers must belong to the union before they can be hired.

**Union shop:** Non-union hires must join the union within a specified period of time.

**Agency shop:** Employees are not required to join the union, but must pay dues to compensate the union for its services.

**Right-to-work laws:** Laws created by the Taft-Hartley Act that permitted states to outlaw union shops.

---

## STEP 3     Work Through the Chapter Tutorials

# Investment in Human Capital

### Frequently Asked Questions

Q: **How do workers invest in themselves? How do firms invest in their workers?**

A: Workers invest in themselves by going to school or learning a trade. Firms invest in workers through on-the-job training or in-house training for employees.

Q: **How can we calculate the return to human capital investment?**

A: The value of human capital investment can be determined using investment analysis. Investments in education involve the direct costs of education and forgone earnings. The benefits of such investments are then spread over the individual's working life.

**Q:** What influences the supply and demand for human capital investment?

**A:** Anything that reduces the availability of funds will reduce investments in human capital. The demand for human capital, meanwhile, is influenced by an individual's abilities and learning capacity. Human capital improves an individual's productivity, thereby resulting in higher lifetime earnings. Productivity thus links education and earnings.

**Q:** Why can a college degree be considered a signaling device rather than an investment in human capital?

**A:** Some economists suggest that investments in human capital do little more than serve as screening or signaling devices for employers. With this view, a college degree is merely a proxy for trainability, discipline, good work habits, and intelligence.

**Q:** What are the two types of on-the-job training, and why do firms tend to offer one and not the other?

**A:** On-the-job training falls into two categories: general and specific training. General training improves productivity at all firms, while specific training improves productivity only at one specific firm. Firms rarely provide general training; workers must get this training on their own. Firms will, however, provide specific training if the returns are high enough.

## Keep in Mind

We saw earlier that over the longer term, productivity determines an individual's standard of living. Investment in human capital typically determines individual productivity, so making investments in ourselves is extremely important. Since you are in college, you probably have a general sense of this.

# Investment in Human Capital Quick Check

## Circle the Correct Answer

1. (T/F) The major costs of attending college are the direct costs such as tuition and books.

2. (T/F) Firms typically pay for specific training for their workers.

3. (T/F) Learning a trade through an apprenticeship program is a form of human capital.

4. (T/F) Firms are generally reluctant to provide their employees with general training because recouping the investment is difficult given that employees can take the training and apply it elsewhere.

5. To determine the supply of investable funds for college, students will tend to use the following funds in what order?
   a. Government subsidized loans, government unsubsidized loans, private market loans, mom and dad.
   b. Government unsubsidized loans, government subsidized loans, private market loans, mom and dad.
   c. Private market loans, government subsidized loans, government unsubsidized loans, mom and dad.
   d. Mom and dad, government subsidized loans, government unsubsidized loans, private market loans.

6. Economists who believe that college degrees have little connection to future worker productivity argue for all *except* which one of the following?
   a. All that college degrees do is let employers know which potential employees have a certain level of trainability, discipline, and intelligence. The degree does not guarantee success.
   b. College degrees are solely screening and signaling devices.
   c. College degrees help the degree holder only, not the general public.
   d. Public support for higher education should be minimal.

7. Young people are more likely to seek further education than older people because
   a. they are smarter than their elders.
   b. the opportunity costs of seeking further education are higher for older people.
   c. their parents push them.
   d. it is easier for young people to get loan money.
8. Older people are less likely to go to medical school than younger people because of all except which one of the following?
   a. Older people face higher opportunity costs.
   b. The time it takes to become a doctor is so long that it leaves much less time for older people to earn income and "pay back" the costs of education.
   c. Younger people are better at screening and signaling.
   d. Older people are much more likely to have family commitments.

9. Which of the following is *not* an example of specific training?
   a. instruction on shipping procedures
   b. training on budgeting formulas used by the firm
   c. knowledge of the inventory system
   d. instruction on using Microsoft Word
10. Which one of the following would you *not* consider in deciding whether to invest in human capital?
    a. the interest costs of loans
    b. the expected rate of return
    c. the cost of earnings forgone, if any
    d. clothing costs for the time you are in school

Score: ____

**Answers: 1. F; 2. T; 3. T; 4. T; 5. d; 6. c; 7. b; 8. c; 9. d; 10. d**

### If You Got 9 or 10 Correct

Go on to Economic Discrimination in the next section.

### If You Didn't Get at Least 9 Correct

You may be going through this material too quickly. It is not difficult, and it reflects to some degree (no pun intended) why you are taking this course. Be sure you know how to set up the costs and benefits of investment in human capital. This is an important concept. Fortunately, the sections in this chapter cover different issues, and each section stands on its own and does not rely on earlier material. Review the material again and then go on to the next section, Economic Discrimination. ■

# Economic Discrimination

## Frequently Asked Questions

Q: **What is economic discrimination?**

A: Economic discrimination occurs whenever workers of equal ability and productivity are paid different wages or otherwise discriminated against in the workplace because of their race, color, religion, gender, age, national origin, or disability. Lower wages, segregation into different occupations, and restrictions on entry into professions are all examples of economic discrimination.

Q: **What is Gary Becker's analysis of economic discrimination, and why does economic discrimination persist?**

A: Gary Becker offered an account of economic discrimination that assumes some employers have a taste for discrimination. Becker concluded that employers who discriminate lose profit opportunities; therefore, competitive pressures should end this discrimination. Competitive forces, however, may not be enough to end discrimination because of the significant costs associated with hiring and firing and otherwise restructuring a firm's workforce. Some workers, moreover, are less mobile than others. If this is true of a group of workers, such as women, this could lead to wage differences that are not clearly discriminatory.

**Q:** **How can segmented markets cause economic discrimination?**

**A:** Another approach to analyzing economic discrimination in labor markets rests on the existence of segmented markets. Various forces can segment workers from different groups into different, noncompeting sectors of the labor market. The labor market can be split into primary and secondary markets (the dual labor market hypothesis); it can broken into predominantly male and female jobs (the job crowding hypothesis); or it can be split into union and non-union or unemployed workers (insider-outsider theory). All these approaches predict separate job markets and different wages for different groups.

Figure 1 shows how segmented markets can lead to wage differentials. Initially, both labor markets pay $W_0$ (point $e$ in both panels) and no wage differential exists. Assume in one segment (labeled High-Paying Employment in panel A) government restrictions (licenses, discrimination, or union membership) reduce the supply of labor to $S_1$. This raises wages in that market; excluded workers move to the other market, increasing supply and reducing wages. The result is a wage differential equal to $W_1 - W_2$.

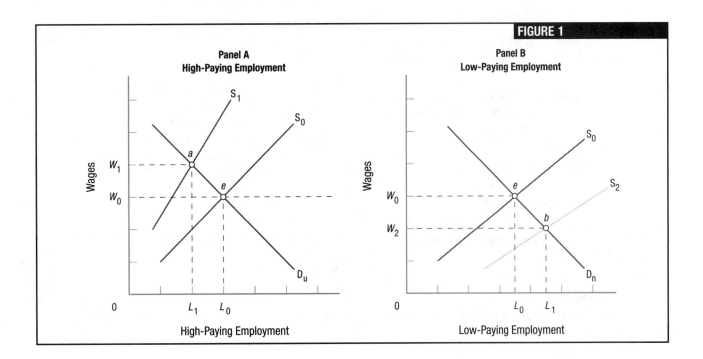

**FIGURE 1**

**Panel A**
**High-Paying Employment**

**Panel B**
**Low-Paying Employment**

**Q:** **What public policies prevent economic discrimination?**

**A:** Public policies and laws have been enacted to counter economic discrimination. These include the Equal Pay Act of 1963, Civil Rights Act of 1964, Executive Order 11246 on affirmative action, Age Discrimination in Employment Act of 1967, and Americans With Disabilities Act of 1990.

## Key Point to Remember

Economic discrimination not only harms the person discriminated against, but also the firm discriminating loses, and society at large loses the higher output that the individual could have produced.

# Economic Discrimination Quick Check

## Circle the Correct Answer

1. (T/F) The surprising conclusion of Gary Becker's theory of economic discrimination is that discrimination hurts discriminating employers as well as the workers who are discriminated against.

2. (T/F) Male–female wage differentials may persist if females are less mobile than males.

3. (T/F) Gary Becker argued that economic discrimination is economically inefficient, causing discriminating employers to miss profit opportunities.

4. Dual labor markets lead to wage differentials because
   a. women prefer more flexible work.
   b. union workers are more productive than non-union employees.
   c. those excluded from one market retire or leave the labor force.
   d. restrictions in one market reduce the labor supply in that market and increase the supply in the other market.

5. Which segmented labor market theory of economic discrimination divides the workforce into unionized and non-union or unemployed workers?
   a. insider-outsider theory
   b. the job crowding hypothesis
   c. the dual labor market hypothesis
   d. the comparable worth hypothesis

6. Affirmative action for firms doing at least $50,000 in business with the federal government is required by
   a. the Taft-Hartley Act of 1947.
   b. the Equal Pay Act of 1963.
   c. the Civil Rights Act of 1964.
   d. Lyndon Johnson's Executive Order 11246 (1965).

7. Competitive forces may not eliminate economic discrimination because of all except which one of the following?
   a. Significant costs may be associated with hiring and firing and otherwise restructuring a firm's workforce.
   b. Women may be less mobile than men.
   c. Women may choose more flexible career paths that do not heavily penalize extended absences from the labor market, and these jobs will tend to pay less.
   d. Women continue to work at different levels of productivity than men in a significant number of jobs in our economy.

8. Which of the following is *not* an example of a segmented labor market theory of economic discrimination?
   a. the job crowding hypothesis
   b. insider-outsider theory
   c. the Becker hypothesis
   d. the dual labor market hypothesis

9. What law required that men and women receive equal pay for equal worth?
   a. The Equal Pay Act of 1963
   b. The Comparable Worth Act of 1964
   c. Executive Order 11246 (1965)
   d. The Taft-Hartley Act of 1947.

10. What law made it unlawful to "refuse to hire or to discharge any individual . . . because of such individual's race, color, religion, sex, or national origin?"
    a. the Taft-Hartley Act of 1947
    b. the Equal Pay Act of 1963
    c. the Civil Rights Act of 1964
    d. Executive Order 11246 (1965)

Score: _____

Answers: 1. T; 2. T; 3. T; 4. d; 5. a; 6. d; 7. d; 8. c; 9. a; 10. c

## If You Got 9 or 10 Correct

Go on to the next section, Labor Unions and Collective Bargaining.

## If You Didn't Get at Least 9 Correct

You didn't read this material very carefully. Economic discrimination is a major public policy issue, and you should understand its various aspects. This is not difficult material; review it again. The next section on unions provides an overview of collective bargaining, its history, and why union memberhip has declined. ■

# Labor Unions and Collective Bargaining

## Frequently Asked Questions

Q: **How are labor unions defined?**

A: Labor unions are legal associations of employees formed to bargain collectively with employers over the terms and conditions of employment.

Q: **What are the benefits and costs to workers of unionization?**

A: Collective bargaining provides workers with increased job security, a more structured work environment, and potentially higher wages. The benefits of unionization, however, do not come free. Monthly dues must be paid to the union, flexibility on the job is often restricted, and infrequently strikes are required, resulting in a loss of wages and possible job loss.

Q: **What are the different types of unions in the workplace?**

A: A closed shop requires workers to be members of a union before they can be hired. A union shop permits union and non-union hires, but requires new employees to join the union within 30 days. In an agency shop, employees are not required to join the union, but they must pay union dues to reimburse the union for its services. The Taft-Hartley Act of 1947 outlawed the closed shop and permitted states to pass right-to-work statutes that prohibit union shops.

## Labor Unions and Collective Bargaining Quick Check

### Circle the Correct Answer

1. (T/F) A union's power comes from its willingness to strike to obtain a work agreement with employers.

2. (T/F) In the 1920s, labor unions in the United States were popular with the public and distrusted by government.

3. (T/F) The Taft-Hartley Act of 1947 required unions to bargain in good faith.

4. (T/F) An agency shop is a workplace where workers are required to be members of the union before they can be hired.

5. (T/F) A significant factor in recent labor markets has been the increase in immigration rates.

6. Unions tend to
   a. increase wages for their members but reduce the number of union jobs.
   b. drive up wages for their members and increase the number of union jobs.
   c. go on strike often.
   d. be stronger in the retail service sector than in the automobile manufacturing sector.

7. What is a closed shop?
   a. Workers are required to be a member of the union before they can be hired.

b. Workers are not required to join the union, but they are required to pay union dues to compensate the union for its services.

c. Workers are not required to join the union or to contribute to it in any way.

d. Both union and non-union hires are allowed, but non-union hires are required to join the union within 30 days.

8. Why has union membership declined as a percentage of wage and salary workers since World War II?
   a. Strikes have become more frequent, leading to public disapproval.
   b. The service sector has grown substantially, and it is harder to organize.
   c. Unions never recovered from the Taft-Hartley Act of 1947.
   d. Young people are not interested in being union members.

9. Which of the following did the National Labor Relations Act of 1935 not do?
   a. require employers to "bargain in good faith" with unions
   b. establish the National Labor Relations Board

c. require unions to "bargain in good faith" with
   employers
d. prohibit yellow dog contracts

10. Which of the following are *not* among the accomplish-
    ments of the 20th-century labor movement?
    a. stronger work safety legislation
    b. Social Security

c. minimum wage laws
d. increases in the number of union jobs

Score: ____

## If You Got 9 or 10 Correct

Move on to the Hints, Tips, and Reminders, the next step.

## If You Didn't Get at Least 9 Correct

You probably went through the material too quickly. It is not difficult. Do a quick review of this section on unions. Although unions today have less than half (as a percent of the labor force) of their peak membership of the 1930s, they are still an important force in our economy, both politically and economically. New strategies are enabling unions to organize the service sector, the fastest growing sector of our economy. As a quick check, list the benefits and costs of unions to workers, and make sure you know how unions affect the labor market.

After you have completed this quick review, go on to next section on Hints, Tips, and Reminders. ■

## STEP 4          Consider These Hints, Tips, and Reminders

1. This chapter covers three distinct issues that affect labor markets. Investment in human capital and economic discrimination are more analytical than the section on labor unions, so you may need to spend a little more time on these first two sections of the chapter.

2. The analyses of segmented labor market and union–non-union wage differentials are essentially the same. Learn it once, use it twice. Separating labor markets into two different markets and then restricting entry (supply) in one market increases wages in that market but shifts some workers to the unrestricted market, thus increasing supply and reducing wages. This is how a wage differential is created.

3. It is important to keep in mind that labor unions are to some extent victims of their own success. Many of the labor market protections we take for granted are the result of collective bargaining that was later passed into law, and others were supported and lobbied for by unions. But changes from globalization and a shift to a more service-oriented economy have reduced manufacturing employment, a traditional stronghold of unions.

## Do the Homework for Chapter 12
## Labor Market Issues

## STEP 5

Instructor _____ Time _____ Student _____

---

**Use the answer key below to record your answers to these homework questions.**

| | | | |
|---|---|---|---|
| 1. _____ | 6. _____ | 11. _____ | 16. _____ |
| 2. _____ | 7. _____ | 12. _____ | 17. _____ |
| 3. _____ | 8. _____ | 13. _____ | 18. _____ |
| 4. _____ | 9. _____ | 14. _____ | 19. _____ |
| 5. _____ | 10. _____ | 15. _____ | 20. _____ |

---

1. Which of the following is *not* a direct cost of a college education?
   a. course textbooks
   b. college tuition
   c. student lab fees
   d. earnings from a full-time job instead of attending college

2. Which of the following does *not* represent general training?
   a. college education
   b. high school education
   c. learning your firm's inventory management system
   d. on-the-job computer software training to use Microsoft PowerPoint

3. Firms will generally not provide general training because
   a. the firm gets no benefit from providing this type of training to employees.
   b. these skills can be used in any firm, not just the firm providing the training.
   c. all employees already have all the general training they can absorb.
   d. management is generally concerned primarily with the bottom line, and the costs of general training will subtract from reported profits.

4. Firms will generally provide specific training because
   a. the firm gets most of the benefit from providing this type of training to employees.
   b. these skills can be used in any firm, including the firm providing the training.

   c. it is a significant fringe benefit to employees.
   d. employees often demand this type of training as a condition of employment.

5. From the view of human capital theory, most people attending college are in their 20s because
   a. college is fun, and people in their 20s want to have fun.
   b. younger people are better at taking tests.
   c. after people have worked for an extended period, their opportunity costs to attending college fall, and so the return from college is too low to be attractive.
   d. younger people have a longer expected work life.

6. Some economists see human capital as just a signaling or screening device. By this, they mean
   a. human capital just builds the resume but adds nothing to the productivity of workers.
   b. human capital enhances productivity of the individual but nothing else.
   c. human capital in the form of higher education adds to productivity, but more important, it indicates to prospective employers that the individual has skills that the employer can immediately profit from.
   d. human capital in the form of higher education adds to productivity, but more important, it indicates to prospective employers that the individual has discipline, is intelligent, and is trainable.

7. Economic discrimination involves
   a. paying different wages to workers of equal ability and productivity.

b. paying workers different wages based solely on the basis of their race, color, religion, gender, age, national origin, or disability.

c. segregating members of a group into an occupation that is paid a different wage.

d. all of the above.

8. Economic discrimination occurs when

a. major league baseball pitchers are paid widely different wages.

b. executive assistants to CEOs are paid higher wages than union organizers.

c. women are restricted to nursing and teaching, resulting in occupational crowding and low wages.

d. college professors with advanced degrees earn less than insurance salespeople with high school diplomas.

9. Which of the following is *not* a major Act or public policy to combat discrimination?

a. Equal Pay Act of 1963

b. Civil Rights Act of 1964

c. Comparable Worth Act of 1965

d. Age Discrimination in Employment Act of 1967

10. Economic discrimination in the United States

a. was never a really serious problem that needed to be solved.

b. has been gradually rising over the last half century.

c. changed little in the face of public policy like the Civil Rights Act of 1964.

d. can cause some people to underinvest in human capital.

11. The segmented market analysis

a. breaks the labor market into union and non-union workers.

b. splits occupations into primary and secondary markets.

c. splits occupations into predominately male and female jobs.

d. all of the above.

12. Unions often try to increase the demand for their labor by suggesting that we "buy the union label." This is usually done to

a. help employers increase demand for their products and increase profits.

b. keep employers from outsourcing computer-programming and high-tech jobs.

c. increase demand for the product and increase wages for members.

d. increase demand for the product, so volume can grow high enough to reach economies of scale and thus result in lower prices.

13. Union membership as a percent of employment

a. steadily declined over the last century.

b. peaked during the depression as individuals needed a union to protect their jobs.

c. has steadily declined since the end of World War II.

d. is rising now as more service and technical workers join unions.

14. Work stoppages or strikes

a. occur frequently.

b. rarely occur.

c. inevitably lead to violence.

d. are outlawed for those in the airline industry.

15. A secondary boycott occurs when

a. a company is struck for the second time.

b. a firm's competitors are involved in a strike.

c. a firm involved in a strike has its suppliers pressured by the striking union.

d. consumers boycott a firm involved in a strike with its workers.

16. A closed shop is one in which

a. union members are not allowed to work.

b. workers must join the union within a month after they are hired.

c. workers do not have to join the union, but they must pay dues to the union representing the company's workers.

d. workers must be members of the union to get hired.

17. An agency shop is one in which

a. union members are not allowed to work.

b. workers must join the union within six months after they are hired.

c. workers do not have to join the union, but they must pay dues to the union representing the company's workers.

d. workers must be members of the union to get hired.

18. Union have the most bargaining power when they have a

a. union shop

b. agency shop

c. closed shop

d. can organize a secondary boycott

19. Approximately what percent of workers belong to a union today?
    a. 6%
    b. 15%
    c. 30%
    d. 45%

20. Since World War II, labor union membership as a percent of those employed in the United States has steadily declined because of which of the following?

a. Unions have been shown to be inherently corrupt.

b. Unions have been unable to increase the wages of their members.

c. Unions may have been too successful in the public policy arena by pushing improvements in working conditions, safety, and minimum wages.

d. Government policies have been decidedly anti-union over the last half century.

| | Use the ExamPrep to Get Ready for Exams | STEP 6 |

This sheet (front and back) is designed to help you prepare for your exams. The chapter has been boiled down to its key concepts. You are asked to answer questions, define terms, draw graphs, and, if you wish, add summaries of class notes.

## Investment in Human Capital

### Education

Describe the relationship between education and earnings:

How do we determine if investment in education is worth it?

Describe the factors that determine the equilibrium levels of investment in human capital:

### On-the-Job Training

Describe the following types of on-the-job training.
General training:

Specific training:

Explain why firms will provide specific training, but workers must pay for general training:

## Economic Discrimination

### Becker's Theory of Economic Discrimination

Describe Gary Becker's theory of discrimination:

What made this analysis unique when it was first proposed?

### Segmented Labor Markets

Describe the three segmented labor market theories:

Use the two grids below to illustrate how a wage differential can result from segmented labor markets:

**Labor Market 1**

**Labor Market 2**

- In both panels, begin with the same labor market supply and demand curves $S_0$ and $D_0$ and the same equilibrium wage, $W_e$. This would be the world without discrimination or market segmentation.
- Now assume that employers and Labor Market 1 discriminate against the group shown in Labor Market 2. Show the new supply curve and equilibrium wage ($W_1$) for Labor Market 1.
- Those workers discriminated against in Labor Market 1 offer their labor to Labor Market 2. Again, illustrate the new supply curve an equilibrium wage ($W_2$) for this market.
- Where initially there was no wage differential, what is the wage difference now?



- Describe some market where this type the discrimination still exists today:



### Public Policy to Combat Discrimination

Describe the major Acts and executive orders designed to eliminate discrimination:

## Labor Unions and Collective Bargaining

Describe the two general types of unions:

Describe some of the benefits and costs of union membership:

Describe the following.
Closed shop:

Union shop:

Agency shop:

Secondary boycott:

Yellow dog contract:

Describe how a union–non-union wage differential can occur:

## Additional Study Help Chapterwide Practice Questions

### Matching

Match the description with the corresponding term.

___ 1. Investment in human capital
___ 2. Screening/signaling
___ 3. On-the-job training
___ 4. General training
___ 5. Specific training
___ 6. Economic discrimination
___ 7. Segmented labor markets
___ 8. Union shop
___ 9. Agency shop
___ 10. Closed shop
___ 11. Right-to-work laws

a. A workplace that permits union and non-union hires, but requires that non-union hires join the union within a given period.

b. Improves productivity equally at all firms. It can range from instruction in typing or computers to apprenticeships in plumbing or carpentry. Most employers will not provide this to their workers, who must pursue it at their own expense.

c. Some economists argue that higher education does not raise worker productivity significantly, but it indicates to employers that the graduates possess certain degrees of trainability, discipline, and intelligence.

d. A workplace that requires workers to be union members before they can be hired.

e. Intended to increase worker productivity and raise the wages a worker commands though investing in education, vocational training, or on-the-job training.

f. Improves productivity at one firm only; for example, teaching employees about a company's specific ordering procedures. Employers will often absorb the cost of it if returns from this investment compare favorably to other investment possibilities.

g. Can take many different forms, from instructions by a supervisor on how to help customers or run a cash register to seminars in a more formal setting away from the job.

h. A workplace that does not require union membership, but does require that employees pay union dues to reimburse the union for its services.

i. Theories about this have been developed along several different lines, including the dual labor market hypothesis, job crowding hypothesis, and insider-outsider theory.

j. Workers of equal ability and productivity are paid different wages or are otherwise discriminated against in the workplace because of race, color, religion, gender, age, national origin, or disability.

k. Prohibitions against union shops, thus ensuring that workers need not join unions as a condition of employment.

### Fill-In

Circle the word(s) in parentheses that complete the sentence.

1. Individuals and firms invest in human capital to increase (employment opportunities, working conditions, productivity, all of these) _____. Individuals typically must invest in (general, specific) _____ training, but firms will often provide (general, specific) _____ training.

2. Economists have found that there is a (negative, positive) _____ relationship between education and earnings. If higher education is simply a screening/signaling device, it provides employers information that educated workers are (highly productive, expensive, trainable) _____.

3. According to Gary Becker's theory of discrimination, employers (gain, lose) _____ from discrimination, and he felt that (government, competition, the U.S. Chamber of Commerce) _____ would eventually eliminate it.

4. Theories of economic discrimination have been developed using segmented markets. The theory where the market is divided (segmented) by company customs, norms, and policies to inspire employee loyalty is known as (dual labor market hypothesis, job crowding hypothesis, insider-outsider theory) _____, but when labor markets are split into "good jobs" (the primary market) and "not so good jobs" (the secondary market) the theory is (dual labor market hypothesis, job crowding hypothesis, insider-outsider theory) _____.

5. A workplace where any employee can work (union or non-union), but all workers must pay union dues is known as a (closed, union, agency) _____ shop; if only union members are hired, the workplace is a (closed, union, agency) _____ shop. A shop where anyone can be

hired, but all workers must eventually join the union is a (closed, union, agency) _____ shop.

## True-False

Circle the correct answer.

T / F   1. The earnings forgone in attending college are typically insignificant as compared to the direct costs of college.

T / F   2. The primary determinants of the decision whether or not to invest in human capital are the interest costs to borrow funds and the rate of return on investments in human capital.

T / F   3. Empirically, the rate of return on college education as an investment in human capital is estimated to be around 40% or 50%.

T / F   4. One reason doctors are highly paid is that, as medical students, they must forgo earning a regular salary for many years.

T / F   5. To finance their education, college students typically turn to private sources of funding first, only turning to government-subsidized loans or family funds as a last resort.

T / F   6. Gary Becker's theory of economic discrimination concludes that discriminatory practices hurt discriminating employers as well as those workers discriminated against.

T / F   7. Any appearance of wage differentials indicates that economic discrimination must be taking place.

T / F   8. One explanation of contemporary male–female wage differentials is that men currently earn far more bachelor's degrees than women.

T / F   9. Affirmative action programs have their origin in Executive Order 11246, issued by President Lyndon Johnson in 1965.

T / F   10. The Civil Rights Act of 1964 provided for equal pay for men and women for equal work.

T / F   11. The ultimate source of a union's power is its willingness to strike if a satisfactory work agreement is not reached with employers.

T / F   12. The Taft-Hartley Act of 1947 required that employers "bargain in good faith" with unions.

T / F   13. A closed shop is a workplace where workers are required to be members of the union before they can be hired.

T / F   14. Over the past 50 years, union membership as a share of the workforce has generally increased.

T / F   15. Union bargaining tactics often result in higher wages for union members but fewer union jobs.

T / F   16. The increasing influx of immigrants and the growth of the high-tech economy have reduced income inequality in the United States.

## Multiple Choice

Circle the correct answer.

1. Which of the following is *not* one of the direct costs of a college education?
   a. books
   b. tuition
   c. forgone wages
   d. student fees

2. In what order will most college students turn to various sources of funds to finance their schooling?
   a. Family funds first, then government-subsidized loans, private loans last.
   b. Private loans first, then family funds, government-subsidized loans last.
   c. Government-subsidized loans first, then private loans, family funds last.
   d. Family funds first, then private loans, government-subsidized loans last.

3. As workers get older and gain more on-the-job experience, the opportunity costs of seeking further education
   a. increase.
   b. remain about the same.
   c. decrease moderately.
   d. fall to zero.

4. Advocates of the screening/signaling view of higher education argue that college degrees give rise to wage differentials primarily by
   a. raising worker productivity.
   b. letting employers know which potential employees have a certain level of trainability, discipline, and intelligence.

c. improving the communications skills of workers.

d. putting more money into the pockets of wealthy professors.

5. Which of the following is *not* an example of general training?
   a. a class in public speaking
   b. typing instruction
   c. a carpentry apprenticeship
   d. instruction in a firm's warehousing procedures

6. Which of the following is *not* an example of specific training?
   a. instruction on running a store's cash register
   b. orientation with a company's shipping procedures
   c. weekend classes in spot welding
   d. going over a restaurant's menu with the wait staff

7. Who will generally absorb the costs of specific training?
   a. the people receiving the training
   b. the firm that employs those receiving the training
   c. the parents or family members of those receiving the training
   d. the U.S. Department of Labor

8. Why are firms typically reluctant to provide their employees with general training?
   a. General training does not increase worker productivity.
   b. General training is invariably more expensive than specific training.
   c. Few firms ever provide their employees with any training, general or specific.
   d. Recouping investments in general training is difficult for firms, because employees can take this training and apply it elsewhere.

9. Gary Becker's theory of economic discrimination assumes that
   a. some employers have a taste for discrimination.
   b. men are generally more productive than women.
   c. labor markets frequently divide themselves into noncompeting segments that support different wage rates.
   d. economic discrimination is likely to be around forever.

10. Gary Becker argues that economic discrimination is
    a. highly efficient, helping employers to get the most qualified people on the job.
    b. economically inefficient, causing discriminating employers to miss profit opportunities.

c. just plain common sense, given that different groups often have different levels of productivity.

d. likely to be around forever, assuming market forces are allowed to operate freely.

11. Which of the following is *not* an example of a segmented labor market theory of economic discrimination?
    a. the job crowding hypothesis
    b. insider-outsider theory
    c. the Landrum-Griffin hypothesis
    d. the dual labor market hypothesis

12. The job crowding hypothesis
    a. breaks occupations into predominantly male and female jobs.
    b. splits the labor market into primary and secondary sectors.
    c. divides the workforce into unionized and non-union or unemployed workers.
    d. divides a firm's workforce into newcomers and employees brought up within the firm.

13. Which of the following is *not* among the reasons male–female wage differentials may well be around for some time?
    a. Women may be less mobile than men, often choosing to accept lower wages rather than moving for a job.
    b. The costs to firms of restructuring their workforces in nondiscriminatory ways may be significant, and competitive markets provide little incentive for change.
    c. Many women may continue to choose occupations with more flexible career paths but lower wages.
    d. For most jobs in our economy today, men and women work at different levels of productivity.

14. What law made it unlawful to "refuse to hire or to discharge any individual . . . because of such individual's race, color, religion, sex, or national origin?"
    a. the Taft-Hartley Act of 1947
    b. the Equal Pay Act of 1963
    c. the Civil Rights Act of 1964
    d. Executive Order 11246 (1965)

15. Economic discrimination in the United States
    a. has been gradually increasing over the past 40 years.
    b. remained more or less constant throughout the 20th century.
    c. has been gradually declining over the past 40 years.
    d. was eliminated with the Civil Rights Act of 1964.

16. The Equal Pay Act of 1963 requires that
    a. all jobs be compensated equally.

b. men and women receive equal pay for equal work.

c. workers of all ages receive equal pay for equal work.

d. workers of all races receive equal pay for equal work.

17. Which of the following is *not* true of labor unions?

a. They are required to bargain in good faith with employers.

b. Their primary purpose is to engage in collective bargaining with employers.

c. They are legally barred from charging their members dues.

d. They sometimes use strikes to achieve their goals.

18. In the 1920s, labor unions in the United States were

a. small, weak, and distrusted by the public.

b. disliked by the public, but politically and economically powerful.

c. both popular with the public and powerful.

d. protected by numerous prolabor laws and sympathetic courts.

19. Which of the following did the National Labor Relations Act of 1935 *not* do?

a. require employers to bargain in good faith with unions

b. establish the National Labor Relations Board

c. prohibit yellow dog contracts

d. prohibit unions from coercing or discriminating against workers who chose not to join the union

20. In what type of workplace are both union and non-union hires allowed, though non-union hires are required to join the union within 30 days?

a. an open shop

b. a closed shop

c. a union shop

d. an agency shop

21. What defines an agency shop?

a. Workers are required to be members of the union before they can be hired.

b. Workers are not required to join the union, but they are required to pay union dues to compensate the union for its services.

c. Workers are not required to join the union or to contribute to it in any way.

d. Both union and non-union hires are allowed, but non-union hires are required to join the union within 30 days.

22. Since World War II, union membership as a percent of those employed in the United States has

a. steadily declined.

b. remained more or less constant.

c. steadily increased.

d. grown intermittently but significantly.

23. Which of the following are *not* among the accomplishments of the 20th-century labor movement?

a. stronger work safety legislation

b. Social Security

c. guaranteed employment for those who wish to work

d. minimum wage laws

24. Approximately what percentage of American workers belonged to unions in the 1990s?

a. 7%

b. 15%

c. 32%

d. 48%

25. If the union's bargaining unit is a small portion of the firm's workforce, the

a. union will have little bargaining power.

b. the firm will be willing to give them anything they want without worrying about the effect on other employees.

c. union's bargaining power is unaffected.

d. union can bargain for higher wages before the firms demand for union labor is affected.

26. Which of these trends has *not* been a factor in the recent evolution of the labor market?

a. There are more two-earner households.

b. There have been dramatic gains by trade unions.

c. There is a growing interest in telecommuting.

d. Immigration rates have increased.

## Essay-Problem

Answer in the space provided.

Labor issues affect all of us. The following questions are designed to extend your understanding of these issues. Use our answers as guides to these extensions.

1. What is the essence of the concept of human capital?

2. Stafford Education loans currently have a fixed interest rate of 6.8%. However, for loans disbursed before July 1, 2006, the rate changes every year but is capped at just under 9.825% maximum per

year. Explain the cap in light of what you have learned about human capital.

3. Does it make sense for retirees to go back to college?

4. In light of what you learned about general and specific training, what skills would you expect a firm to request in a want ad for an office worker?

5. In competitive markets, how do employers who discriminate shoot themselves in the foot?

6. Why do unions set up picket lines during strikes?

7. Why are there so many last-minute settlements between unions and employees?

8. What is one possible reason for the decline in major strikes?

9. What is the rationale behind an agency shop?

## What's Next

After completing this chapter and the last chapter, you now have a deeper understanding of labor markets and some of the complex issues facing workers and employers. Since labor income accounts for 70% of our national income, each of us will confront these issues at some point in our working lives. In the next chapter, we look at the environment and apply economic analysis to environmental issues. Given that the population of the United States now exceeds 300 million and warnings about global warming approach alarmist proportions, economics provides an analytical framework to apply to these issues.

## Answers to Chapterwide Practice Questions

### Matching

| | | | |
|---|---|---|---|
| 1. e | 4. b | 7. i | 10. d |
| 2. c | 5. f | 8. a | 11. k |
| 3. g | 6. j | 9. h | |

## Fill-In

1. all of these, general, specific
2. positive, trainable
3. lose, competition
4. insider-outsider theory, dual labor market hypothesis
5. agency, closed, union

## True-False

| | | | |
|---|---|---|---|
| 1. F | 5. F | 9. T | 13. T |
| 2. T | 6. T | 10. F | 14. F |
| 3. F | 7. F | 11. T | 15. T |
| 4. T | 8. F | 12. F | 16. F |

## Multiple Choice

| | | | |
|---|---|---|---|
| 1. c | 8. d | 15. c | 22. a |
| 2. a | 9. a | 16. b | 23. c |
| 3. a | 10. b | 17. c | 24. b |
| 4. b | 11. c | 18. a | 25. d |
| 5. d | 12. a | 19. d | 26. b |
| 6. c | 13. d | 20. c | |
| 7. b | 14. c | 21. b | |

## Essay-Problem

1. Investing in people (education, on-the-job training) will lead to increases in productivity. It makes people better workers and increases their earnings.

2. To invest in human capital, one must weigh the projected benefits against the projected costs. Projected benefits over one's lifetime are very sensitive to the interest rate. The higher the cost of capital—in this case, the interest rate on borrowed funds—the lower the benefit of investing in human capital. High interest rates will drive people away from attending college or continuing their education later in life. The government caps the interest rate to encourage people to go on to college.

3. The theory of human capital links investments in human capital with productivity over one's working lifetime. Also, the benefit of college to a retiree might be more psychological, but this is a benefit nevertheless. It is up to the retiree to weigh whatever benefits the education would give against the actual costs.

4. The ad should request skills that just about any firm would want, such as typing, filing, knowledge of word-processing programs, maybe some familiarity with Excel.

5. They pay market wages and yet do not get the best workers because they restrict their worker pool. In effect, they give themselves a higher cost structure.

6. There are two major reasons for picket lines. First, during strikes, employers may try to hire replacement workers, called scabs by the union. The union legally cannot prevent these replacement workers from going to work, but they can organize picket lines to put pressure on replacements who have to cross the picket line to get to work. Second, picket lines are used as information tools for potential buyers of the firm's products, telling the public that a strike is going on. If the picket line leads to public shunning of the firm's products, the firm's decline in sales puts added pressure on it to settle with the union.

7. A union's ultimate power comes from the threat of striking. Its members would prefer not to strike because their income vanishes. On the other hand, a firm would prefer not to suffer from the disruption of a strike. Also, once a strike starts, positions tend to harden and become more radical, adding uncertainty to the possibility of a settlement.

It is in the interests of both parties to come to an agreement before a strike occurs. Brinksmanship—waiting until the last minute to settle—is a negotiating tactic that each side uses to get the best possible deal.

8. The federal government has shown a greater willingness to step in and order a cooling-off period, which it can under the law, for potential strikes it considers against the public interest. This willingness has ebbed and flowed, but it is present and must be taken into consideration by major unions contemplating a strike.

9. In an agency shop, one does not have to join the union but has to pay dues to the union to compensate it for its services. The union is the sole negotiator with the firm and negotiates for higher wages and benefits. A non-union worker is the recipient of the higher wages and benefits. If the non-union worker did not pay dues, the worker would be getting these benefits for free, while union members had to pay for them. Out of fairness, the non-union member should contribute toward the union's cost of securing higher wages and benefits for all.

# Public Goods, Externalities, and Environmental Economics

Tim Foley Illustration

## Using Economic Analysis to Understand Environmental Problems Caused by Market Failures

Environmental economics takes economic concepts such as consumer surplus, producer surplus, and market failures, and applies them to environmental problems such as air and water pollution. This will give you a useful framework for analyzing environmental issues. You will get a good understanding of why pollution occurs in markets and what public policy can do to improve the situation. We end the chapter with a look at the economic aspects of climate change.

| This Is What You Need to Know | STEP 1 |

**After studying this chapter you should be able to**

■ Describe the market failures that lead to environmental problems.

■ Describe the impact of negative and positive externalities on society.

■ Describe the Coase theorem on social costs and the role transaction costs play in the optimal allocation of resources.

■ Describe government failures in dealing with market failures.

■ Recognize the importance of the discount rate in assessing the intergenerational costs and benefits of environmental policies.

- Use marginal analysis to determine the optimal level of pollution.

- Describe the differences between command and control policies and market-based approaches to environmental regulation.

- Understand the economic issues surrounding global climate change.

| STEP 2 | Review the Key Terms |  |

**Consumer surplus:** The difference between what consumers (as individuals or the market) would be willing to pay and the market price. It is equal to the area above market price and below the demand curve.

**Producer surplus:** The difference between market price and the price at which firms would be willing to supply the product. It is equal to the area below market price and above the supply curve.

**Social welfare:** The sum of consumer and producer surplus.

**Market failures:** When markets are not competitive or involve public goods, externalities, or common property resources, markets will fail to provide the optimal level of output, and will provide output at too high or low a price.

**Public goods:** Goods that, once provided, no one person can be excluded from consuming (i.e., nonexclusion), and one person's consumption does not diminish the benefit to others from consuming the good (i.e., nonrivalry).

**Nonrivalry:** The consumption of a good or service by one person does not reduce the utility of that good or service to others.

**Nonexcludability:** Once a good or service is provided, it is not feasible to exclude others from enjoying that good or service.

**Cost-benefit analysis:** A methodology for decision making that looks at the discounted value of the costs and benefits of a given project.

**Tragedy of the commons:** Resources that are owned by the community at large (e.g., parks, ocean fish, and the atmosphere) and therefore tend to be over-exploited because individuals have little incentive to use them in a sustainable fashion.

**Externalities:** The impact on third parties of some transaction between others where the third parties are not involved. An external cost (or negative externality) harms the third parties, whereas external benefits (positive externalities) result in gains to them.

**Coase theorem:** If transaction costs are minimal (near zero), a bargain struck between beneficiaries and victims of externalities will be efficient from a resource allocation perspective. As a result, the socially optimal level of production will be reached.

**Government failure:** The result when the incentives of politicians and government bureaucrats do not align with the public interest.

**Command and control policies:** Environmental policies that set standards and issue regulations, which are then enforced by the legal and regulatory system.

**Market-based policies:** Environmental policies that use charges, taxes, subsidies, deposit-refund systems, or tradable emission permits to achieve environmental ends.

## Work Through the Chapter Tutorials

### STEP 3

# Public Goods

## Frequently Asked Questions

Q: **What are consumer surplus and producer surplus?**
A: Consumer surplus is the difference between what people are willing to pay for a product and what they actually pay for it. Producer surplus is the difference between the revenues firms earn from a product and the costs they would be willing to bear to supply it.

Q: **When does market failure occur?**
A: Market failure occurs whenever a market does not provide the socially optimal quantity of a product at the socially optimal price. Market failure can occur because of public goods, externalities, or common property resources.

Q: **What are public goods?**
A: Public goods exhibit both nonrivalry in consumption and nonexcludability. Nonrivalry means that one person's consumption of a good does not reduce the availability of that good to others. Nonexcludability means that once a product has been provided, no consumers can be excluded from consuming the product. Candy bars are a rival and exclusive product; clean air is nonrival and nonexclusive.

Q: **What is the problem with common property resources?**
A: Because common property resources are owned by the community, individuals tend to overuse and overexploit them, as has happened with ocean fishing and some national parks. Solutions to such problems involve either direct government regulation or establishing private property rights.

## Key Point to Remember

Public goods and common property resources are examples of characteristics of products or markets that keep private markets from providing the socially optimal output. These markets often require government intervention of some sort to ensure socially optimal outcomes.

# Public Goods Quick Check

## Circle the Correct Answer

1. (T/F) Total social welfare is equal to consumer surplus minus producer surplus.
2. (T/F) Radio transmissions are a public good because they exhibit both nonrivalry and nonexcludability.
3. (T/F) Consumer surplus is the difference between what people are prepared to pay for a product and what they actually pay for it.
4. (T/F) Downloadable music exhibits nonexcludability because no one is excluded from buying and downloading it.
5. Public goods are
   a. rival in consumption.
   b. goods where some consumers can be excluded.
   c. goods like public television.
   d. both rival in consumption, and some consumers can be excluded from enjoying the benefits of the goods.
6. Which of the following is *not* a public good?
   a. a lighthouse
   b. National Public Radio
   c. national defense
   d. military aircraft
7. What environmental problem arises from common property resources?
   a. negative externality
   b. overexploitation
   c. government failure
   d. high transaction cost

8. Common property resources
   a. face a major problem in that they generate negative externalities.
   b. benefit society and therefore are used at optimal levels.
   c. are often overexploited.
   d. cost so much to exploit that Congress has to step in.
9. If a good exhibits both nonrivalry and nonexcludability, it is
   a. a valuable resource that must be conserved.
   b. a common property resource.
   c. a purely private good.
   d. a public good.
10. "The tragedy of the commons" refers to which of the following practices?
    a. a factory releasing sewage into a river
    b. a factory releasing smoke into the air
    c. a city adding to the number of parks, but not as many as the voters want
    d. people walking their dogs in public parks and not cleaning up after them

Score: ____

**Answers: 1. F; 2. T; 3. T; 4. F; 5. c; 6. d; 7. b; 8. c; 9. d; 10. d**

## If You Got 9 or 10 Correct

You have a good grasp of the concepts of public goods and common resource problems. These issues and concepts form half of the foundation of environmental analysis. Externalities in the next section are the other half. After that you will be ready for the more complex material on environmental policy.

## If You Didn't Get at Least 9 Correct

You should have answered most of these questions correctly. If this is not the case, review this section carefully. Make sure you know why you missed a question. Understanding this section is important for understanding the environmental policy material later on. Do a quick review of the figures in this section; be sure to read the captions under the figures and make sure you understand what is presented. Make sure you understand why private markets will *not* provide public goods.

Environmental policy builds on the analysis of public goods and externalities (covered in the next section) so you will want to get this material straight before proceeding. Take a moment and work through the solved problem below on public goods. Admittedly, it is a relatively simple problem, but if you are missing questions in this area, it will be worth your time to make sure you get the concept of public goods down pat. When you are confident that you can handle public goods, go on to the next section, Externalities. ∎

## Solved Problem: Public Goods

Using the table below, which shows the demand for a public good by individuals a, b, and c, answer the following questions.

| Price | $Q_a$ | $Q_b$ | $Q_c$ | Supply |
|-------|-------|-------|-------|--------|
| 65    | 0     | 0     | 0     | 55     |
| 60    | 0     | 0     | 0     | 50     |
| 55    | 0     | 0     | 0     | 45     |
| 50    | 0     | 0     | 0     | 40     |
| 45    | 0     | 5     | 0     | 35     |
| 40    | 0     | 10    | 0     | 30     |
| 35    | 10    | 15    | 0     | 25     |
| 30    | 20    | 20    | 0     | 20     |
| 25    | 30    | 25    | 20    | 15     |
| 20    | 40    | 30    | 40    | 10     |
| 15    | 50    | 35    | 60    | 5      |
| 10    | 60    | 40    | 80    | 0      |
| 5     | 70    | 45    | 100   | 0      |
| 0     | 80    | 50    | 120   | 0      |

a. In the blank grid below, plot all three demand curves.

b. Plot the total demand for this public good.

c. Given the supply curve, how much at what price will be the public good equilibrium?

### Solution-Discussion

a. See Figure 1 below.

**FIGURE 1**

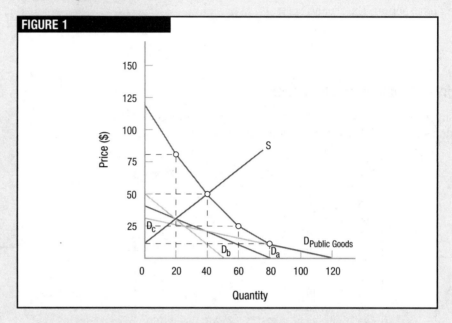

b. Putting together the market demand curve for public goods is a little more challenging than doing the same for normal goods and services. Since all parties get enjoyment from the public good, we essentially need to select a quantity and see how much each person is willing to pay. The three demand curves $D_a$, $D_b$, and $D_c$, correspond to the demands for individuals a, b, and c. Thus, we are adding together the prices they are willing to pay for each quantity. So, for a quantity of 40, person a is willing to pay $20, b is willing to pay $10, and c is willing to pay $20, for a total of $50. This corresponds to the price of $50 when quantity is 40 units.

c. Given the supply curve in the table, and the market demand shown in Figure 1, equilibrium is 40 units at $50 total payments.

# Externalities

## Frequently Asked Questions

Q: **What are externalities?**

A: Externalities, or spillovers, arise when a transaction benefits or harms parties not involved in the transaction. Pollution and littering are examples of negative externalities, or external costs. Positive externalities, or external benefits, include education and vaccinations.

Q: **What is the Coase theorem, and why is it important?**

A: The Coase theorem suggests that if transaction costs are near zero, how property rights are allocated (to pollute or to be free from pollution) will not affect the efficiency of the ultimate allocation of resources. The resulting bargain between the parties will lead to an optimal allocation of resources. Benefits, however, will be distributed differently, depending on the original assignment of property rights.

## Key Point to Remember

Externalities are another reason why markets often do not provide the optimal level of output. They represent spillovers (both negative and positive) to people who are not part of the market transaction.

## Externalities Quick Check

### Circle the Correct Answer

1. (T/F) Littering is a negative externality.
2. (T/F) When China, Europe, India, and the United States generate large amounts of greenhouse gases, they are generating negative externalities.
3. Which of the following is *not* true for externalities?
   a. They can be either negative or positive.
   b. They arise when two parties engage in a transaction and some third party unrelated to either is harmed or benefited by it.
   c. They are called "the tragedy of the commons."
   d. Negative externalities in an unregulated market will lead to the production of too much of a good at too low a price.
4. The Coase theorem suggests which of the following?
   a. Private negotiations over polluting rights will produce efficient results only if these rights are initially distributed evenly among potential polluters.
   b. Private negotiations over polluting rights will produce efficient results only if these rights are initially distributed to the victims of pollution.
   c. Private negotiations over polluting rights will produce efficient results regardless of the transactions costs.
   d. Private negotiations over polluting rights will produce efficient results if transactions costs are low.
5. Which of the following is an example of a negative externality?
   a. Central Park in New York is too crowded to enjoy.
   b. Residents of a community located near a large factory develop respiratory problems attributable to the factory's smoke.
   c. Lake Ontario sees its fishing population depleted by over-fishing.
   d. A community is vaccinated against the flu.
6. When pollution rights are privately negotiated according to the Coase theorem, what condition must be met for the socially optimal allocation of resources to be brought about?
   a. The initial distribution of pollution rights must be equitable.

   b. The victims must hold the distribution of pollution rights.
   c. Transaction costs must be minimal.
   d. Bargaining must be done in good faith.
7. Negative externalities are
   a. the result of a private exchange that imposes costs on others.
   b. the result of product prices being too high for low-income consumers.
   c. the benefits society gets from students in college.
   d. the negative aspects of international trade and out-sourcing.
8. Negative externalities
   a. lead to too little production at market prices that are too high.
   b. are the same as the tragedy of the commons.
   c. lead to too much production at market prices that are too low.
   d. are both nonrival in consumption and nonexclusive once the good is provided.
9. Positive externalities
   a. lead to too little production at market prices that are too high.
   b. are the same as the tragedy of the commons.
   c. lead to too much production at market prices that are too low.
   d. are both nonrival in consumption and nonexclusive once the good is provided.
10. Which of the following goods generates substantial positive externalities?
    a. four-wheeling in the backcountry
    b. eating at McDonalds
    c. getting a college education
    d. traveling to China

Score: ____

**Answers: 1. T; 2. T; 3. c; 4. d; 5. b; 6. c; 7. a; 8. c; 9. a; 10. c**

## If You got 9 or 10 Correct

You picked up the concept of externalities quite well. These concepts, along with the concepts in the previous section, are the basis for America's approach to environmental policy. Before you move on to the next section on environmental policy, make a quick run through the solved problem below.

### If You Didn't Get at Least 9 Correct

These are not particularly difficult questions. You should have done better. Take a moment to write down what is the essence of an externality. Next write down why it is important that private markets provide too much of a product with negative externalities at too low a price. Why should we care about this? (Hint: It has to do with product prices reflecting the full cost of their production.) Next write down why it is important that private markets provide too little of a product with positive externalities at too high a price. Again, why is this important?

After your review of this section and when you are confident you are getting the concept of externalities under control, work through the solved problem below. If you do not understand the problem, start through the section again. When you are done, move on to the next section on environmental policy.

### Solved Problem: Positive and Negative Externalities

Using the table below, which shows the private demand (without externalities) for a product, answer the questions that follow.

| (1) Private Supply | (2) Private Demand | (3) Price | (4) Social Supply Price | (5) Social Demand Price |
|---|---|---|---|---|
| 120 | 0 | 30 | _____ | _____ |
| 100 | 20 | 25 | _____ | _____ |
| 80 | 40 | 20 | _____ | _____ |
| 60 | 60 | 15 | _____ | _____ |
| 40 | 80 | 10 | _____ | _____ |
| 20 | 100 | 5 | _____ | _____ |
| 0 | 120 | 0 | _____ | _____ |

a. In the blank grid below, plot the private demand and supply curves. Show equilibrium price and quantity and label the equilibrium point *e*. What is equilibrium price and output without externalities?

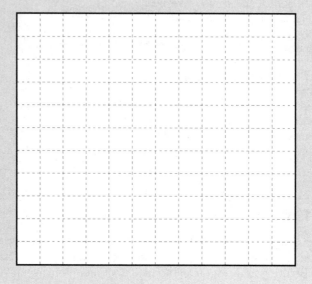

b. Now assume that for each price and output supplied privately, external *costs* are equal to 20% of the per unit price. List the supply price that includes social costs in the fourth column. Graph the social supply curve and label it S$_S$. Label the new equilibrium point *a*. What is the new price and output where this product sells for its full cost, including external cost?

c. Now, beginning again with the original private supplies and demands, assume this product is education that has external benefits equal to $5 a unit. List the demand price that includes social demand in column 5. Plot the new social demand curve and label it D$_S$. Label the new equilibrium point *b*. What is the level of education that is socially optimal? What is the level of subsidy that society needs to provide to education to ensure that the socially optimal level of education is provided?

## Solution-Discussion

a. See Figure 2. Private equilibrium price is $15, and output is 60 units.

**FIGURE 2**

b. See the completed table below. Notice that the price in column 4 is 20% greater than the private price shown in column 3. This added price (cost) represents the external costs imposed by the production of this product. The new S$_S$ curve is shown in Figure 2. The new equilibrium price is around $16.50, and the new output level is 53. Paying full cost for a product, including any negative external costs, results in a higher price and lower output.

| (1)<br>Private<br>Supply | (2)<br>Private<br>Demand | (3)<br><br>Price | (4)<br>Social<br>Supply<br>Price | (5)<br>Social<br>Demand<br>Price |
|---|---|---|---|---|
| 120 | 0 | 30 | 36 | 35 |
| 100 | 20 | 25 | 30 | 30 |
| 80 | 40 | 20 | 24 | 25 |
| 60 | 60 | 15 | 18 | 20 |
| 40 | 80 | 10 | 12 | 15 |
| 20 | 100 | 5 | 6 | 10 |
| 0 | 120 | 0 | 0 | 5 |

c. See the table and Figure 2. The new social demand curve is labeled $D_S$ in the figure. Seventy units of education are now socially optimal, and a $5 per unit subsidy that would shift the private supply curve to the right and pass through point $c$ would be sufficient.

# Environmental Policy

## Frequently Asked Questions

Q:   **What is government failure, and when does it occur?**

A:   Government failures occur when the incentives of policymakers and bureaucrats do not coincide with the public interest. Government regulators are often captured by the industries they regulate, resulting in regulations that benefit the industry rather than consumers.

Q:   **What is the intergenerational aspect of environmental issues, and how do policymakers determine this?**

A:   When developing environmental policies, policymakers must consider and evaluate different possible futures. This intergenerational aspect of environmental issues requires a balancing of interests and complicates policymaking. The decisions made will depend on the discount rate chosen. The higher the discount rate, the lower the value we place on events farther into the future, which can result in significant burdens being placed on future generations. Conversely, if we select a low discount rate, the current generation may be overburdened in paying for benefits to be enjoyed by future generations.

Q:   **Is the optimal pollution level zero?**

A:   Some pollution is acceptable to society. Optimal pollution levels are found where marginal abatement costs equal the marginal benefits. These costs and benefits vary for different types of pollution, industries, and regions of the country. Figure 3 graphs marginal abatement costs against a marginal damages curve; note that the optimal quantity of pollution is not zero.

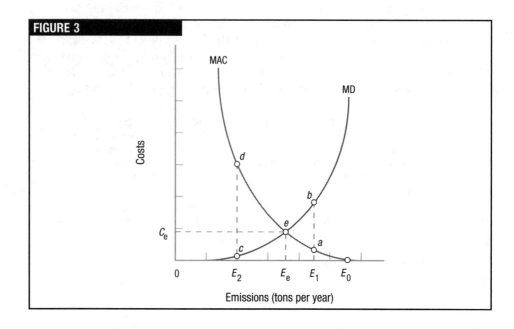

FIGURE 3

Emissions level $E_0$ represents no abatement at all and at that level marginal damages are high, as shown by the MD curve. As abatement or cleanup occurs (moving left from $E_0$), marginal damages drop and marginal costs of cleaning up the pollution rise. At emissions level $E_1$, marginal damages still exceed costs ($b > a$), but once point $e$ is reached, marginal damages and costs are equal. If additional abatement is required, say to $E_2$, costs greatly exceed the benefits ($d > c$), and we are wasting society's resources. As a result, some pollution ($E_e$) typically is socially optimal.

**Q:** What has been the standard approach to environmental policy in the United States?

**A:** Environmental policy in the United States has largely been based on command and control. Command and control policies set standards for polluters—acceptable levels of effluents, for instance—that are systematically enforced through inspections and reports. Another option, though rarely used, is to enact effluent taxes that lead to optimal pollution levels. This is the approach that has been recommended to tackle global climate change—get acceptable levels of carbon dioxide emissions and use marketable permits.

**Q:** What are market-based policies, and how do they work?

**A:** More recently, market-based policies have been recognized as being more efficient than many command and control policies. First, the government determines a permissible pollution level (ideally, near the optimal level); then, firms are allocated permits to pollute, which they may buy, sell, and trade. Pollution is then limited to this permissible level, and the price of permits adjusts to the costs of abatement.

## Key Point to Remember

The optimal level of pollution will not be zero except in extreme cases of highly toxic substances. Some level of pollution, determined where marginal benefits equal marginal costs, will be acceptable to society. In the past, environment protection was based heavily on command and control policies (regulations and prohibitions), but today there is a movement to more market-based solutions that typically lead to better results at lower costs.

# Environmental Policy Quick Check

## Circle the Correct Answer

1. (T/F) Government failure occurs when the incentives of politicians and government bureaucrats do not coincide with the public interest.
2. (T/F) If policymakers use a low discount rate when setting environmental policies, future generations will bear most of the costs of these policies.
3. (T/F) Government failure occurs when the market does not provide the socially optimal amount of a good at the socially optimal price.
4. (T/F) If marginal abatement costs are higher than the marginal damage caused by pollution, society would be better off with some pollution, not zero pollution.
5. When would a pollution tax be likely to achieve pollution-reduction goals more efficiently than command and control policies?
   a. when the type of pollution is water pollution
   b. when firms have different abatement costs
   c. when abatement costs are low
   d. when abatement costs are high
6. In a marketable permits system for reducing pollution, the government
   a. sets the price of each permit.
   b. forbids anyone except polluters from holding the permits.
   c. calculates marginal abatement costs.
   d. sets a maximum quantity of pollution and issues permits granting the "right" to pollute a certain amount.
7. A regulatory body that requires local factories to limit their discharges into nearby rivers to a specific level is an example of what kind of regulatory policy?
   a. marginal abatement cost
   b. command and control

　　c. abatement taxes
　　d. marketable permits
8. Which one of the following is *not* true for a command and control environmental policy?
　　a. It was favored by policymakers before the 1990s.
　　b. It usually sets standards of conduct that are enforced by the legal or regulatory system.
　　c. It often uses abatement taxes.
　　d. Standards treat all firms in an industry the same.
9. Which of the following is *not* a market-based environmental policy?
　　a. plastic-bottle refund systems
　　b. rules for usable technologies

　　c. tradable permits
　　d. user charges for water and wastewater management
10. One benefit of marketable permits is that regulators
　　a. do not have to determine marginal abatement costs.
　　b. can set any price they want for the permits.
　　c. can restrict permit-holding to the polluters only.
　　d. can restrict the technologies used for pollution control.

Score: ＿＿＿＿

Answers: 1. T; 2. F; 3. F; 4. T; 5. b; 6. d; 7. b; 8. c; 9. b; 10. a

## If You Got 9 or 10 Correct

You have done well on a difficult area of analysis. Keeping the curves straight in this section is a difficult chore. The reward, of course, is that you have a good grasp of the general types of environmental policies used to combat market failures in the environment. Go on and review the Hints, Tips, and Reminders.

## If You Didn't Get at Least 9 Correct

Review the material slowly. The graphs and concepts in this section are difficult, so spend a little extra time to make sure you understand the following:

■ Government failure can happen just like market failure. When bureaucratic goals are not aligned with society's interests, governments can make a mess of the environment.

■ The balancing of interests between generations adds significant complexity to environmental policies. Policymakers and politicians must consider the interests of not only their children and grandchildren but also the grandchildren of their great-grandchildren. This is especially a factor with an issue like climate change that takes a long time to develop. Economists use discount rates to balance these types of interests. If too high a discount rate is chosen, future generations will bear an unconscionable burden. If too low a rate is selected, the current generation will sacrifice much, and many in the future will reap the benefits. There is no absolutely correct solution to this problem.

■ Optimal pollution levels are not zero! Policymakers should adjust policies to the point where *marginal* abatement costs are just equal to *marginal* benefits from pollution abatement. Review the discussion surrounding Figure 3 and make sure you understand the reasoning.

■ Policies to reduce pollution fall into two broad categories: command and control and market-based policies. With command and control policies, policymakers set standards (like the 2004 ozone air quality standards set for most metropolitan areas), and local and regional governments must develop plans and policies to meet these requirements over the next decade. Market-based policies use effluent charges, taxes, deposit-refund systems, and tradable permits to reach similar results, typically at lower costs and faster. These approaches often give firms and industries additional incentives to develop and implement the most technically efficient means of reducing pollution.

■ Market-based policies have the advantage of encouraging an industry to meet the goals of pollution reduction at the lowest cost. When taxes are used to encourage pollution reduction, the costs associated with paying taxes on effluents encourage firms and industries to find additional ways to reduce pollution and thus avoid paying the taxes.

■ The idea of tradable permits is not new. It took a long time for policymakers, environmentalists, and the public to accept the idea. Giving corporations the right to pollute went against the grain. Several successful pilot projects, however, changed many minds, and permits are now part of the standard arsenal for policymakers. Market demand and supply adjust to set the price for the allowable pollution permitted. In most instances where permits have been used, the eventual price of permits has been lower than forecasted, suggesting that cleanup costs were less than expected. Marketable permits (based on allowable $CO_2$ emissions) are the chief mechanisms being used today by Europe to implement the Kyoto accords. In the United States, carbon-trading markets are developing, and California recently introduced mandatory carbon limits (with permit trading) for its power and other industries.

To make sure you have a good handle on these issues, go back to the text and make sure you know the difference between market-based policies and command and control policies. Then take some time to read the Hints, Tips, and Reminders below.

## Economic Aspects of Climate Change

The last section of the chapter on the economic aspects of climate change is essentially a case study using many of the tools of economics applied to this important issue. Every year we learn more about the issue, but the economics aspects seem to remain relatively constant. Use it as a way to guide your thinking about this issue as well as other issues that have worldwide implications. ■

## Consider These Hints, Tips, and Reminders                          STEP 4

1. Economists use the terms *externality* and *spillover* synonymously. Negative externalities (e.g., pollution) involve added costs in excess of market prices; hence they are called "spillover costs." Positive externalities (education and vaccinations) involve added benefits to society; hence the name "spillover benefits."

2. When analyzing negative externalities or spillover costs, the focus is on costs, so we use the supply curve; supply involves costs of production. Negative externalities impose higher costs on society, and this is shown by a social supply curve with higher costs. Positive externalities or spillover benefits confer added benefit to society that can be shown by a greater demand for the good or service.

3. Don't let the concept of public goods throw you for a loop. Admittedly, they are a little complex, but keep public goods like national defense and lighthouses in mind when you're faced with a public good problem. My consumption of military protection or the lighthouse's warning does not reduce its value to you (the nonrival characteristic), and once these are provided, no one can be excluded from their protection (the nonexcludability characteristic). Private markets do not provide these products because the public would not be willing to pay (voluntarily) for such services or would pay too little.

**4.** The fact that the optimal level of pollution is not zero may come as a shock, but it is just a straightforward application of "thinking at the margin" that has been consistently applied throughout this course. No one (neither society nor individuals) wants to spend $100 to get a $5 benefit. That is wasting society's limited resources.

## Do the Homework for Chapter 13
## Public Goods, Externalities, and
## Environmental Economics

**STEP 5**

Instructor _____ Time _____ Student _____

**Use the answer key below to record your answers to these homework questions.**

1. _____    6. _____    11. _____    16. _____
2. _____    7. _____    12. _____    17. _____
3. _____    8. _____    13. _____    18. _____
4. _____    9. _____    14. _____    19. _____
5. _____    10. _____    15. _____    20. _____

1. Market failure
   a. occurs, for example, when companies fail to provide enough beef to the market, so prices rise.
   b. occurs, for example, when government fails to regulate the market sufficiently such that not enough output is forthcoming.
   c. occurs only in capitalist economies.
   d. can be caused by externalities associated with the production or consumption of some particular good.

2. Public goods are
   a. rival in consumption.
   b. goods where some consumers can be excluded.
   c. goods like public television.
   d. both rival in consumption, and some consumers can be excluded from enjoying the benefits of the goods.

3. Which of the following is a public good?
   a. a van that holds 14 people

   b. Yellowstone National Park
   c. cable television
   d. national defense

4. The Coase theorem suggests that
   a. air pollution is not a serious problem if only the government would allow bargaining between the parties involved.
   b. regulating pollution is the only workable solution to reducing pollution.
   c. where bargaining costs are small, the resulting agreements between polluters and victims will be efficient, no matter which party is allocated the rights.
   d. where bargaining costs are small, the resulting agreements between polluters and victims will be efficient, no matter which party is allocated the rights; and more important, the distribution of benefits or income will be the same.

Use the table at right and Figure HW-1 to answer Questions 5–8. The table shows the demands by three individuals for a good.

5. At a cost of $8, how many *public* goods will be produced?

6. At a price of $8 how many *private* goods would be purchased?

7. What total amount would these three people be willing to collectively pay for 4 units of the public good?

8. To sell 14 units of the private good, what would the price have to be?

| Price ($) | Amy | Bob | Sue |
|-----------|-----|-----|-----|
| 8 | 0 | 0 | 0 |
| 7 | 0 | 0 | 1 |
| 6 | 3 | 0 | 2 |
| 5 | 4 | 0 | 3 |
| 4 | 5 | 2 | 4 |
| 3 | 6 | 3 | 5 |
| 2 | 7 | 4 | 6 |
| 1 | 8 | 5 | 7 |

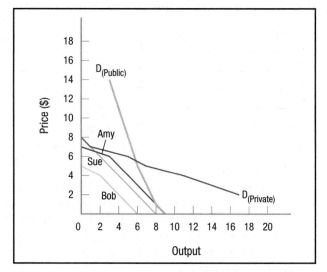

**HW-1**

9. Positive externalities come from which of the following?
   a. industrial effluent in a stream
   b. a child eating a pizza and a cola
   c. the benefit from one more motorist entering the freeway during rush hour
   d. private sector efforts to develop space flights to the moon

Use Figure HW-2 to answer Questions 10–13.

10. If this product generated *negative* spillovers equal to $4 per unit, what would be the socially optimal output level?

11. If a $4 per unit tax were imposed on this product, what would be the new socially optimal equilibrium price?

12. Why did the equilibrium price not increase by $4 when the $4 per unit tax was imposed?
    a. Because the supply curve isn't perfectly elastic (horizontal).
    b. Because the demand curve isn't perfectly inelastic (vertical).
    c. Both consumers and firms share the burden of the tax.
    d. All of the above.
    e. None of the above.

13. If this product generated a $4 per unit *positive* externality, how would the socially optimal output level differ from the initial equilibrium (rise, fall, remain the same)?

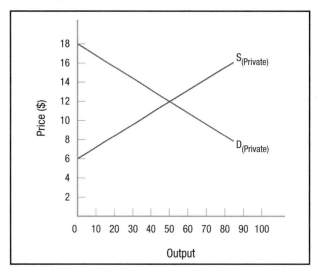

**HW-2**

14. Government failure often results from
    a. taxing the rich less than the poor.
    b. public policymakers' incentives not always being consistent with the public interest.
    c. too much money chasing too few goods.
    d. politicians discounting future results with too low an interest rate.

15. When policymakers make policy today that affects generations into the future, the use of a very low discount rate means that
    a. policymakers will take the benefits of future generations not yet born into consideration, and will be less likely to use debt today to finance programs that benefit mostly the present generation.
    b. policymakers will be more likely to go into debt today to fund benefits to the present generation.
    c. policies that benefit the present generation will have been paid for by a previous generation.
    d. politicians and policymakers will entirely finance any programs with user fees.

16. The optimal level of pollution
    a. is equal to zero for society.
    b. is that level at which total costs of pollution are minimal.

    c. is that level at which marginal abatement costs equal marginal benefits.
    d. is that level at which total benefits from pollution abatement are maximized.

17. An environmental policy in which the government sets levels, then determines the most efficient policies, sets those rules, and enforces them through regulation
    a. is the best approach to take to solve complex environmental issues.
    b. is a market-based policy.
    c. has historically not been typical of environmental regulation.
    d. is a command and control policy.

18. Setting air quality standards is an example of
    a. market-based policy.
    b. abatement tax.
    c. tradable permit.
    d. command and control policy.

19. One of the arguments against market-based environmental policies is that
    a. they are too efficient.
    b. using market forces to solve a problem created by markets seems inconsistent.

c. market-based policies can only be used on a tiny fraction of environmental problems.

d. market-based polices have been shown to not work.

20. The optimal level of pollution is not zero because
   a. policymakers cannot get their act together.
   b. trees need carbon dioxide to survive.
   c. the costs to society would be too high.
   d. government environmental budgets are too low.

Use the ExamPrep to Get Ready for Exams          **STEP 6**

This sheet (front and back) is designed to help you prepare for your exams. The chapter has been boiled down to its key concepts. You are asked to answer questions, define terms, draw graphs, and, if you wish, add summaries of class notes.

## Public Goods

### Producer and Consumer Surplus

Define producer and consumer surplus and illustrate both in the grid at right:

### What Are Public Goods?

Describe the two major aspects of public goods.
Nonrivalry:

Nonexcludability:

Why will the market fail to provide these goods?

### Common Property Resources

Describe the "tragedy of the commons":

What are some of the solutions to these types of problems?

## Externalities

Describe and provide examples of the following:
Negative externalities:

Positive externalities:

Both producers and consumers produce externalities. Complete the table below by providing examples of these externalities. (*Note:* Examples can be of either positive or negative externalities.)

| Origin of Externality | Impact | Victims and Beneficiaries of Externality |
|---|---|---|
| | Consumers | Producers |
| Consumers | | |
| Producers | | |

Use the grid below to diagram the impact of negative externalities. Begin with the private market supply and demand curves labeled $S_P$ and $D_P$ with equilibrium at point $e$, equilibrium price at $P_e$, and equilibrium quantity at $Q_e$.

- Draw the new supply cure $S_1$ that includes the full cost to clean the negative externalities. Label the new equilibrium point $a$; the new price, $P_1$; and output, $Q_1$.
- Show why consumer and producer surplus is larger when output is $Q_1$ rather than $Q_e$. (*Hint:* Look back at the analysis of Figure 4 in the text.)
- Under what conditions would society want to prohibit the production of some product?
- Why might monopolies mitigate the effects of negative externalities?
- Describe the case for subsidizing the production of those products that have positive externalities. Give some examples of products that are subsidized and some that should be subsidized.

### The Coase Theorem

Describe the Coase theorem and its implications for public policy:

## Environmental Policy

Describe government failure:

### Socially Efficient Levels of Pollution

Why are some levels of pollution efficient?

### Environmental Policies

List and describe the two most common types of environmental policies:

Describe how tradable permits work and why they are often highly effective:

## Economic Aspects of Climate Change

Describe the economic concepts applicable to climate change:

## Additional Study Help Chapterwide Practice Questions

### Matching

Match the description with the corresponding term.

___ 1. Consumer surplus
___ 2. Producer surplus
___ 3. Market failure
___ 4. Public goods
___ 5. Externalities
___ 6. The Coase theorem
___ 7. Common property resources
___ 8. Government failure
___ 9. Command and control policies
___ 10. Marketable permits

a. Environmental policies that set limits on pollution; all firms must comply with these standards.
b. The difference between what people are willing to pay for a product and what they actually pay for it.
c. Occurs when markets do not provide the socially optimal output at the socially optimal price. Either too much or too little of the good is produced, or it is offered at too high or too low a price.
d. The difference between the revenues firms earn from a product and the costs they would be willing to bear to supply it.
e. Goods that exhibit both nonrivalry and nonexcludability.
f. Occurs when government policies fail to bring about optimal resource allocation.
g. Owned by the community rather than subject to individual property rights.
h. Spillovers that arise when two parties engage in a transaction, and some third party uninvolved in the transaction either benefits or is harmed.
i. They grant firms the right to generate pollution and can be bought, sold, or exchanged.
j. Suggests that if externalities are present and transaction costs are small, the market output will be socially optimal no matter whether polluters are given the right to pollute or victims are given the right to be free of pollution.

### Fill-In

Circle the word(s) in parentheses that complete the sentence.

1. When producers are able to sell their output for a market price exceeding what they would have been willing to sell the output for, economists refer to this as (consumer surplus, producer surplus, market failure) _____. When markets involve externalities and provide too much output at too low a price, economists call this (consumer surplus, producer surplus, market failure) _____, and when buyers get products for prices that are lower than they would be willing to pay, this is referred to as (consumer surplus, producer surplus, market failure) _____.

2. An oatmeal cookie is a good that is both (rival, nonrival) _____ and (exclusive, nonexclusive) _____ in consumption, whereas Lake Powell in Utah is both (rival, nonrival) _____ and (exclusive, nonexclusive) _____. Public television (PBS) and radio (NPR) are examples of services that are both (rival, nonrival) _____ and (exclusive, nonexclusive) _____.

3. Spillover benefits result in too (little, much) _____ of a good produced at too (high, low) a price; spillover costs lead to too (little, much) _____ production and the resulting output sold at too (high, low) _____ a price.

4. When policymakers are considering policies that have benefits over a long time horizon and their cost-benefit calculations use a low discount rate, they will be (more, less) _____ likely to approve the project.

5. The federal government's approach to reducing pollution from the tailpipes of automobiles has typically been from a (command and control, market-based) _____ perspective, whereas the world's approach to reducing carbon emissions to combat global warming has relied on a (command and control, market-based) _____ perspective.

### True-False

Circle the correct answer.

T / F   1. Producer surplus is equal to the price consumers are willing to pay for a product minus the price they actually pay for it.

T / F   2. Total social welfare is equal to consumer surplus plus producer surplus.

T / F  3. If firms supply a product to the market at the socially optimal quantity and price, there will be no consumer surplus.

T / F  4. Nonrivalry means that once a good has been provided, it is not feasible to exclude some consumers from using it.

T / F  5. Spillover costs arise when two parties engage in a transaction, and another party unrelated to the transaction is harmed by it.

T / F  6. The Coase theorem suggests that private negotiations over polluting rights will produce efficient results only if these rights are initially distributed evenly among potential polluters.

T / F  7. Monopoly production levels may be more socially desirable from an environmental standpoint than competitive levels, though not necessarily.

T / F  8. Providing government subsidies for higher education will be both economically efficient and socially equitable if higher education results in positive externalities.

T / F  9. If a resource is nonrenewable, this means the current stock of it available for use can never be increased.

T / F  10. If policymakers use a high discount rate when setting environmental policies, future generations will bear most of the costs of these policies.

T / F  11. For most pollutants, the socially efficient level of pollution is zero.

T / F  12. Abatement costs are the costs to society resulting from a certain level of pollution.

T / F  13. When various firms have different abatement costs, a pollution tax is likely to achieve pollution reduction goals more efficiently than command and control policies.

T / F  14. Marketable permits for pollution have been around in theory since the 1960s, but they were rarely used before the 1990s.

T / F  15. One problem with marketable permits is that regulators must be able to determine marginal abatement costs precisely to sell the permits at a price that will achieve the desired results.

## Multiple Choice

Circle the correct answer.

1. Consumer surplus is
   a. the difference between the revenues firms earn from a product and the costs they would be willing to bear to supply it.
   b. the number of consumers who want to buy a product but are unable to because supplies have run out.
   c. the difference between what people are prepared to pay for a product and market price.
   d. the excess inventories consumers can purchase at sale prices when supply exceeds demand.

2. Producer surplus is
   a. the difference between market price and the costs firms would be willing to bear to supply it.
   b. the firms in a market that cannot profitably stay in business because the market is overloaded.
   c. the difference between what people are prepared to pay for a product and market price.
   d. the excess inventories producers are left with when supply exceeds demand.

3. Total social welfare is measured as
   a. pollution costs plus abatement costs.
   b. consumer surplus plus producer surplus.
   c. positive externalities minus negative externalities.
   d. abatement costs minus pollution costs.

4. In Figure MC-1, what area represents total social welfare?
   a. $0P_eeQ_e$    c. $0P_0eQ_e$
   b. $P_0P_ee$    d. $P_0P_1e$

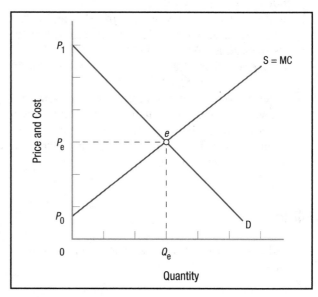

**MC-1**

5. Which of the following exhibits both nonrivalry and nonexcludability?
   a. positive externalities
   b. public goods
   c. common property resources
   d. negative externalities

6. Which of the following goods exhibits nonrivalry?
   a. candy bars
   b. seats at a ball game
   c. laptop computers
   d. cable or satellite television service

7. Which of the following is *not* a public good?
   a. network television broadcasts
   b. radio transmissions
   c. cable or satellite television transmissions
   d. national defense

8. Which of the following is an example of a spillover cost?
   a. fish being killed by a power plant dumping hot water into a stream
   b. a fish population being depleted by overfishing
   c. a stream's fish population being revived when farmers living along the stream take erosion control measures
   d. a government-imposed moratorium on fishing in certain waters

9. When pollution rights are privately negotiated, according to the Coase theorem, what condition must be met for the socially optimal allocation of resources to be brought about?
   a. The initial distribution of pollution rights must be equitable.
   b. Transaction costs must be minimal.
   c. Command and control policies must be instituted to ensure that the proper transactions are made.
   d. A large number of parties must be involved in the transactions.

10. When building a dam expands the wetland habitat housing a previously endangered species of bird, this new wetland is an example of a
    a. positive externality.
    b. public good.
    c. common property resource.
    d. negative externality.

11. To what does the "tragedy of the commons" refer?
    a. negative externalities
    b. the failure of a community to provide public goods
    c. the overexploitation of common property resources
    d. positive externalities

12. Which of the following practices, common in the developing world, is an example of the overexploitation of common property resources?
    a. farmers clearing their own lands using slash and burn methods
    b. unfiltered factory emissions polluting the air
    c. untreated sewage being released into rivers
    d. deforestation of public lands by villagers in need of firewood

Figure MC-2 shows negative externalities in a market. Use this figure to answer question 13.

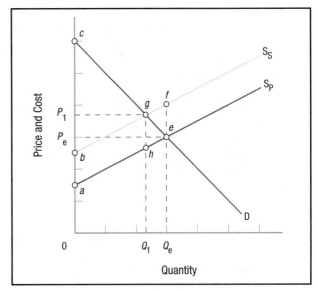

**MC-2**

13. At output $Q_e$, social welfare is given by
    a. area *ace* minus area *egf*.
    b. area $P_1cg$.
    c. area *bcg* minus area *egf*.
    d. area *bcg* minus area *abgh*.

14. Which of the following natural resources is exhaustible, yet capable of renewal?
    a. natural gas
    b. trees
    c. wind energy
    d. gold

15. Government failure results from which of the following?
    a. Government regulators gather large quantities of relevant information on which to base their decisions.
    b. The market does not provide the socially optimal amount of a good at the socially optimal price.
    c. Policymakers are unable to get sufficient information to make good policy.
    d. Economists are allowed to voice an opinion on matters of environmental regulation.

16. A law that requires all power plants to limit their $CO_2$ emissions to certain specified levels is an example of what sort of environmental policy?
   a. command and control
   b. market-based
   c. tradable permits
   d. charges/taxes

17. In a marketable permits system for reducing pollution, the initial distribution of permits affects
   a. the ability of the system to meet the pollution reduction targets.
   b. the efficiency with which the pollution reduction targets can be met.
   c. the distribution of income among participants in the system.
   d. the market price at which permits eventually come to be bought and sold.

18. In what area of pollution control have marketable permits been most successful to date?
   a. toxic waste
   b. sulfur dioxide emissions that create acid rain
   c. recyclable products
   d. solid wastes

19. Prior to the 1990s, what types of environment policies were most favored by policymakers, both in this country and abroad?
   a. command and control policies
   b. marketable permit systems
   c. taxes and charges on effluents
   d. subsidies for pollution reduction

20. In Figure MC-3, if emissions were at quantity $E_1$, society would

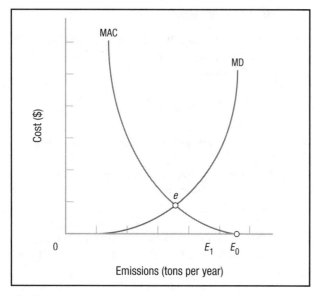

**MC-3**

a. reduce emissions until they are zero.
b. reduce emissions because the marginal benefit of abatement is greater than its marginal cost.
c. do nothing, because this level is optimal.
d. increase emissions to $E_0$, because optimal pollution is never zero.

## Essay-Problem

Answer in the space provided.

The questions below are designed to extend the concepts from the chapter. Use the suggested answers as a way to assess your progress and extend your ability to use this analysis to better understand environmental economics and policy.

1. What is the essence of market failure?

2. Must government always step in when there is market failure?

3. Pollution from automobiles rises when people are stuck in traffic jams during rush hour. Some local authorities have proposed two bridge toll rates: a higher rate for rush hour and a lower rate for non-rush-hour times (remember our discussion of price discrimination in Chapter 9, Monopoly?). Will this two-tier toll structure have any effect on pollution levels?

4. To deal with the "tragedy of the commons" ocean-fishing problem, why doesn't the United States simply restrict the amount of fish each boat can bring into U.S. fish markets at the end of each day?

5. What is a common argument for market-based environmental policies as opposed to command and control policies?

6. National Park rangers at the Grand Canyon have determined that the current level of tourists visiting the park in the summer is causing damage to

the canyon because the air quality is being hurt by automobile exhaust. Devise a command and control policy to deal with this. Devise a market policy.

7. What is a common way to deal with "the tragedy of the commons" as concerns local fishing in nearby rivers?

8. The Blue Ridge Mountain Parkway and Skyline Drive in Virginia offer some breathtaking views of the valleys below. The National Park Service charges usage fees that are very low. Why can the 35-mile-per-hour speed limit be seen as a nonmonetary pollution control policy?

9. The federal government uses a command and control policy to deal with pollution caused by automobile emissions. It divides autos into classes, then sets standards for each class. SUVs were placed in the light truck category because they were seen originally as off-road vehicles. Light trucks have lower standards than autos—they are allowed to emit more pollution than autos, generally. But with the overwhelming majority of SUVs used as primary vehicles, some critics have said that this categorization has led to unnecessary additional pollution. Construct an argument for leaving SUVs as part of the light truck category. Then construct an argument for placing SUVs in the standard auto category.

10. Are the costs from rent-seeking behavior likely to be higher with command and control environmental policies than with market-based policies such as tradable pollution permits?

## What's Next

You now have seen how economic analysis can be used to understand environmental problems. We used the concepts of consumer surplus and market failure, and looked at possible government responses to market failure. In the next chapter, we look at income and wealth distribution and discuss whether it makes sense to think of income disparities in terms of market failure.

## Answers to Chapterwide Practice Questions

### Matching

| | | | |
|---|---|---|---|
| 1. b | 4. e | 7. g | 10. i |
| 2. d | 5. h | 8. f | |
| 3. c | 6. j | 9. a | |

### Fill-In

1. producer surplus, market failure, consumer surplus
2. rival, exclusive, nonrival, exclusive, nonrival, nonexclusive
3. little, high, much, low

4. more
5. command and control, market-based

## True-False

| | | | |
|---|---|---|---|
| 1. F | 5. T | 9. F | 13. T |
| 2. T | 6. F | 10. T | 14. T |
| 3. F | 7. T | 11. F | 15. F |
| 4. F | 8. T | 12. F | |

## Multiple Choice

| | | | |
|---|---|---|---|
| 1. c | 6. d | 11. c | 16. a |
| 2. a | 7. c | 12. d | 17. c |
| 3. b | 8. a | 13. c | 18. b |
| 4. d | 9. b | 14. b | 19. a |
| 5. b | 10. a | 15. c | 20. b |

## Essay-Problem

1. There are situations when markets as institutions as they are currently constituted do not provide the socially optimal quantity of a product at a socially optimal price. Three types of market failures were discussed in this chapter: public goods, externalities, and common property resources.

2. No. There are costs to government activity. The benefit from alleviating the damage from the market failure may not surpass the cost of government intervention. This is why local governments usually do not get involved with small companies that have low levels of pollution. And remember, as the analysis by Coase suggests, when transactions costs are low and the number of individuals involved is small, simple bargaining or legal recourse may be sufficient.

3. It should affect pollution levels by giving incentives to drivers to avoid the bridges at rush hour or seek alternative routes, and in this way it will reduce traffic jams and thus reduce pollution, because pollution climbs when cars are stuck in traffic. It is not popular, however, with those who think they are stuck with driving at a certain time and on a certain route. This is equivalent to peak load pricing and price discrimination, where prices at peak time are higher. Theaters charge higher prices for movies at night, and some utilities charge higher prices when power demands are typically higher (early morning and early evening).

4. The fishing problem is international in scope. Restricting local fishing boats will do little to solve the problem because it will have no effect on international fishing boats that prowl international waters. The "tragedy of the commons" results from the fact that no one person or group has any incentive to fish sensibly as long as others do not have to and do not.

5. Cost. Continual regulation can be expensive, and regulators can be captured by the interests they are supposed to control (government failure). Administration costs of market-based policies can be comparatively low compared to command and control policies. Also, market-based policies and the price of permits give those who value a cleaner environment the easy ability to purchase permits to reduce pollution beyond levels originally set by government.

6. A command and control policy would limit the number of tourists who could visit, or limit the number of tourists in automobiles, or restrict automobiles from areas close to the canyon. Electric-powered buses could be used to transport tourists to the canyon. Similar restrictions on helicopter flights into the canyon have already been proposed to reduce noise pollution and make descending into the canyon a more enjoyable experience. A

market-based policy would raise user fees for those tourists with automobiles, or charge higher prices the closer one drove to the canyon itself.

7. Localities deal with the common property rights problem by requiring permits to fish and restricting permit holders to a certain number of fish of a certain size. Localities can still miscalculate, but they are tied in to a state's animal husbandry program.

8. It can be seen as a nonmonetary pollution control policy in two ways. First, if automobiles give off less pollution going 35 miles per hour than at higher speeds, the lower speed limit will have an immediate effect on the pollution level. Second, for those who want to see the vistas but are in a hurry, the 35-mile-per-hour speed limit will tend to push them to leave after a comparatively short period of time, again lowering potential pollution. The parkway is full of curves, so the lower speed limit may be justified for this reason alone, but the lower limit would seem to have positive externalities as well.

9. Leave SUVs as light trucks: Many of the large SUV engines are similar to light truck engines, not standard family autos, so the costs of pollution abatement are higher for SUVs than family autos; it is not fair to put a higher burden on SUV owners than family auto owners.

   Place SUVs in the family auto category: Many of the SUVs use family car engines, not light truck engines. The Toyota Rav4 uses a Camry engine, not some special light truck engine. Therefore, the SUVs should be treated as if they were family autos. Furthermore, if they were so treated, this would be an incentive for auto manufacturers to develop technology to cut back on SUV pollution because SUVs are very profitable for auto makers.

10. The costs of rent-seeking behavior are likely to be higher with command and control policies because regulators, if they are the ones to set and enforce the policies, will need to meet on a continual basis. Government bodies that establish the permits might be lobbied heavily, but once the permits are established, it is much easier for government to resist the call for additional permits and go into regulatory hibernation.

# Poverty and Income Distribution

# 14

Ross Pictures/Corbis

## Why Do Some People Make More Money Than Others?
## Is Poverty Inevitable?

Some people are fabulously rich and spend money extravagantly. Other people are poor, sometimes desperately poor. Why are income and wealth distributed the way they are? Should we redistribute them? Or just help those on the bottom of the income ladder? And when we look at those on the bottom, can we determine the causes of poverty? Will poverty ever be eradicated? These are the types of issues covered in this chapter on income distribution and poverty. Economic analysis can help us formulate some answers to these questions.

| | | |
|---|---|---|
| This Is What You Need to Know | | STEP 1 |

**After studying this chapter you should be able to**

■ Describe the difference between wealth and income.

■ Describe the effects of life cycles on income.

■ Analyze functional, personal, and family income distributions.

■ Use a Lorenz curve and Gini coefficient to graphically depict the distribution of wealth and income.

- Describe the impact of income redistribution efforts.
- Describe the causes of income inequality.
- Describe the means for determining poverty thresholds.
- Describe the two measures for determining depth of poverty for families.
- Describe the prevailing theories on how to deal with poverty and income inequality.

## STEP 2          Review the Key Terms

**Income:** A flow measure reflecting the funds received by individuals or households over a period of time, usually a week, month, or year.

**Wealth:** A stock measure of an individual's or family's assets, net of liabilities, at a given point in time.

**Functional distribution of income:** The distribution of income for resources or factors of production (land, labor, capital, and entrepreneurial ability).

**Personal or family distribution of income:** The distribution of income to individuals or family groups (typically quintiles, or fifths, of the population).

**Lorenz curves:** A graphical method of showing the income distribution by cumulating families of various income levels on the horizontal axis and relating this to their cumulative share of total income on the vertical axis.

**Gini coefficient:** A precise method of measuring the position of the Lorenz curve, defined as the area between the Lorenz curve and the equal distribution line divided by the total area below the equal distribution line.

**Poverty thresholds:** Income levels for various household sizes, below which people are considered to be living in poverty.

**Income deficit:** The difference between the poverty threshold and a family's income.

**Ratio of income to poverty:** The ratio of family income to the poverty threshold. Families with ratios below 0.5 are considered severely poor, families with ratios between 0.5 and 1.0 are considered poor, and those families with ratios between 1.0 and 1.25 are considered near poor.

## STEP 3          Work Through the Chapter Tutorials

# The Distribution of Income and Wealth

### Frequently Asked Questions

Q: **What is the difference between income and wealth?**
A:  Income is a flow; it measures the receipts of funds by individuals or households over time. Wealth is a stock; it measures a family's assets net of liabilities at a given point in time.

Q: **Why does income vary over the life cycle?**
A:  Family and individual incomes vary significantly over the course of their life cycle. Young people just starting their careers and their families usually have modest incomes. As people grow older and gain experience, their incomes usually rise,

peaking between the ages of 45 and 55. Incomes then normally decline with retirement, as do family responsibilities.

**Q: What is the functional distribution of income?**

A: The functional distribution of income refers to the income distribution among inputs (factors of production). The share of national income going to labor has gradually risen since 1929; it is now fairly stable at around 70%. The remainder of the national income is divided among proprietor's income (small business profits), rent, corporate profits, and net interest.

**Q: What is the personal distribution of income, and how is it calculated?**

A: Personal or family income distribution refers to the percentage of income flowing to families in specific segments of the population. To analyze family income distribution, the U.S. Census Bureau arranges households in quintiles, or fifths, ranging from the 20% of households with the lowest incomes to the 20% with the highest. After totaling and averaging household incomes for each quintile, the Census Bureau computes the percentage of income flowing to each quintile. Since the 1970s, the income distribution in the United States has become more unequal.

**Q: What are the primary methods for measuring inequality?**

A: Economists have developed two primary methods for measuring inequality: Lorenz curves and Gini coefficients.

**Q: What is a Lorenz curve?**

A: Lorenz curves cumulate and plot the percent of people below various income levels on the horizontal axis, relating this to their share of income on the vertical axis. Perfectly equal distribution results in a Lorenz curve that bisects the axes, and deviations from this equal distribution curve indicate inequality. Figure 1 is a Lorenz curve for the United States, showing both income and wealth. Note that income is distributed much more evenly than wealth.

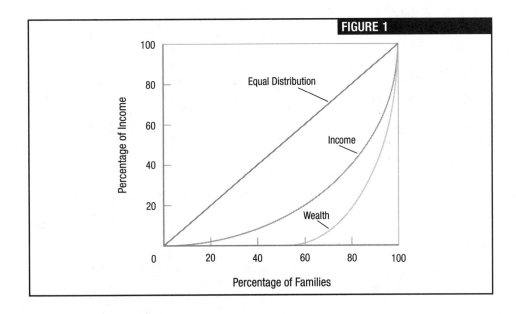

FIGURE 1

**Q: What is the Gini coefficient?**

A: The Gini coefficient is a precise method of measuring income inequality. The Gini coefficient is defined as the ratio of the area between the Lorenz curve and the equal distribution line in the numerator, and the total area below the equal distribution line in the denominator. When distribution is perfectly equal, the Gini coefficient is zero; when distribution is as unequal as possible, the coefficient rises to 1.0.

Q:  **How is income distribution affected by redistribution policies?**

A:  Income distribution is influenced by redistribution policies that include progressive taxes as well as cash and in-kind transfer payments. Redistribution policies are contentious. Those on the political left tend to push for greater redistribution of income and wealth, and those on the right argue that such policies are harmful to economic growth.

Q:  **What causes income inequality in the United States?**

A:  Income inequality in our society has many causes. Individuals and families invest in human capital to varying degrees, some placing a strong emphasis on education, and others failing to do so. Different education levels are a major factor determining inequalities in income and wealth. Economic discrimination can lead to an income distribution skewed against those suffering discrimination. The growth of two-earner households over the last three decades is a major reason for rising income inequality.

## Keep in Mind

Incomes and wealth vary substantially over the life cycle of individuals and families. Lorenz curves and the Gini coefficient are the primary measures of inequality. Income inequality is related to levels of investment in human capital, economic discrimination, and most recently the growth of two-earner households.

# The Distribution of Income and Wealth Quick Check

## Circle the Correct Answer

1. (T/F) Income is a stock measure whereas wealth is a flow measure.
2. (T/F) Income tends to peak for most people between the ages of 35 and 45.
3. (T/F) American workers currently receive approximately 70% of the national income.
4. (T/F) A Gini coefficient of 1.0 indicates that distribution is perfectly equal.
5. Consider family income distribution from 1970 to 2008, shown in Table 2 in the text (it ignores taxes and transfers). Which group has increased its share of income in this time span?
   a. the lowest quintile
   b. the middle quintile
   c. the highest quintile
   d. the poor
6. The Gini coefficient, used to measure the inequality of income, is
   a. higher in the United States than in most European countries, meaning that income in Europe is more evenly distributed.
   b. lower in the United States than in Canada and Australia.
   c. around 0.111 in the United States, meaning that income is relatively unevenly distributed.
   d. above 2.0 in the United States.
7. Which of the following factors are *not* among the causes of economic inequality in the United States?
   a. living in or near a large city
   b. individuals and families making different investments in human capital

   c. rising numbers of two-income households
   d. economic discrimination
8. Which one of the following is *not* correct?
   a. A progressive income tax will tax higher incomes at a higher rate than lower incomes.
   b. Food stamps are a transfer payment.
   c. Progressive taxation does not affect income distribution.
   d. Adding transfer payments to the calculation makes income distribution more equal.
9. Which one of the following is *not* correct?
   a. The political left favors greater taxation of income and wealth.
   b. The political right sees income differences as the natural result of a market system.
   c. The political left has been more effective in the United States than in Europe in its redistribution efforts.
   d. The political right is relatively unconcerned about the distribution of income unless it becomes so unequal that it discourages incentives and reduces efficiency.
10. Which of the following factors is *not* among the causes of economic inequality in the United States?
   a. People have different natural abilities.
   b. People have different education levels.
   c. There have been a growing number of two-income households.
   d. Income is taxed at progressive rates.

Score: ____

## If You Got 9 or 10 Correct

You have a good working knowledge of the concept of income distribution, how it is measured, and what can be done to change it. Go on to the next section, Poverty.

## If You Didn't Get at Least 9 Correct

Check and make sure you understand why you missed the questions you did. This is relatively easy material, and you probably need to pay a little closer attention. We are near the end of microeconomics, and you have been through much harder material. Pay special attention to the Lorenz curves material; it is the most difficult material in the section. Fortunately, the next section, Poverty, really stands on its own.

If you had trouble with Lorenz curves, work through the solved problem below; it won't take long, and you will get a quick refresher on how they are constructed and interpreted. ∎

## Solved Problem: Lorenz Curves

The table below lists the income distribution (by quintile) for the United States in 1950 and 2000, and for Brazil and Sweden in 2005. Using these data, construct Lorenz curves for each country and plot them in the blank grid provided.

| Quintile | United States 1950 | | United States 2000 | | Brazil 2005 | | Sweden 2005 | |
|---|---|---|---|---|---|---|---|---|
| | Fifth | Cum. | Fifth | Cum. | Fifth | Cum. | Fifth | Cum. |
| Lowest | 4.6 | _____ | 3.6 | _____ | 2.5 | _____ | 9.6 | _____ |
| Second | 11.9 | _____ | 8.9 | _____ | 5.5 | _____ | 14.5 | _____ |
| Third | 17.5 | _____ | 14.9 | _____ | 10.0 | _____ | 18.2 | _____ |
| Fourth | 23.6 | _____ | 23.0 | _____ | 18.2 | _____ | 23.2 | _____ |
| Highest | 42.4 | _____ | 49.6 | _____ | 63.8 | _____ | 34.5 | _____ |

## Solution-Discussion

Lorenz curves plot the cumulative sum of income on the vertical axis and the cumulative sum of families on the horizontal axis. The first thing you need to do is cumulate each quintile for each income distribution as shown in the table on the next page. Note that the table now has a cumulative column for each distribution. The fifths of income are summed from the lowest to the highest. For example, in the U.S. 1950 distribution, the first sum for the lowest is just equal to that fifth's income or 4.6. For the second fifth, we sum the previous fifth (4.6) and the second fifth (11.9) to get 16.5, and so on, until the last fifth's sum equals 100.0.

| Quintile | United States 1950 | | United States 2000 | | Brazil 2005 | | Sweden 2005 | |
|---|---|---|---|---|---|---|---|---|
| | Fifth | Cum. | Fifth | Cum. | Fifth | Cum. | Fifth | Cum. |
| Lowest | 4.6 | 4.6 | 3.6 | 3.6 | 2.5 | 2.5 | 9.6 | 9.6 |
| Second | 11.9 | 16.5 | 8.9 | 12.5 | 5.5 | 8.0 | 14.5 | 24.1 |
| Third | 17.5 | 34.0 | 14.9 | 27.4 | 10.0 | 18.0 | 18.2 | 42.8 |
| Fourth | 23.6 | 57.6 | 23.0 | 50.4 | 18.2 | 36.2 | 23.2 | 66.0 |
| Highest | 42.4 | 100 | 49.6 | 100 | 63.8 | 100 | 34.5 | 100 |

Each of the four cumulative columns are plotted in Figure 2 along with an equal distribution line.

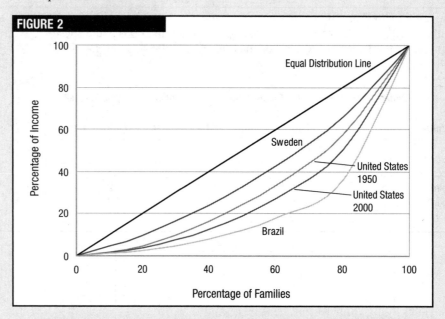

**FIGURE 2**

A quick glance at the figure makes it clear that Sweden has the most equal distribution, followed by the United States in the 1950s, the United States in 2000, and Brazil, the country with the most unequal distribution in income of the four shown. This is the benefit of Lorenz curves. A quick glance and you can tell which distributions are most equal.

# Poverty

## Frequently Asked Questions

Q:  What is the poverty threshold, and how is it calculated?

A:  The poverty threshold was first determined by the U.S. Department of Agriculture (USDA). Surveying the food-buying patterns of low-income households, the USDA used these data to estimate the cost of financing a nutritionally balanced diet. It then multiplied the cost of this food plan, adjusting for family size, by 3. The resulting dollar amount is the income threshold beneath which families are officially deemed to be living in poverty. When the Census Bureau calculates the official poverty rate, it counts as income all money income *before taxes,* including cash benefits, but does not include capital gains or noncash benefits such as public housing or food stamps.

**Q: How has the poverty rate changed since 1959?**

A: The poverty rate in the United States fell rapidly between 1960 and 1975, but it has remained roughly stable since then, fluctuating around 12% to 15%, following the business cycle. Over most of this period, the poverty rate for blacks and Hispanics was roughly twice the rate for whites.

**Q: What are the two major depth-of-poverty measures?**

A: Economists have developed two depth-of-poverty measures that describe the economic well-being of lower-income families: the income deficit and the ratio of income to poverty.

**Q: What is the income deficit?**

A: The income deficit measures how far below the poverty threshold a family's income lies. In 2001, the average income deficit for families living in poverty was just over $7,200.

**Q: What is the ratio of income to poverty, and what does it designate?**

A: The ratio of income to poverty compares family income to the poverty threshold and expresses this comparison as a ratio. The ratio for families with incomes equal to the poverty threshold is 1.0; the ratio for those living at half the threshold income is 0.5. The Census Bureau considers people who live in families with ratios below 0.5 to be "severely or desperately poor," those between 0.5 and 1.0 to be "poor," and those with ratios above 1.0 but less than 1.25 to be "near poor." In 2001, nearly 5% of Americans lived in severely poor families.

**Q: What do experimental measures of poverty consider?**

A: Many researchers have criticized the Census Bureau's official method of determining poverty thresholds. In response, the Census Bureau has developed experimental measures that differ from the old in basing their estimates on after-tax income and counting as income such noncash benefits as food stamps and housing subsidies. Work-related expenses, such as transportation and child care, are deducted from income, as are out-of-pocket medical expenses. When these new measures were applied, poverty rates fell.

**Q: Is poverty a relative or absolute measure, and what are the policy implications of the answer?**

A: Poverty can be a relative or an absolute measure. The official measure of poverty in the United States is based on an absolute number, the poverty threshold. Some researchers, however, think a relative measure would be more useful—for instance, labeling the bottom 20% of American households "poor." Defined this way, poverty can never be eliminated.

**Q: How should we reduce poverty?**

A: The question of how to go about reducing poverty is controversial. The political left sees income and wealth redistribution as the main tool for curing poverty. They suggest expanding welfare-related programs and enhancing the progressivity of the tax system. Those on the right argue that such an approach is too expensive and that it significantly reduces the incentives to work and produce, thereby reducing the economy's output. These people maintain that the best way to cure poverty is by implementing policies that increase the economic pie shared by all, not just by splitting the current pie more evenly.

**Q: What do current theories say about the possibility of a fair income distribution?**

A: There is no unified theory of income distribution that takes all issues into account, or that tells us what distribution is the fairest. Some contemporary philosophers have weighed in on this issue. John Rawls has argued that low inequality is the fairest, since this is what everyone would choose if they did not know where in the income distribution they would fall. Robert Nozick has replied that it is unfair to use the coercive power of the state to deprive people of their private property to redistribute it to others.

## Keep in Mind

The poverty threshold varies by family size and is based on an estimate of a nutritionally balanced, low-income food budget that is adjusted for inflation. Controversy surrounds the various methods for curing poverty. Some see income redistribution as the solution, while others argue that economic growth is the answer.

# Poverty Quick Check

## Circle the Correct Answer

1. (T/F) In general terms, the poverty threshold is defined as the cost of feeding a family a nutritionally balanced diet, multiplied by 3.
2. (T/F) The Census Bureau classifies a family with an income to poverty ratio of 0.70 as severely or desperately poor.
3. (T/F) A poor family's income deficit is the poverty threshold for a family of that size.
4. (T/F) Most of the families classified as poor do not have running water in their homes.
5. The Census Bureau has begun using an experimental measure of poverty that
   a. has virtually eliminated measured poverty.
   b. considers before-tax income.
   c. ignores noncash benefits such as food stamps and housing subsidies.
   d. counts work-related transportation costs.
6. Which one of the following is *not* correct?
   a. The political left sees income and wealth redistribution as the chief means of reducing poverty.
   b. The political right argues that welfare significantly reduces the incentive to work and produce.
   c. The political left believes the possibility of failure is a strong incentive to work and invest.
   d. The political right believes economic growth will alleviate much poverty.
7. Which of the following is correct concerning income distribution?
   a. John Rawls is right and Robert Nozick is wrong: Equity is more important than efficiency.
   b. Robert Nozick is right and John Rawls is wrong: Efficiency is more important than equity.

c. Neither is right nor wrong: There is a tradeoff between equity and efficiency.
d. John Rawls is closer to the correct political policy because he uses the "maximin" principle.
8. When the Census Bureau began using its new, experimental measure of poverty,
   a. it ignored the effects of taxation.
   b. measured poverty rates generally fell.
   c. it simply took the poverty thresholds from 1963 and updated them for price changes.
   d. it treated cash and noncash benefits differently.
9. Rawls's "maximin" principle focuses on
   a. maximizing welfare for the minimum cost.
   b. maximizing poor people's share of income while minimizing the taxes they pay.
   c. maximizing the welfare of the least-well-off individuals.
   d. maximizing welfare for a minimum number of the poor.
10. Economic analysis
    a. helps us determine the fairest policies for reducing poverty and income inequality.
    b. helps us devise the most effective policies for reducing poverty and inequality.
    c. helps us see that incentives are unimportant in considering policies to reduce poverty and income inequality.
    d. helps us determine whether equity or efficiency is more important.

Score: ____

**Answers: 1. T; 2. F; 3. F; 4. F; 5. d; 6. c; 7. c; 8. b; 9. c; 10. b**

If you didn't get all of these questions correct, a patient review of the material should be all you need before you move on to the Hints, Tips, and Reminders below. It is fairly easy material that is used to explain the nature and extent of poverty. If you missed any questions, review your answers to make sure you know why they were wrong, then move on. ■

## Consider These Hints, Tips, and Reminders          STEP 4

**1.** This chapter is one of the analytically easiest you will study this semester. The only part that requires some serious work is computing (and graphing) Lorenz curves. The key is to remember to accumulate the income shares from the lowest quintiles to the highest. Lorenz curves provide a quick visual reference for income distributions versus just looking at a table of numbers.

**2.** The Gini coefficient is not as easy to compute, but it is widely used because it results in a specific number that varies directly from 0 to 1.0, where 0 is an equal distribution and 1.0 is the most unequal. This is very useful for comparisons between countries at a moment in time and over time.

**3.** Topics like income distribution and poverty involve heavy doses of politics, emotion, and value judgments. Economists do not attempt to suggest what is the "best "or "fairest" distribution of income or wealth (with the exception of extreme distribution levels).

**4.** Poverty thresholds for the United States are substantially higher than those used by the World Bank and other agencies to measure poverty in the rest of the world. Annual incomes between $350 and $700 are the norm for poverty measurement in developing nations. The material well-being of the poor in the United States vastly exceeds that of the poor in these other nations.

| Do the Homework for Chapter 14 Poverty and Income Distribution | STEP 5 |

Instructor _____ Time _____ Student _____

**Use the answer key below to record your answers to these homework questions.**

1. _____  6. _____  11. _____  16. _____
2. _____  7. _____  12. _____  17. _____
3. _____  8. _____  13. _____  18. _____
4. _____  9. _____  14. _____  19. _____
5. _____  10. _____  15. _____  20. _____

1. Which of the following is true of income?
   a. Most people earn their maximum income when they are 25.
   b. It is a stock.
   c. It is a flow.
   d. Income and wealth are the same.

2. Which of the following is true of wealth?
   a. Wealth is fairly evenly distributed in the United States.
   b. It is a stock.
   c. It is a flow.
   d. Income and wealth are the same.

3. Which of the following is *not* one of the distributions of income studied by economists?
   a. functional distribution of income
   b. personal distribution of income
   c. family distribution of income
   d. annual distribution of income

4. The distribution of income and wealth
   a. are essentially the same thing.
   b. are measured in similar ways, but the distribution of wealth is more unequally distributed.
   c. are measured in similar ways, but the distribution of wealth is more equally distributed.
   d. are measured in similar ways, but the distribution of income is more unequally distributed.

Use Figure HW-1 to answer questions 5–7.

5. The Lorenz curve $0c$ represents
   a. the most unequal distribution possible.
   b. the Gini coefficient.
   c. the most equal distribution possible.
   d. an unequal distribution that might roughly approximate that of the United States.

6. The Lorenz curve $0dc$ represents
   a. the most unequal distribution possible.
   b. the Gini coefficient.
   c. the most equal distribution possible.
   d. an unequal distribution that might roughly approximate that of the United States.

7. Area $A$ divided by area $(A + B)$ is
   a. the most unequal distribution possible.
   b. the Gini coefficient.
   c. the most equal distribution possible.
   d. an unequal distribution that might roughly approximate that of the United States.

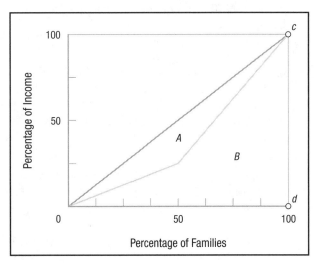

**HW-1**

8. When income and wealth are redistributed with a progressive income and estate tax,
   a. it has no effect on the Gini coefficient.
   b. the Lorenz curve moves away from the line of equal distribution.
   c. the Lorenz curve doesn't move.
   d. the Lorenz curve shifts inward toward the line of equal distribution.

9. When the Gini coefficient approaches zero,
   a. the income distribution becomes more unequally distributed.
   b. the Lorenz curve moves away from the line of equal distribution.
   c. the people in the society become richer and have a higher gross domestic product.
   d. the distribution of income approaches that of equal distribution.

10. Which of the following factors does not seem to be a cause of income inequality in the United States?
   a. different levels of investment in human capital
   b. the progressive income tax
   c. households with two people working
   d. economic discrimination by race, age, or gender

11. When comparing the distribution of income with the distribution of wealth in the United States,
   a. the income distribution is more unequally distributed than wealth.
   b. both have Gini coefficients that are about the same value.
   c. wealth is more unequally distributed than income.
   d. since income is a flow and wealth is a stock, the two cannot be compared.

12. When comparing the characteristics of the lowest income quintile and highest income quintile in the United States
   a. both had the same percentage of householders working full-time.
   b. both included a lot of two-earner households.
   c. the percentage of elderly in the low-income households was higher.
   d. both were equally likely to include individuals who did not work.

13. Poverty in the United States
   a. has steadily risen over the last three decades.
   b. fell dramatically during the 1960s.
   c. tends to fall during recessions and rise in other times.
   d. is unaffected by economic growth because the benefits of economic growth do not "trickle down" to the poor.

14. Poverty in the United States tends to be the highest
   a. in married-couple families.
   b. in white families.
   c. in female householder families.
   d. in male householder families.

15. Families that the Census Bureau considers to be "severely poor" have a ratio of family income to the poverty threshold of
   a. greater than 1.5.
   b. greater than 1.0 but less than 1.5.
   c. greater than 0.5 but less than 1.0.
   d. less than 0.5.

16. Reducing poverty in the United States
   a. has fallen principally on state and local governments.
   b. has often been accompanied by controversy.
   c. could be eliminated entirely by income redistribution efforts at the local level.
   d. could best be handled by strengthening the laws enabling the poor to join unions.

17. John Rawls proposed the "maximin principle," which suggests that
   a. the maximum economic effort must be extracted from those at the bottom of the income ladder.
   b. maximum incomes must only be permitted for the top 20% of wage earners.
   c. the highest-income people should pay the maximum in taxes.
   d. society should maximize the welfare of the least-well-off individual.

18. Which of the following policies might *not* reduce poverty in the United States?
   a. improving the rate of economic growth
   b. reducing economic discrimination
   c. moving to a flat income tax structure
   d. lowering interest rates on educational loans

19. Today, a family of four has a poverty threshold in the United States
   a. of roughly $12,000.
   b. a little over $30,000.
   c. a little over $22,000.
   d. of just below $8,000.

20. In general terms, poverty thresholds in the United States are based on
   a. the minimum of what families need to live comfortably in a modest rental.
   b. the USDA's least expensive food plan developed in the 1960s, then adjusted for inflation.
   c. extensive surveys of how poor families live and feed family members.
   d. the least expensive food budget adjusted for regional differences in costs.

| Use the ExamPrep to Get Ready for Exams | STEP 6 |
|---|---|

This sheet (front and back) is designed to help you prepare for your exams. The chapter has been boiled down to its key concepts. You are asked to answer questions, define terms, draw graphs, and, if you wish, add summaries of class notes.

## The Distribution of Income and Wealth

Describe the following income distribution concepts.
Functional:


Personal:


Use the grid below to diagram the following:

■ Draw a Lorenz curve with equal distribution of income.
■ Draw a Lorenz curve with less than equal distribution.
■ Use the Lorenz curve to define the Gini coefficient.
■ What is the impact of income redistribution on the Lorenz curve?

List some of the programs that lead to income redistribution in the United States:


List some of the causes of income inequality:

## Poverty

Describe how poverty is measured:

Describe the two depth-of-poverty measures and their implications for public policy:

Discuss the new measures of poverty and how useful they are to policymakers:

### Eliminating Poverty

Discuss how poverty could be eliminated:

### Rawls and Nozick

Describe the two philosophical approaches taken to developing theories of a "fair" income distribution by Rawls and Nozick:

## Additional Study Help Chapterwide Practice Questions

### Matching

Match the description with the corresponding term.

___ 1. Income
___ 2. Wealth
___ 3. Life cycle effects
___ 4. Functional distribution of income
___ 5. Personal or family distribution of income
___ 6. Lorenz curve
___ 7. Gini coefficient
___ 8. Progressive tax
___ 9. Transfer payment
___ 10. Poverty threshold
___ 11. Income deficit
___ 12. Ratio of income to poverty
___ 13. Maximin principle

a. A measure of a household's assets and net liabilities at a given point in time.
b. Compares family income to the poverty threshold and expresses this comparison as a ratio.
c. A means of graphically representing the income distribution by plotting the cumulative percentage of people below various income levels on the horizontal axis and relating this to their cumulative share of total income on the vertical axis.
d. The variation of income for an individual or family during different phases or stages of life.
e. The percentage of income flowing to families in specific segments of the population.
f. The ratio of the area between the Lorenz curve and the equal distribution line, and the total area below the equal distribution line.
g. The income level beneath which families are officially deemed to be living in poverty.
h. Income distribution among inputs (factors) of production.
i. Taxes higher incomes at a higher rate than lower incomes.
j. Measures the receipt of funds by individuals or households over some period of time, usually a week, month, or year.
k. A measure of the depth of poverty; that is, it measures how far below the poverty threshold a family's income lies.
l. An idea proposed by philosopher John Rawls that maintains that a society should seek to maximize the welfare of its least-well-off individual.
m. Cash payments or in-kind benefits, such as housing subsidies or food stamps from government to individuals or families.

### Fill-In

Circle the word(s) in parentheses that complete the sentence.

1. Income and wealth vary significantly over families' (portfolios, lifetimes) _____. Income is a (stock, flow) _____, whereas wealth is measured (over time, at a given point in time) _____.

2. Looking at income distribution from the point to view of individuals or families represents the (functional, personal) _____ distribution of income, but when looked at from the viewpoint of factors of production, it is a measure of the (functional, personal) _____ distribution of income.

3. Lorenz curves represent the (cumulative, total, marginal) _____ distribution of income or wealth. Gini coefficients are computed using (factor incomes, Lorenz curves, thresholds) _____ and vary from zero where income is (equally, unequally) _____ distributed to 1.0 where income is (equally, unequally) _____ distributed.

4. The ratio of income to poverty is one way to measure the (incidence, depth, threshold) _____ of poverty.

### True-False

Circle the correct answer.

T / F   1. Wealth is a flow of funds measure.

T / F   2. Most individuals and families have very different incomes at different points in their lives.

T / F   3. Since 1929, the share of the national income accruing to corporate profits has hovered somewhere around 10%.

T / F   4. The wealthiest 20% of Americans have about 50% of the national private wealth.

T / F   5. In deriving its official measure of income distribution, the Census Bureau bases its estimates on after-tax income, including cash transfer payments, but not including such noncash benefits as food stamps.

T / F 6. Over the past 30 years, the percentage of income earned by the top quintile of Americans has risen, while the percentages earned by all of the lower quintiles have fallen.

T / F 7. A Lorenz curve plots all of the people below a given income level on the horizontal axis, relating this to their dollar income on the vertical axis.

T / F 8. A Gini coefficient of 0.0 indicates that distribution is perfectly equal.

T / F 9. The United States has one of the lowest Gini coefficients in the world.

T / F 10. The rising technological complexity of the American workplace has been one factor contributing to rising levels of income inequality.

T / F 11. The poverty threshold is determined as the cost of feeding a family a nutritionally balanced diet, multiplied by 4.

T / F 12. The Census Bureau's official measure of poverty treats in-kind benefits such as subsidized housing and food stamps as income.

T / F 13. Although African American and Hispanic poverty rates are still higher than the rate for whites, the poverty rate for both minority groups fell significantly during the 1990s.

T / F 14. A poor family's income deficit is equal to the poverty threshold for a family of that size minus the family's income.

T/F 15. The Census Bureau classifies a family with an income to poverty ratio of 0.45 as "poor."

T / F 16. The official U.S. poverty rate, based on income thresholds, is a relative measure of poverty.

T / F 17. Although politicians frequently disagree on the best approach to reducing poverty, economists virtually all agree that the most effective approach involves favoring redistribution over growth-oriented policies.

T / F 18. Economic analysis can help us to devise the most effective policies for reducing poverty and inequality, but it cannot tell us which of these policies is fair or unfair.

## Multiple Choice

Circle the correct answer.

1. After laboring for years in obscurity, a novelist finally publishes a book that shoots to the top of the sales charts. At this moment in her career, she likely has
   a. both a low income and little wealth.
   b. a high income, but little wealth.
   c. a low income, but considerable wealth.
   d. both a high income and considerable wealth.

2. At what point in the life cycle does income peak for most people?
   a. when just entering the workforce, usually in one's early 20s
   b. between ages 25 and 35
   c. between ages 45 and 55
   d. upon retirement, usually around age 65

3. A breakdown of the income flowing to different inputs (factors) of production is referred to as the
   a. functional distribution of income.
   b. operational distribution of income.
   c. personal distribution of income.
   d. family distribution of income.

4. Approximately what share of the national income do American workers currently receive?
   a. 10%
   b. 20%
   c. 50%
   d. 70%

5. Approximately what percentage of the national income does the lowest quintile of Americans earn?
   a. 0–1%
   b. 1–1.5%
   c. 3–4%
   d. 7–8%

6. As measured by the Gini coefficient, the inequality of income distribution in the United States has been _____ since 1970.
   a. steadily falling
   b. steadily rising
   c. holding steady
   d. fluctuating erratically

7. The distribution of income in the United States is _____ the distribution of wealth.  ·
   a. more equal than
   b. more unequal than
   c. about the same as
   d. completely unrelated to

8. A Gini coefficient of 0.1 indicates that distribution is
   a. perfectly equal.

b. relatively equal.

c. relatively unequal.

d. as unequal as possible.

9. Which of the following factors is *not* among the causes of rising economic inequality in the United States?
   a. economic discrimination
   b. individuals and families making different investments in human capital
   c. rising number of two-income households
   d. free public education

10. The Lorenz curves for the United States in Figure MC-1 show that
    a. income is less evenly distributed after adjusting for taxes and transfers.
    b. income is more evenly distributed after adjusting for taxes and transfers.
    c. income is relatively evenly distributed before and after adjustment.
    d. wealth is more evenly distributed than income.

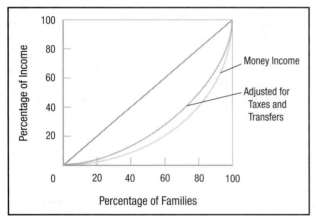

**MC-1**

11. The Gini coefficient for the distribution shown in Figure MC-1 will likely be
    a. around 0.10 before adjustment and 0.05 after.
    b. around 0.05 before adjustment and 0.10 after.
    c. around 0.40 before adjustment and 0.45 after.
    d. around 0.45 before adjustment and 0.40 after.

12. In very general terms, the poverty threshold is defined as
    a. the cost of renting adequate housing, multiplied by 2.
    b. the cost of buying a family's groceries for a month, multiplied by 2.
    c. the cost of feeding a family a nutritionally balanced diet, multiplied by 3.
    d. median household income, divided by 3.

13. Since 1970, African American and Hispanic poverty rates have been roughly _____ those of non-Hispanic whites.
    a. 4–5 times
    b. 2–3 times
    c. the same as
    d. one-third

14. The Census Bureau would classify a family with an income-to-poverty ratio of 0.65 as
    a. severely or desperately poor
    b. poor
    c. near poor
    d. not poor

15. Approximately what percentage of Americans does the Census Bureau classify as "severely poor"?
    a. 2%
    b. 5%
    c. 8%
    d. 11%

16. Which of the following policies has the political left traditionally *not* supported?
    a. a more progressive tax system
    b. greater spending for public education
    c. growth-oriented tax cuts
    d. increases in in-kind transfer payments

17. Rawls's "maximin" principle holds that a society should strive to
    a. maximize its total output.
    b. maximize the percentage of income flowing to the upper quintile of households.
    c. maximize its average income deficit.
    d. maximize the welfare of its poorest individuals.

## Essay-Problem

Answer in the space provided.

Use these questions as another way to assess your progress and, more important, to dig deeper into income distribution and poverty.

1. Why is it important to consider life cycles when analyzing income distribution?

2. Why is it important to look at the functional distribution of income?

3. We have discussed income distribution as if an equal distribution is to be expected. Is it really?

4. The estate tax is a tax paid by the estate of someone who dies. Its original purpose was to break up wealth holdings passed from generation to generation: Think of the Rockefellers. In the 1990s, estates greater than $600,000 had to pay the estate tax. Congress increased this trigger point, in part because of the bad effect it had on small businesses: On the death of a small business owner, the heirs often had to sell the business to come up with the estate tax, because many small businesses were worth over $600,000. The Democrats argued that the ceiling should be raised to $2,000,000 and left there; if there was need to raise it in the years ahead, this could be done by a future Congress. Republicans argued that the estate tax should be abolished completely because it was a disincentive to people to work hard and establish a dynasty. Which party has the better argument?

5. Consider the way poverty was determined in the 1960s. Construct an argument in favor of this procedure. Now, construct an argument against it.

6. In the late 1800s and early 1900s, there was a large outpouring of private charity. Hull House, education for immigrants, and the Salvation Army all started during this time period. The text talks about public policies to deal with poverty and income distribution problems. Why not rely on private charity?

7. An argument against the use of progressive taxation to redistribute income is that progressive taxation encourages rent-seeking and tax-avoiding behavior, and so encourages inefficiencies. Don't all taxes encourage such behavior?

8. Every now and then, arguments for "workfare" surface in the hope of getting "welfare cheaters" off the welfare rolls. Based on what you have learned in this chapter about the poor, what might go wrong with forcing people on welfare to take various jobs?

9. People who talk about the disincentive effects of welfare point to unemployment insurance. Studies have shown that there is a large amount of job-seeking activity in the weeks before the unemployment insurance runs out, much greater than in the months before. In times of economic slowdown, what can we predict will happen if unemployment insurance is extended from 26 weeks to 52 weeks?

10. What can economics tell us about the efficiency-equity tradeoff?

## What's Next

With this chapter completed, you now are near the end of microeconomics. You have used supply and demand analysis to understand how markets work. You have seen how consumers choose to buy goods and services, and why and how firms provide those goods and services. You have seen how market structure affects prices and quantities produced, and how it affects the markets for inputs. You have then gone on to see economic analysis applied to labor issues, environmental issues, and issues of income distribution and poverty.

## Answers to Chapterwide Practice Questions

### Matching

| | | | |
|---|---|---|---|
| 1. j | 5. e | 9. m | 13. l |
| 2. a | 6. c | 10. g | |
| 3. d | 7. f | 11. k | |
| 4. h | 8. i | 12. b | |

### Fill-In

1. lifetime, flow, at a given point in time
2. personal, functional
3. cumulative, Lorenz curves, equally, unequally
4. depth

### True-False

| | | | |
|---|---|---|---|
| 1. F | 6. T | 11. F | 16. F |
| 2. T | 7. F | 12. F | 17. F |
| 3. T | 8. T | 13. T | 18. T |
| 4. F | 9. F | 14. T | |
| 5. F | 10. T | 15. F | |

### Multiple Choice

| | | | |
|---|---|---|---|
| 1. b | 6. b | 11. d | 16. c |
| 2. c | 7. a | 12. c | 17. d |
| 3. a | 8. b | 13. b | |
| 4. d | 9. d | 14. b | |
| 5. c | 10. b | 15. b | |

### Essay-Problem

1. We have seen that people earn different amounts of income, depending on their age. Much of this has to do with the gain in experience and skills as people grow older, up to the point where many people start to slow down physically. If one general population group were much younger than another population group, we would expect this younger group to generate less income than the older group. Not recognizing this fact

could lead to poor public policy that attempted to deal with a problem that really was not a problem.

2. Looking at the functional distribution helps to dispel myths about workers' share of income versus corporations' share. Respondents to surveys generally believe that corporate profits are a much larger share of income than the 9% or 10% it has been for the past 30 years, and workers' share is less than the 70% it has been in the same period.

3. The text discussed many factors that would lead one to expect that the income distribution will be unequal: innate abilities, family wealth, schooling, possible discrimination, two-earner households. Luck may be a factor as well. The bothersome thing about income distribution for most is not the likelihood that income will forever be distributed unequally, but the vast differences in income. For many, this is the issue behind income distribution, not the fact that any inequality exists.

4. There is no right answer to this. Republicans are correct in that the estate tax is a disincentive to working hard and accumulate wealth; this is an efficiency argument. But the Democrats speak for many who think the estate tax is a fair (equitable) measure to prevent the accumulation of wealth and the possible privilege it brings with it. This is an example of the efficiency-equity tradeoff, a question to be decided by the voters, not economic analysis.

5. One of the best things about this procedure was its simplicity: Determine a nutritional food budget and multiply by 3. There was no need to determine costs for clothes, housing, medical care, entertainment, and a host of other potential expenditures. On the other hand, over time, living standards change, so it can be argued that food no longer represents one-third of a poor family's budget. The procedure should be revised to reflect this.

6. The simple answer is that private charity is not enough. The private charities suggest as much when they request more and greater donations.

7. All taxes encourage rent-seeking and tax-avoidance behavior. The question is whether a progressive tax has rates so high that this behavior swamps the desire to work harder and generate more income. In the 1980s, when the United States' marginal tax rate on the highest incomes was cut by more than half, tax revenues on these income classes grew, suggesting that progressive taxes have high disincentive effects for certain tax rates.

8. Many people on welfare are likely not to have invested in human capital—they may not have the skills to do the job. A better alternative would be to offer training in the skills needed for various jobs, before forcing a job on someone. Build up the human capital first.

9. We can predict that the unemployment rate will rise because people will tend to put off a big job-seeking push until near the end of 52 weeks rather than 26 weeks. However, it should be pointed out that there is no magic number of weeks of unemployment insurance. A society must weigh the efficiency aspects of unemployment insurance with the equity aspects. It is equitable to help people who are out of a job by no fault of their own; but what is a fair number of weeks of help?

10. Economics can tell us about the efficiency aspects of public policies. It cannot tell us what is fair; this is what we as voters have to decide.

# International Trade

## Free Trade: Blessing or Not?

A key tenet of globalization is that trade is beneficial. Why is this so? Who benefits and who loses from trade? What are the arguments against free trade? We looked at the benefits from trade in Chapter 2. Here we take a deeper look. We analyze the benefits that trade brings, show who gains and who loses from trade, describe the common methods used to restrict trade, and then explore some arguments against free trade and globalization.

| | | |
|---|---|---|
| | This Is What You Need to Know | STEP 1 |

**After studying this chapter you should be able to**

- Describe the benefits of free trade.

- Distinguish between absolute and comparative advantage.

- Describe the economic impacts of trade.

- Describe the terms of trade.

- List the ways in which trade is restricted.

- Discuss the various arguments against free trade.

- Describe the issues surrounding increasing global economic integration.

387

## STEP 2          Review the Key Terms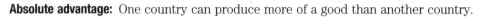

**Absolute advantage:** One country can produce more of a good than another country.

**Comparative advantage:** One country has a lower opportunity cost of producing a good than another country.

**Terms of trade:** The ratio of the price of exported goods to the price of imported goods ($P_x/P_m$).

**Tariff:** A tax on imported products. When a country taxes imported products, it drives a wedge between the product's domestic price and its price on the world market.

**Quota:** A government-set limit on the quantity of imports into a country.

**Infant industry:** An industry so underdeveloped that protection is needed for it to become competitive on the world stage or to ensure its survival.

**Dumping:** Selling goods abroad at lower prices than in home markets, and often below cost.

## STEP 3          Work Through the Chapter Tutorials

# The Gains from Trade

### Frequently Asked Questions

Q: **What has happened to the volume of foreign trade in the past 25 years, and why?**
A: Worldwide foreign trade has quadrupled over the past 25 years. Improved communications and transportation technologies have worked together to promote global economic integration. Most governments around the world have reduced trade barriers in recent years.

Q: **Have people always been keen about free trade?**
A: Free trade has not always been popular. In 1929–1930, as the world economy collapsed, many countries attempted to protect their domestic industries by imposing trade restrictions that discouraged imports.

Q: **In the past century, what happened when the United States restricted trade?**
A: In 1930, the United States enacted the Smoot-Hawley tariffs, which imposed an average tax of 60% on imported goods. This hurt industries around the world and has been credited with adding to the depth of the global depression.

Q: **Is trade a zero-sum game, and if not, why not?**
A: In a zero-sum game such as poker, for one party to gain, the other party must lose. Voluntary exchange and trade is a positive-sum game, meaning that both parties to a transaction can gain. These gains arise because of comparative advantage.

Q: **What is the difference between absolute advantage and comparative advantage?**
A: One country has an absolute advantage over another if it can produce more of some good than the other country. A country has a comparative advantage over another if its opportunity cost to produce some good is lower than the other country's.

Q: **How are trade and comparative advantage linked?**

A: Even when one country has an absolute advantage over another, both stand to benefit from trade if each focuses on the goods or industries with a comparative advantage.

Q: **What are the constraints on trade that every country faces?**

A: There are some practical constraints on trade. First, every transaction involves costs. Second, production is governed by increasing costs and diminishing returns. This makes it difficult for countries to specialize in the production of just one product. Indeed, specializing in one product is risky, since the market for a product can always decline or its production can be disrupted. Third, even though countries that engage in trade benefit, some individuals and groups can be hurt by trade.

## Keep in Mind

People generally benefit from trade because trade is a *voluntary* act, and they would avoid it if they did not gain. Although nations as a whole benefit from trade, there are winners and losers within each country, and the losers are far more vocal than the winners. This explains the controversy that sometimes surrounds globalization.

---

# The Gains from Trade Quick Check

## Circle the Correct Answer

1. (T/F) International trade is a zero-sum game because both trading countries equally benefit from trade.

2. (T/F) The Smoot-Hawley tariffs imposed by the United States in 1930 worsened the Great Depression.

3. (T/F) If the United States has an absolute advantage over Spain in producing oranges and wine, it will never benefit from trading with Spain for these two products.

4. (T/F) Two countries can gain from trade if one has a comparative advantage over the other in the production of one good, while the other country has a comparative advantage in the production of another good.

5. Comparative advantage is based on
   a. one country being able to outproduce another country in some good.
   b. differences in opportunity costs between two countries.
   c. comparing physical endowments, such as mineral resources, of two countries.
   d. comparing the capital accumulation of two countries.

6. Assume the United States produces two goods: movies and computers. If the United States can produce 100 movies and 20,000 computers each year, what is the opportunity cost of producing one movie?
   a. 1/200 of a computer
   b. 100 computers
   c. 200 computers
   d. 2,000 computers

7. Which one of the following is *not* correct?
   a. Even when one country has an absolute advantage over another, both stand to benefit from trade if each focuses on the goods or industries with a comparative advantage.
   b. Trade is constrained because production faces increasing costs and diminishing returns.
   c. Everyone benefits from trade.
   d. Trade is a positive-sum game.

8. If the United States can produce 100 movies and 20,000 computers in one year, and Canada can produce 5 movies and 2,000 computers, which of the following is true?
   a. The United States will not benefit from trading with Canada, and Canada will not benefit from trading with the United States.
   b. Canada will benefit from trading with the United States, but the United States will not benefit because it has an absolute advantage in producing both items.
   c. Trade will benefit both because Canada has a comparative advantage in producing movies, and the United States has a comparative advantage in producing computers.
   d. Trade will benefit both because Canada has a comparative advantage in producing computers, and the United States has a comparative advantage in producing movies.

9. France has a comparative advantage in the production of perfume, and the United States has a comparative advantage in the production of running shoes.
   a. The United States should try to catch up to France in the production of perfume.
   b. Both countries will benefit if they specialize in the product in which they have comparative advantage and trade with each other.
   c. It is risky for any country to concentrate in producing goods, so France should increase its production of running shoes, and the United States should increase its production of perfume.
   d. Trade will not occur because it will be a zero-sum game in this instance.

10. Which one of the following is *not* a constraint on trade?
    a. Production is limited by increasing costs and diminishing returns.
    b. There are transaction costs with every trade.
    c. Trade can hurt some group or individuals, even if it is beneficial for most people.
    d. Some countries produce few products and don't have an absolute advantage in any of them.

Score: ____

**Answers: 1. F; 2. T; 3. F; 4. T; 5. b; 6. c; 7. c; 8. d; 9. b; 10. d**

## If You Got 9 or 10 Correct

You have the basics of the benefits of trade and how these benefits derive from comparative advantage. Go on to the next section, The Terms of Trade.

## If You Didn't Get at Least 9 Correct

- Give yourself a maximum of 5 minutes and write a one-sentence definition of absolute advantage and comparative advantage.
- After you do so, check the text and revise or complete your definition of absolute advantage and comparative advantage. You might want to put your revised definitions into the ExamPrep in Step 6.
- Then go back to the text and review Figures 2 and 3 and Table 1, making sure you see how both countries can benefit from trade.

The next section, The Terms of Trade, is more complicated (not just a review of the material in Chapter 2), and it builds on this section. Make sure you understand why people and countries trade so that determining the terms of trade will be easier to pick up. Review the solved problem below, then move on to the next section. ■

## Solved Problem: Mangoes and Motorcycles

Amy Yee, in the *Financial Times* (April 28, 2007, p. 2) reported, "After months of negotiations the U.S. has agreed to import Indian mangoes for the first time after clearing concerns about insect importation." She further noted, "In exchange for mangoes India is considering relaxing restrictions to allow the import of Harley-Davidson motorcycles, barred from India because of emissions standards and high taxes." Currently, the United States imports mangoes from Mexico and other Central American countries. This agreement is expected to double trade between India and the United States in the next several years.

Who stands to benefit and lose from this recently negotiated agreement between India and the United States?

### Solution-Discussion

Clearly, American consumers will benefit because the supply of mangoes will rise and price will undoubtedly fall. The other beneficiaries will be Harley-Davidson and its workers because it will enjoy a new market for its products. One suspects that Harley-Davidson was probably lobbying hard for this agreement.

Since there isn't a huge U.S. mango industry and most mangoes are imported, the losers will be other importers from Mexico and Central America and their American agents.

# The Terms of Trade

## Frequently Asked Questions

Q:  **What are the terms of trade?**

A:  The terms of trade determine the prices of imports and exports. If a country exports computers and imports coffee, with two computers trading for a ton of coffee, the price of a computer will be one-half the price of a ton of coffee. When countries trade many commodities, the terms of trade are defined as the average price of exports divided by the average price of imports.

Q:  **What happens to the price of a good when countries trade?**

A:  When two countries begin trading, the price charged for one good may be different in the two countries. In Figure 1, clothing is priced at $P_1$ in China and $P_2$ in the United States. As market forces lead each country to focus its production on the goods and industries at which it has a comparative advantage, that good's price will tend to equalize in the two countries, moving to an equilibrium level somewhere between the two original prices. In Figure 1, the equilibrium price after trading, $P_e$, is between the initial lower price in China and the initial higher price in the United States.

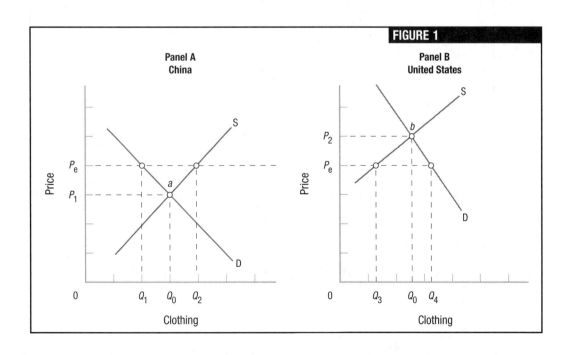

FIGURE 1

Panel A
China

Panel B
United States

Q:   Who gains from trade? Who loses?

A:   Though beneficial to both countries, trade can produce winners and losers. In Figure 1, China has a comparative advantage over the United States in the production of clothing, and so it begins exporting clothing to the United States. Chinese manufacturers and workers will benefit from this increased business, but their domestic consumers will be hurt as the price of clothing rises from $P_1$ to $P_e$ to meet American demand. In the United States, where clothing had been more expensive, textile manufacturers and workers will be hurt by the competition from the Chinese, but American consumers will benefit as clothing prices fall from $P_2$ to $P_e$. Notice that at equilibrium, Chinese exports of $Q_2 - Q_1$ are just equal to American imports of $Q_4 - Q_3$.

Q:   What are the most common forms of trade restrictions?

A:   The most common forms of trade restrictions are tariffs and quotas.

Q:   What is a tariff?

A:   A tariff is a tax on imports. Most tariffs are *ad valorem taxes,* meaning that a product is taxed a certain percentage of its price as it crosses the border. Other tariffs are *unit taxes,* meaning that a fixed tax per unit of the product is assessed.

Q:   Who benefits from a tariff? Who is hurt by a tariff?

A:   Tariffs generate revenues while driving a wedge between a product's domestic price and its price on the world market. When a tariff is imposed on a product, its price will rise. This benefits domestic producers, increasing their sales and the price they can charge, but the resulting price increase hurts domestic consumers. The government collects tariff revenues. In Figure 2, a tariff (T) added to the world price of $P_w$ generates revenue for the government equal to the shaded rectangle.

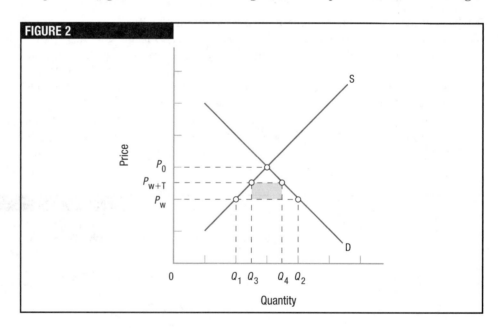

**FIGURE 2**

Q:   What are quotas, and how do they differ from tariffs?

A:   Quotas restrict the quantity of imports into a country. Quotas have much the same effect as tariffs, except that they do not generate revenues for the government.

## Keep in Mind

Trade tends to equalize prices in both countries after trade. Tariffs and quotas are the two most common forms of trade restrictions, and they lead to roughly the same outcomes except that tariffs produce revenue for governments, so they are the most frequently used.

# The Terms of Trade Quick Check

## Circle the Correct Answer

1. (T/F) The terms of trade are defined as the average price of exports divided by the average price of imports.
2. (T/F) A quota is similar to a tariff, except that the government collects revenues under a quota but does not under a tariff.
3. (T/F) An ad valorem tax is a tariff calculated as a specific percentage of a product's price.
4. (T/F) A tariff and a quota have the same effect on imports.
5. The United States and Japan both produce cameras. Japan has a comparative advantage over the United States in the production of cameras. After trade, we know that
   a. the price of cameras will rise in both countries.
   b. the price of cameras will fall in both countries.
   c. the price of cameras will rise in Japan and fall in the United States.
   d. the price of cameras will rise in the United States and fall in Japan.
6. The United States becomes convinced that Mexico is dumping its lettuce on the U.S. market and institutes an ad valorem tariff.
   a. This tariff benefits U.S. consumers.
   b. This tariff does not help U.S. lettuce producers because it should be a unit tariff, not an ad valorem tariff.
   c. This tariff benefits U.S. lettuce producers.
   d. This tariff benefits Mexico's lettuce producers.
7. Which one of the following is *not* a reason why governments use tariffs?
   a. Traditionally, governments have used tariffs to generate revenues.

b. Firms that lose from trade seek tariffs as a means of protection from competition.
   c. Unions might seek tariffs as a way to protect jobs.
   d. Consumers seek tariffs to keep out foreign goods.
8. Germany has a comparative advantage over the United States in the production of camera lenses. If Germany and the United States trade,
   a. German consumers will be hurt by a higher price.
   b. U.S. consumers will be hurt by a higher price.
   c. U.S. producers will benefit.
   d. German producers will seek tariff protection.
9. If the United States institutes a tariff on Swiss digital watches,
   a. it will have no effect on the quantity of Swiss watches exported to the United States.
   b. it will have no effect on the price of Swiss watches exported to the United States.
   c. it will benefit U.S. consumers.
   d. it will benefit U.S. digital watch companies.
10. When faced with an influx of cheap foreign goods, consumers will
    a. seek to have an ad valorem tariff instituted.
    b. seek to have quotas instituted.
    c. seek to have a unit tariff instituted.
    d. seek to lower trade barriers.

Score: ____

**Answers: 1. T; 2. F; 3. T; 4. T; 5. c; 6. c; 7. d; 8. a; 9. d; 10. d**

## If You Got 9 or 10 Correct

You have done well on a difficult area. Go on to the next section, Arguments Against Free Trade.

## If You Didn't Get at Least 9 Correct

You should have answered at least nine correctly in this quiz. If this is not the case, review this section and the first section on gains from trade again. Start by making sure that you understand the gains from trade, then jot down the difference between a tariff and a quota. Then go back to the text, paying special attention to Figure 4. Be sure you know who benefits and who loses from trading in this case. This will help you understand the arguments against free trade covered in the next section.

If you do not understand the benefits from trade and who might lose from trade, separating which arguments are valid and which are not is difficult. Once you finish this review, work through the solved problem below before you go on to the next section, Arguments Against Free Trade. ∎

## Solved Problem: Tariffs and Quotas

Using the data for domestic supply and demand for luxury sport utility vehicles (SUVs) in the table below, answer the questions that follow. Note that prices are in thousands of dollars, and quantities demanded and supplied are also expressed in thousands.

| Price | Quantity Demanded | Quantity Supplied |
|-------|-------------------|-------------------|
| 140   | 0                 | 240               |
| 120   | 40                | 200               |
| 100   | 80                | 160               |
| 80    | 120               | 120               |
| 60    | 160               | 80                |
| 40    | 200               | 40                |
| 20    | 240               | 0                 |
| 0     | 280               | 0                 |

a. Plot both curves in the blank grid below.

b. Assume the prices for 109 series Land Rovers (sold in Africa, Australia, etc.) and other foreign luxury SUVs are $40,000. How many will be imported into the United States at this price, and how many domestic luxury SUVs will be produced?

c. Now assume that the United States levies a $20,000 per unit tariff to protect domestic Hummers and other luxury SUVs from competition from Land Rovers and other foreign luxury SUVs. What is the reduction in imports of luxury SUVs to this country?

d. How much revenue does the government collect from this tariff? Could the government accomplish the same level of protection by putting an 80,000-unit quota on foreign imports?

## Solution-Discussion

a. See Figure 3 below.

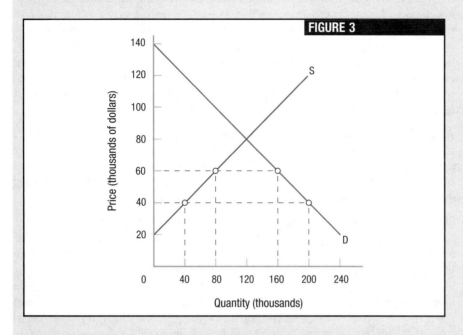

**FIGURE 3**

b. At a $40,000 price, consumers will buy 200,000 units, of which 40,000 are supplied by the domestic industry and 160,000 are imported.

c. SUV prices rise to $60,000, and 160,000 are purchased, 80,000 are produced domestically, and 80,000 are imported. Thus imports are cut in half.

d. A $20,000 tariff on 80,000 vehicles generates $1,600,000,000 in revenue. Yes, the same level of protection could be accomplished if the government was willing to give up the revenue (not likely).

# Arguments Against Free Trade

## Frequently Asked Questions

Q: **What is the infant industry argument against free trade?**
A: Despite the many benefits of free trade, some arguments exist for restricting trade. One is that infant industries require some protection. These are industries that are too underdeveloped to achieve a comparative advantage or perhaps even to survive in the global marketplace.

Q: **What is dumping, and why are there laws against it?**
A: Some American trade laws target dumping, which occurs when a foreign firm sells its good cheaper and typically below cost in the United States than in its domestic market. One goal of such dumping may be to drive American firms out of business, thus allowing the foreign firm to come back and impose higher prices on American consumers in the long run. Another may just be to gain a foothold or market share in a foreign market. Or dumping may simply be a form of subsidized price discrimination. If the federal government determines that a

foreign firm is dumping products onto the American market, it can impose antidumping tariffs on the offending products.

**Q:  Do we need to restrict trade to be protected from cheap foreign labor?**

A:  Some advocates of trade barriers maintain that domestic firms and their workers need to be protected from displacement by cheap foreign labor. Without this protection, it is argued, foreign manufacturers that pay their workers low wages and benefits will flood the market with low-cost products. On balance, however, most economists estimate that the benefits of lower-priced imported goods exceed the costs of lost employment. The federal government has resisted imposing protection measures to protect jobs. Instead, the government funds programs that help displaced workers transition to new lines of work.

**Q:  What is the national defense argument against free trade?**

A:  In times of national crisis or war, the United States must be able to rely on key domestic industries such as oil, steel, and the defense industry. These industries may require some protection even during peacetime to ensure that they exist when a crisis strikes and importing resources may be difficult.

**Q:  Should trade be restricted if it leads to job losses for domestic workers?**

A:  Some critics argue that increased trade and globalization spells job losses for domestic workers. Firms unable to compete with imports will be forced to lay off workers or even close their doors. Increased trade, however, allows firms that are exporters to expand their operations and hire new workers. For workers who lose their jobs, switching industries can be difficult and time consuming and often requires new investments in human capital. American trade policy recognizes this problem. The Trade Adjustment Assistance (TAA) program provides workers with job search assistance, job training, and some relocation allowances.

**Q:  What is the environmental argument against free trade?**

A:  Concerns about globalization, trade, and the environment usually take one of two forms. Some people are concerned that expanded trade and globalization will lead to increased environmental degradation as companies take advantage of lax environmental laws abroad, particularly in the developing world. Others worry that attempts by the government to strengthen environmental laws will be challenged by trading partners as disguised protectionism. Environmental protection is an income elastic good: As incomes rise, the demand for environmental protections rises faster. And because trade increases incomes in developed and developing countries, free trade may further the cause of environmental protection.

**Q:  Should a country stop trading with another country where wages are low and working conditions poor?**

A:  Some antiglobalization activists argue that for the United States to trade with developing countries where wages are low and working conditions are deplorable simply exploits workers in these developing countries. But restricting trade with these countries would probably do more harm than good. Low wages reflect low investments in human capital, low productivity, and low living standards characteristic of developing nations. Blocking trade with these nations may deprive them of their only chance to grow and thus improve in these areas.

## Keep in Mind

Most of the arguments against voluntary free trade do not have a solid empirical basis. Trade benefits individuals and nations, or they would not engage in it. Remember, in general, the losers from trade are a small segment or industry, and the nation as a whole gains, but the losers are far more vocal than the winners. Infant industries and national defense requirements are situations where nations may wish to restrict trade to protect their industries, but nations must be vigilant to see that these industries continue to be (or become) competitive given their protection from global competition.

# Arguments Against Free Trade Quick Check

## Circle the Correct Answer

1. (T/F) The national defense argument against free trade claims that key domestic industries such as oil, steel, and manufacturing must be protected even in peacetime to make sure that they are established and ready if called upon during a crisis.

2. (T/F) Concerning jobs lost because of foreign trade, the United States government has tended to focus on job retraining rather than protectionist measures.

3. (T/F) Restricting trade with countries that do not raise their wages to what we consider to be acceptable levels or bring working conditions up to certain standards would probably harm the foreign workers involved, because it would block what might be their only chance to escape poverty and misery.

4. Concerning the infant industry argument against free trade, which one of the following is *not* correct?
   a. An infant industry may be too small or undercapitalized to compete in world markets.
   b. Infant industries may be coddled by protection and never mature.
   c. Infant industry protection tends to focus on capital-intensive manufacturing.
   d. Countries with huge labor supplies need to develop capital-intensive industries first to use the labor.

5. Concerning the antidumping argument against free trade, which one of the following is *not* correct?
   a. Firms can use dumping to lower prices so much that foreign companies will be driven out of business; the dumping firm would then raise its prices, offsetting its short-term losses.
   b. If Japan dumps cameras on the U.S. market, U.S. consumers will be hurt.
   c. Firms can use dumping to gain market share.
   d. Dumping violates U.S. trade laws.

6. Concerning the low-foreign-wages argument against free trade, which one of the following is *not* correct?
   a. The argument often arises when workers in advanced economies are displaced by low-wage foreign workers.
   b. The costs of lost employment are usually lower than the benefits of lower-priced goods.
   c. Proponents fail to include the cost of benefits such as health care when calculating the wages for foreign workers.

   d. The United States has tried to help displaced workers transition to new lines of work rather than impose protectionist measures.

7. Concerning the environmental argument against free trade, which one of the following is *not* correct?
   a. One concern is that environmental regulations should not unfairly discriminate against the products of another country.
   b. Freeing trade in agricultural products may lead to less environmental damage (e.g., overuse of land, excessive use of pesticides), not more.
   c. Rising incomes in developing countries, over time, will lead to increased interest in environmental protection.
   d. As incomes rise, the demand for environmental protection rises faster because it is an income inelastic good.

8. The infant industry argument against free trade might prove detrimental to countries with huge labor supplies if it
   a. encouraged capital-intensive manufacturing rather than labor-intensive industries.
   b. encouraged large industries rather than small ones.
   c. encouraged large countries rather than small countries.
   d. used quotas rather than tariffs.

9. Which one of the following is *not* correct concerning globalization?
   a. Increased globalization has led to some job losses for domestic workers.
   b. Increased globalization usually leads to increased job creation for exporters.
   c. Globalization has pressured firms to increase their comparative advantages.
   d. Globalization has been a mixed bag for consumers.

10. What is the rationale for U.S. antidumping laws?
    a. Dumping hurts American consumers.
    b. Dumping hurts foreign exporters.
    c. Dumping gives foreign firms an unfair advantage over U.S. firms.
    d. Dumping may reflect legitimate instances of lower cost production.

Score: _____

**Answers:** 1. T; 2. T; 3. T; 4. d; 5. b; 6. b; 7. d; 8. a; 9. b; 10. c.

## If You Got 9 or 10 Correct

You picked through these tricky little questions quite well. Separating the valid from the invalid arguments in the area of free trade and globalization can be difficult because the rhetoric can sound compelling. Take a few moments to read through the Hints, Tips, and Reminders in the next section.

### If You Didn't Get at Least 9 Correct

You should have correctly answered at least nine of these questions. If you didn't, you will want to review this chapter one more time. First, review the questions you missed and make sure you understand why you missed the questions you did. The arguments against trade often sound good, and it can be difficult to separate the valid from those that sound reasonable.

Second, review the section on Arguments Against Free Trade. Many of these arguments have valid points, whereas others are simply nice-sounding rhetoric. It is important that you leave this course with the ability to keep them straight. It is always a good idea to look at each argument with your eye on knowing what group is prone to make the argument, and why. Work through the Hints, Tips, and Reminders in the next section; you may find something that helps you get the arguments in this chapter under control. ∎

## STEP 4          Consider These Hints, Tips, and Reminders

1. The key difference between absolute and comparative advantage is that comparative advantage rests on *opportunity costs*. One nation (firm or individual) can produce a product at a lower opportunity cost than another.

2. Remember that trade is a *voluntary* activity. No nation (or firm or individual) would voluntarily engage in trade unless it expected to benefit. This is why trade is called a positive-sum game.

3. The most difficult material in this chapter is the discussion of the terms of trade; the ratio of the price of exported goods to the price of imported goods. Spend some time with the discussion around Figure 4 in the text. That discussion illustrates why there is often opposition to international trade—some industries (and workers) lose when faced by competition from international firms with a comparative advantage.

4. Don't let tariffs and quotas throw you—they are just two ways to restrict imports and are very similar. Tariffs are taxes, and quotas restrict the amount of imports into a nation. Both result in the same impact (imports are reduced), but tariffs yield revenue to governments. Guess which one governments prefer?

| Do the Homework for Chapter 15 International Trade | **STEP 5** |

Instructor _____  Time _____  Student _____

**Use the answer key below to record your answers to these homework questions.**

1. _____    6. _____    11. _____    16. _____
2. _____    7. _____    12. _____    17. _____
3. _____    8. _____    13. _____    18. _____
4. _____    9. _____    14. _____    19. _____
5. _____    10. _____   15. _____    20. _____

1. An absolute advantage exists when
   a. one country exports more to another country than it imports from that country.
   b. one country can produce more of one product than another country.
   c. one country can produce absolutely less of one product than another country.
   d. one country's opportunity cost is less for one product than for another country.

2. A comparative advantage exists when
   a. one country exports more to another country than it imports from that country.
   b. one country can produce more of one product than another country.
   c. one country can produce comparatively less of one product than another country.
   d. one country's opportunity cost is less for one product than for another country.

3. The Smoot-Hawley tariff passed in 1930
   a. helped to moderate the economic consequences of the Depression.
   b. imposed an average tax on imported goods approaching 200%.
   c. had only a modest impact on the world economy.
   d. added to the severity of the global depression.

4. International trade exists because
   a. most countries could not survive without the global flow of goods.
   b. governments force it on its citizens.
   c. nations expect to gain.
   d. treaties negotiated during the 1920s require trade between nations.

5. When one country has an absolute advantage over another country,
   a. trade will never be worthwhile for either country.
   b. that country will push its advantage over the other country and force trade.
   c. both countries may still benefit from trade.
   d. trade will lead to losses for each country.

6. The terms of trade
   a. determine the legal rules for trading between two countries.
   b. are the definitions of comparative and absolute advantage.
   c. set the limits to trading between two countries and are defined as the maximum exports minus the minimum imports.
   d. are defined as the average price of exports divided by the average price of imports.

7. International trade
   a. is voluntary, so everyone involved must benefit.
   b. is involuntary, so no one really gains.
   c. leads to gains overall to nations, but there will be winners and losers within nations.
   d. reduces product choice for consumers.

8. Which of the following does *not* constrain trade?
   a. There are both winners and losers within nations from trade.
   b. Diminishing returns limit production.
   c. Most countries can only produce one product.
   d. Every trade involves transactions costs.

9. A tariff is
   a. shipping charges associated with international trade.
   b. rules that govern exports.
   c. a limit on the amount of specific goods that can be imported into the country.
   d. a tax on imported goods.

10. A quota is
    a. shipping charges associated with international trade.
    b. rules that govern exports.
    c. a limit on the amount of specific goods that can be imported into the country.
    d. a tax on imported goods.

11. One advantage of a tariff over a quota is
    a. tariffs lead to higher prices, whereas quotas do not.
    b. governments prefer tariffs because they are easier to negotiate and administer.
    c. governments prefer tariffs because they generate revenue.
    d. tariffs lead to less lobbying than quotas because the stakes are lower.

12. Tariffs and quotas
    a. are the backbone of our international economic policies and are designed to help developing countries grow faster.
    b. lead to large-scale lobbying efforts by the companies and industries affected.
    c. have had little effect on the automobile industry, for example.
    d. lead to a better allocation of resources in the United States since these policies protect our smaller and more vulnerable companies and industries.

13. The major beneficiaries from a U.S. tariff on French wine are
    a. French winemakers and American consumers.
    b. American consumers and the government.
    c. California winemakers and the government.
    d. California and French winemakers.

14. Which of the following is *not* an argument against free trade?
    a. Trade keeps consumer prices too low.
    b. Small industries need protection to achieve comparative advantage in a global environment.
    c. Workers need protection from low-wage foreign workers.
    d. Some industries need protection to ensure that we have them in times of national emergency.

15. When the United States imports products from a country with a wage of less than $2 a day,
    a. that country's workers are harmed.
    b. U.S. workers in the same industry are harmed.
    c. consumers in the United States are harmed.
    d. tariffs must be instituted in the United States to protect the workers in the foreign country from exploitation by multinational corporations.

16. When wages and incomes in developing countries rise,
    a. tariffs on that country's products can be increased without harming workers and incomes in that country.
    b. U.S. workers will have nothing to fear from outsourcing.
    c. consumers in the United States will want to see quotas instituted to keep prices from rising.
    d. the demand for environmental protections will rise.

17. Use the table at right for wine and olive oil production in Greece and Australia. The opportunity cost of one barrel of olive oil in Greece is
    a. two casks of wine.
    b. half a cask of wine.
    c. three casks of wine.
    d. one-third cask of wine.

18. Use the table at right for wine and olive oil production in Greece and Australia. The opportunity cost of one barrel of olive oil in Australia is
    a. two casks of wine.
    b. half a cask of wine.
    c. three casks of wine.
    d. one-third cask of wine.

|           | Wine (casks) | Olive Oil (barrels) |
|-----------|--------------|---------------------|
| Greece    | 10           | 20                  |
| Australia | 30           | 10                  |

19. Use the table on the previous page for wine and olive oil production in Greece and Australia. Assume each country initially produced and consumed half of its possible production of both commodities. Now assume that Greece produces only olive oil and Australia produces only wine, and the two countries agree to split the resulting output. As a result,
    a. Greece will gain an additional 10 casks of wine.
    b. Australia will lose 5 casks of wine.
    c. Australia will gain 10 barrels of olive oil.
    d. Greece will gain 5 barrels of olive oil.

20. Use the table on the previous page for wine and olive oil production in Greece and Australia. Assume each country initially produced and consumed half of its possible production of both commodities. Now assume that Greece produces only olive oil and Australia produces only wine, and the two countries agree to split the resulting output. As a result,
    a. Greece will gain an additional 5 casks of wine.
    b. Australia will lose 5 casks of wine.
    c. Australia will gain 5 barrels of olive oil.
    d. Greece will gain 5 barrels of olive oil.

| | Use the ExamPrep to Get Ready for Exams | **STEP 6** |

This sheet (front and back) is designed to help you prepare for your exams. The chapter has been boiled down to its key concepts. You are asked to answer questions, define terms, draw graphs, and, if you wish, add summaries of class notes.

## The Gains from Trade

Define the following.
Absolute advantage:

Comparative advantage:

Describe the gains from trade associated with comparative advantage:

Describe some of the limits to trade and specialization:

## Terms of Trade

Describe the process of determining the terms of trade between two industries in two countries:

Describe the impact that trade has on both consumers and workers in the two countries:

## Restricting Trade

Use the grid below to illustrate the effects of a tariff. Begin with domestic demand and supply with an equilibrium price of $P_0$. Then put in the world price of the product $P_w$ below the domestic equilibrium price.

How much of this industry's product is imported?

How much is sold by domestic firms?

Add a tariff (T) to this product.

How much is now imported?

How much is now sold by domestic firms?

Shade in the revenue received by the government from the tariff.

Who benefits from the tariff?

Who are the losers from the tariff?

If the government substituted a quota for the tariff and reduced imports by the same amount, how would this quota differ from the tariff?

## Arguments Against Free Trade

Describe the following arguments against free trade.
Protection of infant industries:

Antidumping:

Protection from low foreign wages:

Providing for the national defense:

### Concerns about Globalization

Discuss the following concerns about globalization, listing both sides of the argument.
Impact on domestic employment:

Impact of trade on the environment:

Impact on working conditions in developing nations:

# Additional Study Help Chapterwide Practice Questions

## Matching

Match the description with the corresponding term.

___ 1. Absolute advantage
___ 2. Comparative advantage
___ 3. Terms of trade
___ 4. Tariffs
___ 5. Quotas
___ 6. Infant industry argument
___ 7. Antidumping

a. Determine the prices of imports and exports. When countries trade many commodities, this is defined as the average price of exports divided by the average price of imports.

b. When one country can produce more of some good than can the other country.

c. A tax on imports. It can be an ad valorem tax: a certain percentage of its price. Or it can be a unit tax: a fixed tax per unit of the product.

d. When one country's opportunity cost to produce some good is lower than the other country's.

e. When a foreign firm engages in predatory pricing and sells its goods cheaper in the United States than in its domestic market, the U.S. government can impose tariffs on the offending products.

f. An industry that is too underdeveloped to enjoy a comparative advantage or to survive in the global marketplace. Some advocates argue that they require some initial trade protection, usually tariffs or quotas, to allow them to grow and achieve global competitiveness.

g. Restricts the quantity of imports into a country. It has much the same effect as a tariff, except that it does not generate revenues for the government.

## Fill-In

Circle the word(s) in parentheses that complete the sentence.

1. When one nation can produce a product at a lower cost than another, it has a(n) (comparative, absolute) _____ advantage over the other country. But just being able to produce more than another country only confers a(n) (comparative, absolute) _____ advantage. Diminishing returns, the market risk associated with specializing in producing one product or commodity, and (transactions costs, terms of trade, low labor costs) _____ place some practical limits on trade.

2. Excise taxes on imported products are (the terms of trade, quotas, tariffs) _____; the price of exports divided by the price of imports is equal to (the terms of trade, quotas, tariffs) _____; and just restricting imports is done with (the terms of trade, quotas, tariffs) _____.

3. Underdeveloped industries that are often protected are (low-wage, infant, capital-intensive) _____ industries, and some antitrade advocates argue that domestic workers need protection from foreign (low-wage, infant, capital-intensive) _____ industries.

4. Selling products at different prices in domestic and foreign markets is referred to as (exploitation, globalization, dumping) _____. Although trade can produce losers among specific industries, overall (workers, consumers, governments) _____ stand to benefit.

## True-False

Circle the correct answer.

T / F   1. Roughly one in five American workers owes his or her job to foreign consumers.

T / F   2. Free trade policies have steadily grown more popular around the world since World War II.

T / F   3. In international trade, one country can gain from trade only if another country loses.

T / F   4. If Japan has an absolute advantage over China in the production of automobiles, this means Japan can produce more cars than China.

T / F   5. If France has a comparative advantage over Germany in the production of cheese, this means France is capable of producing more cheese than Germany.

T / F   6. If France has a comparative advantage in the production of wine and Germany has a comparative advantage in the production of beer, both countries can enjoy more wine and beer if each specializes in the area of production where it has a comparative advantage, and the two countries then trade.

T / F   7. If Australia has an absolute advantage over New Zealand in the production of crocodile-skin boots, this means Australia will definitely want to focus some of its resources on producing crocodile-skin boots.

T / F   8. If the United States has been trading baseball caps to Great Britain for years and they are not subject to significant tariffs, the price of baseball caps in Britain will likely be quite close to their price in the United States.

T / F   9. Calculating the terms of trade between two nations is a relatively simple task for economists.

T / F   10. If the United States is a net exporter to Taiwan, Taiwanese producers will generally be hurt by this trade, but Taiwanese consumers will benefit from it.

T / F   11. As a general rule, tariffs benefit domestic producers but hurt domestic consumers.

T / F   12. A quota is an ad valorem tax assessed on imports as they cross the border.

T / F   13. When consumer groups try to lobby for tariff reductions, they are usually outspent and outlobbied by industry groups supporting the tariffs.

T / F   14. A quota generates more revenues for the government than a tariff.

T / F   15. The infant industry argument for trade barriers suggests that countries with young industries should erect permanent trade barriers to protect these industries.

T / F   16. Developing nations often try to protect their capital industries on the infant industry rationale, even if they would be better served by promoting their more labor-intensive industries.

T / F   17. If China begins selling T-shirts in the United States at a lower price than American producers because China can produce T-shirts less expensively, the federal government is likely to invoke antidumping laws and impose a tariff on Chinese T-shirts.

T / F   18. If the United States were to boycott Burmese textiles because Americans decided wages in Burma were unconscionably low, this move would probably help American textile workers far more than Burmese workers.

T / F   19. Although many industries are vital to securing U.S. national defense, most of them seem capable of thriving even without any special trade protections.

T / F   20. Expanding our trade with other nations typically has the effect of lowering American wages.

T / F   21. Although economic development has clearly caused some environmental degradation, most evidence now suggests that increasing income levels around the world would serve the cause of environmental protection.

T / F   22. The best way to promote higher wages in developing nations is generally to threaten them with a cutoff of trade if they do not start paying their workers more.

## Multiple Choice

Circle the correct answer.

1. Approximately what is the combined value of annual U.S. imports and exports?
   a. $500 billion
   b. $800 billion
   c. $1.5 trillion
   d. $3 trillion

2. What was the name of the tariff the United States imposed in 1930 with disastrous results?
   a. Baxter-Taylor
   b. Smoot-Hawley
   c. Jackson-Landreau
   d. Hart-Smalley

3. Which of the following is an example of a positive-sum game?
   a. football
   b. poker
   c. war
   d. international trade

4. If Chile has a comparative advantage over Peru in coffee production, what does this mean?
   a. The opportunity costs of producing coffee are lower in Chile than in Peru.
   b. Chilean coffee is of higher quality than Peruvian coffee.
   c. Chile is capable of producing more coffee than Peru.
   d. The price of Chilean coffee is higher than that of Peruvian coffee.

5. If Chile has an absolute advantage over Peru in coffee production, what does this mean?
   a. The opportunity costs of producing coffee are lower in Chile than in Peru.
   b. Chilean coffee is of higher quality than Peruvian coffee.
   c. Chile is capable of producing more coffee than Peru.
   d. The price of Chilean coffee is higher than that of Peruvian coffee.

6. If Ireland can produce 10,000 additional tons of potatoes every year only by forgoing the production of 100,000 barrels of ale, what is the opportunity cost of 1 ton of potatoes in Ireland?
   a. 0.1 barrel of ale
   b. 10 barrels of ale
   c. 100 barrels of ale
   d. 10,000 barrels of ale

7. Trade between two countries will benefit both
   a. when one country has a comparative advantage over the other in one type of production.
   b. when one country has an absolute advantage over the other in one type of production.
   c. when one country has an absolute advantage over the other in numerous types of production.
   d. in all of the above instances.

8. The United States and South Africa trade cars for diamonds. If 1 car trades for 3 diamonds and each car costs $15,000, what is the price of a diamond?
   a. $5,000
   b. $15,000
   c. $20,000
   d. $45,000

9. If Chile has a comparative advantage over Peru in the production of coffee and Peru drops its barriers against the importation of Chilean coffee, which two groups will be adversely affected by this new arrangement?
   a. Chilean producers and Peruvian consumers
   b. Chilean producers and consumers
   c. Chilean consumers and Peruvian producers
   d. Peruvian producers and consumers

10. If Japan has a comparative advantage in electronics production and China has a comparative advantage in textile production, what will happen to the price of electronics in Japan if the two countries start trading electronics for textiles?
    a. It will drop.
    b. It will rise.
    c. It will hold steady.
    d. Any of the above possibilities is equally likely.

11. If a tariff takes the form of an ad valorem tax, this means:
    a. a fixed tax is assessed for every unit of the product that is imported.
    b. imported goods are taxed every time they are featured in advertisements.
    c. a limit is placed on the quantity of a certain product that may be imported.
    d. imported products are assessed a tax equal to a certain percentage of their price.

12. If a tariff takes the form of a per unit tax, this means:
    a. a fixed tax is assessed for every unit of the product that is imported.
    b. imported goods are taxed every time they are featured in advertisements.
    c. a limit is placed on the quantity of a certain product that may be imported.
    d. imported products are assessed a tax equal to a certain percentage of their price.

13. Who are the two primary beneficiaries of a tariff?
    a. foreign producers and domestic consumers
    b. domestic consumers and the government
    c. domestic producers and the government
    d. foreign and domestic producers

14. What is the primary difference between tariffs and quotas in terms of their final effects?
    a. Tariffs help domestic producers whereas quotas do not.
    b. Tariffs generate revenues for the government whereas quotas do not.
    c. Tariffs help domestic consumers whereas quotas hurt them.
    d. Tariffs are difficult to repeal for political reasons whereas consumer groups can get quotas repealed easily.

15. "We should protect the oil industry because we will need to have a secure domestic source of oil if we ever go to war." This is an example of which of the following arguments for trade barriers?
    a. the infant industry argument
    b. the antidumping argument
    c. the low foreign wage argument
    d. the national defense argument

16. "We need to slap a tariff on Japanese televisions because Sony is selling its TVs below cost in the United States." This is an example of which of the following arguments for trade barriers?
    a. the infant industry argument
    b. the antidumping argument
    c. the low foreign wage argument
    d. the national defense argument

17. "Mozambique needs to protect its steel industry until it attracts enough capital so that it can be competitive in the global marketplace." This is an example of which of the following arguments for trade barriers?
    a. the infant industry argument
    b. the antidumping argument
    c. the low foreign wage argument
    d. the national defense argument

18. Which of the following is *not* one the arguments *against* erecting trade barriers on the infant industry rationale?
    a. Capital-intensive industries are usually the ones protected on this rationale, whereas many developing nations would be better off promoting the development of their labor-intensive industries.
    b. Many industries have proven themselves perfectly capable of developing without costly protectionist measures.
    c. If a young industry is protected for a short time, this can help it to grow large enough to be competitive in the global market.
    d. Many countries coddle their infant industries so much that these industries never really mature and become competitive.

19. If the United States begins importing textiles from Burma, where workers may be paid only $1 per day, which group will this likely hurt the most?
    a. Burmese textile workers
    b. Burmese textile producers
    c. American consumers
    d. American textile workers

20. In recent years, when American jobs have been lost due to competition from abroad, the most common response of the federal government has been to:
    a. help displaced workers transition to other industries.
    b. impose tariffs against foreign products.
    c. impose quotas on foreign products.
    d. provide domestic producers in the affected industries with subsidies.

21. As incomes rise, especially above the subsistence level, the demand for environmental protections typically:
    a. falls.
    b. remains constant.
    c. rises, though more slowly than the rise in incomes.
    d. rises faster than the rise in incomes.

22. Which of the following policies would probably help workers in developing countries least?
    a. expanding political and economic freedoms

b. strengthening the rule of law, especially in the area of property rights
c. instituting rigid trade barriers to protect domestic industries
d. taking measures to promote the influx of foreign capital

## Essay-Problem

Answer in the space provided.

Use the questions below as another way to assess your progress. Your answers may differ from ours, but they should not be too far apart. These questions should give you more perspective on issues in international trade.

1. Why is comparative advantage so important for trade?

2. When we hear an argument against free trade, who likely is making the argument?

3. Consider a charge of dumping against two products: cameras and eggs. Why might the charge be mistaken in the case of eggs?

4. We have seen that dumping may put domestic firms at an unfair advantage with a subsidized foreign producer. From the point of view of the domestic consumer, is dumping bad?

5. What did the Smoot-Hawley tariff teach us?

6. What is the difference between buying cheese from a farmer in Wisconsin and from a farmer in Saskatchewan?

7. What groups are hurt if the United States puts a tariff on French wine? What groups benefit?

8. Why would an underdeveloped country be apt to have looser environmental regulations than developed countries?

9. When an infant industry is protected, who suffers?

10. Often in this chapter, we have talked about trade without mentioning specific products. Name five products that the United States exports.

11. Use Figure EP-1 to answer the following questions. Points e are the initial equilibrium in both markets, and note that camera lenses are measured in thousands.

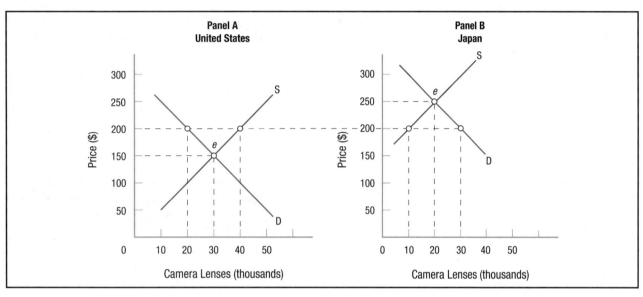

**EP-1**

a. Initially, how much revenue do U.S. firms make?

b. After trade with Japan, how much revenue do U.S. firms make?

c. Initially, how much revenue do Japanese firms make?

d. After trade with the United States, how much revenue do Japanese firms make?

e. Which country's firms gain from trade?

f. Initially, how many camera lenses are bought at what price by U.S. consumers?

g. After trade with Japan, how many camera lenses are bought at what price by U.S. consumers?

h. Initially, how many camera lenses are bought at what price by Japanese consumers?

i. After trade with the United States, how many camera lenses are bought at what price by Japanese consumers?

j. Which country's consumers gain the most from trade?

12. Use Figure EP-2 to answer the following questions. The figure illustrates the effects of a tariff of $5 per unit on the world price of $20.

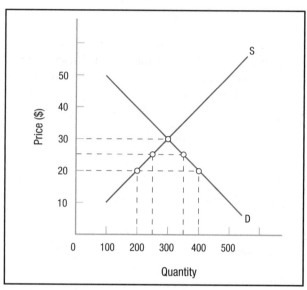

**EP-2**

a. What is the original equilibrium price and quantity in the home country?

b. If the price in the home country fell to the world price, $20, what quantity would be demanded? What quantity would be supplied by firms in the home country? What quantity would be supplied by foreign firms?

c. If the government imposes a $5 tariff, what quantity is demanded? What quantity would be supplied by firms in the home country? What quantity would be supplied by foreign firms?

d. How much revenue is generated by the $5 tariff?

e. Comparing the world price to the world price plus tariff, who in the home country benefits from the tariff? Who in the home country is hurt by the tariff?

## Answers to Chapterwide Practice Questions

### Matching

| | | | |
|---|---|---|---|
| 1. b | 3. a | 5. g | 7. e |
| 2. d | 4. c | 6. f | |

### Fill-In

1. Comparative, absolute, transactions costs
2. Tariffs, the terms of trade, quota
3. Infant, low-wage
4. Dumping, consumers

## True-False

| | | | |
|---|---|---|---|
| 1. F | 7. F | 13. T | 19. T |
| 2. T | 8. T | 14. F | 20. F |
| 3. F | 9. F | 15. F | 21. T |
| 4. T | 10. T | 16. T | 22. F |
| 5. F | 11. T | 17. F | |
| 6. T | 12. F | 18. T | |

## Multiple Choice

| | | | |
|---|---|---|---|
| 1. d | 7. d | 13. c | 19. d |
| 2. b | 8. a | 14. b | 20. a |
| 3. d | 9. c | 15. d | 21. d |
| 4. a | 10. b | 16. b | 22. c |
| 5. c | 11. d | 17. a | |
| 6. b | 12. a | 18. c | |

## Essay-Problem

1. Comparative advantage is important because it means that a country does not have to have an absolute advantage over another to trade: trade should take place as long as there is a difference in opportunity costs. This lets poor countries trade even though richer countries are more efficient in all matters of production.

2. Firms and workers who are hurt by free trade. Their concern is legitimate. Their solution, however, may not be in the best interests of everyone.

3. Perishables must be sold in a limited time period. When they start to rot, the value of the product goes down to zero. Lowering the price might be a way to get rid of the product before it goes bad. No such issue of perishability occurs with cameras.

4. No. The domestic consumer obtains a product at a lower price. What is the harm to the consumer in that? For example, why should an American consumer care if Japanese taxpayers are subsidizing a Japanese producer, and so in effect Japanese taxpayers are subsidizing American consumers?

5. High tariffs can destroy trade, and plummeting trade can lead to immediate drops in national income and output. This can cause or worsen adverse macroeconomic situations, turning a recession into a depression, for example.

6. None, unless the products are vastly different. There is no difference to the consumer in buying a product produced in another state as compared to a product produced in another country. The division between states and countries is arbitrary.

7. French wine producers will sell less wine in the United States, so they are hurt by the tariff. U.S. consumers will see the price go up. American wine producers, on the other hand, will be helped by the tariff because they will face diminished competitive pressures, and the U.S. government will benefit because it collects the tariff revenues.

8. There is a cost to environmental regulation. For a foreign firm thinking about investing in an underdeveloped country, the higher the cost, the less chance it will invest. This does not mean there will be no environmental regulation at all, nor does it mean that foreign investors will always be less particular about the environment in an underdeveloped country than a developed one. Consider, for example, a firm that wants to build a factory in an underdeveloped country. If it already has an environmentally friendly design, it is probably cheaper to use this design again than to incur the redesign cost. In this sense, foreign investors may improve the environment, not harm it.

9. First, the infant industry may suffer if it is coddled and never learns how to deal with competitive pressures. Second, if the infant industry is subsidized, taxpayers are hurt. Third, consumers are hurt by having the infant industry's product price higher than the market price.

10. There are many American products valued overseas. Here are only a few: Intel computer chips, IBM computers and servers, Coca-Cola, Gap clothes, Nike athletic shoes, agricultural machinery such as John Deere tractors, Caterpillar heavy machinery.

11. a. $4,500,000
    b. $8,000,000
    c. $5,000,000
    d. $2,000,000
    e. United States
    f. 30,000 @ $150
    g. 20,000 @ $200
    h. 20,000 @ $250
    i. 30,000 @ $200
    j. Japan's

12. a. $30 and 300 sold
    b. 400, 200, 200
    c. 350, 250, 100
    d. $500
    e. Domestic firms and the government; consumers